THE

PUBLICATIONS

OF THE

SURTEES SOCIETY

VOL. 217

THE

PUBLICATIONS

OF THE

SURTEES SOCIETY

ESTABLISHED IN THE YEAR
M.DCCC.XXXIV

VOL. CCXVII

Portrait of John Buddle (by courtesy of the North of England Institute of Mining and Mechanical Engineers)

LETTERS OF
JOHN BUDDLE TO
LORD LONDONDERRY
1820–1843

EDITED
BY
ANNE ORDE

THE SURTEES SOCIETY

THE BOYDELL PRESS

First published 2013

A Surtees Society Publication
published by The Boydell Press
an imprint of Boydell & Brewer Ltd
PO Box 9, Woodbridge, Suffolk IP12 3DF, UK
and of Boydell & Brewer Inc.
Mt Hope Avenue, Rochester, NY 14620–2731, USA
website: www.boydellandbrewer.com

ISBN 978–0–85444–072–6

ISSN 0307–5362

A catalogue record for this book is available
from the British Library

Details of other Surtees Society volumes are available
from Boydell & Brewer Ltd

The publisher has no responsibility for the continued existence or
accuracy of URLs for external or third-party internet websites
referred to in this book, and does not guarantee that any content
on such websites is, or will remain, accurate or appropriate

Papers used by Boydell & Brewer Ltd are natural, recyclable products
made from wood grown in sustainable forests

Printed and bound in Great Britain by
CPI Group (UK) Ltd, Croydon, CR0 4YY

CONTENTS

Frontispiece: Portrait of John Buddle (by courtesy of the North of England Institute of Mining and Mechanical Engineers)

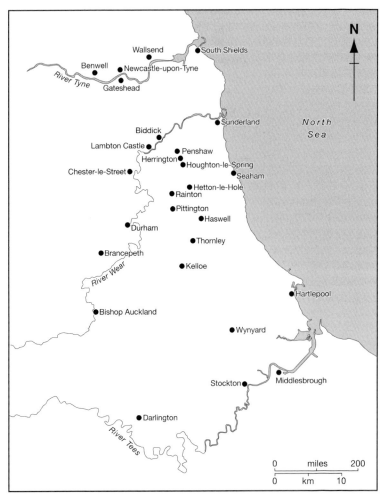

The Durham coalfield

ABBREVIATIONS

DCM	Durham Cathedral Muniments
DCRO	Durham County Record Office
DUJ	*Durham University Journal*
Hist Parl. 1790–1820	R.G. Thorne (ed.), *The History of Parliament: the House of Commons, 1790–1820* (5 vols, London, 1986)
Hist Parl. 1820–1832	D.R. Fisher (ed.), *The History of Parliament: the House of Commons, 1820–1832* (7 vols, Cambridge, 2009)
NEIMME	North of England Institute of Mining and Mechanical Engineers
NRO	Northumberland Archives (formerly the County Records Office)
ODNB	*Oxford Dictionary of National Biography*
Parl. Deb.	*The Parliamentary Debates* (Hansard)

INTRODUCTION

John Buddle was viewer and colliery manager to the third Marquess of Londonderry from 1820 until his death in October 1843. In the course of those twenty-three years he wrote to his employer some 2000 letters, of which the following are a selection. The letters printed here are representative, in their subject-matter, of the correspondence as a whole. It is not the primary purpose of this edition to give a picture of the relationship between the two men, although that does emerge. Nor can it be to give a complete picture of Buddle's career, since it covers only a part. The purpose is to present a picture of North East England at a time of social and economic change, seen through the eyes of a well-informed participant. The main focus, naturally, is on coal and related matters – the industry, colliery affairs, the coal trade, property, the building of Seaham Harbour, industrial relations. A second subject that received a great deal of attention was Lord Londonderry's financial affairs. Thirdly there are reports on local public affairs, notably politics. Taken together the letters give a picture of North East England at a time of far-reaching change.

Buddle was born at Kyo near Tanfield in Co. Durham on 15 November 1773. His father, also called John, was a school master of a scientific cast of mind, who is said to have helped friends engaged in mining with their calculations and estimates, and thus to have taught himself the technical knowledge to become a viewer, a mining engineer.[1] The older Buddle's first appointment as a viewer was at Greenside near Ryton. Later he worked for a number of employers, including the Bishop and the Dean and Chapter of Durham; and in 1792 he was appointed by William Russell as resident viewer at Wallsend, one of the great new collieries opened on the Tyne downstream from Newcastle in the last quarter of the eighteenth century. He wrote *An Historical Account of the Fire-Engine for raising Water,*

---

1 T. Fordyce, *Local Records, or Historical Register of Remarkable Events*, vol. 3 (Newcastle upon Tyne, 1867), p. 180; Richard Welford, *Men of Mark 'twixt Tyne and Tweed* (London, 1895), p. 425.

which was published in Newcastle in 1813, after his death. He developed, helped by his son, a system of segmented cast-iron tubbing for lining pit shafts to prevent the influx of water.

There were six children, among whom John Buddle junior was the only son.[2] He began working with his father as a very young boy, 'not quite six years old';[3] and he always maintained that to get to know coal it was necessary to start young.[4] By 1802 the younger John was working on his own account as well as as his father's assistant. On the latter's death in 1806 he succeeded to the post at Wallsend, and by 1815 he was viewer also at Hebburn, Percy Main, Jarrow, South Shields, Heaton, Benwell and Elswick collieries on the Tyne, and Lambton and Washington on the Wear.[5] He represented several of these collieries on the Joint Northumberland and Durham Coal Owners Association and was secretary of its Tyne committee. He bought shares in a number of collieries, taking in 1835 a one-third share in the Stella Coal Co.[6] The Tyne collieries were particularly subject to inflammable gas, and as a viewer Buddle was much concerned with improvements to ventilation. He was involved with the Society for the Prevention of Accidents in Mines set up after a disaster at Felling in 1812, and took part in Sir Humphry Davy's work on the safety lamp.[7]

Starting work as young as he did, Buddle is not likely to have received much formal schooling; but his letters show that along the way he acquired the style and vocabulary of a well-read man. His journals give evidence of cultivated tastes. He attended the theatre and, when in London, the opera; he went to scientific lectures in

2   Christine M. Hiskey, 'John Buddle (1773–1843): Agent and Entrepreneur in the North East Coal Trade' (M.Litt. thesis, University of Durham, 1978), ch. 1; *Oxford Dictionary of National Biography* (Oxford, 2004) (hereafter *ODNB*).

3   Buddle to Londonderry, 14 Jun. 1842, a letter read out in the House of Lords on 24 Jun. and reproduced in the *Morning Post* of 25 Jun., but not printed in Hansard. See letter No. 173 (the letters are numbered, and are cited by number).

4   See No. 174.

5   Matthias Dunn, 'Sundry memoranda of my own transactions and other occurrences in the coal trade of Newcastle upon Tyne in the manner of a journal', MS, North of England Institute of Mining and Mechanical Engineers (hereafter NEIMME).

6   Durham County Record Office (hereafter DCRO), NCB 1/SC/466(10); Hiskey, 'John Buddle', ch. 14.

7   See his evidence to the Select Committee on Accidents in Mines in 1835, Report of the Select Committee on Accidents in Mines (1835), vol. 5 (603), pp. 131–59.

Newcastle; he was a founder member of the Newcastle Literary and Philosophical Society. He was a good musician, playing chamber music with friends; and he hosted and attended musical evenings.[8] In 1827 he spent £150 on a cello, evidently a good instrument, and had it sent up from London by sea.[9] Buddle never married. After his father's death he continued to live at Wallsend with his mother and an unmarried sister. Later he also had a house at Penshaw among the Londonderry collieries, where another sister, a widow, kept house for him.

Charles William Stewart was born on 18 May 1778, the second son of the first Marquess of Londonderry. He was commissioned in the army at the age of sixteen, and served in the Netherlands and the Peninsula, reaching the position of adjutant-general. Wellington and Sir John Moore, under both of whom he served, acknowledged his gallantry, but neither wholly trusted his judgement. Disappointed at the absence of further promotion Stewart turned to diplomacy and was appointed minister to Prussia, where he served in the campaign of 1813. In 1814 he was raised to the peerage as Baron Stewart and appointed ambassador to Vienna, where he worked closely with his half-brother Robert, Lord Castlereagh, the Foreign Secretary.[10] In 1819 he married, as his second wife, Frances Anne Vane Tempest, twenty years his junior and heiress to the Vane Tempest properties in Co. Durham.[11]

Frances Anne's father, Sir Henry Vane Tempest, had died in 1813, leaving his daughter as a ward in Chancery. During her minority the property was managed by trustees, though not as well as it could have been. The coal in particular was managed by Arthur Mowbray, who was not a coal expert but a banker whose business failed in 1815.[12] The most important colliery, Rainton, was leased from the Dean and Chapter of Durham who, suspecting bad management, threatened not to renew the lease when it next expired and asked Buddle's advice. He replied that, whilst the lessees were not actually in breach

8   NEIMME, Buddle Collection, NRO 3410, Bud//48/1–15 *passim*, Place Books.
9   DCRO, NCB 1/JB/319–20.
10 *ODNB*, *s.n.* Vane.
11 *ODNB*; see also Edith, Marchioness of Londonderry, *Frances Anne. The Life and Times of Frances Anne, Marchioness of Londonderry, and her husband Charles, Third Marquess of Londonderry* (London, 1958).
12 Mowbray was a partner in the bank of Richardson and Mowbray, Darlington. Maberly Phillips, *A History of Banks, Bankers and Banking in Northumberland, Durham and North Yorkshire* (London, 1894), pp. 353–60.

of the requirement in the lease that the colliery should be worked well in accordance with best local practice, their present methods of working were wasteful and would not be used by a prudent owner working his own freehold.[13] Stewart, evidently resolved from the start to manage his wife's property actively, dismissed Mowbray, (who remained aggrieved at his treatment), and appointed Buddle, first as viewer and on 1 January 1822 as sole colliery manager.

During Buddle's lifetime the coal industry of North East England expanded on a very large scale. In 1750 the region's estimated production was 1,955,000 tons out of a national total of 5,230,000 tons. In 1775 it was 2,990,000 tons; in 1800 4,448,000 tons; in 1815 5,383,000 tons; in 1830 6,914,000 tons; in 1850 15,200,000 tons out of a national total of 68,400,000 tons.[14] Much of the increased demand for coal came from new industry, increasing use of steam power, and, after 1820, new transport. The principal product of the North East, however, was still house coal for the London market. This was what the Londonderry collieries specialised in, and Buddle's letters discuss the achievements, problems, and organisation of this sector of the industry. There is little mention of the land sale that accounted for up to one third of the region's production, apart from some small coal – coal that passed through the screens used to separate the better quality large lumps. In the last years of the correspondence there are mentions of new markets and new products – exports to the continent of Europe, and steam coal.[15]

Buddle did not write a great deal about the day-to-day working of the collieries; but he did write about new machinery such as the transferer for lifting tubs of coal off keels into a ship.[16] He was much occupied with wayleaves[17] for transporting coal from the collieries to the shipping points, working out routes for new waggonways and negotiating the terms of leases. He reported on major accidents, both

13 NEIMME, NRO 3410/Bud/6, pp. 160–4, 171–6, T. Fenwick to Buddle, 25 May 1816; Buddle to Fenwick, 8 Jun., 15 Jun.

14 M.W. Flinn, *The History of the British Coal Industry, Vol. 2: 1700–1830* (Oxford, 1984) (hereafter Flinn, *Coal Industry*), pp. 26, 35; Roy Church, *The History of the British Coal Industry, Vol. 3: 1830–1913* (Oxford, 1986) (hereafter Church, *Coal Industry*), p. 3.

15 See Nos. 145, 186.

16 See Nos. 5, 9, 11, 12, 21, 52. Keels were flat-bottomed boats used to convey coal unloaded from waggons at the staiths – loading quays, generally with storage facilities – out to sea-going ships.

17 A wayleave was the right to transport coal and other goods across the land of another proprietor, on payment of an agreed rent.

a few that affected Londonderry directly and others that involved Buddle himself, including the Wallsend disaster of June 1835.[18]

By contrast a large proportion of Buddle's letters are concerned with the sea sale that was the mainstay of the North East coal trade and of the Londonderry collieries. This trade was organised by the Joint Northumberland and Durham Coal Owners Association, constituted in 1805. There was a committee each for the Tyne and the Wear, and a joint general committee. The Tyne committee was elected by the member collieries. Since there were fewer owners on the Wear, all could attend the committee. The joint committee fixed the total 'vend' or permitted quantity of coal sold by sea, the quantity representing their judgement of what the market could take without forcing prices down. This total was then divided between the rivers on a proportion based on output, and then further subdivided between collieries on a 'basis' for each, resulting in its 'issue'. The issue could be adjusted fortnightly or monthly, according to the state of the market. All member collieries were expected to adhere to the regulation. Shortfalls in sales could be made up; over-selling was subject to penalties.[19] It was a producers' cartel, designed to manage competition and keep up prices. On the whole it benefited the coal owners, and marginally disadvantaged the London consumers; but probably did not greatly affect the economy as a whole.[20]

The practice of the trade was that owners sold their coal to fitters at the ports: these then sold the coal to ship-masters. Some fitters worked for a number of owners; others worked exclusively for one. Inducements of various kinds were often offered to ship-masters, and a great deal depended on their judgement of the market, as well as on hazards such as the weather. When trade was particularly difficult owners also resorted to freighting, that is, hiring ships themselves to take their coals – a practice which Buddle considered invariably led to loss. In London the coal was bought by factors working on behalf of the owners, and sold by them to merchants both wholesale and retail.[21]

From the beginning the system was subject to strains, which

---

18 See Nos. 30, 148.
19 Flinn, *Coal Industry*, pp. 254–73; Paul M. Sweezy, *Monopoly and Competition in the English Coal Trade 1550–1850* (Cambridge, MA, 1938).
20 See Elaine S. Tan, 'Market Structure and the Coal Cartel in Early Nineteenth-Century England', *Economic History Review*, new ser., lxii (2009), pp. 350–65.
21 Raymond Smith, *Sea Coal for London: History of the Coal Factors in the London Market* (London, 1961).

feature throughout Buddle's letters. There were disputes between the Tyne and the Wear about their respective proportions. There were rivalries between owners and collieries. Buddle and Lambton's viewers, as agents for the two leading Wear owners, were generally in favour of co-operation, but their principals were not always of the same mind. New collieries were opening in both Northumberland and Durham, and they demanded a share. Matthias Dunn, a leading viewer, estimated that between 1800 and 1830 the number of sea-sale collieries rose from forty-seven to fifty-nine; and by 1843, with the addition of collieries shipping from the Tees, it had reached 130.[22] In the early 1820s the newly established Hetton Coal Co., led by Arthur Mowbray, was particularly aggressive, aiming for and eventually achieving parity with Lambton and Londonderry. In the 1830s the Hetton Co. became more co-operative, but their place was taken by another new company, Thornley. Unless the market expanded as fast as the new producers entered the field, they could only be accommodated by reducing the share of the vend allotted to existing collieries. Regulation broke down frequently during the 1820s and 30s; but for a good many years no one welcomed the prospect of unbridled competition, and so it was as frequently patched up. Eventually regulation was virtually abandoned in 1844–5, largely because Londonderry, during the miners' strike of 1844, minimised his losses by over-selling and refusing to pay the penalty imposed.[23] Buddle, as he made plain on a number of occasions, favoured regulation as generally beneficial.[24] Londonderry was by temperament less inclined to co-operate with others.

When he took on his wife's property Londonderry evidently resolved to be a major coal owner, at least equal to his neighbour and political opponent John George Lambton, later first Earl of Durham. The basis for this ambition was not, however, quite as strong as was desirable. The Vane Tempests owned coal property at Penshaw and some near Durham; but the largest colliery was Rainton, which, as has been seen, was not owned outright but leased from the Dean

---

22 Matthias Dunn, *An Historical, Geological and Descriptive View of the Coal Trade of the North of England* (Newcastle upon Tyne, 1844), pp. 202–3.

23 Church, *Coal Industry*, pp. 66–8; D. Large, 'The Third Marquess of Londonderry and the End of the Regulation 1844–7', *Durham University Journal* (hereafter *DUJ*), new ser., xx (1958–9), pp. 1–9.

24 See No. 6; Lord Londonderry's position on regulation is re-examined by C.E. Hiskey, 'The Third Marquess of Londonderry and the Regulation of the Coal Trade: the Case Re-opened', *DUJ*, new ser., xlv (1983–4), pp. 1–9.

and Chapter of Durham and was therefore not entirely secure. An important object in the early years of the marriage was therefore the purchase of more coal property. This was achieved by buying the Biddick and Seaham estates in 1821, and land at West Herrington. Buddle would have liked to aim for Hetton as well, but that was beyond the ambitions of the family. A further lease was taken in 1825, of the coal at North Pittington; and other possibilities were explored from time to time. As Buddle put it: 'We must always bear in mind that we are essentially a Coal family, and that therefore nothing but the most urgent necessity should by rights compel us to alienate any of that type of property, which ... gives infinitely more political influence than the mere landed property, under which it lies.'[25]

The Dean and Chapter of Durham, as well as the bishop, owned large quantities of coal-bearing land all over the coalfield. The coal in many cases had been worked since the Middle Ages, and now it was producing impressive revenues. The system by which ecclesiastical property was leased was distinctive: it had been settled since the seventeenth century. Lessees paid a certain rent, which in most cases was that laid down in 1541. Coal property was treated in exactly the same way as agricultural land. Most Dean and Chapter leases were for terms of twenty-one years (forty years for urban house property), and were usually renewed every seven years. A lessee who wished to renew could normally expect to do so, but he had no legal right. On the issue of a new loan, or a renewal, the lessee paid a lump sum or fine, which was intended to compensate the lessor for the difference between the certain rent and the current market value of the property – a difference which by the nineteenth century might have become large. The most common fine for agricultural land was one year's (later one and a quarter) clear improved rent, i.e. the full market value less the certain rent. This sum amounted in effect to a loan from the lessee which the lessor could invest; so the custom arose of allowing the lessee a discount or notional interest on the fine, at a rate which in the early seventeenth century was more or less equivalent to the interest obtainable on government bonds, but by the nineteenth century was considerably higher except at times of heavy government borrowing.[26] For agricultural land this system worked without much question, and operated on the whole to the

---

25 See No. 170.
26 See P. Mussett with P.G. Woodward, *Estates and Money at Durham Cathedral 1660–1985* (Durham, 1988), pp. 4–5.

benefit of the lessees, who came to regard themselves and to be regarded as virtual proprietors. Problems of valuation arose from time to time but on the whole there was enough comparable land in secular ownership to allow market rates to be calculated without difficulty. For coal property it was, however, less straightforward, and the fine became a matter for serious negotiation. Rents payable to secular landowners were available for comparison, but calculation of the fine depended on figures for money invested, output, quality and prices. Until about 1820 the Dean and Chapter based their calculations on known production: they then went over to using estimates of future profit as a basis. Buddle thought this outrageous, and it undoubtedly made the process more speculative, especially at a time when the trade was under strain and prices under pressure. Buddle's relations with the Dean and Chapter mining agent, Thomas Fenwick, were friendly; but Fenwick had little authority and Buddle regarded members of the Chapter as insufficiently open to professional advice. Their position, however, was the stronger, for Londonderry needed Rainton to maintain his position as a leading coal owner, whilst he was not the only possible lessee. The renewal of the Rainton lease was a recurrent headache for Buddle.

Seaham Harbour, which Londonderry built to ship his coals, bypassing the constricted facilities of Sunderland, was the subject of a good many letters, from the inception of the project to the design and building of the harbour, the laying of the foundation stone, the first shipments, and the gradual build-up of trade. Although not responsible for the work, Buddle took a keen interest in it, from both the engineering and the business points of view. He had a ship, the *Lord Seaham*, built to share in the trade.[27]

After the repeal of the Combination Acts in 1824 trade unions grew in the North East coalfield. Relations between the owners and the pitmen were governed by a system of annual bonds. The men were bound not to strike and not to leave their jobs during the year. In return they were guaranteed a stipulated wage (but not guaranteed work) and accommodation.[28] Owners agreed wage rates among themselves, but at a time of rapid expansion skilled men were in demand and were able to move in search of better conditions, and owners might find it difficult to retain an adequate workforce. Binding negotiations gave the pitmen experience of collective action,

27 See No. 104.
28 See Flinn, *Coal Industry*, pp. 329–38.

and their generally isolated lives encouraged solidarity; but the early unions were ephemeral and collapsed after setbacks.[29] Buddle, like all owners and managers, was opposed to unions. In the strike of 1831 his own safety and property were threatened with violence. He wanted the owners to present a united front, and was chagrined when Londonderry, first among the Wear owners, conceded the men's wage demands.[30]

A large number of Buddle's letters are devoted to Londonderry's financial affairs. As colliery manager he handled much of the money that was the family's main income, and had to arrange payments on a variety of their obligations. At no time was this a simple task. Often the payments that were due took up most of the month's receipts from coal, and Buddle had to ask Londonderry's Sunderland banker, Edward Backhouse, to increase the amount of his overdraft, and to juggle between the creditors with the most pressing demands. At the beginning, Buddle was confident, and was able to assure Backhouse that the costs of the mortgages for buying Biddick, Seaham and West Herrington would be paid off in a few years of good trade. But then a great London house was bought and needed extensive repairs and refurbishment; Wynyard Park, the Vane seat near Stockton, was rebuilt at a cost of £147,000; more money was borrowed for Seaham Harbour; elections were expensive. It became apparent that the scale of expenditure was constantly rising.

In the absence of full sets of accounts, it is not possible to construct a complete picture, but some papers show aspects of the situation at different times. A paper of 1824 shows outstanding mortgages to a total of £219,589.6.8, on which payments of £13,227.0.0 were currently due; and other debts outstanding of £91,000.[31] Another paper of October 1829 shows sums owing by Londonderry for purchases since he came into the property as totalling £162,990. His annual income, in round figures, was £52,000, of which the collieries provided £30,000, the English estates £10,000 and the Irish estates £18,000. His annual outgoings were £21,000 including annuities payable under his marriage settlement to Lady Londonderry, her mother the Countess of Antrim and her aunt Frances Anne Taylor, and the allowance to Londonderry's son by his first marriage, Lord

---

29 See Flinn, *Coal Industry*, pp. 396–41; Richard Fynes, *The Miners of Northumberland and Durham* (London, 1873), chs. 2–3; E. Welbourne, *The Miners' Unions of Northumberland and Durham* (Cambridge, 1923), ch. 2.

30 See Nos. 98, 99, 100.

31 D/Lo/B310.

Castlereagh.[32] A later paper of 1836 shows total debts of all kinds as £526,867.12.6.[33]

From time to time Buddle felt obliged to urge Londonderry to retrench, whilst acknowledging that he must keep up a suitable life-style. From time to time Londonderry promised to economise, but without noticeable result. Matters came to a head in 1834. There had been a proposal ten years earlier to put the English properties into the hands of trustees, so that, while the family lived off the Irish estates, any surplus revenues after mortgages and annuities were paid could be devoted to paying off the debts.[34] That proposal had not been carried out, but now, with the Joint Stock Bank threatening to seize the collieries to cover their claims, a trust was set up under which all the English properties except Seaham and the London house were handed over to trustees – Edmund McDonnell, second husband of the Countess of Antrim, Thomas Batson of the bank, and Robert Scurfield a fitter. They were given the task of reducing Londonderry's bank overdraft and raising £200,000 towards paying off his other debts.[35]

One of the items of expenditure that caused Buddle trouble at intervals was electoral politics. For much of the eighteenth century the Tempest and Lambton families had shared political influence over the City of Durham. From 1819, following his marriage, the families were represented by Londonderry and John George Lambton, a neighbour and rival coal owner, a prominent Whig of a radical bent, son-in-law of the second Earl Grey.[36] The unreformed electorate for Durham City consisted of the freemen, members in name of the various guilds. Many of them were not now residents of the city; and since voters had to be brought to the poll with their expenses paid, producing the outvoters, in some cases from as far away as London, could be an expensive addition to the normal expenditure on food and drink. Buddle had to manage the money

---

32 D/Lo/C310(2).

33 D/Lo/E21.

34 D/Lo/B310, 1824.

35 Trust deed, 21 Mar. 1834, D/Lo/E51. See Hiskey, 'John Buddle', ch. 13. The trust replaced that of the marriage settlement of 1822: see R.W. Sturgess, 'The Londonderry Trust 1819–54', *Archaeologia Aeliana*, 5th ser., x (1982), pp. 179–92.

36 *ODNB*; R.G. Thorne (ed.), *The History of Parliament: the House of Commons, 1790–1820* (5 vols, London, 1986) (hereafter *Hist. Parl. 1790–1820*), ii, pp. 151–5; D.R. Fisher (ed.), *The History of Parliament: the House of Commons, 1820–1832* (7 vols, Cambridge, 2009) (hereafter *Hist. Parl. 1820–32*), vi, pp. 25–37.

involved and deliver the 'household troops' – employees and clients – to the polls. He did not himself have a vote in Durham, and did not share Londonderry's ultra-Toryism, but did this duty. The 1832 Reform Act divided the county of Durham into two, and enfranchised Sunderland and several towns on Tyneside. In Durham City, the non-resident freemen lost the vote, and the newly enfranchised £10 householders were less amenable to aristocratic influence . The tacit arrangement by which Londonderry and Lambton shared the representation of the city came to an end. Londonderry's influence continued to secure one of the two seats, but he had greater difficulty in making his influence felt. In 1837 he contemplated trying to secure both, and did intervene in North Durham. In 1843 he fell out with the local Conservatives, and as a result in the next election both seats went to the Liberals.[37]

The development of railways in the 1820s and 30s was a matter of considerable public and personal interest. Buddle's letters reflect the development, and his attitude to railways, from the first project for the Stockton and Darlington Railway through plans for a number of lines, both from the Tees into the southern and eastern parts of the coalfield and from the Durham area to the Tyne.[38] Buddle also observed, sceptically, the early stages of the development of Hartlepool and Middlesbrough as coal ports.[39] Projects for lines from the Tees were an object of suspicion to the established Wear coal owners, because they aimed to open up areas such as that round Bishop Auckland, where the coal had long been worked but the collieries were limited to land sale for lack of access to a river, and also to allow the sinking of new pits. Some of the railway lines were opposed by Londonderry and Lambton; but it was difficult to do so, as Buddle pointed out, with parliamentary opinion running in favour of freer trade and lower prices.[40] Railways from the Durham area to the Tyne might disadvantage coal owners who were paying

---

37 See Nos. 153, 188; A.J. Heesom, 'The "Wynyard Edict" of 1837', *Durham County Local History Society Bulletin*, no. 21 (Apr. 1978), pp. 2–7; A.J. Heesom, *Durham City and its MPs 1678–1992* (Durham, 1992), p. 25; David Large, 'The Election of John Bright as MP for Durham City in 1843', *DUJ*, new ser., xvii (1955–6), pp. 21–7; A.J. Heesom, '"Legitimate" vs "Illegitimate" Influence: Aristocratic Electioneering in mid-Victorian Britain', *Parliamentary History*, vii (1988), pp. 282–305.

38 For the whole subject see William Weaver Tomlinson, *The North Eastern Railway, its Rise and Development* (Newcastle upon Tyne, 1914).

39 See No. 125.

40 See No. 65.

substantial wayleave rents to private landowners; but some offered prospects of improved outlets for the same owners. Other goods, too, might usefully be received by rail.[41] Personal travel by train began. Londonderry took a train, possibly to Carlisle, in 1839,[42] and Buddle increasingly did so, both for local journeys (as from Penshaw to Gateshead, across to Percy Main and back to Wallsend on 14 May 1839) and for longer distances. It was not possible to go to London by train via York until 1841, but in May 1840 Buddle took a train to Carlisle, coach to Preston, and then train to London via Birmingham. From 1838 he had been able to go from Leeds to Gloucester via Manchester and Birmingham, in order to visit the mines in the Forest of Dean.[43]

In the autumn of 1831 Buddle had some kind of breakdown, the exact nature of which is not known but which was probably caused, at least in part, by the strain of the strike of that year.[44] When he returned to work he was relieved of the tasks of making payments and collecting bills for Londonderry, but he began to find the task of dealing with Londonderry's demands increasingly burdensome. In March 1832 his friend the Newcastle solicitor Armorer Donkin wrote to him: 'Much as I respect the feelings which prompt your exertions, I am satisfied that this description of business is more likely to be injurious to your health than any other, and I am also convinced that all your exertions will be *useless* to the party they are intended to serve, who is evidently incorrigible.' Donkin went on to report a story, that was generally believed, of Londonderry's attempts to borrow money from a corn merchant. There would be no difficulty, he said, in raising £3000 or £4000 on Biddick for anyone who would pay the interest; but if anyone in Newcastle was asked, the answer would be: 'I cannot think of trusting my money, however ample the security, to a party who would not pay a shilling of interest except *by compulsion.*'[45] A year later Buddle evidently asked advice from Sir Henry Browne, a former aide-de-camp of Londonderry's who was now a trusted friend. Browne replied, encouraging Buddle to be firm in refusing to use any of the money borrowed under an Exchequer loan scheme for building Seaham Harbour, for any other purpose.

---

41 See No. 160.
42 See No. 159.
43 NEIMME, NRO 3410 Bud/48/3–13, Place Books, 30 Sep. 1838, 14 May 1839, Jun. 1840, 16 May 1841.
44 See No. 108.
45 A. Donkin to Buddle, 15 Mar. 1832, DCRO, NCB 1/JB/406.

'Yours is a hard and difficult position at the moment, my dear Friend – and I can say nothing but this – if you have health to go on with your invaluable services to Lord L. without loss to your character and credit, well and good. Character and health are the first things to be considered. If friends or employers require from us the sacrifice of either the one or the other, it is our decided duty to choose others.'[46]

Then in 1834 came the subjection of the Londonderry properties to a trust. Londonderry obviously found this intensely frustrating, even though his lifestyle does not seem to have been much affected. He was anxious that the trust should be wound up when his son Lord Seaham came of age in 1842. It was usual for an estate to be resettled when the eldest son reached twenty-one;[47] but that did not prove possible. In February 1841 there was a bad fire at Wynyard, and Londonderry immediately resolved to rebuild the house at a cost of £40,000 to £50,000, and pressed Buddle to find the money. This Buddle said he could not do without the consent of the trustees, which was not forthcoming. Instead he advised Londonderry to shut the house for four or five yeas and let the gardens and park, a course which Londonderry rejected.[48] On 24 May Buddle, accompanied by John Gregson the solicitor, had a difficult interview with Londonderry which he, unusually, recorded in his journal. Londonderry launched into a long series of complaints and grievances about the management of his affairs, by the trustees and by Buddle, the effect of which, he said, was to keep him subjected to the trust longer than was necessary. There was a great deal of unnecessary expenditure at Seaham; the colliery agents were not helping him and cared only for their large salaries. Buddle said that he would welcome an enquiry into the accounts, his own salary was in arrears, and he would have to consider whether he could continue any longer in a state of 'such annoyance'. Londonderry's language was such that Buddle resolved not to hold any further correspondence with him, and the breach continued until November, when receipt of a conciliatory letter enabled Buddle to take up correspondence again.[49] Londonderry was known for quarrelling with all kinds of people, and Buddle had in the past had occasion to apologise for couching

46 Browne to Buddle, 29 May 1833, DCRO, NCB 1/JB/181.
47 See F.M.L. Thompson, 'The End of a Great Estate', *Economic History Review*, 2nd ser., viii (1955), pp. 36–52.
48 NEIMME, NRO 3410 Bud/48/13, Place Book, 12–13 May 1841.
49 NEIMME, NRO 3410 Bud/48/13, 14, Place Book, 23 May, 12 Nov. 1841. See No. 162.

his advice in somewhat blunt terms, always with the explanation that he did it with the best interests of the family at heart. He always accepted Londonderry's policy decisions even if he did not wholly agree with them.[50] It is quite possible that his financial administration was flawed. As noted above, the system of payments between fitters, ship-masters and owners was complicated and open to confusion or abuse. Buddle was overworked and may well have been unsystematic; too many functions were combined in too few hands; but there could have been no doubt of either his integrity or his zeal. An auditor, Nathaniel Hindhaugh, was now taken on, and eventually Buddle's own post was suppressed. Meanwhile relations were re-established, but for the next two years they were noticeably more formal than they had been earlier.

Buddle died on 10 October 1843 after a very short illness. The following day R.H. Brandling, the chairman of the Northumberland and Durham Coal Owners Association, wrote to the colliery representatives asking them to attend the funeral.[51] That took place at Benwell, where Buddle had bought some property and had given the land for the new church, although he never lived there and was a Unitarian. The funeral procession went from Wallsend through Newcastle, attended by fifty gentlemen on horseback, nine mourning coaches, and sixty-eight private carriages. The Mayor of Newcastle was there, coal owners and colliery representatives, and workers from collieries of which Buddle was viewer, but not, it would seem, from Londonderry collieries.[52] Buddle died a rich man, leaving an estate worth at least £150,000. He left the bulk of his property to two nephews, Robert Atkinson and Thomas Bennett, the house at Wallsend to his sister Elizabeth Bennett for her life, and bank shares to great nieces and nephews.[53] He has gone down in local memory as King of the Coal Trade. The judgement of one of his fellow viewers, Matthias Dunn, was more nuanced. Dunn listed Buddle's technical improvements in mining practice – cast-iron tubbing, the working of pillars, improved ventilation; his habit of going down the pits two or three times a day, even into his last years; his appearing as expert witness at parliamentary enquiries. He also noted Buddle's appetite for fame and money, and his pride in managing the coal trade until

---

50 See for example Nos. 105, 123.
51 Northumberland Archives, NRO 263/A2.
52 *Newcastle Chronicle*, 7 Dec. 1843; J. Sykes, *Local Records, or Historical Register of Remarkable Events* (2nd edn, Newcastle upon Tyne, 1866), iii, p. 180.
53 Buddle will, 7 Oct. 1843, DCRO D/X/410.

the strikes of 1831–2 when his nerves suffered and it was thought he would not work again. After that Dunn suggested that he only held his place on sufferance. He thought that Buddle outlived his fame, and that when he died 'his employers considered that instead of suffering a grievous loss they were released from a species of thraldom'.[54]

Acknowledgements

Buddle's letters to Londonderry are preserved in the Londonderry Papers in the custody of Durham County Record Office. I am most grateful to the late Marquess of Londonderry for his permission to publish this selection. Some of Londonderry's fewer, shorter and less informative letters in reply are also in the County Record Office, in Buddle's papers deposited by the National Coal Board. I am very grateful to the County Archivist, Mrs E.M. Bregazzi, and her staff, for facilitating my access to these archives and for much help in the course of my work on them. I also wish to thank the staff of the North of England Institute of Mining and Mechanical Engineers, Newcastle upon Tyne, where more of Buddle's papers are preserved among a rich archive of coal industry history. The Institute facilitated my use of these archives and their library, and have kindly given permission for the reproduction of the portrait of Buddle in their possession. Other archives and libraries where I have received assistance are Durham University Library (Archives and Special Collections), Durham Cathedral Muniments, and the Northumberland Archives at Woodhorn. I am very grateful to them all.

Note on the text

Spelling, punctuation and capitalisation are as in the original. Words underlined in the text are printed in italics. Except for standard abbreviations, contracted words are expanded using square brackets.

The letters for the month of April 1822 are printed in extenso, as an example of complete coverage.

---

54 Matthias Dunn, 'History of the Viewers', MS, NEIMME, pp. 18–21.

LETTERS OF
JOHN BUDDLE TO
LORD LONDONDERRY
1820–1843

1.

D/Lo/C142/1(1)   Pensher Colliery Office 22 Jan[uar]y 1820

My Lord

I had the honor to receive your Lordship's letter of the 28th Ult. on my return from Cumberland on the 19th Inst.

I perceive that at the time of writing your Lordship had not received my letter of 5th Dec[ember][1] in which I expressed my sentiments on the affair of the Renewal[2] very freely; and trust – in essential points – that they will accord with your Lordship's ideas.

It is impossible not to feel, that through the whole of this affair, the conduct of the Chapter, has been most unbecomingly rapacious, and such as deservedly to excite feelings of resentment, and a desire of retaliation, or at least, of self-defence.

However strong, and just, those feelings may be, I submit, that it would not be prudent, to betray them at present; but to temporize – at least 'till after the next *grand* Chapter[3] in July, when, if they give us the opportunity, which is by no means unlikely, we may again try the chance of negociation. And indeed as there is the least chance of succeeding, we need not openly commit ourselves in any *offensive* measures; but at the same time, we should steadily, pursue those of *defence*, which are pointed out in my letter of the 5th Dec[ember].

Prudential motives ought also, to lead us to keep up the appearance of being on amicable terms with the Chapter, as *we* ought not, I think on any account suffer it to escape us, that we dispair of being able to induce them to acceed to our terms As should an idea of this sort get abroad, we should in all probability, be teazed with troublesome Competitors – either real, or *prickers* – brought up by the Chapter themselves to *push us on*. On this point therefore, it behoves us to be guarded. In all my conversations with the D[ean] & Chapter's Viewer,[4] I have uniformly declared, that I could not possibly advise your Lordship to exceed the offer made. But this declaration

---

1   Not found in Londonderry Papers.

2   Of the lease of Rainton Colliery from the Dean and Chapter of Durham.

3   Two 'grand' meetings of the Chapter were held each year, on 20 July and 20 November, when major business was conducted. All prebendaries were supposed to attend, and more actually did so than at the regular meetings.

4   Thomas Fenwick.

has always been coupled with the expressing of a firm expectation, that the Revd. Body would, after mature deliberation feel the propriety of renewing, on the terms offered.

As yet the business remains perfectly secret, and I hardly think the Chapter will divulge it themselves; as I do not think they are quite so far lost, to every sense of decency, as to let it go forth to the world (especially in these *times*) that they have refused a Fine of £40,000 for the renewal of a Colliery Lease.

This affair has dwelt constantly on my mind since my last interview with the Chapter. And although I do not dispair of renewing the Lease in the long run, in one way or other, yet it would be presumptuous to calculate upon it as a certain event. And when I consider, in case the Rainton Mines should pass into other hands, at the expiration of the Lease, in 1826, that it would be impracticable, by any means for the Freehold Colliery, in it's mangled state – even with the annexation of the Baronet's coal[5] – to support your Lordship's present rank in the Coal Trade, I am excited to very uncomfortable feelings.

To find out a substitute for Rainton, in the event of a complete rupture with the Dean & Chapter, has often occupied my most serious attention. And I cannot find any unoccupied Tract of Coal, so likely to assure that purpose, as Hetton. Indeed whether we remain with the Chapter, or not, it has always been my opinion, that the Hetton Coal Mining, ought to be possessed by your Lordship's Family; and I have only been restrained from calling your Lordship's attention sooner to the subject, by the desire of getting our present Concerns put upon an eligible footing and out of all pecuniary difficulties, before any fresh investment of Capital should be contemplated. Besides, the advantage of a personal intercourse with your Lordship during the negociations for taking the Mine, together with the Way-leaves &c. and also while planning the mode of conducting such an operation, weighed greatly with me, in wishing to defer the business – at least 'till your Lordship's return to England, altho' I would prefer that the matter should lie dormant for about four years longer.

My wishes in this respect have however been, in some degree disturbed, by Mowbray's[6] *nibbling* about the concern. For altho' I

---

5   A small tract of land at West Herrington, adjacent to Penshaw Colliery, owned by Sir Ralph Milbanke, Sir Francis Blake and Sir John Thorold, which Lord Stewart was buying.

6   Arthur Mowbray, 1755–1840, had been manager of Frances Anne Vane

don't believe that he has made any progress yet his *fistlling* about it, has excited the attention of the public to the subject. And as it is well known that Mr Lyons[7] is labouring under great pecuniary difficulties, it is natural to expect, that he must be inclined to listen to any terms that may be offered for the Mines. And as an idea prevails, that the Coal is as good, as the Rainton Coal – immediately adjoining, it is equally probable, that some monied adventurer may come forward to make him an offer for it.

All these considerations embarrass my judgment considerably. I feel that I should not like to advise your Lordship to make a premature offer, so as to incur an unnecessary expense before our affairs are in a condition to bear it, with perfect convenience. Whilst at the same time I am satisfied, that I should feel very unhappy if by an ill judged economy, I should be the cause of letting slip, the opportunity of securing a concern which ultimately may prove highly beneficial to your Lordship.

In this state of perplexity, the following view of the subject has occurred to me, which I beg leave to submit to your Lordship's serious attention. And as I send this letter open, to Mr Iveson,[8] he will also be prepared to judge it and to discuss the subject when we meet.

From what I know of the feelings of Mr Lyon's Trustee and his Agent, I have little doubt, but I could secure the Hetton Colliery, to your Lordship, at a certain rent of £1000 a year for a 21 years' lease. And I think I could negociate to be allowed 18 months, or two years, *rent free* – to *win* or open the Colliery. But to be at liberty to give up, in case way-leave could not be obtained on eligible terms.

Now as the £1000 a year Rent must be for an equivalent number of *Tens* of Coal, at such a tentale Rent,[9] as may be agreed for – with the privilege of *making up the short workings* – that is, if we should not work a sufficient number of Tens, in any one year, or years, of

---

Tempest's collieries during her minority. He was dismissed after her marriage, and was now leading the launching of the Hetton Coal Co. See John Banham, 'Arthur Mowbray – Adventurer or Entrepreneur: a North East Business in the Industrial Revolution', *Durham County Local History Society Bulletin*, no. 48 (1992), pp. 27–47; no. 49 (1992), pp. 45–68.

7   John Lyon, owner of the Hetton estate.

8   John Iveson, land agent for the Vane Tempest properties.

9   A rent based on colliery output. A ten was a measure of varying size, used in leases, generally between 46 and 49 tons. See Flinn, *Coal Industry*, p. 462. The rent for a colliery normally took the form of a certain rent for a given quantity of tens, plus a further sum for an additional quantity. See Introduction, p. xvii.

the term, at the stipulated price per ten, to amount to the £1000, we may have the privilege, of working up the arrears in any succeeding year, or years of the Lease. It follows that if it should not be deemed prudent to make the Winning within two years, your Lordship might hold the Mine for £1000 a year until it might be thought proper to win and work it; and then the arrear of short workings might be made up. Or in other words, the *Loan* of Tentale Rent advanced, prior to the opening of the Colliery might be liquidated by extending the workings to such a pitch, as circumstances might permit.

As the details of a correct estimate of the expenses of *winning* Hetton Colliery, would require a good deal of time, I shall at present only state an outline of the business to your Lordship.

When Mr Lyons embarked in the Winning, in 1810, it was estimated to cost some way about £53000, but his plan was to deliver the Coals at Sunderland, by a long line of Rail-way – to join Nesham's way[10] – through a difficult line of country. Mr Lyons proceeded 'till he expended £13000, and the pit was sunk to the depth of 20 fathoms and secured through a formidable quick sand. A smith and carpenter's shop, a store house, and four workmen's houses (which your Lordship's workmen inhabit at present) were built; but no part of the Rail-way was executed.

Now according to this plan £40000 might be supposed to complete the Winning by any party possessing only the same means as Mr Lyons. But by the facilities which your Lordship's Collieries would afford and by bringing the Waggon-way, in the *first instance,* to your Lordship's present staiths, I think I may safely venture to say, that it might be accomplished for £25000.

The distance from your Lordship's staiths to the Hetton Pit, is very little more than from the staiths to our Hazard Pit – not quite five miles.

Supposing your Lordship to have secured Hetton Colliery, the following would seem to present itself as the most proper plan of procedure.

1. In the event of not renewing Rainton Lease, to push the working of Hetton and the Freehold Colliery to the utmost extent, in order as far as possible to supply the place of Rainton.

---

10 A waggonway running from Newbottle Colliery to the Wear just above Sunderland. It was the first waggonway on the south side of the Wear, opened in 1812 by John Dowthwaite Nesham, lessee of Newbottle. See Colin E. Mountford, *The Private Railways of County Durham* (Melton Mowbray, 2004), pp. 148–9.

2. But in the event of renewing Rainton Lease (in which case we should be limited to the yearly quantity of 80,000 Chs.)[11] then to work the whole yearly Vend[12] from Rainton and Hetton; and discontinue the Freehold Colliery altogether, so as to preserve it as long as possible. In this case all the live and moveable stock of the Freehold Colliery would be applicable to Hetton, and lessen the actual expenditure of Capital for that Establishment.

And in like manner a sufficient quantity of live and moveable stock might be withdrawn from Rainton, to stock Hetton, if the Lease of the former should not be renewed.

It is for consideration how far the report of your Lordship's being in negociation for Hetton Coal might not operate in our favour with the Dean & Chapter. They might easily be startled by an application for way-leave from Hetton through Rainton grounds (which by-the-by we could either do with, or without) without seeming to aim it as a hostile movement. But at the same time it would without doubt put them upon the qui vive.

I find that I have extended this letter to too great a length to admit of adding other matters without risking confusion. I shall therefore trouble your Lordship with another communication on the more immediate Colliery affairs, in the course of a few days.

I am very glad indeed to learn so favourable an account of my Lady Stewart's health, especially as certain persons in this neighbourhood are constantly spreading reports of a very contrary nature.

The right honble
Lord Stewart,
Vienna[13]

I have the honor to be
My Lord
with the greatest respect,
Your Lordship's
most obedient
humble servant
J^{no} Buddle[14]

11 For the system of regulating sales from collieries see Introduction, p. xv. The Newcastle chaldron was equivalent to 53 cwt.
12 Allowed sale. See Introduction, p. xv.
13 Stewart was British ambassador to Austria at this time.
14 Buddle subscribed the great majority of his letters in this fashion, or 'with great respect', or 'most obedient faithful servant'. Other variations are noted.

2.

D/Lo/C142/C142/1 (2)
Colliery Office Pensher
Jan[uar]y 28th 1820

My Lord

I am happy to inform your Lordship that the Ice, which stopped the Navigation of the Wear, on the 24th Dec[ember] broke up on the 24th Inst. and has set our Keels at liberty again. We have not however been able, owing to the Flood occasioned by the Thaw, to do much business yet; but in two or three days, I hope we shall be at full work again.

The *lack* of Vend this month will try the mettle of our Fitters; at the next Receipt on 1st Feb[ruary]. They have not been shipping any Coals, and must therefore provide the *Supplies* out of other 'ways and means', and will not I hope find any deficiency.

In consequence of the want of Vend a considerable quantity of Coals has accumulated, at the Pits and Staith. And notwithstanding the pains which have been taken in depositing the Walls-end[15] – in the manner stated to your Lordship in a previous Letter, I fear that a considerable loss, will be sustained in filling them up again – as the utmost care must be taken, not to injure the character of the Coals, by sending them in a small or crushed state to market.

As this is an inconvenience to which we shall in a greater or less degree be subject every Winter, it is most desirable that we should be able to adopt some effectual mode of avoiding it.

This may be effected by taking the Coals from Nesham's Rail way to Sunderland, by which not only the breakage of the Coals would be avoided; but we should have the advantage also of being able to ship them regularly at *all Seasons, as wrought.*

As far as I can ascertain the machinery, on Nesham's Way, is capable of conveying from 30,000 to 40,000 Chs. a year, more than their own quantity which would do for our Walls-end, and probably a certain portion of Eden-main also. It happens that our Waggons fit Nesham's Way, and a few hundred yards of our Way, would connect our rail-way and theirs. So that our waggons might be made either to go to Sunderland, or the present Staiths, as occasion might require.

---

15 The top quality house coal, so called after Wallsend Colliery, where it was produced from the High Main Seam. Coal owners marketed their coals under proprietary names, Wallsend with a prefix being used for the best. Eden Main was the Vane Tempest second best house coal.

In this case we should only have Nesham's to pay for the *use of their way*. And to pay Way-leave to the Land proprietors – at the same rate as Nesham's pay, I should presume.

The expence of erecting a Shipping Spout,[16] at Sunderland, a few additional Waggons & Horses, and an Inclined Plain Engine, would fall upon your Lordship. But the *Lighterage*, *Fittage*, and casting would be saved, and an additional price may be obtained for the Coals. I have had my eye upon this business for some time, but before I give your Lordship a distinct opinion on the subject I am wishful to make a detailed, and as correct an Estimate of the cost, and savings as possible. As I however think it prudent, that my views on this business, should remain secret, until from an Estimate of the expence, and other considerations your Lordship may be enabled to decide, whether it might be carried into effect, or not, I am obliged to seek the requisite information with great caution, and cannot therefore proceed with my estimate so expeditiously as I should otherwise do. I hope however to be able to complete it with sufficient accuracy in the course of a few Weeks.

In the event of this plan being adopted, I believe, that the shipping spout, will have to be erected in the Revd. Dr Gray's property.[17] The Doctor is a member of the Chapter and as I am on very friendly terms with him, I have no doubt of being able to agree with him on fair conditions.

It happens that a Tract of about 104 acres of Coal, belonging to the Doctor's Stall,[18] lies in front of our Resolution Pit's Workings. And altho' we can do without it, yet it will be a convenience to take it. I therefore submit that we should endeavour to take it (on fair terms) as the tentale rent for which we may agree with the Doctor, will be a precedent for the D[ean] & Chapter. And besides as it is the Doctor's private property, we may by taking it, altho' we have plenty of the D[ean] & Chapter's Coal adjoining, make him *our friend in the Body*. Indeed I think the more your Lordship can get connected with the Prebend[arie]s individually, in this sort of way, the more firmly will the interest of the Body be connected with that of your Lordship, and the more likely to facilitate the main object – the renewal.

16 A chute for delivering coal from shore to sea-going ship.
17 Robert Gray, 1762–1834, Prebendary of Durham 1804–34, Rector of Bishopwearmouth 1805–27, Bishop of Bristol 1827–34. *ODNB*.
18 i.e. his Prebendal stall in the Cathedral. See Anne Orde, 'The Dean and Chapter of Durham's Coal Interest 1541–1872', *Durham County Local History Society Journal*, no. 77 (2012), pp. 5–20.

As I have so often occasion to refer to the several Pits by name, I have prepared a pocket plan of Rainton Colliery which I shall forward to your Lordship; but I am desirous in the first place, if I can to annex the Hetton Estate to it.

I have great pleasure in reporting to your Lordship, that all the operative Departments of our Colliery concerns are in a very favorable situation, although we have been reduced almost to a state of torpor for the last month; but are at length cheered, by the Thaw having set our wheels in motion again.

I hope to have the pleasure of seeing Mr Iveson here on the 31st Inst. when we shall fully discuss the affair of Hetton &c.

I am glad to say that the spirit of Radicalism is still declining amongst our Colliers; and will by-and-by I hope be extinguished, if not re-excited by the imprudence of Mr Lambton[19] and his partizans. He dined in Newcastle with a Physician of the name of Hedlam,[20] on the 19th Inst. and on the following day, a requisition was presented to the Mayor to call a meeting, 'to consider the propriety of petitioning Parliament for a Reform in the representation of the House of Comm[on]s.' This the Mayor very properly refused to do, and in consequence the requisitionists resolved to hold the meeting in a private Room which I understand they can do by the late Act.[21] Mr Lambton is said to have promoted this business. Mr James Losh,[22] the late Receiver for my Lady's landed property, was at the head of the requisitionists.

The general opinion even of a very great number of people, who entertain the same political principles as Mr Lambton is, that the agitating the question of parliamentary Reform, at the time, whilst the embers of radicalism, are still smoking[23] is exceedingly injudi-

19 John George Lambton, 1792–1840. MP for Co. Durham 1813–28. His property adjoined Rainton; his coal interest was of importance comparable to the Vane Tempests'. *ODNB*; *Hist. Parl. 1820–32*, vi, 28–37.

20 T.R. Headlam.

21 One of the 'Six Acts' of December 1819 not only severely restricted the holding of public meetings but strictly regulated all places where the public could hear lectures or take part in debates.

22 James Losh, 1763–1833, Newcastle barrister and reformer, Recorder of Newcastle 1832. He had been Receiver for the Vane Tempest properties 1814–19. See *The Diaries and Correspondence of James Losh*, ed. Edward Hughes, Surtees Society, lxxi, lxxiv (Durham, 1962, 1963); *ODNB*.

23 Widespread agitation in the summer of 1819 for parliamentary reform, mostly peaceful, culminated on 16 August in the Peterloo massacre at Manchester, when eleven people were killed and several hundred wounded. Durham

cious. But in point of political prudence Mr Lambton stands very low in the public estimation. And his intemperate conduct in public matters, together with his hauteur in private life have rendered him exceedingly unpopular in this County.

His conduct at the late public meetings, at Durham & Sunderland – particularly at the latter, was very rash and offensive, and has lost him the good opinion even of the Radicals.

Amongst the respectable inhabitants of Sunderland, there is a great wish for a Member to represent the Co. of Durham, who would be decidedly Ministerial – they deem it absolutely essential to their maritime interests. The cry therefore is, with them 'We must have Mr Lambton out at the next Election'.

Mr Lambton's making use of my name in the Cause, in the manner he did was neither fair, nor correct, as he *knew* that other Colliery Viewers, as well as myself (who had the same opportunities of ascertaining the fact) had also declared that the pitmen were arming as fast as they possibly could.

I do not envy him his feelings on that occasion, but feel the satisfaction of self approval, as on reflecting on all that has passed in this neighbourhood during the last four months, I am convinced that the line of conduct which I have pursued, was what I should repeat under similar circumstances.

Mr Lambton is president, for the year of the public rooms at Sunderland. These rooms are held in shares of £35 each and Members subscribe £1.11.6 yearly, each individual. Mr Lambton holds two shares.

When last at Sunderland it was communicated to me, that a very general desire prevails, that your Lordship should become a proprietor – to as great an extent at least as Mr Lambton. And I understand that when the year expires next May, it is the wish of the Loyal party, to elect your Lordship President. The addition of your Lordship's name would be an Host to this party, who have long been victims of an arrogant and domineering spirit, and who have almost been subdued, for want of a Chief. The ground on which the public Rooms are built, was as I am informed given to the proprietors by the late Sir Henry Vane Tempest.[24]

During the late Frost the poor inhabitants of Sunderland, have

---

was one of the 'disturbed counties' listed in another of the Six Acts, which empowered magistrates to search for and seize arms dangerous to the public peace.

24 Sir Henry Vane Tempest, 1771–1813, father of Lady Stewart.

suffered much from the want of Fuel. They must have literally starved to death but for the assistance of the Coal owners who sent them a regular supply of small Coals by Carts, the delivery of which was under the management of a Committee. The same practice has been followed on former occasions, and the quantity of small Coals, sent by each Coal owner bears a proportion to his Vend. On this occasion we have sent the same quantity as Mr Lambton, which I hope your Lordship will approve.

The right honble   I have [&c.]
Lord Stewart   Jno Buddle
Vienna

3.

D/Lo/C142/1 (5)   Colliery Office Pensher
                                                      28th Mar[ch] 1820

My Lord
    I had the honor of receiving your Lordship's letter of the 3rd Inst. yesterday, and shall immediately set about the Hetton business.
    My letter of the 11th Feb[ruary]25 will have informed your Lordship of certain peculiar circumstances relative to the Hetton coal, which did not come to my knowledge 'till after my first communication thereon to your Lordship.
    I hope there are no insuperable difficulties in the way, and I will without delay take such steps as I think best calculated to forward the negotiation, both with Mr Lyons and Clutterbuck's26 party. The manager for the latter is an indecisive, trifling character, and I anticipate considerable trouble and difficulty in bringing him to a point; but still I expect to be able to manage him. And a little delay in the negotiation, so long as we *keep together*, is of little consequence; as I conceive it to be of more importance, to keep *others out*, than to get into the concern ourselves for the present.
    This opinion is strengthened by an occurrence which has just taken place, and which I hasten to communicate to your Lordship.
    There is a mutiny in the Chapter!!! The *old ones* have absolutely

25 D/Lo/C142/1(3).
26 The coal on the Hetton estate was owned jointly by John Clutterbuck (Lyon's brother-in-law) and Alexander Emerson together with John Lyon.

mutinied, in consequence of the *young ones* holding them back from pocketing the Rainton fine. Our silence and reserve on the subject, has so disconcerted and puzzled them, that they are no longer able to bear it; and on Saturday last this discontent broke out into open *insurrection*.

I met T. Fenwick at Sunderland yesterday in search of me, having been dispatched for that purpose, by the *Insurgents*, to enquire whether your Lordship had declined all idea of further Treaty for the Renewal, or whether the Door was still open to negotiation – adding a great many anxious wishes for a continuance of that union of interests, which had so long subsisted between your Lordship's Family and the Chapter.

I replied that altho' *we* on the part of your Lordship, had been much discouraged by the unfavourable reception which the Revd. Body had given to our very liberal offer; and which had almost compelled us to relinquish the hope of being able to effect a renewal yet I was so well aware of the sincerity of your Lordship's wishes to cultivate that reciprocity of interests with the Chapter which must result from a renewal of the Rainton Colliery Lease, that I felt no hesitation in saying we were ready to renew the treaty whenever the Revd. Body themselves should feel inclined to do so. I then *pushed home* all our strong points of *self-defence* in case we should be *driven*, by the impracticability of effecting a Renewal; but carefully avoided placing them in an *offensive* point of view.

Fenwick told me that an express had been sent for him on the Evening of the 17th Inst. to attend at the Chapter Room next morning, which he accordingly did, and found the Honble --- Gray, and Mr Boyer and Dr Price[27] there. The meeting was private, i.e. Bowlby[28] was not admitted and Fenwick was enjoined to secrecy. All that he was permitted to communicate to me is stated above, from which I think it is not difficult to make out, that a part of the Revd. Body, at least, are quite as anxious for the Renewal as we are. Phillpotts[29] was not at this meeting – he was from home that day, and Fenwick thinks the meeting was called purposely in his absence.

Fenwick is to communicate the substance of our conversation to

---

27 Hon. Anchitel Grey, 1774–1833, Prebendary of Durham 1809–20; Reynald Bouyer, 1741–1826, Prebendary of Durham 1792–1826, Archdeacon of Durham; Robert Price, 1748–1823, Prebendary of Durham 1794–1823. *ODNB*.

28 John Bowlby, Deputy Register [= Registrar] to the Dean and Chapter.

29 Henry Phillpotts, 1778–1869, Prebendary of Durham 1809–20, 1831–69, Rector of Stanhope 1820–31, Bishop of Exeter 1830–69. *ODNB*.

the Archdeacon who will in consequence convene a special Chapter next Saturday 1st April, from which I foresee that it will not be long, before we shall be engaged again *yard arm & yard arm* with the Revd. Body.

I told Fenwick that if the Chapter were really sincere in their wish to renew, and to have all things in readiness for that purpose by 20th July next, no time should be lost in setting about it, as we could not calculate upon a shorter space than six weeks for referring any point, or making any communication which it might be requisite to have with your Lordship on the business.

Fenwick is very sanguine in his expectation that we shall now agree with the Chapter; and is also I believe sincere in his wishes that we may do so. And really I am of opinion myself that we shall make a bargain with them, after haggling a little, and probably having to advance £2000 or £3000 on the Fine, just for the sake of getting the matter set at rest.[30]

I shall not trouble your Lordship with any further speculation on this affair at present; but as soon as any further movement takes place, I will write immediately.

Mr Iveson read to me the D[raf]t of your Lordship's proposed letter to the Chapter which the hurry of Electioneering matters would not at the time allow us to go into with sufficient deliberation. But the hasty opinion which we then formed, was, that no harm could result from delaying it 'till we could have an opportunity of giving it more deliberate attention; and I now feel very glad indeed that it has been postponed – the first move on this occasion has come from the *right side.*

I am happy to inform your Lordship that all our Colliery affairs are going on well; and I hope to see the *Black Diamonds* shine brilliantly this year, if their lustre is not tarnished by the absurdity and folly of the Tyne Coal owners, amongst whom every particle of common sense seems for the present to be extinguished.

We have got 'the Binding'[31] very well over, and I hope our vend this month will reach 10,500 Ch. Saturday next is our receipt day at Sunderland, after which I shall have the pleasure to write your Lordship the particulars of the Binding, the Vend, the receipt, &c.

---

30 The Rainton lease was renewed on 26 December 1820: Durham Cathedral Muniments (hereafter DCM), B/BA/ 102, fols 1v–12v. The Dean and Chapter originally asked for a fine of £56,000, but eventually settled for £40,000, paid in instalments.

31 The system of signing annual contracts for pitmen. See Introduction, p. xviii.

Our Electioneering Campaign is over, but the result for the County is not so favourable as might have been wished.[32] The prodigious Swarm of petty Freeholders with which the County of Durham abounds, has carried Mr Lambton thro' with éclat – by no means from personal respect to him I believe; but from downright detestation of the Clergy. Nor is it to be wondered at when the oppressive conduct of the Dean and Chapter is taken into consideration. I know several of their Tenants who would not vote at all, merely to thwart the wishes of their Landlords, whom they were afraid to go directly against by voting for Mr Lambton.

The oppressive conduct of the Clergy in the Diocese of Durham is much to be regretted,[33] as it tends, together with all the other unfavourable circumstances of the times greatly to increase that spirit of dissatisfaction, which still lurks in the minds of the lower orders in this Country, and which appears to be gaining ground amongst the middle classes of society also with great rapidity. I am delighted to hear so good an account of my Lady's health, and have the Honor to remain [&c.]

The right honble   J^no Buddle
Lord Stewart
Vienna

---

32 In the election of 1820 for County Durham, Lambton polled 1731 votes, the other Whig candidate W.N. Powlett 1137, the Tory Richard Wharton 874. For Durham City, the Tory candidate Sir Henry Hardinge and the Liberal Michael Angelo Taylor were elected unopposed: *Hist. Parl. 1820–32*, ii, 353–5, 362–4. The contest cost Lambton £30,000. See Chester W. New, *Lord Durham* (Oxford, 1929), pp. 58–63.

33 Buddle's criticisms anticipated by a year the so-called libel on the Durham clergy, published by the *Durham Chronicle* on 18 Aug. 1821. W.L. Burn, 'The Libel on the Durham Clergy', *DUJ*, new ser., vii (1945), pp. 25–9. *The Trial of John Ambrose Williams for a Libel on the Clergy …* (Durham, 1822). See below, letter 119, when Buddle proclaims his desire for reform of the Church.

4.

D/Lo/C142/2   Colliery Office Pensher
                                                      4th Jan[uar]y 1821

My Lord

I now have the honor to lay before your Lordship, a statement of the Vend &c for the year 1820, and I most heartily wish, that the new year may prove, in every respect as good as the old one – the enclosed return shows the state of the vend &c.

The amount of the Cash Balance as stated in the last return, 8th Dec[ember] is reduced by the two subsequent pay Bills. But we received £12,086.0.3 ½ on the 2nd Inst. which will commence our Cash Account for the new year. The Amount of the Coals vended in December, about £10,250, which we shall receive on the 1st Feb[ruary] added to the surplus of the receipt on the 2d Inst. after paying the current expences of the present month, will leave ample Funds, I expect, to carry us through the *dead* months of March and April. I call these heavy months, because I am apprehensive from the present state of the Season, as well as from the general aspect of the Trade, that the Vend during the present and next month will be *shy,* and that in consequence, the receipts on the 1st Mar[ch] and 1st April, will be proportionably deficient. I don't however like to forbode evil; but at the same time it is right to anticipate probable events.

Fortunately for us the River kept open till the 2nd Inst. and few Lynn vessels dropping in, enabled us to push up the December Vend to better than 9,000 Ch. whilst every other Colliery on the River has been completely at a stand still for nearly a Fortnight.

A severe Frost commenced on the 2d Inst. which closed the River, and all our Waggon-ways, being completely blocked up by a heavy fall of Snow yesterday, we have laid the Pits off – to give the Pitmen the holydays, which we owe them for Christmas.

Below ground, I am glad to say that everything is in a favourable state, in consequence of which, the proposed reduction in the establishment of Horses &c in the Dunwell pit, was carried into effect, on the 1st Inst. 7 Horses are now doing the work there instead of 34.

We have fortunately got the Masonry of the new Engine house at the Meads finished before the Frost set in. The roofing will be on in a few days when the Engineers will be able to proceed with the fitting up of the Machinery.

As it is probable that the Workings may exceed the vend during this and next month, the accumulation of resting coals may be expected; but as I don't think the Eden-main will take much injury from exposure to the weather I think of allowing them to remain at the Pits, and will reserve the Staith for the Walls-end – to keep them under cover.

I have been requested by the 'Davy plate Committee' to hand the accompanying paper to your Lordship and a similar one has been sent to Mr Lambton. The following is a brief history of this affair.

It was agreed by a general meeting of the Coal-owners of both Rivers to compliment Sir H. Davy with a Service of Plate, for the invention of the Safety Lamp,[1] and a Service of £2000 value was accordingly ordered. Several pretenders to the invention of Safety Lamps immediately sprung up, and the consequence was, that a party squabble took place amongst the Coal-owners, and thro' the spirit of party feeling many declined subscribing to Sir Humph[ry].'s Plate altho' they fully admitted the utility of his invention, and thro' private opposition subscribed £1000 to another person who had made some attempts at a Safety Lamp; and ultimately pyrated Sir Humphrey's. This schism caused a defalcation in the Subscription, and in the end left £1210 short of paying the Silversmith for the Plate. The subscription from the *whole* trade of the Wear, of which my Lady's Collieries paid in proportion to the quantity vended, was only £190 and as all the principal Coal-owners on the Tyne, who were of Sir H's party doubled their original subscription, the Committee now request the aid of the principal Owners on the Wear, to enable them to settle the Balance with the Silversmiths who in consequence of wanting their money so long, have become very clamorous. And they will feel very greatly obliged by any assistance your Lordship may think proper to afford them in this difficulty.

In consequence of a communication from Mr Iveson, we are making arrangements for celebrating my Lady's Birth-day, in a manner becoming the occasion – paying due regard to economy at the same time.

Nothing further has come to my knowledge respecting the Hetton affair. But we are entering into arrangements for purchasing Story's Farm[2] on the principle which I formerly named to your Lordship,

---

1   For Sir Humphry Davy, the safety lamp, and the controversy about priority in its invention see Flinn, *Coal Industry*, pp. 137–42; *ODNB*.

2   A farm at Moorsley belonging to John Storey, which Lord Stewart was buying.

viz. that the purchase money shall remain on Mortgage – the Value to be fixed by disinterested persons.

I don't think we have any domestic news of much importance in this quarter at present. We have been all very quiet in political matters since the Durham meeting. But the Whigs are going to kick up a fuss in Northumb[erlan]d in consequence of the High Sheriff having refused to call a County meeting to take the late proceedings against the Q—n[3] into consideration, at the request of Lord Grey,[4] Sir C. Monk,[5] Mr Lamton [sic] &c. Mr Lambton is a 40/- Freeholder in Northumb[erlan]d and is now stopping with Lord Grey.[6] They have called a meet[in]g to be holden at Morpeth on the 10th Inst. I believe, when we shall no doubt have the Durham song, sung over again.

The affair of the Q—n is now getting very thread bare and stale, and is losing all interest with the lower classes; and I should not wonder to see the Tide completely turned ere long. When any fresh prey is sprung by the Jackalls of the opposition papers, the Radicals yelp loudly, for a while like well thrashed puppies, but soon forget it again.

The right honble	I have the honor, [&c.]
Lord Stewart	Jno Buddle
Vienna	

---

3   On his accession in 1820 George IV asked ministers to institute divorce proceedings against his estranged wife Princess Caroline of Brunswick. Her cause was taken up by Whig politicians amid popular tumult. In January 1821 she accepted an offer of a settlement, but the king's coronation in July gave her an opportunity to claim the right to be crowned. She was refused admission to Westminster Abbey and died the following month. Her death caused further controversy in Durham when the cathedral bells were not tolled in the customary manner.

4   Charles, second Earl Grey, 1764–1845, Northumberland landowner and prominent Whig, Prime Minister 1830–4. ODNB.

5   Sir Charles Monck, 1779–1869, Whig MP for Northumberland 1812–20. ODNB; Hist. Parl. 1790–1820, iv, 610–12.

6   Lambton was married to Earl Grey's daughter Louisa.

5.

D/Lo/C142/2   Colliery Office Pensher
                                                            7th April 1821

My Lord

I have received your Lordship's letter of the 13th Ulto: from the tenor of which I am led to hope that we may soon expect to hear of my Lady as well as yourself being relieved from those anxieties, which the existing circumstances of the Family must naturally excite – by the happy consummation of your best wishes.[7]

I have delayed writing longer than usual, in expectation of being able to inform your Lordship, that we had garnered the first Fruits of the Regulation – an advance on Eden-main Coals.

This I now have the pleasure to say is accomplished, as an advance of 1/- per Ch. took place on the 1st Inst. I have never lost sight of this object since the agreement for the regulation took place; but could not get Croudace[8] to *take the Leap*, till the evening of the 30th Ulto: when finding him in the *Vein* the 'Iron was struck whilst it was hot'.

The Fitters have made no material objection to the advance, and no more oaths have been sworn by the Captains than might reasonably have been expected on the occasion. The violence of the gale will soon be over, and we shall then have water again.

The price of the best coals is getting up fairly enough at London; but the demand for the inferior sorts, still continues slack; and so far as I can learn, no material improvement is likely to take place 'till about the middle of May, as the large stocks laid in, by the Merchants, in anticipation of a severe Winter, are not yet cleared off. We may therefore expect rather scanty pickings for a Month or so, to come.

The present short Vend is cramping our Finances a little at a time when money is wanted to meet the Dean & Chapter's instalment, and to pay Longridge & Pringle's[9] Assignees. But it is a great satisfaction to think that we shall get *safely* paid for what Coals are sold; and that we have also obtained an advance of 1/- per Ch. on Eden-main which will be equal to a gain of £4000 a year even if we should not get another shilling, which I don't entirely dispair of doing.

---

7 George Henry Robert Charles William Vane, the Stewarts' first son, was born on 21 April 1821. From 1823 he had the courtesy title of Lord Seaham.

8 Thomas Croudace, viewer to J.G. Lambton.

9 Unidentified.

In the course of May, or beginning of June, I have little doubt but that we shall have a free demand for Coals again, and I firmly expect that when your Lordship arrives you will find us as busy as a Hive of Bees. Vending a less quantity of Coals than any body else, is quite out of the question. We have got the lead and *will* keep it.

In consequence of the limited Vend, the Whitefield Pit – in the Freehold will be laid off on the 10th Inst., and all our workings will then be from the Dean & Chapter's and Mr Davison's property,[10] as stated in a former letter. And the extraordinary Expences of Coal-work, will be reduced as much as circumstances will permit; but our extra work – at the Meadows, the Quarry, and the Tub apparatus will not admit of any abatement at present.

Everything is going on, as well as possible at the Meadows – in four or five weeks' time I expect to see the new Engine vomiting out 1000 gallons of water a minute from the old Waste.

The Quarry[11] is in a very promising state; and will I hope turn out a good Concern. We are getting blocks of excellent stone of 2 to 5 Tons weight; and only wait the completion of the Cranes &c. for delivering them into the barges, to commence a regular supply to the Pier. The Quarry offers a good source of employment for a number of Durham freemen.

We are working away very hard at the loading Machine,[12] for the old Tub system; and I hope to have one Branch of it in operation and the other branches, considerably advanced by the time when we may expect to be honoured with your Lordship's presence. I am very glad that your Lordship will be at home before it is to be carried into full operation; for as it will be the means of bringing about a most material reduction in the Expences, incurred by the Fitters, in shipping the Coals; your Lordship must participate in such reduction, to compensate for the expence of the Apparatus. We may therefore look forward to a very material change in the whole system of Fitting the Coals, to commence with the year 1822, in the discussion and arrangement of which, the early communication with your Lordship will be very satisfactory.

I have had a good deal of conversation, with the most respectable of our Fitters on this affair. And two of them, Scurfield and Tanner,[13]

---

10   John Davison, Beamish. The property was at Herrington Mill.

11   At Penshaw.

12   A machine, devised by Buddle, for loading coal in containers {tubs} directly from the keels into the ship, instead of casting it by hand.

13   Robert Scurfield and William Tanner, fitters at Sunderland.

are anxious to contract – to take all the Walls-end at a reduced Fittage of 2/- which will be equivalent to an advance of 2/- per Ch. on the price of the Coals.

Now assuming that we shall ship 30,000 Ch. a year in this way – in the first instance, which may be done with our floating Engine, and 30 Keels fitted up with Tubs – the reduction in the Fittage will amount to £3000.

I calculate the cost of the Apparatus for the Tub system, including the floating Engine &c. at £4000. And the actual expence of working and keeping it in repair at £1000 – including 10 per cent. Interest, to liquidate the capital expended in the outfit.

Then this sum, deducted from the £3000 of reduced Fittage – leaves a neat saving of £2000 a year to your Lordship.

I have little doubt that, allowing two or three of our most respectable Fitters, to vend the whole of the Walls-end Coals, would be the most eligible plan, in point of convenience and profit; but how far the granting of an exclusive privilege of this sort, may be the most politic line to adopt, is for future discussion.

With respect to South Biddick I must confess that I should like to see it in your Lordship's possession, altho' I should not like to see it bought too dear. The chief consideration, in my mind, which makes it valuable to your Lordship, is to enable you to preserve the *balance of power*, in the scale of your Colliery Politics, as explained in a former Letter. In any other point of view I should hardly think it worth your Lordship's attention. I have never been in 'the Hall', but it seems a comfortable sort of House, and might suit a private Gentleman's Family very well, if it should not come within the arrangement of your Lordship's plans, to make it an occasional residence whenever you might feel disposed to look into the detail of your operations.

Croudace has frequently talked to, or rather talked *at* me, on the subject, with a view I imagine of endeavouring to *fish* out whether your Lordship is likely to become a competitor, with Mr Lambton; but he has never been able to get even a *nibble*. As far as I can make out from him Mr Lambton would not like to give more than £15000 to £16000 – he values it at £12000 to £13000, but would give the larger sum on account of it's contiguity. I suspect that the latter word, will admit of a *very extensive* meaning. A few days ago he observed to me, that he should not wonder if some Fool or other, might run it up to considerably more than it's value, at the Sale, in which case Mr L. would certainly not buy it. I am not however disposed to give much credit to this assertion as it is very evident to me from Croudace's manner that he is very anxious it should come into Mr Lambton's

possession. Mr Iveson will be down here before the day of sale, when
we must consider what is best to be done. My present notion is that,
no person ought to appear at the sale, who could at all be suspected
of bidding for your Lordship. But that some person, totally uncon-
nected with your concerns, ought to be employed, confidentially to
bid for your Lordship. This in my opinion is the most likely plan of
avoiding a violent competition with Mr Lambton.

I can say little more at present respecting Hayton and Horn,[14]
than what I have already communicated. If any opportunity occurs
of making use of them, in the way your Lordship suggests, it shall
not be *slipped*. But I by no means think it unlikely that the whole *pack*
may be *swamped* before ever they get a Coal. They have been stopped
for several weeks past by a feeder of water; and cannot advance
an inch further 'till they get an Engine. Scruton[15] is advertising for
£28000 to borrow, on 'good security' which it is well understood to
be applied to the winning of Hetton Colliery. There [*sic*] position
at present, therefore is, that the sinking is at a stand, and they are
endeavouring to borrow a large sum of money to carry on the works
with.

I never had any great opinion of Hayton's stability; and circumstances which have recently come to my knowledge, have by no
means improved that opinion, but the contrary.

And as I have every reason to believe that the two persons who
have been his Bondsmen for some years past, are merely men of
Straw, I deemed it requisite a few days ago, to inform him, that
unless he procured Bondsmen of whose stability I should approve,
I could not feel justified in continuing to supply him with Coals.
In consequence of this he offers to give the security of his Son in
Law Mr Stobart[16] and a Ship-owner of the name of – Thompson.[17]
The former I think I cannot well object to, and I don't as yet know
whether the other will be satisfactory, or not; but I have enquiries
on foot, to ascertain the point. If he does not give satisfaction in this
point he will not continue to get his Coals, as we can never part with

---

14 William Hayton and Thomas Horn, Sunderland fitters, were shareholders in
the Hetton Co.
15 Walter Scruton, solicitor in Durham.
16 William Stobart, viewer, shareholder in the Hetton Co., leased Rickleton
Colliery from Lambton.
17 There were two ship owners in Sunderland of the name of Thompson. Buddle
was evidently not sure which one was concerned here.

him at a better time, i.e. when we have less money (about £3000) at risk with him.

I am glad to observe that all our underground operations are going on well. We now only want an increased Vend to make us flourish; and this I hope a few Weeks will bring.

Our political Foes, it is said, are preparing to give us battle for the President-ship of the Rooms at Sunderland – the first Monday in May. We must provide against the worst, as well as we can, and I should not wonder, if like the Carbonari,[18] they disband them-selves before we meet them fighting in the Field. The present year under your Lordship's auspices, has been the most tranquil since the commencement of the Institution. I wish Sir C. Sharp[19] may get here against the day of Election. He will be a powerful partizan in case of need. Hoping very soon to have a good account of my Lady

The right honble	I have the honor [&c.]
Lord Stewart	J^{no} Buddle
Vienna	

6.

D/Lo/C142/3   Colliery Office Pensher
                                        29th April 1821

My Lord

I have the honor to acknowledge the receipt of your Lordship's letter of the 5th inst. which came to hand on the 26th. I am happy to learn that we are soon likely to have the pleasure of seeing your Lordship in this Country; but I must confess that it would have been a very great additional pleasure, to have learnt that my Lady was safely in her bed – an event which we are anxiously hoping daily to hear of, and which we trust will not now be long delayed.

I feel obliged by the frank and candid manner in which your Lord-ship expressed your sentiments, respecting the regulation of Vend; and shall state my own views thereon in reply, without reserve, as I shall always be glad to do, on every subject whenever your Lordship may feel disposed to enter into detail.

18 An Italian republican secret society, responsible for unsuccessful revolts in Naples and Piedmont in 1820 and 1821.
19 Sir Cuthbert Sharp, 1781–1849, Collector of Customs in Sunderland 1823–45, historian of Hartlepool. *ODNB.*

The sole question, to the solution of which, our attention was directed, during the preliminary considerations, which led to an acquiescence, in the Regulation, on the part of your Lordship, was, How should we manage to make the most money?

After the most mature consideration, the vending of a certain quantity, at a certain price, *well paid*, appeared to be much more likely to attain that end, than striving for an indefinite quantity at an uncertain price, and *doubtful* Payment. Could we have been certain of vending, ad libitum, with any reasonable prospect of obtaining our full price, the entering into any regulation of quantity, would have been highly injudicious. The converse of this proposition was however, our dread, and the apprehension of the probable consequence of preventing a general Regulation which could not have been carried into effect, without your Lordship's concurrence, impelled us to acquiesce in the measure.

If the Regulation had not taken place, I am under the strongest conviction that a reduction of Price, must inevitably have ensued. The very idea of which is terrific, as even a couple of Shillings a Chaldron, on our quantity would amount to £11,000 to £12,000 a year; but the worst of it is, when a decline once takes place, there is no knowing when it will end, as it never fails to scatter ill blood, and angry feeling in the Trade.

Under existing circumstances, our choice was suspended between Quantity, and Price; and considering how much more easy, it is to make up a temporary deficiency of Quantity than to overcome a reduction of Price, the plan which ensured the maintaining of the Latter was preferred.

Although we stand the same quantity, on the Basis of Regulation, as Mr Lambton yet our actual vend for the year will stand about the same ratio *ahead* of him as last year, as we shipped more Coals than he did, before the Regulation took place. The regulation will expire on the 28th Feb[ruary] 1822 when our future arrangements as to the vend, will I hope be under your Lordship's immediate direction.

We got the lead of Mr Lambton during the first months of the year, by the exertions of our Fitters, who stowed the Coals on board of their Ships, in the harbour, when some of them lay several weeks, and in consequence they had not left the harbour, yet the Coals shipped counted as vend.

There is great truth in your Lordship's remark, as to the benefits resulting to the smaller Collieries from a Regulation. But at the same time, it is to be remarked, that it scarcely ever happens, that any of them are placed hors de combat, when there is no Regulation. And when forced to a reduction of Prices, either by direct, or indirect means, and to make the best *scramble* they can, they seldom fail to cripple their more powerful Neighbours, to an extent fully commensurate, with their own distresses. The scheme of *extermination* has been tried, at various periods, by the more potent proprietors, but always without success. The establishments of the inferior Collieries are small, and they always contrive in difficult times to make a better *fend* than might be imagined, whilst the great concerns cut dreadfully to waste.

The prospect of the Trade, at the commencement of last year, was certainly very bad; and we were all mistaken as to the unprecedented demand which took place in the fore end of the summer. It is possible the same thing may happen again this year (altho' I very much doubt it from the very nature of circumstances) in which case we shall enjoy the full benefit of it. For it is by no means the intention of the Regulation to retard the vend, when there is a *real demand* – it is only to prevent the Coals from being crammed upon the market, when it is over stocked. And consequently the vend is restrained, at this time, from the want of demand. I also hope that as the Coals are not *forced off*, we shall soon have, an increased, and *material* demand, and that in June and the following months, we shall be at full stretch again.

My candid opinion of the present regulation is, that it will be the salvation of the Shipping and Mercantile Interests of the North of England, if it is but well conducted. And that it will put the whole Machine so completely in order, that it will work well, by it's own impulse, for some time to come. And that after two years of privation (ending with the present) are completed, we shall still fill our cornucopiae before we have these voracious *black* Cormorants to feed.

I have no apprehension whatever, of the consequences which your Lordship predicts, from your *presence*, but the contrary. When on the spot your Lordship will be the better able to judge of the whole economy of the Trade as it may be modified by particular circumstances and will I am sure direct judiciously.

I assure your Lordship that I have always felt myself the most comfortable when acting under the immediate direction of my employers. And I feel the most entire confidence, that I shall feel the same satisfaction when my endeavours are the more immediately under the control of your Lordship.

I am happy to say that all our underground works are going on to my entire satisfaction; and the Meadows Engines, will *attack* the large body of stagnant water, on the 4th May – in due time I have little doubt but we shall be completely upon velvet in this quarter.

Storey's affairs[20] will be settled in a day or two, on eligible terms I hope. The whole amount will not exceed £3300 I expect. This is a position of importance as I hope to have the pleasure of pointing out to your Lordship on the spot.

I have nothing more to say on the Hetton affair at present, than that they are still sticking fast, 'till the Engine is ready – long may they stick is my prayer.

Hayton now having produced unexceptionable security, we cannot with decency set him a drift this year. I am exceedingly glad that he has brought forward better Bondsmen as I am informed through a private channel, that his Finances are in a very deranged state; and that it is highly improbable that he can *keep his legs* 'till Hetton is launched.

I shall now go to a more agreeable subject than the above – I mean South Biddick. I hope if your Lordship's mind is not already set to rest on this affair, it will very soon be so, by communications already forwarded. And I feel the highest satisfaction in stating, that the more I reflect on the consequences, which might eventually have ensued, had Mr Lambton been the purchaser, the more I am delighted to think that your Lordship has become the proprietor.

When your Lordship comes to see the importance of this Position, I am sure you will be impressed with the same sentiments. All that I shall say further on the subject, 'till I have the honor of pointing out it's importance to your Lordship *on the spot* is, that all your Lordship's Collieries may now be put in communication, with the *best part of the River, without passing through Mr Lambton's ground at all.* Whereas Mr Lambton *cannot possibly ship his present quantity of Coals, without having a Way-leave through your Lordship's grounds.* I would not 'for all the shoes in my shop' see your Lordship change places with Mr Lambton in this respect.

Mr Lambton is now fully sensible of the importance of this matter, and fortunate it is for us that his eyes were not sooner opened to it. Croudace never came near me since the day of sale, 'till the 27th Inst. when he exhibited the most evident marks of the deepest chagrin, and even dread of Mr Lambton's feelings on this occasion. He said he was sure Mr Lambton would be highly dissatisfied, that they had not got it; and he really did not know what to *say* to him about it. The only consolation he had, was that the blame of missing it was not his. From the questions he put – what use can it be to Lord Stewart – he

---

20   See n. 33.

surely never can intend to live in it – it is too small a property to be an object to him, Mr L. would be glad to give your Lordship something handsome for the bargain. And I venture to suggest that, if any such application should be made, and that your Lordship should be disposed to listen to it, that the reservation of a free Way-leave, to the River, with a sufficient Staith-room thereon, should be made a sine qua non. Croudace says they would have given £18,000 for it, which he considers to be the full value of the Land.

I have great pleasure in informing your Lordship, that I have made out, very much to my own satisfaction, from the examination of the old Colliers who wrought in the So. Biddick Colliery, that a considerable trail of Coal, which is accessible from the Pensher Pits, still remains unwrought there in the Maudlin, and Hutton Seams. I make it out at a moderate calculation, to contain upwards of 40,000 Ch. of Eden-main Coals, which in it's situation, being close to the River, ought to leave a Profit of £6000 at a low Estimate.

I have been through the House &c. and find it, to use a North Country phrase, to be a very *canny Place*. The House is in good repair – the Furniture excellent, and the Rooms a good size and height. The better to enable your Lordship to judge of the House, I have enclosed a rough plan of the first and second Floors &c., with the dimensions of the Rooms. And as they are anxious to know whether your Lordship feels disposed to take any part, or the whole of the Furniture I have made a schedule of it.

The present monthly payment to the Poor is £28.2.0. but I hope we may be able to reduce it by giving employment to some of the Paupers.

I shall have the honor of writing again after the *Battle* of the Rooms on the 7th May, when I hope we shall beat the Carbonari. We are very busy with the loading Machinery.

The right honble	I have the honor [&c.]
Lord Stewart	Jno Buddle
Vienna	

7.

D/LO/C142/4   Walls-end 1st Jan[uary] 1822

My Lord

Just as I am on the point of setting out for Pensher, I have received your Lordship's letter of yesterday's date, which informs me of the change your Lordship has thought it expedient to make, as far as relates to the management of your Colliery property, and informing me of your Lordship's intention, to confide the sole management of it to my care. Although I feel the full weight of the additional responsibility which is attached to me, on this occasion, I feel at the same time most sensibly, the gratifying indication of your Lordship's approbation of my conduct, which it conveys, and that tacit sort of expression of your Lordship's confidence, which kindles upon my mind, with the most ardent desire, to execute those Duties, committed to my charge, in a manner that may be satisfactory to your Lordship, and merit the continuation of that good opinion, the attainment of which has always been the summit of my ambition. I am sure that your Lordship will consider my saying any thing more on the subject quite unnecessary.

I shall always have great pleasure, and indeed it will be a great relief to my mind, to communicate freely and without reserve, to your Lordship every material circumstance connected with the concerns under my charge. And I cannot anticipate the least doubt of a continued co-operation with those, to whom your Lordship may confide the administration of your other affairs.

The general Coll[ier]y accounts shall be made out in any way that your Lordship may suggest – the more comprehensive the better, especially as they may for some time to come, have to be transmitted to your Lordship at a distance. But this as well as other points, would be for discussion when I next have the honor of seeing your Lordship.

Gregson[1] may probably be rather too sanguine in his idea, as to the value of Seaham,[2] but still considering that the property had

---

1   John Gregson. Solicitor to the Vane Tempest properties. He also had an office in London. He had a number of other clients in Durham, and property interests of his own.

2   The Seaham estate, bought by Lord Stewart from Sir Ralph Milbanke in 1821.

been totally neglected for so many years past, it is only reasonable to assume, that it must be capable of considerable improvement.

I don't exactly like Mr Wood's[3] silence, but I suspect that all may yet end well. I shall shew Groom's[4] note to Gregson tomorrow.

I begin to be rather anxious for Croudace's return, as I want to propose some plan of retrenchment to him, to be carried into effect at our next Binding, 5th April, and which I cannot accomplish in our Works, without his co-operation. And as he generally requires about 3 months of *drilling* to bring him to *stand fire* in a case of this sort, I wish to begin with him in good time.

The Lord Stewart	I have the honor [&c.]
Wynyard	Jno Buddle

8.

D/Lo/C142/4   Sunderland 1st April 1822

My Lord

Croudace came here this morning too late for the Post. Mr Lambton, Lorain,[5] & himself have gone through the articles of the agreement,[6] together, and Mr Lambton approves of them. He is going to London again almost immediately and Lorain is going also; and Mr L. thinks it may be proper to see your Lordship in London, and hopes there will not be the least difficulty in completing the Agreement.

I proposed to Croudace that he and myself should get our Law-men here, to draw the agreement properly, under our inspection, and then send it to London for your Lordship's & Mr Lambton's approval & signature. But he demurred, and said that Mr Lambton wished in the first place to have some private conversation with your Lordship either personally or through Lorain – observing at the same time, that Mr Lambton instructed him, to assure me, that he was most anxious, to have the agreement carried into full effect, and that he wished of all things, to be on amiable terms with your Lordship.

---

3 Unidentified.
4 William Groom, London lawyer, solicitor to the trustees of the Stewarts' marriage settlement.
5 William Lorain, agent to J.G. Lambton.
6 An agreement recently negotiated by Buddle and Croudace for a mutual accommodation of wayleaves.

Croudace was not at liberty to inform me what the object of Mr Lambton's intended conversation, with your Lordship is; but I firmly believe, it is respecting Biddick. Whether he means to offer something in exchange for it, or to ask it as a boon at your Lordship's hands I don't know. I also suspect from the manner in which Croudace glared at our Dalden project,[7] that they are under some sort of alarm about it. I could not however find out what it is; but I feel confident that *whatever it may* be, it cannot be well founded, and that of course it will not be difficult to answer.

It therefore appears that the matter must rest where it is, until your Lordship hears further from Mr Lambton in London. Croudace says Lorain is to start for London next Sunday or Monday at latest, and if I understood Croudace rightly, he has first to wait upon your Lordship to broach the subject of Mr Lambton's communication.

We have got our receipt very pleasantly over here, considering what has occurred on the Tyne. The amount £8535. 11. 7½. The vend in March was 2974 Ch. Walls-end and 5282 Ch. Eden-main – together 8256 Ch. Amount £10,025. 8.0 besides £833.15.9 of Small, to tradesmen.

E. Backhouse[8] was however much disappointed at the small amount he received. He came to me, and although exceedingly civil, and smooth, shewed evident signs of being much dissatisfied, with the state of the account, and more particularly, at not receiving the whole of the Fitters' Bills. I told him that I now expected our receipts to increase considerably, and that they would continue larger, during the year. He was evidently however, much dissatisfied, and I really fear will be turning *restive* if the balance is any further increased. Not satisfied with what he said to me, he sent the enclosed[9] in the Evening.

I omitted to notice in my last that Gregson told me of Mr Groom's idea of paying off the Dean and Chapter. I did not say to Gregson that I did not see any advantage to arise out of it to your Lordship, unless the Money can be had at 4 per cent. Two objections occur to

---

7   The project of building a harbour at Dawden Cove on the Seaham estate, eventually Seaham Harbour.

8   Edward Backhouse, 1771–1860, Lord Londonderry's banker in Sunderland, partner in the Quaker family bank based in Darlington. See M. Phillips, *A History of Banks, Bankers and Banking in Northumberland, Durham, and North Yorkshire* (London, 1894), pp. 134–54; John Banham, *Backhouse's Bank of Darlington 1774–1830*, Papers in North Eastern History (Durham, 1997).

9   Not found in the Londonderry Papers.

me, 1st that by paying off the D[ean] & C[hapter] at once, when *not called for*, it will lead them to think at least, if it does not *confirm* the notion, that we are making enormous profits of their Colliery, and 2nd the expence of borrowing the Sum – Mortgage deeds, Stamps, Law expences and *procuration money* will be *outrageous*. By paying off the instalments *quietly*, we fulfil our engagement to the Chapter, without making any *parade* of our prosperity, and save all further Expence and plague of Law. I don't know the motives, which may have to do with this suggestion, but taking it in the abstract, it appears to me more likely to benefit the Lawyers, than your Lordship.

I regret to say that the Coal-owners on the Tyne seem determined to play the D—l with the trade completely. They lowered the price 2/- a Ch. on the 28th Ulto. And this morning Bell's & Brown's Wallsend[10] were put down 5/- per Ch. more, i.e. 7/- per Ch. in all, the price to the Ship-owners being 26/- instead of 33/-. I have received an express, to inform me of this *folly*. It has occasioned a great sensation and I don't know what the consequences will be. If this reduction becomes general and continues six months, this Country will be placed in the same state of distress as Staffordshire was, a few years ago from the retrograding of the iron trade. My only hope is, that this step of Bell's is so decisive, that it may bring all parties to their senses, before it is *too late*. I shall however be able to form a better opinion in the course of a day or two. If this reduction is general and continues a year, it will amount to upwards of £270,000 on the Tyne *alone*. And this I know to be far more than the aggregate profit of all the Collieries on the River. Some of Bell's family connections will be the most severely hit, by this blow.

The Board of Customs are prosecuting some Ship-owners here for certain irregularities in the signing of their *Coasting* Bonds, and a deputation is coming to London to wait on the Lords of the Treasury on the affair.[11] Mr John White[12] one of our Fitters is one of the deputation, and will wait upon your Lordship, to explain the matter & to

---

10 Coal from Willington and adjacent collieries owned by the partnership of Bell and Brown.

11 The coastwise coal trade was subject to a number of taxes and duties, paid to Customs at the ports of shipping, and varying according to the type and (from 1816) size of the coal shipped. The duties added very substantially to the cost of sea coal in London. Campaigns for their reduction or abolition led to the appointment of a House of Lords Select Committee in 1830. Flinn, *Coal Industry*, pp. 279–85, and see below.

12 John White and Sons, Sunderland fitters.

crave your Lordship's aid. There is no fraud found in the case, but some sort of explanation and adjustment is requisite.

Would a Pipe of Port wine be an object to your Lordship, the same as the last sent to Wynyard – payment ⅓ Cash and ⅔ Small Coals? It can be delivered either in London or Wynyard. I expect that a Pipe of Madeira should some time now be delivered at St James' Square from Featherstonehaugh.[13] I should like to know when it comes to hand, as I shall not *part with* the Coals 'till the Wine is forthcoming. I will notice Tommy Fenwick's affair in a few days – craving your Lordship's indulgence for all inaccuracies – considering it is written after a *Fitters' Dinner*

The Lord Stewart K.B.   I have the honor [&c.]
St. James' Square   J[no] Buddle
London

9.

D/Lo/C142/4   Newcastle 6th April 1822

My Lord
    I did not receive your Lordship's Dispatches of the 4th Inst. 'till after I had sent my Letter of this morning[14] to the Post. I immediately rode over to Durham, to consult with Gregson, on D. Lambton's[15] affair, and to impress on him, the necessity of obtaining an extension of time for the 1st instalment. He will do the best he can, to accomplish this point, and thinks he may be able to prevail with them, to defer it 'till May 1823. This I should hope will meet your Lordship's wishes, but he will write you fully tomorrow, on the business.
    I regret that I did not know when I saw Croudace, last Monday, that Williams[16] has resumed his old tricks, or I think I should have

---

13 Marmaduke Featherstonehaugh, Sunderland merchant.
14 Not found in the Londonderry Papers.
15 John Dawson Lambton, owner of Biddick.
16 John Ambrose Williams, editor of the *Durham Chronicle*, a radical newspaper patronised by Lambton. On 20 Oct. 1921 the paper reported at length an article in the *Irishman* giving an unfavourable account of relations between Lord Stewart's half-brother the second Marquess of Londonderry and a Presbyterian minister at Newtonards. At the Durham Assizes in March 1822 Lord Stewart had Williams indicted for libel, alleging that the paper had embarked on a career of libel against him. In the issue of 16 Mar. Williams asserted that in the original article he had disclaimed knowledge of the truth

handled the subject in such a manner as would have made due impression upon him. But the fact is, that I have always had such a singular disgust to this publication – from the accounts I have heard of it, that I never read a line of it in my life. I shall however make a point of seeing Croudace about it, & feel confident, that if he can put a stop, to Williams' abuse of your Lordship's Family he will. I really cannot imagine that the blackguard articles to which your Lordship alludes, can possibly have been inserted, either by Mr Lambton's or Croudace's privity. I shall however know more by-and-by – to talk of being on amicable terms with your Lordship, and at the same time, even to connive at, much less to encourage such scurrility, would be humbugging indeed to all intents and purposes.

Mr Lambton is still at Lambton and is to set off for London, I was told in passing thro' Chester-le-Street today, either on Monday or Tuesday next, and in all probability Billy Lorain will start in the morning. Your Lordship may therefore expect a call from him very soon. I feel very confident, that they will not wish to disturb the arrangement made with Croudace, in any essential point, and think it must be something, in the way of a favour, or matter of accommodation, which they wish of your Lordship. Their object must however soon be known and as dispatch in this affair is of importance to us, I shall hold myself in readiness, and if your Lordship finds my presence at all necessary you will find me with you by *return of post*.

I must say that Mr Groom's style of business correspondence, is very ambiguous, and unsatisfactory. He certainly ought, under existing circumstances, to enter into your Lordship's feeling, and be as explicit as possible on every point. May is fast approaching, and there is no time for trifling. If he had exerted himself a little more for the last three months, there surely could have been no necessity for working *eight hours* a day at this time. I should however feel alarmed at the idea of putting these affairs into other hands, as such delay might, eventually in that case, take place as might occasion almost insurmountable difficulties. Your Lordship has now performed the greater part of *this* Voyage with him; and I really think under all the circumstances, it will be advisable to continue under his pilotage, until it is finished.

He must be aware of the necessity of being punctual in the Seaham affair, where we have our greatest Enemies to deal with. And it is not

---

or otherwise of the *Irishman*'s story, and accused Lord Stewart of trying to muzzle the press.

likely, from the pressure of the Bank Creditors, that Sir F. Blake[17] *can want* his money. These considerations I should think would stimulate Groom, to use his very best exertions to set your Lordship at ease on these important matters, with all possible dispatch.

I understand your Lordship's explanation of the Financial Scheme, but don't still see any advantage in paying off the Dean & Chapter sooner than agreed for. It can make no difference whether the Interest of the Money is paid to them, or to any body else; but the transfer of a debt of it's magnitude cannot well be liquidated in a more easy way, than by £500 instalments.

I have no apprehension of Backhouse breaking with us, provided the balance is not further increased. And when your Lordship wishes remittances to be made, I should advise that they should go from the bank, and not in the Fitters' Bills, as I really think Backhouse was more annoyed by the loss of Discount on the £1000 Bills – some 12/6 or so, than he was by the largeness of the advance, although he said if they had not been so largely in advance, they could have made £400 more of the money in another way. I will look in upon him (Edward) in two, or three days and state to him, your Lordship's feelings on the subject, which I have no doubt will sooth him. I should not like to change Backhouses, as they can do our business much better than any other house. Indeed I scarcely know where we could go to, in the event of quitting them. In all the County of Durham there is none but Hutchinson's[18] to whom we could look. And in Northumberland and Newcastle, there are none but Lambton's[19] and Sir M. White Ridley.[20] And they, since the failure of Reids and Blake,[21] have got the ball so much at their feet, that they won't accommodate any body. This was the reason why the Hetton Co. quitted Ridley's – they would not advance a single guinea.

---

17 Sir Francis Blake Bt 1775–1860, part owner of the West Herrington property bought by Lord Stewart, partner in the Northumberland Bank, which failed in 1821, MP for Berwick 1820–34. *Hist. Parl. 1820–32*, iv, 288–92; Phillips, *History of Banks*, pp. 163–73.

18 Hutchinson and Place, Tees Bank, Stockton. The bank failed in 1825. See Phillips, *History of Banks*, pp. 287–91.

19 Lambton's Bank, Newcastle. Phillips, *History of Banks*, pp. 239–64.

20 Sir Matthew White Ridley Bt 1778–1836, MP for Newcastle 1812–36, partner in the Old Bank, Newcastle. *Hist. Parl. 1820–32*, vi, 262–71; Phillips, *History of Banks*, pp. 174–95.

21 See n. 17.

I will keep the Pay Bills, as low as I possibly can – consistently with the credit & respectability of the Works.

I expect the transferring machine to be ready in the course of next week. We shall require another week or so, to *drill* the men who have to manage the Machine and to get the Tubs fitted into the Keels. I therefore hope that in a Fortnight, or three weeks we shall be fairly under way with the Tubs. I examined the harbour last Tuesday morning with the Engineer, and fixed upon a Birth for the Engine Vessel. I also applied to the Chairman of the Commissioners Mr Robinson,[22] for leave to moor her, in the harbour. The mobility seems to have forgot this affair; it is however possible that the appearance of the Vessel, in the harbour may excite their notice again, we will therefore take all measure of precaution, we can, in a *quiet* way.

I will take care to send the Pipe of Port, to Wynyard, and shall be glad to hear of the arrival of the Madeira at St James' Square, as also of the Glass.

I can buy a Pipe of Madeira for Small Coals – your Lordship paying the Duty in Cash. It is lying in the W. India Dock, and if your Lordship will send any person to Messrs White & Greenwell, 54, Black-friars Road, they will give an order for tasting it. When if approved your Lordship may take it out of Bond, on paying the Duty, and I will settle the remainder as above stated.

We have not yet got the better of the water in the Resolution Pit; but even without her, I expect we can produce better than 10,000 Ch. this month, which under existing circumstances is fully as much as I expect to vend. In every other respect we are going on, as well as possible.

Nothing more here, since I wrote this morning, although it is said, that some of the refractory are about to hoist the *Flag of distress*, but I have not this, upon good authority.

The Lord Stewart K.B.   I have the honor [&c.]
St. James' Square   J^{no} Buddle
London

---

22 George Robinson, Sunderland magistrate and chairman of the Harbour Commissioners.

10.

D/Lo/C142/4   Colliery Office Pensher 10th April 1822

My Lord

I have this morning received your Lordship's Letter of the 8th Inst. which has greatly relieved my mind as to Mr Groom's movements, as I think he is likely to accomplish the May-day Plans of Finance altho' it does not seem, by *Law*, that he can compass them exactly in the way that might have been wished for. I am however very glad that he is likely to effect his purpose even in the way your Lordship states as I always have the utmost horror and apprehension of the tedious delay of Law-men in all matters of real business. There is generally something forgot, or something remaining to be done when you come to the very last point; I however trust this will not be the case in the present affair.

The reflections which your Lordship makes on your own personal situation in this great affair, makes me sad. But yet we have a good Ship under us, and although we may encounter some rough Weather, yet I have no apprehension of foundering in the midst of the Voyage. But when it makes bad weather we ought to shorten sail a little and put the vessel under *snug Canvas*. I therefore trust your Lordship will pardon the liberty I took in suggesting the propriety of suspending our operations at the new harbour, and of the buildings at Wynyard for twelve months or so, should your Lordship find that all your great plans – including them, cannot be carried on, at the same time without suffering a greater deprivation of personal comfort, than is consistent with your Lordship's rank in Life

If these operations were suspended for one, or even two years, and the resources of the Collieries applied solely to the liquidation of the mortgages on the new Purchases, it would place your Lordship in a much more comfortable situation, with respect to personal responsibility. And then the harbour & Building might be carried on with greater vigour. In this view of the case we should just be getting into the Marrow of our new Port &c by the time we might expect your Lordship to become resident in the Country. We should then go on with great vigour, and I think the superintendence of our operations would be a great source of amusement, and occupation to your Lordship's active mind. I offer these suggestions with great defference, and I hope your Lordship will not find them impertinent.

With respect to these pecuniary matters I agree with your Lordship, that there is a great similarity between our present   position and that of two years ago. But I see a striking difference between the two cases – two years ago, the Debt was for a *dead weight* of arrears, to be brought up. Now it is a fair legitimate debt, for the purchase and accumulation of a large additional property.

I will do all I can to keep the Pay Bills down, but at our present scale of work, it will be impossible to keep them so low as your Lordship mentions. We must now keep up our workings and vend every Coal we possibly can. At present we feel a want of Ships for Eden-main, owing to a N.E. wind which has kept the light vessels back for ten days. I am however still keeping up our workings, in hopes of running the Coals off, when the light Ships do arrive. A few Ships are off I hear, and will most likely get into the harbour during the night or tomorrow. At Newcastle every think [*sic*] is in perfect confusion and if a fleet of light Ships should arrive in the present state of affairs, there will be a complete race of destruction amongst the Coal-owners there. My only hope is that matters have gone to such an extreme of absurdity there, that they cannot long continue in their present state, and that before the Storm can have time to break over Sunderland, it will have exhausted it's fury at Newcastle.

We must positively make a stand here to support our prices; to follow the Tyne People would be ridiculous, and I hope that Croudace feels as I do on this point, although I have not seen him since the 1st Inst. I shall however feel his pulse again, before I leave here this week.

I am going to Sunderland tomorrow to look about me there, and to talk 'Friend Edward' [i.e. Backhouse] over a little. I want also to see some of the magistrates, to concert measures for keeping the peace when our Transferring Machine goes into the harbour, which will be on Monday week I expect.

I hope to send your Lordship a copy of the Gen[era]l Plan of this neighbourhood on a reduced scale, by the Mail from Newcastle, on Saturday morning. My Draughtsman will begin with it in the morning, and all the Properties your Lordship names shall be distinctly drawn upon it.

The person of whom I bought 40 doz. East India Madeira (Featherstonehaugh) is teasing me for the 1/3 cash, but I don't like to pay him until I know that the wine has arrived at St James' Square. As the poor fellow is much pinched, I shall be glad to hear from your Lordship, as soon as the wine is delivered.

The Lord Stewart K.B.	I have the honor [&c.]
St. James' Square	J^{no} Buddle
London	

11.

D/Lo/C142/4   Colliery Office Pensher, 11th April 1822

My Lord

I called at the bank this morning, and conveyed your Lordship's sentiments relative to the state of our Account (as expressed in your Letter of the 4th Inst.) to Ed[ward] Backhouse. He was very civil, but evidently much dissatisfied with the state of the account, observing that it was so much more over-drawn, beyond what they ever contemplated. He is therefore exceedingly desirous that it should be reduced, and although he did not express himself, exactly to that purport, yet I feel satisfied, from the manner in which he did express himself, that they have made up their minds, not to allow the balance to be further increased.

The present unfavourable aspect of the Coal trade, is evidently giving him uneasiness, and if your Lordship could in your present pecuniary arrangements, contrive to pay in £5000 in reduction of their Balance, I think it would be very well applied. It will be the same thing to your Lordship whether the Interest is paid to them, or to any body else. But it would have the effect of keeping them in humour, and of inducing them perhaps, to lend us assistance in case of any emergency. Which I am very apprehensive they will not do if the Account remains in it's present state.

I also called upon Mr Robinson as a Magistrate, and Chairman of the Commissioners, relative to the placing and protecting of our transferring machine, in the harbour. He most readily offered me every assistance in his power. He will put the River-Watch (10 men) who are under his command, on the alert, and make them all special Constables, as well as the People who have to manage the machine, and also the running Fitters, belonging to Tanner and Beckwith, and Scurfield.

There is a Company of Infantry stationed in the barracks, and he will make immediate application to the commanding officer at Newcastle, to have another Company (or at least as many men as he can spare) sent from thence. Whether he succeeds in the latter object or not, I think we shall have force enough, as above, to protect our machine and keep the Peace.

Croudace called upon me this Evening. Mr Lambton left home, for Catterick yesterday morning, and will be in London on Sat[urda]y or Sunday next. But Lorain is sauntering about no body knows what here, and does not think of starting 'till next Sat[urda]y or Sunday. I expect however from what I said to Croudace, that he will *touch him* with the *Spur*. And accelerate his movements a little.

As far as I can gather from Croudace, Mr Lambton's main, if not his sole object in wishing to have an interview with your Lordship, is to make some sort of proposition or other about Biddick.

I handled Croudace rather tightly about Williams' conduct. He fully admitted the impropriety of it, and really in my opinion felt very properly with respect to it. He declared most solemnly that he has not for some months, had any communication whatever with this vagabond. And he *knows* that Mr Lambton had not had any communication whatever with him, either directly or indirectly, since the Durham Election,[23] except the communication through Croudace himself, expressing his entire disapprobation of Williams' indecent and personal abuse of your Lordship. I told Croudace I was willing to believe the truth of all he said, but as the avowed patron of the paper, it would be very difficult to convince either your Lordship, or your friends, that Mr Lambton did not at least connive at Williams' villainous conduct, unless he immediately mended his manners. Croudace admitted the justness of the remark, and promised to use his utmost exertions to put a stop to Williams' scurrility. But he says that Williams is an impracticable and violent fellow, and wishes most heartily that the paper was suppressed. I told him however that Williams *must be managed* on the point in question, or it will be impossible for us, to go on smoothly together.

Croudace is now more bewildered than ever, with respect to Nesham's Colliery, as the Hetton Co. have become Mr Lambton's competitor for it. This has roused Croudace, and he is for buying at all hazards.

He seems equally determined, I am glad to say, to stick by us in supporting prices. Indeed he says he has Mr Lambton's express directions to co-operate with me, on this point, and that Mr L. has the greatest possible aversion to any reduction of price whatever – especially the best Coals.

If Lorain starts on Sat[urda]y or Sunday he will be in Town on Monday or Tuesday and will most likely call upon your Lordship on Wednesday or Thursday. And if your Lordship should deem my attendance necessary, I shall expect to receive *marching orders* about Sat[urda]y or Sunday, and will of course be in Town on Monday or Tuesday following. Dawson's property being now actually secured

23 Of 1820, see p. 15, n. 32.

gives us a new Fulcrum, to act from, in case Mr Lambton should broach any new Point.

Croudace suspects that Gregson has been concerned in a Plot, with Beckwith & Thompson,[24] to extort from Mr Lambton the extravagant price which he was obliged to give for Beckwith's estate. He is greatly annoyed at the idea of being the dupe of this Plot.

I hear that matters are getting the longer the worse on the Tyne, if possible; but I will go over to Newcastle tomorrow afternoon, to gain intelligence, and will write your Lordship by Saturday's Post.

The Committee for building the new Infirmary at Sunderland[25] are in want of two Stones 8 ft. long by 5 broad, each, on which to cut the Inscription, and will feel obliged if your Lordship will make them a present of two such Stones from our Quarry.

I some time ago made a bargain with Featherstonehaugh for 30 doz. of Sherry. It is now ready for delivery, and I shall be glad to know whether your Lordship would wish to have it sent to Town, or to Wynyard.

The Glass is shipped on board the Durham packet & will I hope shortly arrive safe. C. Johnson has insured £600 upon it.

The Lord Stewart K.B.   I have the honor [&c.]
London   Jno Buddle

12.

D/LO/C142/4   Newcastle 12th April 1822

My Lord

We tried the transferring Mach[in]e this morning, and I am glad to say that it promises fair to answer our best expectations. There are however several little matters which require adjustment, which could not be done 'till the machinery was put in motion. I therefore question that we shall be able to commence regularly with the Tubs on Monday the 22nd Inst. Tanner and Scurfield attended the trial of the Machine, and were much pleased with it. They suggest, that it will be best to set her to work in the harbour, when there is a *throng* of Ships in, and the casters have full employment, which will direct

---

24 William Beckwith, Trimdon; Thomas Thompson, Sunderland lawyer.
25 The first infirmary at Sunderland was built in 1823, to a design by Ignatius Bonomi.

their attention from the machine. I think this is a good idea, and we will adopt it, if circumstances will allow us to do so.

I came here in in [*sic*] the afternoon, to see what was going on, in the Coal trade; and find everything in the utmost possible confusion. With the exception of Walls-end, and Bewicke's Walls-end, which still hold out at 31/-, the prices of all the rest of the Walls-ends, are merely nominal. They are certifying the Coals at 25/- and 26/- per Ch. But the fact is, that they are mostly sending their Coals to market, at their own expence, and risk, by freighting Ships to carry them. Or they are bribing the captains, or giving great measure; in short, they stick at nothing to get their Coals off.

The mischief is not yet however at its height, as there has been for a Fortnight past, and still continues to be, a great scarcity of light Ships, owing to a determined N.E. and E. Wind. But when the Fleet arrives, there will in all probability be a complete Scramble. About 30 Sail of light Ships got in yesterday morning, which were all instantly snatched up, by the freighters, so that Walls-end and Bewicks, did not get a single Ship, and are of course at an entire Standstill.

Should the same thing occur, when the Fleet arrives, Walls-end and Bewicke, will be compelled to reduce, to such a standard as will induce the Ship-owners to load with them, so that at present there is no seeing the end of the mischief.

It is rather extraordinary that the inferior Collieries, are maintaining their prices much better than the first Class.

I shall forward the general Map of the Neighbourhood of Biddick & Painsher by the Mail tomorrow, which will I hope be sufficiently explanatory.

The Lord Stewart K.B.   I have the honor [&c.]
London   J^{no} Buddle

13.

D/Lo/C142/4   Walls-end 15th April 1822

My Lord

I this morning had the honor to receive your Lordship's Letter of the 13th Inst. which is very encouraging, but I must own that the aspect of the times at present makes me rather nervous. Your Lordship's *project* of finance, is exceedingly satisfactory, and I can most sincerely assure your Lordship that it is my most ardent desire, to see all your great plans – so promptly devised, and carried into execution – successfully accomplished. I can only say that neither attention nor exertion shall be wanting on my part, in aiding your Lordship's designs, to the utmost of my power.

Notwithstanding the remarks which I took the liberty to offer in my letter of the 10th Inst. I have not relaxed in the slightest degree in forwarding the preparatory measures for the Wynyard operations; as I have laid it down as a principle, to carry your Lordship's orders into execution, to the very letter at all times, unless I receive counter orders. Your Lordship may therefore rest assured, that I shall never waver in this respect, unless from prudential motives, arising out of new or unexpected circumstances.

With respect to the Wynyard waggon train for loading the Stones, I expect to have it in motion early next month. I only wait for the Stone carts from Leith. On fully reconsidering the subject, I decided in favour of the single-horse cart, used at Edinburgh in the Publick Quarries, as being the best calculated for our purpose. One man drives 3 of them; & I have ordered six – 3 to start from each end, every morning & to meet at Castle-Eden. They are to change carts there, and the Horses will return to their own respective Stables in the Evening. The *Elephant*[26] will start when the Stone carts arrive, and we shall send the Waggon Horses to the Carts. More than half the Stones are already quarried. I am also in treaty for a quantity of Timber; but the merchant's appetite is not so keen for Small Coals as I could wish, which has, as yet, prevented me from closing.

It is utterly impossible to describe the state of the Coal trade on this River, at present, the absurd conduct of the Coal-owners is without parallel, I believe. The Ship-owners taking advantage of their folly, refuse to buy their Coals, and the Coal-owners in their Phrenzy are freighting Ships to carry their Coals to market, at such extravagant rates, as will amount to a reduction on most of the 1st class of Coals of 10/- to 12/- per Ch. This insane conduct in the majority, has compelled Walls-end and Bewicke's Walls-end (the only two Collieries, which have attempted to stem the torrent) to reduce their Coals other [*sic* ?another] 2/- that is 4/- in all. We are therefore now obliged to sell at 29/- instead of 33/- per Ch.

How long this *mania* may continue, is difficult to say, but if it continues any length of time, inevitable ruin to half the Coal-owners on the River must be the consequence. My only hope is, that the Fit of delirium, is too violent to last long. I have not however before seen

---

26 An early form of steam locomotive.

any thing like it, and cannot therefore judge how long the paroxysm may last; but as far as I can guess, it will not last above a month, or six weeks. I think I already begin to perceive the appearance of lucid intervals, in some of the unhappy patients, which may I hope lead to a general convalescing.

It is this hope chiefly, which encourages me to expect, that we may still be able to maintain our prices on the Wear. It is however but too evident, that the struggle for this grand and vital object will be attended with a temporary deprivation of vend – mainly I hope on the Eden-main. I however feel that the object is worth a struggle, as I almost shudder, when I think upon it, that a reduction of even 4/- per Ch. on your Lordship's Coals would not amount to less than £20,000 to £24,000 a year. I dare not reflect upon this, and *something whispers to* me, that *it must not be*.

My chief speculation on this subject is, that from the very low prices at which the best Coals are shipping here, and the extra quantity which will be urged into the market, that the prices will be exceedingly depressed there. Whilst on the other hand your Lordship's, and Lambton's Walls-end, from going in something like the ordinary supply, will maintain their ground, and must of course take a greater lead in point of price than ever. Charles Johnson[27] can however give your Lordship the best opinion on this branch of the subject.

Although I feel a sort of conviction that we shall be able to maintain the prices of the Walls-ends at least, on the Wear, I must confess that I wait the issue of the Conflict on the Tyne, with great anxiety; but I feel great consolation in having been able to narrow my own little personal concerns on that River, while the storm was gathering.

I am glad that Sir C. Sharpe is coming to Sunderland, as he is an active partisan, and will be of great service to us in case of need, in protecting our Tub apparatus. With the best intentions, the Magistrates are at best, but a very pusillanimous set, and require *stirring up* when anything of consequence occurs.

Capt. Harrison the Landing Surveyor of the Customs, is not dead – contrary to all human probability he recovered, after having been given up for some days by the faculty.

I have seen Featherstonehaugh, the Madeira was at Sunderland, intended to be sent to Wynyard. It has be[en] re-shipped for London, and will I expect now very soon be delivered at St James' square,

27 Unidentified.

of which I shall be glad to be informed, as he shall not have either money, or Coals 'till I hear of it's arrival.

In the present state of affairs your Lordship may expect to hear from me frequently. Indeed I shall constantly write, whenever any thing occurs to me, worth communicating.

I have not heard a word of Mr Lambton nor Lorain, since I last wrote your Lordship, but should think the latter *must be* in Town this day, or tomorrow,

The Lord Stewart K.B.	I have the Honor [&c.]
St James' Square	J^no Buddle

14.

D/Lo/C142/4 Newcastle 20th April 1822

My Lord

I am this morning favoured with your Lordship's interesting and amusing Letter of the 12th Inst. Your Lordship has managed *Billy* [Lorain] admirably, the point of view in which you have placed every branch of the subject accords entirely with my own sentiments and I have very little doubt, but that in the End Mr Lambton will come to our terms.

The binding of your successors to the *mutual* accommodation of way-leave, can in no way be prejudicial to the interests of your Lordship's family. It is therefore right to consider it, and it ought to satisfy Mr L. I wish *Billy* may not make some blunder, and should like it better if Mr Lambton would wait upon your Lordship himself, or leave the matter to Croudace and me. We have decidedly the *whip-hand*, especially as Davison's is secure; but at the same time I should like to have the business fairly wound up.

The affairs of the trade here remain in statu quo; but it is rather extraordinary that the inferior Collieries are standing the shock infinitely better than was expected. None of that class have lowered their Prices more than 3/- and several have not lowered at all, and talk boldly about standing out. It is the first Class and second best, that are being *massacred*. Not withstanding the enormous reduction of price they have made, scarcely any of them have been able to get a single Ship without freighting. They are completely discomfited and dispersed. The *small-fry* standing out so *nobly*, is however highly favourable to our views on the Wear. For notwithstanding the grumbling of the Sunderland Ship-owners, and several of them having sent their Ships round to the Tyne for cheap Coals, it is impossible for me, to express the satisfaction I feel, in informing your Lordship that we have not yet felt any material difficulty in vending our Coals. Up to last night our actual vend for the present month was

Walls-end	1874 Ch.	
Eden-main	4392	6266

And according to the best information I can obtain, we have Ships *on to take* as following more

Walls-end	1924	
Eden-main	2690	3714
In all for April	9980	

The amount will be £11,909.15.6 besides £215.2.6 paid to tradesmen in Small. Nothing but some unforeseen accident at the Colliery, or Floods &c. can prevent the accomplishment of the above.

Croudace is not however getting on so well, as he cannot get a single Ship for Harraton, Bourn-end &c. and even Primrose is not so much in favour, as he could wish. He has just sent Smith[28] the Viewer to tell his grief, and I have *comforted* him as much as I can & sent him word to keep up his heart & I will see him in a day or two. The *little chieftains* on the Tyne are making a capital *diversion* in our favour & if Croudace will but stand manfully by us, I really hope we may be able to *hold out* till the scattered Forces on the Tyne can be rallied again.

From the hints which I have received I however think it likely, that your Lordship may expect to be teazed by petitions, or personal applications, to reduce the price of your Coals. I have with all the civility I am master of, *turned a deaf ear* to all suggestions on this subject, as I really cannot with any sort of good grace contemplate a reduction of price.

It is all I can do to save the post with this, & will write again in a day or two.

I am happy to learn so favourable an account of my Lady & the Baby.[29]

The Lord Stewart	I have the honor [&c.]
London	J[no] Buddle

---

28 Thomas Smith, viewer to J.G. Lambton.
29 Frances Anne Emily Vane was born on 15 April 1822.

15.

D/Lo/C142/4   Newcastle 21st April 1822

My Lord

I had not time yesterday morning to inform your Lordship that Tommy Fenwick called upon me to *hint* that if your Lordship felt disposed to purchase the Herrington Mill estate, he *believed* Mr Davison would have no objection to sell it, as it is entirely detached from all his other Property. I told Tommy I thought your Lordship's Plans of purchase were about completed, and I could not say whether you might be inclined to buy any more property in the neighbourhood of Pensher, or not. But at the same time as this little estate was completely surrounded by your property, I was not quite sure whether your Lordship might not think about it if they would set a moderate price upon it.

I do not however much see that this property is much worth your Lordship's notice, unless it can be had *very cheap* indeed, as the Coal is too much exhausted to make it an object as a separate Colliery. Besides which, there is no Way-leave to it, except thro' your Lordship's property, or the Nesham Colliery, but even in the latter way, there is no access to Sunderland by Nesham's Rail-way, without passing through your Lordship's (Dawson's) Herrington. So that in fact, they have not an out-let from the Colliery anyway, except thro' your Lordship's property. The real state of the case therefore is simply this, that unless Mr Davison will let your Lordship work his Coal, on eligible terms, your Lordship *need not* allow any body else to work it. I suspect that Tommy has smell[e]d this Rat since Dawson's was bought, and is desirous to slip his neck out of the noose without appearing to be afraid of it. By referring to the general map your Lordship will see all this distinctly.

I have allowed Tommy to examine the accounts of the workings (certainly not any Document from which he could form the least idea of Profits &c.) out of Herrington Mill, as named to your Lordship some time ago. And am glad to say that he is satisfied, of the full tentale having been paid on all the Coals which have been wrought, and that the Lessor has no claim whatever against the Collieries.

Nothing new has occurred since I wrote yesterday, but some of the greatest advocates for a free trade, are getting very *long Faces* in consequence of the present state of affairs; and even begin to admit that they have erred in judgment. They have not however suffered enough yet, but I don't think it will be long before they will clearly see into their folly, and *draw together* again to save themselves from destruction. For a week past we have had the finest Spring weather imaginable. And there is the finest prospect imaginable for an abundant Crop.

I hope my Lady and young lady Frances continue to go on well.

We have had some vexatious accidents at the new Engine, Resolution Pit, which have thrown us greatly back in getting the water out; but have not deprived us of any vend. I always however wish to have plenty of spare *Pit-room*.

It is said that *old Arthur* [Mowbray] is endeavouring to knock up a subscription Comp[an]y – a sort of Tontine, to buy Nesham's Colliery – to prevent Lord Stewart or Mr Lambton from getting it at their *own Price*.

The Lord Stewart K.B.   I have the honor [&c.]
St James' Square   J^{no} Buddle

16.

D/Lo/C142/4   Pensher 21st Apr[il] 1822

My Lord

I have received your Lordship's Letter of the 19th Inst. – too late to answer it by this day's Post. My view of the Biddick affair is as follows.

The chief object of my recommending it's purchase to your Lordship was to secure a Way-leave to the River – *independently* of Mr Lambton. That object being gained it's importance to the family as a Landed property is not I conceive of material importance.

If therefore any material object can be obtained by the sale of it, to Mr Lambton there can be no impropriety in doing so, on condition, 1st. That Lord Stewart reserves all the remaining Coal in the estate, to his own use and benefit, and 2nd that he reserves a Way-leave through the estate, on the east side of the Dean, to Biddick Haugh, and the old Staith thereon.

The latter clause will however in a great measure be rendered unnecessary by the general convention, which secures to Lord Stewart a Way-leave through Mr Lambton's Property independent of Biddick. Under existing circumstances I cannot view Biddick as in any way essential to your Lordship's immediate or ulterior Plans; further than as an object of importance to be given up, to Mr Lambton, for some object of equal importance, to your Lordship, to be conceded by Mr Lambton. I cannot however find out that Mr

Lambton *at present possesses any such equivalent* and the Scheme to which I look forward, & hinted at in a previous Letter, is that, in the event of Mr Lambton's purchasing Nesham's Colliery, he might on condition of having Biddick ceded to him,, under the reservations already named, grant to your Lordship the S.W. tract of Nesham's Colliery, which adjoins Rainton, or accommodate your Lordship with the easternmost Pit (the Dorothea) in Newbottle Colliery, to facilitate the working of the Baronet's & Dawson's Coal, or both these points.

In the event of giving up Biddick to Mr L. or only the W. part of it, that part E. of the Dean would round out the Pensher Estate very nicely, and the Land would be useful as the Colliery-Farm. In order to convey a more clear idea of the matter, I have sent a rough sketch of Biddick in another Cover and have shewn the *supposed* new Boundary Line of division by a red dotted Line.

As an instrument of Finance, I cannot however see how we can make any great use of Biddick, as I am not Lawyer enough to know, whether Mr Lambton could be called upon to pay us, any more of the purchase money than we have paid to Dawson. I should apprehend not, as I think the mortgage would have to be transferred to Mr Lambton, in which case your Lordship would not derive any pecuniary aid worth mentioning. Mr Groom will be the best able to advise your Lordship on this branch of the subject.

If any fresh idea should strike my mind relative to this affair I will write without reserve.

I have the honor [&c.]
J^{no} Buddle

I have preferred sending this & the Sketch in separate Covers, direct, instead of sending a Packet to the Under Secretary of State's office, lest any delay in the delivery should occur.

The Lord Stewart K.B.
St James' Square
London

17.

D/Lo/C142/4   Colliery Office Pensher, 23rd Apr[il] 1822

My Lord
    I went to Sunderland this morning to see how matters were going on there, but chiefly to see Edward Backhouse.

We talked the affair of our Accc[oun]t quietly over. He was in very good humour and is much satisfied with being allowed to charge the usual banking Commission on the Acc[oun]t but expressed a strong desire to have the bal[anc]e reduced, as it has crept up so much larger, an amount than they ever imagined it would do.

I stated to him, that your Lordship had been led, by an extraordinary concatenation of circumstances, into several large purchases, within the last six months which had thrown you into very heavy payments, and induced you to press much harder upon their Acc[oun]t than you expected would have been necessary. But that I now confidently hoped, the Bal[anc]e would be put in a train of gradual, and regular liquidation, until it was reduced, within the limits of understanding, viz. about as much, as the Fitters' receipts would cover.

He was satisfied, and did not say anything about security; but at the same time expressed himself in such a manner, as to convey to me, that they *will not allow of any further* increase in the Bal[anc]e and that they will be much disappointed if a diminution does not forthwith take place.

I found all our Fitters with, very long faces, and in great uneasiness about the state of the Coal trade. Both them and the Shipowners, are expecting a reduction in the price of Coals, to be made against the 1st May. I did not however encourage them to expect any such thing. The Fitters are in a sort of Panic, to day in consequence of a number of their friends having sent their Ships round to the Tyne for cheap Coals yesterday, and several more are leaving the harbour, this morning for the same destination.

I however find on *cross examining* some of the parties, that it is chiefly the inferior sorts of Coals, on the Wear which are falling short of Ships. And that the best viz. Stewart's & Lambton's Walls-end, Eden-main & Primrose, are getting a fair proportion of Ships. I only heard of two Ships which had actually taken on, for Eden-main, with Roger Watson,[30] having run out of the harbour for the Tyne, this morning. I don't however much like this, as Eden-main stands the Ship-owner to about 29/- or 29/6, and as all the 2nd class of Coals, on the Tyne, viz. Heaton, Hebburn, Killingworth, Willington, Northumberland Walls-end, Coxlodge &c. are put free on board by spout at 25/-. And even Bell's & Brown's Walls-end are put on board at 26/-. I am apprehensive that they may injure us less, or more, particularly

---

30 Sunderland fitter.

the Eden-main. We must however not be panic struck, at the sight of danger, but must meet the enemy firmly, and make the best *fight* we can – a reduction of price will bring the trade back, at any time, but that must be our *last shift*. I shall see how Croudace goes on tomorrow, or next day.

He has had two cargoes of Coal at Lynn, and the account there is, that one of them was tolerably well liked; but that the other, could not be sold, out of the Ship, but was landed to be retailed out on Hayton's own acc[oun]t.

From what I know of Stobart's Coals I have not much fear of Eden-main being injured by Hayton's Scheme. These are however eventful times, and one cannot view such matters with indifference.

Hayton sold one of his Shares of Hetton some time ago, and is now on the point of selling the other – quere if he accomplishes this, will he have *Brass* enough to apply, to be taken into the list of our Fitters again?

Sir Cuth[bert] Sharp had to preside at the King and Constitution Club-Dinner to day. I sought him all over the Town but could not find him; and various matters requiring my presence here, I could not stay to dine with the party.

I shall write again tomorrow, or next day. I hope my Lady and the baby continue to go on well.

The Lord Stewart K.B.   I have the honor [&c.]
St James' Square   J^{no} Buddle
London

18.

D/Lo/C142/4   Colliery Office Pensher, 26th April 1822

My Lord

I am this morning favoured with your Lordship's letter of the 24th inst. enclosing the copy of a Note to Lorain. This movement meets my views exactly, as it is high time, that Mr Lambton should make up his mind, in one way, or the other. This *Shot* will bring Billy to and I have little doubt of Mr Lambton closing the negotiation, as he ought to do, viz. to agree to all the terms of the Convention and to leave the affair of Biddick entirely to your Lordship.

Croudace drank tea with me last night, he is in high good humour, in full expectation of our agreement being ratified; but he has not heard a single word, either from Lorain, or Mr Lambton since they left home!!! He does not therefore, know any thing about what is going on with your Lordship, nor what their feelings are, and I did not enter at all into the matter, seeing that it could be of no use.

Although Croudace is very uneasy, about the present state of the Coal trade, yet I am glad to find him very firm, as to supporting prices. He feels with me, however, that the less we go amongst the Fitters &c. at Sunderland, just now, the better, as we are only teazed with complaints, and questions, we don't like to answer. We think if we can but struggle on, for a month or six weeks longer, even if the fools on the Tyne, don't in the mean time come to their senses, that we shall be able to support our prices, after that period, without much difficulty. And as we have no stocks of Coals on hand, at present, we are in the best possible state, for standing a *Siege*. Croudace thinks the worst that can happen to us, will be to take 1/- off Eden-main & Primrose which we laid on last year. As yet I am happy to say, we have felt little difficulty, as the keels are coming freely to the Staith, which is the best possible proof, that their [*sic*] are Ships at Sunderland to receive the Coals. And this is the only sort of intercourse, that I am any way anxious about, with Sunderland at present.

I met Gregson at Moorsley last Wed[nesday] and rode through the Elemore Country with him. Old Geo[rge] Baker[31] has quarrelled with his Son in law Capt. Tower, and in a *pet* is for selling Elemore. Gregson has a client who wishes to buy it, and our Plan is, to see, if we can contrive to gain your Lordship a preference, in some way, or other, for the Coal. But all this at present is *under the rose*, and *must be kept secret*. Elemore joins Moorsley & N. Pittington, and N. Pittington joins Grange & Gilly-gate moor where your Lordship, as Lord of the Manor has the Coal. If we can secure the Coal in Elemore & N. Pittington, we shall then have the *key* to the whole of the Coal District between Hetton & Durham. This would keep the family *at the head of the Coal trade for a century to come*. We are in a fair line for securing N. Pittington, as your Lordship knows. And we will look as close after Elemore as circumstances will permit.

We tried to hoist a loaden Tub, with the *Transferer*, yesterday, and all was promising; but the *Jib* broke, the Timber of it, proving unsound at the heart. We have decided to make a new one, of oak;

---

31 George Baker of Elemore, 1754–1837. His only daughter Elizabeth married Christopher Tower.

but it will cause a fortnight's delay – this is very vexatious. All other matters are going on well.

The Lord Stewart K.B.	I have the Honor [&c.]
St James' Square	J^{no} Buddle
London	

19.

D/Lo/C142/4   Newcastle 27th April 1822

My Lord

I am quite delighted with your lordship's communication of the 25th inst. You have managed *Billy* most capitally and the issue, is just what I wished.

We shall now know distinctly what we are about with respect to Way-leaves &c, in reference to Mr Lambton, and shall be able to steer our course accordingly.

I think I did not name in my last letter, Croudace's great uneasiness about Mowbray's views on Nesham's Colliery. He is doing all he can, to raise a party to purchase it, and it is said that Shotton,[32] the person, who lately married Scruton's daughter, and who has made a fortune in the E. Indies, is to find the *pewter*. Whether this is true, or not God knows, but certain it is, that *Arthur* is making a *fuss* about it. Croudace is quite in a rage, and is determined to buy if possible. He has now employed two professional Viewers (old Stobart and Steel)[33] to view, & value the Colliery for his government.

We have not any thing fresh astir here today, the good prices obtained last Wednesday have rather revived the drooping spirits of the Coal-owners, but many of them are beginning to feel the effects of the reduction sensibly. And I hope by-and-by, some exertions will be made to prevent the mischief, and ruin, which must sooner, or later overtake them., if the present system is continued.

I met an acquaintance of Mr Lambton's (Mr James) to day, who gives a deplorable account of the iron and Coal trade in Staffordshire. He says they have it in agitation to petition the legislature to reduce the export Duty on Coal – to enable us to send our Coals to

32 William Shotton, a shareholder in the Hetton Co.
33 William Stobart sr, father of William Stobart jr (see p. 22, n. 16); Edward Steel.

the Continent, and to make *room* in the home market for their Coals. This appears to me, to be a sort of *wild-goose* idea.

I have returned your Lordship's correspondence with Mr Lambton, in another Cover.

The Lord Stewart K.B.   I have the Honor [&c.]
St James Square   J^no Buddle
London

20.

D/Lo/C142/4   Walls-end 28th April 1822

My Lord

I have this morning received your Lordship's letter of the 26th Inst. enclosing Mr Lambton's note, relative to Biddick.

It appears that there are two distinct conditions on which Mr Lambton, expects your Lordship to accommodate him with Biddick viz. 1st by an exchange of property, or 2nd by a clear sale for money.

Now to talk of arbitration in the latter case, and the propriety of it, even in the former, is questionable. This affair, ought in my opinion, to stand on it's own bottom – clear and without reference to any other transaction; saving that feeling of obligation which is due to your Lordship, from Mr Lambton, for the spirit of accommodation, which induces you, to part with Biddick, *to him*, on any terms what-ever.

Under this view of the subject, I should say, that if it is to be a matter of *clear* Sale, Mr Lambton ought to give your Lordship *your own price*, and not *higgle* for £1000 or £2000. But if it is to be an offer of an exchange of property, or some matter of Colliery accommoda-tion, there an arbitration could only be necessary, in the event of a difference of opinion between your respective Negotiators.

In short, it does not occur to me, that the parting with Biddick, is at all, a proper subject for arbitration – it is altogether a gratuitous act, on the part of your Lordship, and ought to be appreciated by Mr Lambton accordingly.

At present I cannot see any thing Mr Lambton has to accommo-date your Lordship with (which is not included in *the Agreem[en]t*) that can be considered an equivalent for Biddick. The only thing I look forward to, is to get something *raked up*, out of Nesham's Colliery, in the event of Mr Lambton becoming the purchaser. But that he may be the purchaser, though probable, is by *no mean certain*.

I therefore think, it would be well, if the question of Biddick, could stand over, 'till Nesham's affair is decided; and as we shall most likely, have to go into the Division of the baronet's Property forthwith, in order to settle the proportion of the purchase money, to be paid by your Lordship, and Mr Lambton – according to the extent, and value of the property, which you respectively take, Biddick being kept *hanging in the wind*, in the mean time, would do us no harm.

I shall see Croudace at Sunderland next Wednesday, and altho' I don't at present see any necessity for communicating *all that has* passed in London, about Biddick, I can ascertain whether he can find out any thing, that Mr Lambton has to part with, which we can consider as an equivalent for it. And I will also consult with him, as to the best plan of getting the Agreement executed at the least expence. Indeed I have already talked with him on this point.

I have returned Mr Lambton's note under another cover.

The Lord Stewart K.B.   I have the honor [&c.]
St James' Square   J^no Buddle.

21.

D/Lo/C142/4   Newcastle 30th May 1822

My Lord

On returning to the Barracks last night I was delighted to find the *Waggons rattling* past famously. They had loaden about 60 Keels, both on Tuesday and Wednesday and expect to do as much *every day* during the week. The Custom-house officers are going on measuring the Tubs, in the most tiresome way possible, altho' I believe their rules are such, that they cannot well help it. I however expect, although I have some doubt about it, that they will finish 6 or 7 Keels this week, so as to enable us to make a start next Monday.

I have been to Sunderland, this afternoon to see how matters were going on there. The transferer, is lying very quietly in her *Birth*, and has not been in any way disturbed. She appears so much less than the Casters expected, that she seems for the present, not to be worth their notice. With respect to the general feeling of all parties as to the present state of affairs, matters are by no means so smooth.

There is a general gloom, and dissatisfaction from the highest to the lowest, at our keeping up the price of the Coals. And I heard, although from no good authority, that the Ship-owners had, or were about to address your Lordship & Mr Lambton on the subject.

The account of last Monday's market, which came yesterday, has produced a general sensation. Stewart's Walls-end selling only at 39/- is the worst thing that has happened to us yet. As long as they keep at, or above 40/- they will pay 10/- per Ch. freight, which affords fair general agreement for keeping up the Price; but the worse they fall below 40/- the less tenable our ground becomes.

A very considerable number of Ships is now in the Harbour, and all our Fitters are securing such of them as they have any control over. But all the free Ships – most Lynn-men, are waiting till Saturday 1st of June when they confidently expect a reduction of price will be made. If not they *swear* that every man of them will leave the Port.

All this however does not, at all change my opinion, as to the inexpediency of complying with their wishes, as long as there is any hope of the Tyne people coming to an understanding, or as long as we can sell as many Coals, at present prices, as will make our Pays. This I feel almost confident we may do, if Mr Lambton will but stand by us, with his *best Coals*, until the *refractory* parties on the Tyne are put *hors de combat*. From the very nature of things it does not appear to me that the *war of annihilation* can now be of long duration. To my certain knowledge, some of the most turbulent spirits, are now selling their Coals at 5/- pcr Ch. less than they cost working. And if this does not soon 'take the fight out of them' the D—l is in it.

The more I think of Mr Lambton's – Croudace's plan, I ought to call it I believe – of a reduction of 5/- per Ch. the less I like it. It must evidently arise out of a feeling spirit which ought not to be entertained by any real Gentleman. By yielding to it Mr Lambton would in my opinion lower himself down to the level of the *pettyfoggers* on the Tyne, as it would be impossible, that even *he* could remain for any length of time in that position. Mr L. is surely not aware of the immense reduction an abatement of 5/- per Ch. would make from his monthly receipt. Suppose it to have taken place this month & his Vend to have been 8000 Ch. it would just have reduced his receipt £2000 – I shudder at the idea.

The horror of a reduction haunts my imagination so much, that I can hardly rest anywhere; and I have just come here to see what is going on. The account of last Monday's market, has shaken the nerves of the stoutest hearted, and if the two succeeding markets, keep equally low, of which I think there is little doubt, it will produce the most salutary effect, I foresee, at the meeting on Wednesday. As far as I can gather, there will be much less difficulty with the Coal-owners who attend personally, to represent *their own* interest, than with certain Agents, who attend to represent the interest of others.

I don't recollect that I have ever informed your Lordship, that there are *many of us* on these occasions, *far bigger men* than their Masters. Especially such of us, as have not masters, who give themselves the trouble to become acquainted, in *some degree*, further with their own concerns, than barely knowing when they make *some* profit, and when they make none, expressing satisfaction when they make profit, and grumbling when they make none; but without being able to appreciate the cause, either of the one, or the other. I do not like to be personal on any occasion, and whenever I may happen by way of elucidation, to be led into anything of that sort, in my confidential correspondence with your Lordship, I feel the most entire confidence that it will not, in any way be suffered to operate, to the prejudice of any individual.

I therefore venture to inform your Lordship, that one principal bar to an understanding on the Tyne, is the obstinacy and unbusiness-like conduct of Lord Ravensworth[34] & his Agent Lambert. He is a personal friend of mine, and is, I believe as honest & honourable a minded man, as can be. But in business, a mere Baby, without temper, management, or resource of mind equal to such circumstances as we now have to combat in the trade. He demands a larger quantity from all their Collieries, viz. Killingworth, Burradon, South moor & Low moor, than according to the circumstances of those Collieries and the state of the Trade he is entitled to, and instead of reasoning the matter loses temper & cuts all argument short, by 'I will', or 'I won't'.

Whether he may persist in this line of conduct at our next meeting I don't know, but when Killingworth Coals are selling in London at 34/6, he *must feel*, according to the freights he is now paying, that he will not get more than 19/- per Ch. for the Coals.[35] And Lord Ravensworth must certainly feel at the end of the year that he will get *no profit*. It is quite impossible that he could do so badly, on a quantity that would be allowed him, under a regulation, even if he made no claim at all for quantity. I hope the *mist* will be cleared away from L –'s eyes at our next meeting.

Mr Russell[36] having entailed his estates, his Son cannot sell any

---

34 Thomas Henry Liddell of Ravensworth Castle, 1775–1855, created Baron Ravensworth 1821. His agent was Richard Lambert.
35 Footnote in text: During the regulation Killingworth Coals sold at 30/- per Ch.
36 William Russell, 1734–1817, a Sunderland fitter, leased Wallsend and Washington collieries and employed the elder John Buddle and then his son as viewers. He bought Brancepeth Castle in 1796. His son Matthew, 1765–1822,

part of them, and the Law-men have doubted whether they can, without obtaining an act of parliament for the purpose, give your Lordship a title to the part already sold.

I am going to meet Mr Iveson tomorrow at the barracks, when I hope we shall come to an understanding with Croudace, about the Biddick Furniture.

I have the honor [&c]

J^{no} Buddle

I hear under the *rose* that the Viewers who have been surveying Nesham's Colliery for *old Arthur*, have a very bad opinion of the concern, from which it is supposed, that he will not bid against Mr Lambton, except for the sake of mischief. I *guess* however that there is another reason. Hetton is now very heavy in hand. £54000 have been advanced & the *Chancellor of the Exchequer* is exceedingly put about, to raise the supplies for carrying on the War, someone's being[37]

I saw Ward[38] at Brancepeth yesterday morning, he is now quite reconciled to the Biddick affair & says they will have no difficulty in making the payments.

The Lord Stewart K.B.
London

22.

D/Lo/C142/6   Newcastle 27th July 1822

My Lord

I arrived here yesterday morning and had the pleasure to learn from Hunter[39] who came from Pensher to meet me, that all our Colliery affairs were going on as well as possible. The regulation is also working well, and there are plenty of Ships to take off all the Coals we are allowed; and the whole of the Ships which had gone to

---

the present owner, was MP for Saltash 1802–7, 1808–22, but is not recorded as ever having spoken in the House of Commons. *Hist. Parl. 1790–1820*, **xxxx**, 69–70.

37 This sentence is incomplete.

38 Thomas Ward was partner with Russell in Washington Colliery.

39 George Hunter, Buddle's assistant, resident viewer at Penshaw. He married a niece of Buddle's.

the Tyne for cheap Coals, have now come back again to Sunderland since the prices were raised to their former stand on the Tyne.

I am glad to inform your Lordship that the transferer is now currently at work, and loads 2 keels of Tubs per hour, and Hunter tells me there is no doubt of it's answering our expectations fully.

I have not seen anything of Croudace nor Loraine yet, to learn what they have done with regard to Nesham's Colliery affair, but we have to meet on Coal Trade business at Chester[-le-Street] on the 30th Inst. when I shall hear all about it. Through the course of the week, I will make a thorough inspection of all our Works and will also go to Sunderland to see what is going on there – particularly to see Backhouse and endeavour to prevail with him to provide for the liquidation of London Bills, with a good grace. After I have seen about all these matters I will write your Lordship fully.

On arriving in London Sir Henry Hardinge[40] took me to Mr Vansittart,[41] with whom I had a very satisfactory interview, on the subject of the Sunderland Fitters &c. complaints, as to the hardship of the Custom-house Regulations with respect to the delivery of Coals at the Coasting Ports. Mr Vansittart directed Mr Freeling[42] to introduce me to Mr Dean, a Commissioner of the Customs and altho' I did not find this gentleman so courteous or accommodating as Mr Vansittart & Mr Freeling yet I expect that I have got the business but into such a train, as will ultimately lead to the accomplishment of the Fitters' wishes.

I also saw Messrs Gregson & Groom, on my way through London. The former is considerably tranquililized, but the latter says we have much to do yet. He read me over a list of heavy payments, to be provided for, & said he would send me a copy of it; when I receive it I shall be the better able to judge but I fear our resources in this quarter will not be equal to their liquidation. Economy must be the order of the day with us, and not a farthing must be expended, but what is absolutely necessary for carrying on the *money making mill*, until we get our heads fairly above water and have Funds at command; or we shall not be able to take advantage of any circum-

---

40 Sir Henry Hardinge, 1785–1856, married Lady Emily Stewart, half-sister of Lord Stewart. MP for Durham City 1820–30, later Clerk of the Ordnance, Chief Secretary for Ireland, Governor-General of India 1844–8. Viscount Hardinge of Lahore. *ODNB*; *Hist. Parl. 1820–32*, v, 497–528.

41 Nicholas Vansittart, 1766–1851. Chancellor of the Exchequer 1812–22, Baron Bexley 1823. *ODNB*; *Hist. Parl. 1820–32*, vii, 536–43.

42 Francis Freeling, 1764–1836, Secretary to the Post Office. *ODNB*.

stance that may eventually arise, to make an opening, for a dash at
Hetton &c.

I hope that my Lady and the little ones have, so far, borne their
journey well, and that they will continue to do so.

The Lord Stewart K.B.   I have the Honor [&c]
                                                            J^no Buddle

23.

D/Lo/C142/6   Colliiery Office Pensher 30th August 1822

My Lord
I have the pleasure to inform your Lordship that all our Colliery
Concerns are going on well, both above and below Ground. The only
change of feature under-ground, worth notice, is the bringing down
of a feeder of water, from the roof, in the Plane Pit, by working the
Pillars.[43] This however is nothing more, than one of the ordinary
casualties of mining, and is of the less importance, in this instance, as
we shall apply the spare Machinery, and pumping apparatus, from
the Resolution Pit, to the drawing of this water.

The water is drawn from this part of the Colliery, at present, by
Buckets at the Plane, and Nicholson Pit. But by erecting the spare
Machinery, from the Resolution Pit at the North Pit, we shall draw
the water more advantageously, and leave the 30 Horse rotation
Engine, now occupied in drawing the Water, in Buckets, at Nicholson's Pit disposable. This affair will be accomplished by our ordinary establishment of Artifficers in about four months. The feeder of
water above alluded to, discharges 23 Gallons per minute.

The nine pumping Engines at the Resolution Pit, having completely
mastered the Water, in the Western part of the Colliery, has led to a
change of arrangement in the general working of the Mine, from
what was contemplated, before the event took place.

It was originally intended, to push the immediate future work-

---

43 Large pillars of coal, containing approximately half the total, were initially left
    unworked to support the roof of a seam. They were later 'robbed' according
    to a system devised by Buddle, to allow up to half the remaining coal to be
    extracted. See Flinn, *Coal Industry*, pp. 88–90. One of the complaints about
    Mowbray's management of the Vane Tempest collieries during Frances
    Anne's minority was that they were worked wastefully, an excessive quantity
    being left in the pillars.

ings, from the Meadows. But in consequence of being obliged to effect the complete drainage of the Western Division of the Colliery, by the new Engine, at the Resolution Pit, we are enabled to regain the Adventure Pit – a Pit lost by water, in Sinking, in the year 1817 when within about 12 or 13 Fathoms of the Hutton Seam. This will afford us more immediate relief, in the expence of underground Horses, &c. than the Meadows New Pit, and will besides enable us to suspend our operations there for a while.

The water has for some time, been drawn out of the Meadows 'old Waste', and the next step, is to take out the large (19 in.) pumps which drew it out, at the depth of 47 Fathoms, and to put in smaller (16 in.[)] Pumps, to drain the Hutton Seam at the depth of 85 Fathoms.

As we have to buy the 16 in. Pumps which will cost £500, it will be proper to delay the purchase as long as we consistently can. One of our Fitters J^{no} White (with his Sons) has commenced the Foundry Business at Sunderland, and I have agreed with him, to do a considerable part of our Cast Iron work, at the customary prices – to be paid 1/3 of the amount in Cash, and 2/3^{ds} in Small and inferior Coals. By this I hope to relieve the pressure of money Payments for castings, considerably, next year. The Foundry is not yet finished, and he will not be able to cast the 16 in. Pumps 'till about Christmas. But this is of no consequence, as we can wait without inconvenience.

In consequence of the reasons stated in my last, for extending the Tub System, I have contracted with Hunter and Elliott,[44] two of our Fitters, to fit out 8 Keels with Tubs – 64 Tubs in all, at £7.5.0 a Tub, which will amount to £496. Payment £76 in Cash, when the Tubs are finished, £220 in Small & oversea Coals, and £200 in Cash in May 1823. This is 5/- per Tub less than the last cost.

The next point on which I have to remark, is Shippardsons Coal under North Pittington,[45] respecting which I am again put on the *qui vive*. I had occasion to see Tommy Fenwick, the day before yesterday. He informed me that Thompson, the Attorney of Sunderland, had applied to him a few days ago, to purchase the Coal under this

---

44 Hunter and Thomas Elliott, Sunderland fitters.

45 The Shipperdson family of Pittington Hallgarth had for many years leased the manor, and its coal, from the Dean and Chapter of Durham, but had not worked the coal. On 28 Sep. 1821 Edward Shipperdson was informed that the lease would not be renewed: Durham University Library, Archives and Special Collections, Shipperdson papers, 3293–5.

Estate. Thompson said, that *they* – meaning the Pembertons,[46] as Tommy supposed, had made a Bargain for the Land, and wished to purchase the Coal also. With every disposition to serve us, Tommy did not, however, on this occasion, act with becoming judgment and decision. For instead of cutting the matter short by telling Thompson at once, that another party had the refusal of it – which your Lordship's letter to the Chapter fully authorized him to do, he referred Thompson to the Chapter-office, and then went in quest of Dr Gray, to tell him what had happened; and to advise with, & remind him, that your Lordship had made a previous application!!! Poor Tommy's wits must have been a *wool gathering* on this occasion, I think, or he could not possibly have been so *soft headed*. He did not however find the 'little Doctor' but saw his Son, to whom he explained the matter.

I foresee mischief in this affair. Thompson and the Pembertons, are the same party who plagued Mr Lambton, both in the affair of Beckwith's Estate, and the Nesham Colliery. There is never a bit of Coal Property, in the Country, likely to be brought to market, but they are *nibbling* about it, and with the Chapter they will get into the right Soil for doing us mischief. For there, the *weed* of competition thrives rarely.

I have Tommy's confidence, and will look sharp after him. I should wish him to strangle the *Urchin* in the Cradle, if possible; but am apprehensive that he has let slip the most favourable opportunity. I will however do all I can, to avert this competition, and as soon as Tommy can *unfetter* me, I will take such steps as may appear the best calculated for that purpose. I will try what I can do with Dr Gray, he ought I expect to stand our friend in the Chapter; but whenever the revd. Body has a question of interest to discuss, I'm afraid that they all *pull the same way*, and I doubt the Doctor's voice will be too feeble to make much impression in this case.

Croudace is going on with the Bridge at Floater's Mill. He pressed hard for a money subscription of £50, but I stuck to a contribution of Stones and Labour. He fell to £25 Cash. I stuck to the Stones, and after a pause of three weeks, he has taken to the Stones with a good grace. He is so sadly *bothered* about Nesham's Colliery, nothing further having been yet done, but he does not think, that either Pembertons, or *Arthur* is opposing Mr Lambton, and therefore expects that he has the Field to himself.

---

46 Members of the Pemberton family owned land in the area, including Ramside Hall near Pittington. Two brothers were shareholders in the Hetton Co.

Hayton's Creditors have sent Kidson the Attorney,[47] and a Bow-street Officer after him to France, where he has been seen, both at Paris & Dieppe. It is supposed, that their object is, to endeavour to get some of the money from him, but not to bring him back to justice. The general feeling of the Creditors seems to be that they would rather lose their money, as bring him to the Gallows.

This neighbourhood was quite in an uproar yesterday, on the occasion of the Duke of Sussex[48] coming to Lambton. Mr Lambton's Collieries were laid off, and all the People, Waggon Horses, and all, together with the Tenantry, assembled at Chester-le-Street and proceeded, in grand Cavalcade, to meet the Duke, mid way between Chester & Durham, and to escort him to Lambton Hall. The Publick Houses in Chester were opened at Mr Lambton's expence, and he gave an Ox, and 70 Sheep, to regale all who chose to partake.

Today I hear, that the Duke is going to Newcastle to lay the Foundation Stone of the new Rooms, to be built there for the Philosophical Society,[49] and tomorrow he is to visit Sunderland.

It does not appear that Mr Lambton has divested himself, so much of the feelings of party spirit, as might have been expected. At a meeting of the Commissioners of the River Wear, held at the Publick Rooms at Sunderland, on the 14th Inst., he moved, that the meetings of the Commissioners should in future be holden at the Engineer's office at the Pier, alleging as the reason for such change, 'that the Publick Rooms were not free'. No intimation of this motion having been previously given, and being supported by his particular Friends Mr Lambton's motion was carried. Our friends say, that this is merely a measure of retaliation, in consequence of your Lordship being elected President. They wish to call a full meeting next Board, to endeavour to reverse this motion, of Mr Lambton's; but for my part, I think it will be better let alone, as it is not an object of any consequence – certainly not worth *fighting* about. *Little* Reid,[50] the

47 John Kidson, Sunderland solicitor.

48 Augustus, Duke of Sussex, 1773–1843, brother of George IV. For an account of his visit to the North East see M.A. Richardson, *The Local Historian's Table Book of Remarkable Occurrences*, Historical Division, vol. 3 (Newcastle upon Tyne, 1846), pp. 253–5.

49 A new building for the Literary and Philosophical Society of Newcastle upon Tyne, of which Buddle was a founder member, was completed in 1825. It was designed by John Green.

50 Unidentified.

speech writer who, your Lordship will remember, and Dr Gray, are much annoyed at this affair.

We have got the two young Horses here, they are the best, and handsomest pair, of their age I ever saw; and will I hope be approved, both by your Lordship, and my Lady. If no accident happen to them, I am sure they will double their present value, or more, in less than twelve months. One of them is by X,Y,Z, Dam by a Son of Factors. The other is by Ardrossen, Dam by Podargus.

It is almost a pity to risk them on board of Ship, and if there is any chance of your Lordship returning to England sooner than you originally intended, it would be best to keep them here, and have them ready for work, against your Lordship come home.

I have not heard from your Lordship since the 5th Inst. but can readily imagine how much your time and attention must be occupied at this time.[51]

The Marquis of Londonderry   I have the Honor [&c]
                                                              Jno Buddle

24.

D/Lo/C142/6   Colliery Office Pensher
                                                    27th Sep[tember]: 1822

My Lord

I have had the honor to receive your Lordship's afflicting letter of the 3rd Inst. it is exceedingly distressing to me, to contemplate the extent of domestick affliction, with which it has pleased the Almighty to visit your Family, and I most cordially sympathize with you.

I feel great consolation, however, in the midst of all this great distress, in having it in my power, to state, to your Lordship, that all our Concerns, here are going on comfortably.

The good effects of the Regulation are now felt by all parties. It has secured the price to the Coal-owner, and has obtained remu-

---

51 Lord Stewart's half-brother Robert, Lord Castlereagh, the Foreign Secretary, had succeeded as second Marquess of Londonderry on 6 Apr. 1821. He committed suicide on 12 Aug. 1822. H. Montgomery Hyde, *The Strange Death of Lord Castlereagh* (London, 1959); *Hist. Parl. 1790–1820*, v, 278–96; *1820–32*, vii, 286–300; *ODNB*. Lord Stewart now succeeded as third Marquess of Londonderry.

nerating prices for the Ship-owner – without injuring the Publick. Our Walls-end, and Lambton's have got up to 44/- in London. This is enough, and will pay the Ship-owners amply; and any material further advance ought to be checked by throwing in, an additional quantity. Our Vend must therefore be extended next month.

Nothing of material interest has occurred since my last, in the Works. So that with respect to the *interior*, I have been quite at my ease. I have however been on the alert, about the North Pittingon affair, and have *scared* up, a good deal of information, partly true, and partly false, no doubt, about it. From what I have collected I am now led to think, that it is not either *Arthur* [Mowbray], or his Hetton Associates, who have actually entered the Lists against us. It seems to be an entire new set of adventurers, of larger Caliber, in point of capital than the Hetton Co. who are *manoeuvring*. The parties named are, the Pembertons, Sir Geo. Shee,[52] Col. Bradyll,[53] Major Anderson,[54] and your Lordship's Castle-eden friend Burdon,[55] with several other, whom I think even more unlikely than the latter Gentlemen.

Their plan is, it is said, to unite Belmont, Pemberton's small Freehold estate, which lies between the Grange, and North Pittington, Little-town, Haswell, Pessell, and Elemore, in one magnificent Colliery. And as it were to carry by a coup de main, the whole Field of *unoccupied* Coal, in that part of the County.

This great plan is to be completed, by making a Harbour, at Hawthorn Dean (a little to the South of Dawdon) or by carrying a rail-way to Stockton.

Now I must confess that I feel much more at my ease, since the development of this very magnificent Plan, than I did when it seemed to be confined to N. Pittington, Elemore, and probably Belmont only. It is much too large, and unwieldy, an undertaking and must necessarily fall in pieces by its own weight – considering the *hands* it is in. Indeed I have great hopes that it never will be fairly *launched* from the knowledge I have of some of the parties. Who unless they commit the whole management, to much more efficient hands, than

---

52 Sir George Shee Bt, 1754–1825. He was successively Surveyor-General to the Ordnance, Under-Secretary to the Home Department, Under-Secretary of War and the Colonies, Receiver-General of Customs. *ODNB*.

53 Col. Thomas Bradyll, owner of the Haswell estate. He lived on another property at Ulverston in Cumberland.

54 Major George Anderson, Hawthorn Hive.

55 Rowland Burdon of Castle Eden, 1757–1838.

their own, never will *bring it to bear*. They neither possess sufficient energy, nor activity for such an undertaking – the only requisite they do possess is Capital.

I don't however, mean to allow these considerations to lull me into a false security. For although this party may not be able to bring it to bear, yet it is to be apprehended that their *fumbling* about it, may bring other more efficient enemies into the *Field*. And as there is hazard of their stirring in it, injuring us at any rate, I shall never rest satisfied 'till I either see my way, more clearly, with regard to N. Pittington, or at least have left no stone unturned to do so.

If we had but N. Pittington secure, I should not give myself any concern about the rest. And I don't even look to the securing of Pittington, as an immediate object for the extension of your Lord-ship's Works; but as a measure of security against mischievous Rivals.

Rainton contains a supply of Hutton Seam (exclusive of all other Seams) for 33 Years, as appears by the accompanying Estimates which I made last February.

We need not therefore be under any apprehension about falling short of Coal, even without taking Pensher, the Baronet's and Herrington into the Account.

I saw Tommy Fenwick on the 21st Inst. He could not give me any fresh information, as the 'grand Chapter' will not be holden 'till tomorrow. Tommy is our friend, but with his Masters Interest is to Friendship as 'an Horse is to a Hen'. We must therefore make all the use we can of the information gained through Tommy's friendship. But trust little to the friendship of his Masters.

In a few days I shall expect to learn from Tommy if any regular application has been made to the Chapter, relative to North Pittington Coal, and will act upon the information I receive, to the best of my judgment.

I have to meet Sir H. Williamson's[56] agent, at Sunderland on the 1st or 2d of next Month, when I expect to agree with him for the Tub Engine *Birth*, as named in my last.

Nothing further has been done in the Nesham Colliery affair; but from a communication, which has just appeared from the trustees,

---

56 Sir Hedworth Williamson Bt, 1797–1861, owned property at Sunderland, including a stretch of the river bank. He was MP for Co. Durham 1832–2, North Durham 1832–7, and Sunderland 1847–52. *Hist. Parl. 1820–32*, vii, 795–6.

to the Creditors, I think it probable e'er long that Mr Lambton will become the purchaser.

In a former letter, I informed your Lordship of my agreement with White & Sons, for cast Iron work – payment 1/3 in Cash, and 2/3ds in Small &c Coals. I now hope that I may be able to effect a similar agreement, with Hunter and Elliott for Pit-wood – Props &c. In short I shall let slip no opportunity of pushing this sort of Traffick, as it is very advantageous to us.

I cannot yet get correct information as to the quality of the Main Coal Seam at Hetton. That on which I can, as yet place the most reliance, is, that it is *very bad*.

The Colts are coming on famously. They have been backed, and are as tractable as possible.

I am most anxious to hear better accounts, both of your Lordship, and my Lady's health. I hope and trust she is recovering her health and strength.

The Marquis of Londonderry   I have the Honor [&c]
Vienna   Jno Buddle

25.

D/Lo/C142/6   Colliery Office Pensher 12th Oct[ober] 1822

My Lord

I am happy to inform your Lordship, that all is well here. Our receipt on the 1st Inst. was £10,658.6.9 exclusive of £377.13.10 ½ of Tradesmen's Coals. And our Vend in September was as follows viz.

1535 Ch. Walls-end Tubs	at 30/1½
1480 do.	at 28/½
7091 Eden-main	at 22/1½

10,106 Fitters	£12,237.15.9
373 Ch. Eden-main	at 22/1½
53 Splints	at 8/1½
537 Small	at 6/1½

1,134 Ch. Tradesmen	£736.9.9

capital receipt on the 1st December.

I hope there will be no hazard of our getting this quantity, as the Keelmen's war on the Tyne[57] cannot last much longer I expect and they are too much occupied with their own affairs at home to spare time to invade us here, although strongly inclined to do so. Houghton Feast is also over, so that we have no interruption, except Lambton Races, now to apprehend.

I have not heard anything more of the *grand Coalition*, except that the scheme was sprung by a person of the name of Smith – the same I believe, who has published a Geological map of England.[58] He has found out, according to the Warmian Theory, that the magnesian Limestone, being of much more recent formation, than the independent Coal formation, and being superincumbent, on it, *cannot affect* the thickness, or quality of the Seams of Coal, et irgo, the Coal must be in perfection in Col. Bradyll's *Limestone* Estate of Haswell &c. And I hope he will include Seaham also.

This is all mighty scientific, and tickles the Ears of those who know no better, and wish it to be so. In reply to all this theorizing (as I cannot just now find out scientific reasons, on which to argue against it) I can only oppose an homely North Country Proverb viz. that 'Steel is not to be found in a Steg's head'. Mr Smith has also found out, that a capital Harbour may be made at Hawthorn dean, for *almost nothing*, by rubble Stone Piers, to be formed of the Limestone debris of the neighbouring Shores. This is also a fine subject for table talk, and I am exceedingly glad that the whole affair seems to be taken up on such elementary principles, as I trust it will never get any further.[59]

My friend Tommy assures me that no application has yet been made, to the Dean & Chapter, for the N. Pittington Coal, except your Lordship's. So far then all's well, but I am rather disappointed to find that they did not bring your Lordship's application into discussion, on the 28th Ulto. Tommy promises to give me the earliest intelligence of any movement, in this quarter.

---

57 A major strike of Tyneside keelmen was in progress: see J.M. Fewster, *The Keelmen of Tyneside: Labour Organisation in the North-East Coal Industry, 1600–1830* (Woodbridge, 2011).

58 William Smith, 1769–1839, geologist and civil engineer, pioneered the science of stratigraphy. In 1815 he published the first geological map of England and Wales. Buddle was mistaken in thinking that he was involved in a coal scheme in Co. Durham. Smith was, however, proved right about the coal under the magnesian limestone. *ODNB*. The identity of the Smith involved in this plan is not known.

59 Within a few years, of course, Buddle was himself involved in the construction of Seaham Harbour, some two miles north of Hawthorne Dene.

Mr Lambton gives £70,000 for the Newbottle Colliery, and takes possession as from the 30th June last, so that it is now carrying on, on his account. They contemplate the carrying of a considerable proportion of the Lambton Coals, down the Newbottle Rail-way, to ship them by spout at Sunderland. The only objection is the enormous way-leaves paid on this Line. I have had much conversation with Croudace, on this subject, and have *pointed a great Gun for him to fire off* against the several Land proprietors, through whose property the way lies. And if he only chooses the right moment for *clapping to* the match, his Fire, will produce the desired effect.

Croudace is delighted with this idea as he thinks if we can unite in this manner, it will greatly strengthen our position in reference to the Hetton Banditti, and enable us to keep them much better in check, happen what may. I will not now enter into the development of this *grand junction* scheme fully, until I see my way more clearly. But I foresee the probability of *working up* something, or other out of it, which will prove highly beneficial to our Colliery concerns. And I will not fail to lay the *Foundation Stone* when ever the opportunity occurs – always reserving to your Lordship the option of completing the superstructure, or not, as may seem expedient.

Croudace is quite upon the qui vive, and is anxious to unite with us in any scheme whatever, to keep the Hetton Co. in order. I have seen Tommy Fenwick this morning and told him, to inform Dr Gray that we should, by-and-by, have to come to him for a way-leave and shipping place, at Wearmouth, for the Rainton Coals. And as it was a *Church Concern*, I expected he would deal with us, on the most liberal terms.

The prospect of eventually taking our Coals to Sunderland, by Nesham's Rail-way, will make me pause a little, in taking all Sir H. Williamson's Quay, unless on condition of being at liberty to give it up, again at 12 months notice. I shall however think it prudent to secure *one* Birth at any rate. The agent is sick at present, or I should most likely have done this already.

Last week the flames of civil war, broke out with great violence, amongst the Hetton Co. Pistols were talked of, but most prudently, the wagging of Tongues, was preferred to the pulling of Triggers, and the *elegant epithet* of Scoundrel, Rascal, &c. flew like *Grape-shot*. Cap. Cochran,[60] and Scruton, were the principal *Gladiators*, on the occasion. After much hard fighting, a parly was beaten, and the affair

---

60   Hon. Archibald Cochrane, shareholder in the Hetton Co.

ended, in the dismissal of the commander in chief –old Arthur. The charges preferred against Arthur, by Scruton, were obstinacy, and extravagance; but the main cause of the fracas, is understood to originate, in the difficulty, some, if not all the parties find, in raising money, to carry on the works. I know from undoubted authority, that the Lawyers' pens, are in great activity, drawing mortgage deeds &c. to raise money, for certain members of the Co. while others positively refuse to advance any more money. Their *sinking or swimming*, rests solely on the turning out of the quality of the Coal, on the opening of their present pits. And this is a point which still continues in a state of the greatest uncertainty.

I will keep a sharp look out in this quarter, to see if any opening occurs for carrying the Enemy's position by a coup de main.

I attended Col. Brown[61] to the Altar on the 1st Inst. and regret that he has left our neighbourhood, as I derived great consolation from an occasional conference with him, in the absence of intelligence from your Lordship.

I have enclosed the only printed Documents which have been issued by the Coal-owners of the Tyne, during the present struggle of the Keelmen. The sole object of the latter is to limit the use of Ship Spouts to the loading of small Vessels of 6 Keels instead of all sizes up to 18 Keels or so. Those wishes in this respect can never be complied with.

I have not heard from your Lordship since the 18th Sep. I am most anxiously expecting to hear more favourable news of my Lady, and trust that your Lordship's spirits are recovering their ordinary tone.

The Marquess of Londonderry   I have the Honor [&c]
Vienna   Jno Buddle

---

61 Col. Henry Browne, former aide-de-camp to Lord Londonderry. He married a sister of R.W. Brandling, owner of Gosforth Colliery and chairman of the Northumberland and Durham Coal Owners Association.

26.

D/Lo/C142/6 *Private*   Colliery Office Pensher
18th Dec[ember] 1822

My Lord

I have had the honor to receive your Lordship's letter of the 26th and 28th Nov[ember], but have delayed replying to them as well as to certain parts of your Lordship's *private* letter of the 19th Nov. until I could see Wyatt,[62] and waiting for a reply from Groom, relative to the appropriation of the money for the sales of the settled Estates.

I have the highest opinion of Mr Groom's professional correctness; but there seems to be a sort of irritability of temper about him, which makes him rather ticklish to deal with. And he wants that sort of *je ne sais quoi*, which it is difficult to describe, to make him the agreeable man of business. He has also an attachment to his own opinion which it is difficult to weaken.

It appears from my late correspondence with him, that he has taken up the Cudgels for Gregson, and it is clear that matters will not go smooth again, until Gregson's Bill is paid. This we should if possible do, in the manner stated in my last letter as it is most desirable, in matters of such importance as your Lordship's affairs, that all the parties concerned, should act cordially together, with zeal & energy – any thing like lukewarmness will not do.

Groom's reply to my enquiry, as to the way in which the money for the sale of the Estates, is to be disposed of: is another specimen of his want of distinctness and precision, in business correspondence. Why not at once say, it can be applied in this way, or that, but not otherwise?

It is the occurrence of difficulties alone, in the affairs of human life, which call forth our energies, and when adverse circumstances do beset us, we must not sit tamely down, and wring our hands, and cry to Jove to come and assist us; but set our shoulders manfully to the wheel, and do the very best we can to extricate ourselves.

The prodigious exertions which your Lordship has made, within so short a period, were called forth by circumstances. To have omitted to take advantage of such circumstances, for the purpose of extending and securing the interests of a Family, whose Conse-

---

62 Philip Wyatt, architect, d. 1836, son of James Wyatt, employed by Lord Londonderry to rebuild Wynyard Park. See John Martin Robinson, *The Wyatts, an Architectural Dynasty* (Oxford, 1979), pp. 101–3, 115–23, 253.

quence, in this County, we may reasonably hope, will extend to the latest posterity, could not in my humble judgment, have been justified, on any grounds whatever; but on the other hand, might have entailed censure, on the individual, who is bound by every tie of honor, and by the worthiest feelings of our nature, to promote, and conserve, it's best interests.

The renewal of the Rainton Colliery Lease began, the subsequent purchase of Biddick, Seaham, the baronet's and Dawson's estates *extended*; and the establishment of the Daldon harbour, will complete the *renovation* of the family Colliery property.

To a partial, or timid observer, the present position of your Lordship's affairs, may appear sombre. But let us contrast the present situation of the family property, with that in which it was when your Lordship came to the administration of it's affairs. We shall then be the better able to form an impartial judgment, and find that there is no real cause for despondency, but the contrary.

It cannot be denied, but at the period here alluded to, the main stay of the family-property, was its Collieries. They consisted of a freehold Mine belonging to the family, and a Lease-hold belonging to the Dean & Chapter of Durham. But what was the situation of those Mines? Why the former was nearly exhausted, and the Lease of the latter had only six years to go, without the least prospect of a renewal being effected. Beside which, the workings of this mine were getting into a very cramped state, as it would not have been prudent to have expended large sums of money on their extension, under so short a Lease.

It is not now for us to enquire how matters came to be brought, into this deplorable state. But if we ask any rational man, if it would have been prudent to have allowed them, to remain in such a situation, it would be outraging common Sense, not to suppose that he would immediately reply, *no* –'by no means. Use every possible exertion, within your power, to restore the family to a permanent interest in the Collieries, and to extend and renovate them'.

This my Lord I am satisfied is the true state of the case, and what your Lordship has done, is what the exigencies of the affair, imperiously called for. It is questionable whether such a coincidence of adverse circumstances, ever before occurred in the property of any family.

To extricate the property from this dilemma, great exertions were called for. These exertions have been made, but they have been made for an object worthy of such exertions.

The term of the lease-hold Colliery has been filled up to 21 years and large Sums of Money have been expended, in improving and extending the Works, over and above the Fine of £40,000 for the renewal of the Lease.

A great addition has been made to the Freehold Colliery, by the purchase of Biddick, the Baronet's and Dawson's Estates.

The landed property has also been materially augmented by the purchase of the above Estates, and Seaham. But was all this to be effected, without great pecuniary difficulty, and a reasonable space of time to bring all the requisite resources into operation?

Widely different indeed would have been the state of affairs, if under my Lady's Minority, the property had been so managed as to have produced that accumulation of money, which it ought to have done. What are now mountains to be surmounted, would in that case only have been *mole-hills*.

These reflections are now however of no avail, we must therefore, give our best consideration to the great points, which are the immediate objects of attention.

When we are hard run, and out of breath, by great exertion, the best plan to regain our vigour, is to remain tranquil.

Now, that by remaining tranquil, your Lordship's Finances would soon gain strength and vigour, there cannot be a doubt. But then the chief consideration is, will your Lordship's plans of life, admit of this state of tranquillity for the requisite period?

Two great objects present themselves at the same moment, both probably equally important to your Lordship. The one being for the aggrandizement of the family, the other for it's comfort.

Under existing circumstances, it does not seem practicable to undertake both, and the immediate commencement of one of them, is even inconvenient, unless some extraneous pecuniary aid can be obtained.

As to which should be first accomplished, it is so entirely a matter of feeling, that it's decision, must entirely rest with your Lordship. I can only say, that whatever your Lordship's decision may be, my best exertions shall not be wanting, to aid, and promote it's object.

I hate *croaking*, but at the same time, we must not deceive ourselves, but take a calm view of our real situation. This I have done, and it is really painful to me, to avow, that I cannot see how any efficient aid, can be given from the Colliery Funds, until after Mr Groom's list of demands is cleared off. This with other matters which are always occurring, will anticipate the Colliery Funds, 'till next August. And I am satisfied that Backhouse's accommodation has reached it's fullest extent.

Edward has frequently told me, that they are not money lenders, and that it does not suit their purpose at all to advance money, except on the balance of an Account current. I have also made out very much to my own satisfaction, that the Daldon project, is the last thing, in the world, on which they would advance money.

The Backhouses are large proprietors in the Darlington Rail-way,[63] and are very jealous of the Daldon project. Indeed I believe they are pushing it with all their might at present, to get before hand with us, in the supply of the duty-free part of the Coast, within the port of Stockton. I am persuaded, that if we could have commenced the Daldon Harbour, with vigour last spring; they never would have thought of carrying their Rail-way to the port of Stockton, for the purpose of shipping Coals. They have pushed this undertaking with increased energy of late, in consequence I presume, of my negotiations with Edward, having exposed our want of means: and they no doubt calculate on our inability to accomplish the harbour.

When we cannot do as we could wish, we must do what we can. This consideration has pressed strongly on my mind, and has stimulated me, to the consideration of various schemes, for the accomplishment of Daldon Harbour. The only one however which I think feasible, is the following.

To have the money raised in the way of a Bridge, or Canal Company, by letting it out in Shares, *your Lordship reserving the option of buying up the Share*, at the end of any given period, as seven, or ten years for example. The following outline will better explain my meaning.

Supposing the harbour, with all it's appendages, to complete it for the shipping of Coals, to cost £15000. This sum to be divided into 30 Shares of £50 each.

The Interest to the Share-holders to be say 10 per cent, will amount to £1500 a year. Which stating the yearly Vend, only at 30,000 Ch. will be covered by a Toll of 1/- per Ch. But if the Vend should be extended to 40,000 Ch. a Toll of 9d per Ch. would pay the Interest, and so on. The rate of Toll decreasing, as the Vend increases.

---

63 An Act to allow building of a public railway from Stockton via Darlington to the Bishop Auckland area, with the object of improving the transport facilities of southern Co. Durham and reducing the cost of carrying coal, was passed on 19 April 1821. The Backhouses were major subscribers. See Tomlinson, *North Eastern Railway*, pp. 40–70; M.W. Kirby, *The Origins of Railway Enterprise: Stockton and Darlington Railway 1821* (Cambridge, 1983), pp. 26–39. The line, from Stockton to Brusselton near West Auckland, was opened on 27 Sep. 1825.

I really think if this matter was fairly set about, there would be little difficulty in raising the money, even at a less rate of Interest than 10 per cent. Many people would take more than one Share; and I should not wonder if several people about Sunderland, and this neighbourhood – our Fitters and others would take Shares.

The question is, whether it would not be better to raise the money in London; rather than in the neighbourhood. Although if raised amongst Ship-owners &c. it might give them an interest in the success of the undertaking which would induce them to patronise it, by sending their ships to the Port.

I shall be glad to know your Lordship's opinion of this *project*, and if you should approve of it, I would consult Mr Chapman[64] the Engineer, as to the best mode of setting the subscription agoing, as he has had much experience in matters of this kind.

The most important matter is, the new Building at Wynyard. I spent yesterday morning & the day before, there, with Mr Wyatt. I have made out from him, in the best way I am able, his notion of what should be done, on the *curtailed* plan, to render the House habitable against June 1824. To avoid perplexity, I have written this Statement on a separate paper marked A, and as far as I am able to judge (if anything more than the Foundations, up to the surface level is to be done this spring) less cannot well be done, to admit of the future extension of the Building, to it's intended limits.

Your Lordship's definition of Wyatt's character, is so accurate that I need not say anything on that subject. I don't pretend to have any judgment in the ornamental part of architecture, and am willing to allow Mr Wyatt full credit for his good taste, and knowledge, in arranging the Comforts of a large mansion. But his ignorance in the arrangements of the operative part of his profession, and more especially, with respect to the estimating of the cost of every thing connected with the art of building, is to me, quite marvellous.

He is so vague, and loose – so completely *abroad*, in all points of this description – so very different to every other man of his profession, with whom I have ever had anything to do, that I must fairly acknowledge, to your Lordship, that I cannot place any confidence in his Estimates. I therefore consider them an entire hit, or miss, affair. On looking over the estimate, I observed to your Lordship, that the prices for the different items of the work, appeared to be ample. And

---

64 William Chapman, Newcastle engineer.

the only doubt I had, was as to the *correctness* of the measurements, and that something might be omitted.

Your Lordship will perceive by the enclosed paper, that his Estimate (a copy of which your Lordship sent me) entirely omits an item of £2000 for completing the offices: and I heartily wish that this may be the only omission.

The result of our discussions is, as stated in the enclosed paper, that to finish a certain part of the House, as therein specified – to make it fit for your Lordship's residence – in part execution of the *curtailed*, or £36000 plan, against June 1824, will cost £27000. About £18000 of which will have to be expended in regular weekly payments of £250, in wages, to the different classes of workmen and labourers. The remaining £9000 will be expended in various materials.

It is impossible to estimate how the payment of the £9000 may be called for, or whether any, or what credit may be obtained on any part of the amount. But it is quite clear, that we must either pay, or incur debt, to the amount of £1500 a month, of which £1000 at least per lunar month *must* be paid in *Cash*.

This consideration brings me to the most painful part of my subject; for when I know, that there is nothing to calculate upon from this quarter; but the surplus Balance of the Colliery Account, and being but too well satisfied, that this surplus, is already anticipated, for other purposes, I feel myself under the painful necessity of declaring it, as my opinion, that the Collieries cannot give any efficient pecuniary assistance to the Building; at any rate 'till after July next. By referring to the Schedule of payments and the estimate of our ways & means, of August last, your Lordship will find that Mr Groom's list of payments, will require rather more than the whole probable amount of the Colliery surplus (£13000) up to that period. Besides which, there are other Sums to be provided for, which have occurred since, and are not named in the list.

There is for instance Gregson's £1984.19 which ought to be paid by May, or we shall have no peace with the Lawyers. There is also your Lordship's Draft of £800 which it would sting me to the very quick, not to be able to meet. Webster[65] has also written to Hawkes,[66] for £1640 to pay the Freight, Insurance, and Custom-house dues, on your Lordship's packages from Trieste. Besides which we shall have Dawson's Biddick Interest to pay.

---

65 Shipping agent.
66 William Hawkes, land agent at Wynyard.

The £1640 to Webster is the most pressing, as I see no alternative but to pay it, otherwise the packages will be detained. Thus it appears that £4424.19.0 is to pay, *more than* the probable surplus of the Colliery Balance, between now & the end of next July.

As Backhouse will *decidedly not* allow us to exceed the £20,000, your Lordship will readily see, the narrow limits to which I am confined; and how difficult it will be, not to say, impracticable, to meet such unexpected and pressing payments unless I have assistance from some other quarter. These payments are the more unwelcome at this time, when our resources, are so entirely dependent on the weather.

As it is but too evident that there is not the least probability of the Collieries giving any pecuniary assistance to the Building, at any rate, before next August. If therefore your Lordship determines to go on with it, in the mean time, the Funds must be provided from some other Source.

Hawkes is much depressed, and very low at the enfeebled state of the Finances.

The Tradesmen who want their money are increasingly pressing for payment, and he is afraid that some of them, should be urged on by our blackguard Enemies, to proceed to extremities, which would be a fine subject for Willams's animadversions. Indeed I should think it wrong to conceal from your Lordship that this subject is much talked of every where; and I should advise that the clamour of these people should be quieted if possible, without delay.

I really crave your Lordship's indulgence for the freedom of my remarks, but I should consider myself wanting in duty, to that confidence, with which your Lordship had honored me, were I to withhold such information. But at the same time, I beg to assure your Lordship, that I shall always offer my observations with due deference, and not presume to press them further, than they may coincide with your Lordship's own views.

I beg further to observe, that I shall always consider it my duty, to carry your Lordship's wishes into effect, to the utmost of my power, and execute your orders, to the very letter, as far as our circumstances will permit. I trust by this time your Lordship knows enough of me, to be satisfied that a little extra exertion, at any time when circumstances require it, has no terrors for me. Nature has blessed me with a good constitution, and I have been brought up to habits of industry. I never have been accustomed to measure out my hours of labour, and *dread* no degree of fatigue. I have therefore only to say to your Lordship, 'command me whenever, or wherever you think

I can render service in your affairs, and your Lordship may rely on my best exertions'.

I feel exceedingly obliged by your Lordship's kind wishes, with respect to the payment of my Salary. I have enclosed a Statement B of my account up to the 31st Inst. I commenced the valuation of the Colliery Stock by Mr Whitton's[67] order on the 9th April 1819, and on the 10th June following your Lordship, did me the honor to appoint me to the management of the Collieries. During that period I was occupied in the valuation of the Colliery Stock, surveying the Workings, &c. My professional charge if made by the *job*, would have exceeded the rate of my yearly Salary for that period. But to make it reckon straight, I have charged the Salary from the 9th April 1819. Your Lordship will perceive that I have charged £600 at different periods, in the pay Bills, and that the balance due me on the 31st Inst. will be £2379.7.3.

As I am not in any immediate want of money, and as I hope to see our general affairs more easy in money matters by-and-by, than they are at present, I am willing if it meets your Lordship's approbation to allow £2000 to remain on Interest 'till it may be convenient to pay it – just as your Lordship pleases. The use for which I wish to reserve it, is to pay off the mortgage of a small Estate, I bought in Northumberland some time ago.[68]

In my last packet I sent out a power of Attorney, with the requisite Affidavits for your Lordship's execution, which will have to be done in the presence of a Notary Publick – a creature which is to be found in every part of the world I believe.

I once thought, it might have been expedient, for me, to have had a power of Attorney, from your Lordship, for general purposes; but I am now of a different opinion. The not having such an authority, will always shield me against the importunities of our Lawyers, for *premature* payments of any sort: and in case of any emergency, like Hayton and Douglasse's Bankruptcy, I can always send a special one for your Lordship's execution.

I have given an account of my *reconnaissance* with old Pemberton, and other matters, in my official letter.

It is impossible for me to express the degree of regret I feel, in not being able to give a better statement of the resources for the Building.

67 Unidentified.
68 Buddle had some years earlier bought a property at Benwell on the outskirts of Newcastle.

Wyatt declares that with the exception of a quantity of flooring Deals, there is *already Timber enough on the premises*. I will take every opportunity of laying my Hands on flooring Deals, and of leading Stones. For whether your Lordship decides to push the Building or not, it is always so much done to have the materials ready. The River was frozen last Sunday and Monday, and I had made arrangements for making a *rush* in the leading of Stones, with the Waggon Horses, while the Frost continues. A thaw came on Tuesday however, and put an end to this scheme for the present. But we will manage it so, that when we *cannot* lead Coals, we *will* lead Stones.

Hawkes has every thing in very good order at Wynyard: and the new Foundations so far, are very well done. The worst job is, the failure of the Bricks, as few of them are fit for common purposes. They are too soft not being sufficiently hardened in the burning owing to the nature of the Clay I think or perhaps an over mixture of sand.

The Marquess of Londonderry   I have the Honor [&c]
Verona[69]   J^no Buddle

---

69 Londonderry was serving at the Congress of Verona in his capacity as Ambassador to Austria. He had in fact determined to resign as soon as he learned that George Canning had replaced his late half-brother as Foreign Secretary, but did not present his letters of recall to the Austrian Emperor, Francis I, until 22 December 1822, in Venice, after the conclusion of the Verona conference. He set out for England the next day. Irby C. Nicholls, jr, *The European Pentarchy and the Congress of Verona, 1822* (The Hague, 1971), p. 267n.

27.

D/Lo/C142/7   Colliery Office, Pensher, 28th Mar[ch] 1823

My Lord

I am happy to learn by your Lordship's letter of the 27th Ulto: that we may expect your Lordship, and the family in England, in June, as your Lordship's presence near the scene of our operations here, will be a great comfort to me, and will ensure the means of a regular and quick correspondence at all times.

I am now negotiating with the several Way-leave proprietors, on the Daldon line of rail-way. Croudace agrees to take £50 a year for the Bradleys; but if I cannot get the Rector,[1] and Ironside, to take under £60, we are to give Mr Lambton the same.

The basis which I am endeavouring to establish with all the parties, is the same as Huttons viz. a 63 years Lease (for I hate renewals) *and no rent to be paid 'till we lead Coals.* Of course no Way-leave rent will become payable, until, by the sale of Coals we shall become possessed of the means of paying them. I shall find some difficulty in bringing all the parties to this; but as I have all this year to negotiate in, I don't dispair of bringing them to consent by one means or other. Engaging the way-leaves on this plan will also give us leisure to make the Harbour.

I am also desirous to establish the Harbour, on a *self-paying principle.* My Plan is to raise the Money, by subscription Shares of say £100, the same as for a canal or any other publick work. The interest to be paid by a Chaldron Toll, out of the Vend. I have already submitted the outlines of this scheme to your Lordship's considera-tion in former letters; and have been waiting for your Lordship's observations and instructions thereon, nearly three months. But as it is doubtful, that these letters may ever reach your Lordship; the best plan will now be I think, to let the matter rest, until your Lord-ship's return to England, when the whole plan may be much better discussed in all it's bearings.

By raising the money in this way I think a great many Ship-owners, and Fitters &c. would become share-holders, which would interest them in the success of the undertaking; and induce them to

---

1   Of Bishopwearmouth, Robert Gray (see p. 9, n. 17).

patronize it by loading their Ships there, instead of going to other ports. And by granting building Leases on eligible terms, I think we should very soon see a Colony established, and 'Stewart's Town' spring up, to the great benefit of the Seaham Estate. The Butcher, Baker, Brewer, carpenter, sail-maker &c. would immediately follow the Shipping to Daldon, & establish themselves there.

I have arranged the outlines of the rail-way contract with Thompson,[2] but until the Way-leaves are secured, and the arrangements for the harbour are finally made, it is not necessary to close the agreement with him. Indeed I cannot obtain the requisite data, to enable me to do so, until all these matters are finally settled.

If this project was completed it would give us a decided advantage over our neighbours; as neither Frosts, nor Floods would interrupt us. Gales of Wind certainly might, but these three plagues, would never occur at the same time – such a coincidence could not happen. Croudace *consoles himself* with the idea that this plan will never be accomplished.

I some time ago mentioned to your Lordship, that Tommy Fenwick had informed me, in confidence, that the Revd. Body, had changed their views, as to N. Pittington. Looking forward to all the rail-way schemes which have been talked of – to Daldon, Hawthorn Dean, Hesleden & Hartlepool, they are inclined to look on a little, and will neither let, or sell for the present.

The Hetton Co. continue fighting & scratching as usual; and in consequence there is no subordination, or order at the Colliery. An opinion is gaining ground, that neither their High-main, nor Hutton Seam, is turning out nearly so well, as was at first expected. As yet we don't feel that they have in the slightest degree, infringed upon the Vend of Eden-main; and I have no apprehension whatever about the Walls-end.

To guard against an injurious interference from the 'Lyons-main' at Lynn – with the Eden-main, as much as might be, I widened our Screens, a little at Christmas, so as to take the small Dust, entirely out of them; and in consequence our Fitters say, that they are getting into greater respect than ever.

They have not yet found the Coal beyond the great Slip-Dyke at Hetton, which lies at 180 yards to the S. of their Pit. This is cramping their operations exceedingly and I understand that nothing but that

---

2 Benjamin Thompson, builder of waggonways, engineer for the Seaham railway.

want of unanimity amongst the Co. prevents their making an immediate proposition to your Lordship for a division of the Coal.[3]

This subject will most likely be ready for discussion by the time
your Lordship arrives in England. At any rate, my present feeling is,
that it's discussion, ought to be put off 'till then.

That part of Hetton, which must at any rate be allotted to us,
under a Division; will make *a very pretty little separate Colliery of itself,
to go to Daldon* – independently either of Pensher, or Rainton. But I
shall hope to have the honor of explaining my views on this subject,
personally to your Lordship, in the *Cabinet*, long before any arrangement for taking the Field need be made. The only catastrophe which
we should have to deplore, in this event, would be the death of poor
Croudace, who would scarcely survive the shock of such development, I fear.

Croudace and I have commenced our negotiations, with the
Newbottle Way-leave proprietors, and so far are in as fair a way, as
we could well expect, We have seen Dr Gray, Ettrick, the Fenwicks,
and Hopper. The idea of a reduction from the terms established by
Nesham's people, is by no means palatable – especially with the
Doctor. But as he will in a great degree be governed by Tommy
Fenwick's opinion, I think we shall in the end agree. The most
awkward part of the business with respect to the Doctor's shipping
place, is, that a part of it is occupied by a Lime-Kiln for which a
person pays him £200 or £250 a year. This Kiln occupies the best part
of the shore, and some plan must be contrived for getting quit of it,
either by removing it, or by contriving a spout to ship the lime, so
as not to interfere with the shipping of the Coals. It is agreed that
T. Fenwick is to examine the situation with me, to endeavour to get
these matters accommodated, and I expect that we shall not meet
with any insuperable difficulties.

Ettrick, Hopper, and the Fenwicks will I think be brought to terms;
and we shall see the other parties as soon as convenient.

The following are the parties through whose property, we have to
pass – placed in the order they stand, downwards from the Colliery
to the Harbour,

---

3   The shares of the Hetton coal held by Emerson and Clutterbuck (see p. 12,
     n. 26) had been secured by Buddle for Lord Londonderry. Early in 1824
     Mowbray tried to buy these shares; Lyon agreed to a division of the coal, and
     to sell his share to William Russell, son of Matthew Russell. The negotiations
     were prolonged, but were completed in 1825. See below, p. 137.

1.   General Maxwell
2.   Messrs Widrington & Ackroid
3.   Mr Lambton, late Nesham
4.   Mr Nesham
5.   Mr Lambton, late Nesham
6.   The Marquess of Londonderry, late Dawson
7.   Ditto – late Baronets-Rayne's Farm
8.   Mr Lambton, late Baronet's
9.   Ditto, late Beckwith's
10. Mr Addison Fenwick
11. Mr John Thompson
12. Mr H. Hopper
13. Revd. Ettrick
14. Mr Geo. Fenwick
15. Dr Gray
16. Mr Th. Hopper[4]
17. Dr Gray, through Glebe, and Staith.

The treating with these parties will necessarily occupy a good deal of time, but by patience and perseverance we shall get thro' it. I informed your Lordship some time ago that I had prevailed with Croudace, to adopt the principle, of being at the whole expence of making the requisite alterations and improvements, in the Rail-way, and of conveying our Coals by the Chaldron, according to Thompson's plan, so that the only expence which will fall upon your Lordship, will be the creation of the Spouts, and making the requisite stock of Waggons.

I yesterday received intelligence of S[i]r Henry Hardinge having vacated his Seat,[5] and that he would be in Durham in the morning to commence his canvass.

I went to Durham to see what sort of a sensation this unexpected intelligence had produced on friends and foes there,

Deputations of Freemen had gone to Wilkinson (old *Bunker's* son)[6]

---

4   Thomas Hopper, Bishopwearmouth.

5   On being appointed Clerk of the Ordnance in March 1823 Hardinge was obliged to resign his seat. In the ensuing by-election Hedworth Lambton, brother of J.G. Lambton, was nominated as Whig candidate in his absence and without his consent and, receiving only a few votes, withdrew on the second day of the poll. *Hist. Parl. 1820–32*, ii, 364; Alan Heesom, *Durham City and its MPs 1678–1992* (Durham, 1992).

6   Anthony Wilkinson, Coxhoe Hall.

and to Sheppardson,[7] to intreat them to oppose Sir Henry; but they declined the honor, and we have every reason at present to hope, that we shall have no opposition. This produced a diversity of feeling – the *independent* Freemen, are crestfallen, and we are *delighted*.
I hope they will not be able to bring forward any man of Straw for the sake of a row, and to run us to expence.

Croudace as sincerely wishes to avoid any thing of this kind as I do, and had not up to last night heard any thing on the subject from Mr Lambton. He thinks it fortunate that Mr Lambton's younger Brother is not in the Country, as he thinks it by no means unlikely that he would have opposed Sir Henry.

Sir Henry will be in Durham early in the morning where I shall attend to lend all the assistance I can.

Our Pitmen's binding passed over on the 22nd Inst. without the slightest difficulty and I am glad to say that our vend is going on steadily. I hope it will not be short of 10,000 Ch. this month, and we are getting a very good proportion of Walls-end.

I hope my Lady and the Children continue to enjoy good health.

The Marquess of Londonderry   I have the honor [&c.]
Rome   Jno Buddle

28.

D/Lo/C142/7   *Private*   Colliery Office, Pensher, 23rrd May 1823

My Lord

I notice your Lordship's reflections on the self-paying plan of raising the money for the new Harbour. There is no question but the carrying of this business into effect at your Lordship's private expence, is the most independent plan, and if it could be accomplished, would in the end be the most satisfactory. I only proposed the other as a Succeddaneum, in case it should be imprudent to raise the money otherwise.

No harm is yet however done, as the scheme is only known to your Lordship, Chapman & myself. It may therefore either be adopted, or rejected, as may seem most eligible when we come to the discussion of that branch of the subject.

Chapman is coming down to Scarbro' and will come forward to

7   Edward Shipperdson.

Newcastle next Week. This will give me an opportunity of conferring with him further on the spot, if requisite, relative to the Harbour.

When he sounded the monied men in London, he did not say where the Field of action was.

In the year 1817, I think it was, Parliament granted a large Sum of money to be lent, on certain conditions, to individuals, or Companies, for purposes of this sort – when the object was to give employment to the labouring classes.[8]

Mr Littleton[9] will be able to give full information on the subject, as I know that he was on the Committee for the appropriation of the money. Your Lordship may probably think it right to write to Mr Littleton for information, as to whether the act is still in force, and whether the Case of our Rail-way & Harbour would come under it's meaning. If we could obtain £10,000 or £15,000 from this Fund it would enable us to accomplish our object within ourselves, which I should decidedly prefer, to having either the rail-way or Harbour done by contract. The Rail-way I am sure we can do ourselves at a very much cheaper rate, than any contractor could do it for. I could get the whole of the cast iron work – to pay one half the amount in Small Coals.

I am really very much at a loss to find out, what is to be done with Groom. He is evidently quite unhappy under the liability which he either has, or imagines he has incurred for the £13000, and it is evident that we shall have no peace with him, until he is freed from it, in one way, or other. It is preying upon his mind so, that I am told by a friend in London, who knows him, that he scarcely keep *his own Council*.

The most obvious plan, is, to get Coutts's to accept some security from your Lordship, and to exonerate him. But this I feel it will almost impossible to accomplish without your Lordship's personal exertions & influence with them. Groom sticks to his opinion that the Colliery stock, is not an available security for money. But might not Coutts' be induced notwithstanding to accept it, if not as a *direct*, as a

---

8   On 28 Apr. 1817 Parliament authorised the issue of Exchequer bills up to a sum of £500,000 to make loans for public works and the employment of the poor. *Parliamentary Debates* (hereafter *Parl. Deb.*), 1st ser., xxxvi, cols 27–47. Further sums were authorised later. Lord Londonderry obtained two loans for building Seaham Harbour.

9   Edward Littleton, 1791–1863, MP for Staffordshire 1812–37, South Staffordshire 1832–5, Baron Hatherton 1835: *ODNB*; *Hist. Parl. 1820–32*, vi, 128–39. He was a member of a number of parliamentary committees, including two on finance.

collateral security, with some other property for the amount? Groom seems to look to the Colliery-profits alone for the liquidation of this sum; but if he would refer to my Statement of August last, he would see that the profits of the Collieries were anticipated by the payments therein put down, up to the end of July next. He would then see that £22,911.0.10 had to be paid, and he must know that £16,701.10.10 of this amount has actually been paid, besides several other large sums, not enumerated in the List. He ought therefore to be more sparing in his expectations from that quarter.

I hope & trust that I may be able to remit him the £800 on the 1st August, but as our total means, will I fear fall far short of the demands, the most needful must be first supplied, and the remainder must be deferred. My private memorandum of the 3rd Inst. would shew your Lordship the state of our Finances at that time; and after our Receipt of the 1st June, I will send a corrected statement up to that period, which will enable your Lordship to judge of, and direct the disposal of our means.

S[i]r Henry Hardinge has relieved us greatly by remitting £700 towards defraying the expences of the Election; which leaves us about £400 to pay, £300 of which is already paid. But still I am utterly unable to get Gregson paid, which is a bar to finishing the Seaham purchase, and annoys me greatly.

I have seen Col. Grey[10] who assures me that 'they have not yet got a Whig made of Mr Russell', notwithstanding his voting in the minority on Lord John Russell's motion.[11] It was merely one of those political aberrations into which young Members are liable to fall. He will yet take the right course, I firmly believe.

To The Marquess of Londonderry   I have the honor [&c.]
                                                              Jno Buddle

---

10 Col. Grey, Stockton.
11 On 20 Feb. 1823 Lord John Russell moved in the House of Commons a motion calling for a return of the number of voters in boroughs, and the qualifications for the vote. The motion was defeated by 128 to 90. *Parl. Deb.*, new ser., viii, cols 172–88. Matthew Russell had died in 1822. His son William was not yet an MP. He instructed his agent in Durham to support Hardinge in the election.

29.

D/Lo/C142/7　　　　　　　　　　　Pensher 12th Aug[ust] 1823

My Lord

As my Letters of late have not entered much into the detail of actual Colliery business, I now take the liberty of addressing your Lordship more especially on that subject.

I feel the greatest satisfaction in stating that our Underground affairs are, in as favourable a situation generally speaking, as I would wish for. But at the same time your Lordship will readily conceive that our large Vend, must produce a corresponding extension of the Workings underground; and that it will of consequence be requisite either to sink new Pits, or to employ a great additional number of Horses, to carry the Coals underground, as the Workings are progressively extended.

The working of the Pillars for some time past, has greatly counteracted the necessity of sinking new Pits; but the field of *whole* Coal getting gradually exhausted in the Dunwell, Hazard, Hunter's-house and Resolution Pits renders it necessary to commence the Sinking of a new Pit, or two, to replace them.

The completion of the Adventure Pit, which was prevented by Water, in 1817 is now in great progress, and will in part effect the above purpose; but still another new Pit ought to be put in progress this Autumn.

I had proposed to sink the latter to the Westward from the Adventure; but on exploring the Mine underground I find a more eligible situation, under existing circumstances, in a Southern direction from the Meadows.

As this will be a Pit of great magnitude and importance, I submit that it should be named after some of the Family – in compliment to my Lady, to Lord Henry or any other that your Lordship may approve. We might call her 'The Lady Frances' Pit', 'The Henry,' or 'The Londonderry' or any other name of that sort which your Lordship may think the most appropriate. And I shall be glad to learn your Lordship's decision in the course of a month or six weeks.[12]

We are by no means cramped for the want of new Pits yet; but good management requires that we should be putting them in progress – especially for the purpose of keeping up a regular supply of the Walls-end Coals.

12　The new pit was named the 'Londonderry'.

The next point is the shipping of the Coals. The best plan, provided Way-leaves can be obtained on eligible terms, probably is, to ship by Spout at Sunderland. But as this would only be to the extent of 50,000 Ch. yearly, and as I hardly expect, from Croudace's languid movements, that this can be effected in any definite time, I am strongly inclined to recommend the extension of the Tub system, with all convenient speed, to your Lordship's attention.

I think I can now secure a good situation for a *stationary* loading Machine for about £50 a year; and might have it ready to start when the next Spring Trade opens out, in May.

Our present machine is doing considerably more business than I calculated. She is now loading at the rate of more than 30,000 Ch. a year; and will this year make a neat saving of £2500.

Another Transferer would enable us to Ship *all our Walls-end*, and a considerable quantity of the Eden-main also by Tubs. In this case the Eden-main would be *advanced a Step,* and become more eligible for the London Market – a sort of second Walls-end in short, and if we could not advance the price, we should at any rate make a saving of 2/- per Ch. on the quantity thus shipped.

I shall now make some observations on our Walls-end Coals, as your Lordship has occasionally expressed some degree of disappointment, at their not standing above Mr Lambton's in price at the London Market.

However gratifying it would be to see them standing 3d or 6d per Ch. a head of Mr Lambton's, and admitting it to be practicable, as I really believe it is, to make them do so, I am nevertheless under the entire conviction that it would be highly impolitick, and prejudicial to your Lordship's interest to make the attempt.

I would first beg to call to your Lordship's attention to the *very large* proportion of Walls-end, which we have for some time past been making. We also know that they are sufficiently good to stand upon a level, with Lambton's, and to sell freely at the same price.

Now as a Coal-owner, the latter is the *real & essential point in which your Lordship's interest is mainly concerned*. For if the Stewart's Walls-end, stood even 1/- per Ch. higher in London, than Lambton's, it would not put a *single farthing* into your Lordship's pocket, as the price to the Fitter and Ship-owner *here* is fixed, and stationary, & would of course remain the same. The *grand secret* and true point of gain to your Lordship, therefore is, to send them *as bad as ever we can; barely to get them to stand on a level with Lambton's. By no means to strive to get them to pass his in price at London*, but just to keep them equal, *at as cheap a rate of manufacture as possible.*

I have studied this subject attentively, and I am satisfied, to make our Coals good enough, to beat Lambton's 3d or 6d per Ch. In London for the sole benefit of the Ship-owner, would cost us, at this time, in the sacrifice of quantity, *not less than £600 a month*!!!

This lead would also be of very short duration as Croudace's jealousy would be so raised, that he would most likely, set to work immediately, to make Mr Lambton's Coals better. And let us make our's as good as ever we might, he would be *up to us*, and the result of our efforts, would merely be, a destructive competition for an *ideal* advantage.

I am therefore satisfied, that our *true interest* is to go on *snugly*, getting all the *quantity* we can, and keeping up our *price here*, without straining to lead at market, nor paying more attention to that point, than is requisite to enable us, to gain the above essential object. This is unquestionably the true way to make the most money.

I shall conclude with a few words on the subject of the *new* Coal.

The *cheapest* Coal which we can obtain is the Low-main from the North Pit Rainton. It is of a quality too inferior, to merit any better a name, than S. Main – it is not worth the bestowing of any family name upon. The selling price will be 16/1½ per Ch. but at this price it will leave nearly as much profit, as Eden-main from the cheap rate at which it can be wrought. And I expect it will sell readily coastwise, and to Tradesmen &c. We had better therefore for the present, I think, suspend the idea of making any other sort of inferior Coal. I am just setting off to the Chester meeting and shall write your Lordship an account of it tomorrow.

The Marquess of Londonderry	I have the honor [&c].
London	J^{no} Buddle

30.

D/Lo/C142/7   Pensher Colliery 3rd Nov[embe]r 1823

My Lord

I am grieved to inform your Lordship that one of those catastrophes which but too frequently occur in Coal mining has today befallen us here. At ¼ before 6 o'clock this morning the Plane pit at Rainton exploded, and killed, I fear, about 50 people beside many grievously scorched & wounded. I have just come out of the pit (5 o'clock p.m.) and as far as I can at present make out, we have found 46 dead Bodies – 5 more are said to be missing The explosion had been very heavy, many of the sufferers being so mutilated & mangled that they could not be recognised, and we were obliged to coffin the Bodies in the pit. The Overman Wm Dawson, a valuable man, and his 4 assistants are killed.

We cannot yet ascertain the immediate cause of this accident – the proximate cause was a sudden discharge of inflammable air from the *crushed down* excavations where we were working off the pillars. *No other lights* than the Davy Lamps were used. The inflammable air rushed out of the old inaccessible pillars and filled all the Davy Lamps with fire. Dawson & his assistants were seen by some of the Survivors exerting themselves to extinguish the Lamps, and withdraw the Workmen; but before he could accomplish his design the accident happened. From what cause we shall probably never ascertain; but in all likelihood it had been from some accident to, or mismanagement of a Davy lamp.

Altho' every thing is terribly knocked about in the pit, and 11 or 12 of the Horses out of 17 are killed, yet all may be set to rights again in a few days; but the loss of men & more particularly of the Boys will be difficult to make up again before the next Binding next April.

And as according to custom the other men will not work 'till all the dead are found & buried I hardly expect any more work to be done this week.

This is a cruel cut in upon our operations as I am afraid it will diminish our vend for the month nearly 2000 Ch.

I cannot say more at present than that every possible exertion will be made to lighten this misfortune and to recover the back-cast which it will inevitably give us in point of Vend.

I have much satisfaction in reporting to your Lordship the good conduct of all our Viewers, Overmen &c. on this occasion and am happy to add that no lives were lost, in the dangerous operation of endeavouring to save the lives of the sufferers & in searching for the dead Bodies. Hunter, Robson, Legg & Longstaff shewed the greatest skill & intrepidity, and saved many Lives by their prompt exertions, before I could arrive.

I shall send for the Coroner in the morning, and will have the burials on Wednesday if possible, which may give us the chance of getting to work again on Thursday. Mr Lambton's Viewers came as Volunteers to assist us in getting the dead bodies out. During the night I hope all the missing will be found, unless they should be covered under falls of the Roof, many of which have taken place from the props being blown out by the explosion. In a day or two I shall be able to send your Lordship a correct return of the mischief done on this occasion.

The Marquess of Londonderry   I have the Honor [&c.]
Mount Stewart   J^{no} Buddle

31.

D/Lo/C142/7   Pensher Colliery 4th Nov[embe]r1823

My Lord

The total number of killed, and those who have died of their Wounds up to this Evening amounts to 59, and I fear from the accounts of the Surgeons that more will yet die. One more dead body was found during the course of last night, but 4 still remain in the pit: during this night or tomorrow however I hope they will be found as we know pretty nearly where about they are, and the only chance against their being got, is that they may be buried under Rubbish,

The Coroner's inquest was held this morning and many funerals have taken place to day. The remainder will be buried tomorrow and on Thursday morning I expect some of the pits will start work again.

The conduct of the people is exemplary. I scarcely ever witnessed such decency & propriety of conduct under similarly distressing circumstances; and the examination of the Witnesses, and the verdict of the Coroner's Jury are well calculated to satisfy the minds of our own people, as well as the publick.

By the Inquest it appears to [have] arisen from an accident not attributable to any neglect; but *I have* made it out, very much to my own satisfaction, to have been occasioned by an error of judgement, committed by one of the Deputy overmen, Armstrong, who fell a sacrifice to it.

He had injudiciously dislodged a quantity of inflammable air from some of the old Workings without apprizing Dawson of it. This cloud of gas floated across to leeward with the current of air, amongst the Workmen when it filled all the Davy Lamps with fire. The Deputy, Blackbird in charge of that part of the Workings immediately took measures of precaution, and went in quest of Dawson for further orders. Armstrong learnt from some Boys, who escaped what had occurred, when he instantly became sensible of the error he had committed & hastened to remedy it; but having nearly half a mile to go, the explosion took place before he could accomplish his object, and he perished with the rest.

Notwithstanding this no explosion would have happened, unless the gas had fired at some of the Davy Lamps, and this it *would not have done* if all had been managed right with them. It is quite evident that the fire must have taken place at some of the safety Lamps, as no other lights were there; but whether from accident, or carelessness will for ever remain a Secret.

This unfortunate affair has produced many distressing cases – the male population of many families being wholly swept away: but a correct account cannot yet be made out.

I this m[ornin]g received your Lordship's Letter of the 29th October, and will attend to the various matters contained in it. I observe that your Lordship's Letters never reach me 'till the 5th day after they are dated, which seems a long time considering the distance.

The Marquess of Londonderry   I have the honor [&c.].
Mount Stewart   J^no Buddle

32.

D/Lo/C142/7   Walls-end 16th Nov[embe]r 1823

My Lord

I received your Lordship's letter of the 10th inst. yesterday, and shall now endeavour to reply to the several topicks it contains in the order they occur and first as to a general Fund for the relief of the Widows & children of the persons who are killed in the Collieries in this Country.

Pitmen's Fund.

An establishment of this kind would unquestionably be of incalculable benefit. A grand effort was made in the year 1817 to accomplish this object.

The Coal-owners of both Rivers, with the exception of Mowbray for my Lady, agreed to contribute 1/2d per Ch. on their whole vend and it was proposed that the Workmen should subscribe from 4d to 6d in the pound out of their earnings, according to circumstances. The whole was to be put under the management of Trustees & Governors, and to be sanctioned by act of Parliament. At first the pitmen took to it cordially but when the plan was nearly about matured, the whole body, from some sudden caprice, or jealousy, that it was not intended for *their benefit* opposed it *in masse* and would not have any thing to do with it 'No not upon no account whatever'. So ended the matter at that time, and whether the subject might now be revived with any better hopes of success is questionable. If the matter was originated by the Workmen themselves it might probably succeed, but if by the Coal-owners, I very much doubt their receiving it, as they ought to do.

Vend

Your Lordship's observations as to the superior quality of your Walls-end and Eden-main are quite correct, and there is no doubt of their vending in full proportion to others at all times, at their *relative price*. But if a general reduction should take place on the Wear, it would not be possible to vend our Coals, but at a proportionate reduction.

In mooting the question of quantity with Croudace, he always quotes the number of Collieries they have open; they are as follows

Harraton	Mr Lambton's Freehold
Lambton	Ditto
Burn-moor	Ditto
Murton	Leasehold under the Bishop of Durham
Lumley	Ditto Lord Scarbrough
Cocken	-- Carr Esq.
Pensher	Mr Lambton's Freehold

All the above are included in his *Basis* of 120,000 Ch. and are wrought by himself, independent of Newbottle which is a separate Concern. He lets the following Freehold Collieries

Fatfield	Let to W.M. Lamb
Leafield	do. John Humble
Rickleton	do. William Stobart

His Walls-end & Primrose are produced from Burn-moor, Murton, Lumley & Cocken. Few from Burn-moor, but I believe a few Primrose are sent from Pensher.

Your Lordship says, 'If I remember right we started in our Contest with Hetton, to limit them to 50,000 Ch. and we were to have 120,000. I know not therefore why having gained one point that I must surrender the other, or be accused of turning the trade loose.'

The above statement of the quantities is quite correct, but I don't quite understand the conclusion drawn by your Lordship. At the *memorable meeting at Chester when the Hetton Co. were constrained to take 50,000 Ch. on the* Basis, the general basis of the Wear for one year to end on the 30th June next was fixed as under viz.

Lord Londonderry	120,000 Ch.
Mr Lambton	120
J.M. Davison Esq.	26
W.M. Lamb	28
W. Stobart	20
W. Russell Esq. & Co.	24
J. Humble	18
Nesham	50
Hetton	<u>50</u>
	484,000 Ch.

Now this basis is only an assumed quantity to fix the proportion of Vend between Colliery and Colliery, as the *actual* Vend which may be required by the trade cannot be known before hand. But it may be either more or less than the assumed quantity on the Basis.

At a late meeting of the Committees of the two Rivers, they *conjectured* that the actual Vend on the Basis might be about 900 to the Thousand which would give your Lordship & Mr Lambton each 108,000 Ch. and Hetton & Newbottle each 45,000 Ch. *actual Vend* for the year.

But if instead of 900 to the Thous[an]d the Trade should require 1100 then your Lordship's and Mr Lambton's quantities would be increased to 132,000 Ch. each and Newbottle & Hetton to 55,000 Ch. each. So that in fact the basis is nothing more than a scale of proportion by which to adjust the quantum of Vend to each Colliery. After this explanation I must candidly state to your Lordship that the point which gives me the greatest uneasiness in this affair is, that at the meeting above alluded to, I conceived myself authorized to acquiesce in the arrangement of Basis then established, altho' I did not dispair of getting a modification subsequently by a strong representation, grounded on the large proportion of superior Coal which we Vend, as compared with others – in favour of an additional quantity.

Your Lordship asks me 'If *upon your honor you do not* think Mr Croudace in my position, would talk a very different language?'

I will answer this by premising, that I always make my Communications to your Lordship, upon my Honor. I have from the confidence with which your Lordship has honoured me, always felt myself *bound* to communicate openly & frankly with your Lordship. And if I could imagine that any part of my character or Conduct caused a contrary impression on your Lordship's mind, I should instantly lose heart, and become incapable of rendering your Lordship any further service. Now to Croudace. Were he in our position I make no doubt he would make the best of it he could. He might balance between the questions of profit, or Quantity, for a while, but I have not the least doubt he would decide in favour of the former.

Your Lordship says 'now one word about yourself. I am fully aware that your situation is a very delicate & difficult one &c.' I feel exceedingly obliged by your Lordship's Candour & kind considera-tion on this score; but I beg to offer a few words in explanation, from which I think your Lordship will agree with me that my connexions on the Tyne, do not place me in quite so delicate a situation as might be imagined.

My business on the Tyne is almost exclusively *professional as a Viewer*, or adviser in the mining & Engineering departments. With the exception of Walls-end & old Tanfield-moor I have not *anything to do* with the general management of any Colliery on the Tyne – not even excepting those in which I have an interest.[13] It would be quite impossible for me to interfere in the general policy and management of those Collieries, the mining concerns of which I direct, as they are possessed by various individuals & Companies whose interests are the most conflicting. In short, I no more enter into the management of those Concerns, as to Vends &c. than a physician enters into the private affairs of the several families whom he attends.

Since I had the honor to be employed by your Lordship I have declined several of my regular professional engagements and nearly all occasional business – certainly all but some of my oldest comm[itmen]ts.

On the Wear I have no management at all, except for your Lord-ship, as Wade[14] who has 1/4th of the Washington Colliery with Mr Russell manages it.

With the exception of the two Collieries above named I never would take the management of any Collieries until I had the Honor to be employed by your Lordship. Nothing 'till then of sufficient magnitude offered, as my *independent* profession, was both more agreeable & profitable to me, than tying myself up to the manage-

---

13 Buddle held shares in several collieries – Benwell, Heaton, Sheriff Hill, Backworth, Elswick, Crawcrook and Stella – but took no part in their management. He managed Wallsend and Tanfield Moor. Hiskey, 'John Buddle', ch. xiv.

14 Thomas Ward.

ment, and mere agency of any – even the most extensive Colliery on either River, your Lordship's or Mr Lambton's excepted.

These my Lord are the principal features of my position and when I have the honor of personal communication with your Lordship, I deem it due to that confidence with which your Lordship has honoured me, that you should distinctly be acquainted with the connections &c. of the person in whom you have reposed such confidence. In short that your Lordship should *know the man*, and in this I shall be glad to give every assistance as I have nothing to conceal from your Lordship.

Hetton.

Nothing more on this subject of late, worth attending to, although there are fresh reports daily. Sharpe's information about Baker's Coal[15] is the old story revived. He will let his Coal to any body; but he will have *it's value*, and the Hetton Co. taking it does not seem feasible. They have territory enough & pay heavy certain Rents – the incumbering themselves with more *land* of this sort, unless they have all gone stark mad is not likely. The latest report which I have heard is, that Baker & his son in law, Major Tower are to have Scruton's & Light's shares. No person in my opinion need however offer to buy these shares unless they can actually bring *money* to pay for them, as Edward[16] assured me, that they would not advance a shilling more on any account, nor would they find the money to buy the shares for any body. *If they* would have done so, the shares would have been bought long ago, as he assured me that they had had various applications for assistance in that way.

I therefore presume that in the event of any shares, or even the whole concern being offered to your Lordship, all the assistance that could be calculated upon from the Quakers would be a continuation of their present advance; but certainly not an additional loan.

It is certainly most difficult to decide in the present state of affairs, what may be the most prudent course to take with respect to the two great objects – Hetton and the harbour – now both floating before us. The best plan is probably to do nothing, at least precipitately, but to look on for a while till matters take a more settled form, always keeping in view the provision of pecuniary means, as without this requisite, no great and effectual blow can be struck. To go into all

15 See p. 51.
16 Edward Backhouse.

that might be said on this branch would be too much for the compass
of a Letter, as it furnishes ample matter for close consideration in the
Cabinet.

Backhouse's

As *true Quakers* – to the very Letter I believe, they will fulfil their
engagements I firmly believe but will not go a step beyond *that point*.
We must therefore calculate upon having to act distinctly on either
the one or the other of their propositions. I availed myself of the
points suggested by your Lordship to aid me in bringing them to the
two propositions, of which your Lordship chose the latter. I should
therefore almost dispair of being able to obtain an amalgamation in
the way your Lordship suggests.

   Your Lordship asks 'Would the Bank feel our turning the Trade
loose an advantage or disadvantage to them? I strongly suspect the
latter.' In this your Lordship is perfectly correct, as the Bankers feel
according to all appearances more anxious about the regulation than
the Coal-owners themselves. I mean the whole of our N. Country
Bankers: and I have *very good* grounds for believing that the *persua-
sion of Friends* was much more efficacious than the *threats* of the Coal-
owners in inducing the Hetton Co. to accept the 50,000 rather than
hold out for more.

Groom

It seems this gentleman is determined to dog our heels as much as
possible. I therefore think your Lordship ought to get done with him
if possible. It is impossible for your Lordship's great affairs to go
on uniformly unless every man in his station, does his duty with
promptitude and alacrity. And if any one finds that he cannot so, do
his duty, he ought not to stand in the way, but should allow others
to do it.

   In compliance with your Lordship's orders I wrote Gregson to
obtain the money for the Seaham mortgage and to get the purchase
completed ; but more particularly to write & give your Lordship
some satisfactory information on these important matters. He has
not replied to me & I have not had an opportunity of seeing him; but
I hope he has written to your Lordship.

Accident

Under other Covers I have sent the return of the Casualties on
this occasion, including a List of the Widows & children. As soon
as circumstances will permit an appendix will be sent containing

'Remarks' and a Scale of allowance subject to your Lordship's approbation to the families of the several sufferers.

Pay-Bill

I am glad that your Lordship examines the pay-Bills attentively, and
shall always be ready to give explanations when required. Our transactions & payments are so multifarious that there is not space in the
pay-Bill to explain the several items so well as one would wish. We
are obliged to club them in order to get them into one Sheet.

I return Sharpe's Letters under other covers. I shall probably see
him this Week as if all matters go smooth at the Collieries I mean to
have a look over the Warden-law line & a ramble to Sunderland.

I have secured S[i]r H. Williamson's plan but doubt I shall not be
able to beat Thomas[17] down below the £200 a year.

Oliver[18] is on the look out for the mares according to your Lordship's wishes.

The Marquess of Londonderry   I have the Honor [&c.]
Mount Stewart   J[no] Buddle

---

17 Robert Thomas, Bishopwearmouth.
18 Robert Oliver, land agent for the colliery farms.

33.

D/Lo/C142/8   Colliery Office Pensher 30th Jan[uary] 1824

My Lord

I called upon Gregson on the 27th Inst. and find that there has been a great deal of *bother* between Wharton[1] & Todd and himself, about some technical nonsense raised by them relative to the settlement of the Seaham purchase. He now however expects it is all over, and that he will have the deeds from them this morning. It is most extraordinary that these Lawyers never get on straight forward with their business like other people.

Metcalf is not satisfied with the Seaham Rental, and is not willing to advance the mortgage money, unless he can have some other security. This Gregson thinks can be easily managed by giving them security on one, or two farms in the settled estates and has written Metcalf to this effect, which he expects will satisfy him.

I learn from Gregson, that the half yearly Payment of £125 to Sir J. Thorold[2] is for the interest of a £5000 mortgage on Barmston, taken in part payment of the baronet's estate – a transaction of Groom's. Sir J. Thorold is I understand a client of Groom's; it will therefore be best in future to remit the money to Groom direct, and take his receipt for it, without troubling Coutts with it, in the same way as Lord Middletons's[3] interest is remitted to Nowell.

I called upon Col. Browne also on the 27th Inst. He says that our application for the renewal is a subject of conversation amongst the learned Doctors in the College.[4] He starts for Wales on the 3rd February.

Report gives us Dr Hall, Dean of Oxford for our new Dean at Durham.[5] The appointment is in the Earl of Liverpool.[6] Hall is said

---

1   William Wharton, Dryburn Lodge, Durham.

2   Part owner of the West Herrington property, see p. xvii.

3   Henry, sixth Baron Middleton, 1761–1835, from whom Lord Londonderry was buying Holdernesse House in London.

4   i.e. the Chapter.

5   Charles Henry Hall, 1763–1827, Dean of Christ Church, Oxford, 1809–24, Dean of Durham 1824–7. *ODNB*.

6   Robert Banks Jenkinson, Earl of Liverpool, 1770–1828, Prime Minister 1812–27. *ODNB*.

to be a very poor man, and may not therefore be so bad to deal with. The Dean has two votes in the Body, he must therefore have great influence in their Councils. The deanery is said to be worth £10,000 a year.

The new Rail-way from the Tees below Portrack to Willington in the first instance but ultimately into Weardale, is now very much talked about.[7] It is said that the consent of all the proprietors of the Lands through which the line runs has been obtained and that the money is already subscribed. Col. Browne informs me, he hears from good authority that Mr Russell has subscribed £5000.

Croudace breakfasted with me this morning and read to me a Letter from Mr Cartwright[8] the great organ of the rail-way project, to Mr Lambton stating the leading features of the plan and requesting Mr Lambton to present the Bill. The main object of the plan is to open out the Coal-mines through the heart of the County from Cox-hoe, or as much further E. as Coal may be found, all the way to the western extremity of the Coal District; and to ship the Coals on the Tees. The distance from the shipping place to the first Colliery Cox-hoe, is 12 or 13 miles & to the farthest Willington 22 miles.

Mr Lambton is of opinion that this plan if carried into effect, will injure the trade both of the Tyne & Wear, and therefore wishes to know if the Coal-owners of the two Rivers mean to oppose the Bill, in which case he will decline to present it. But on the other hand if they do not mean to oppose it he will present the Bill. Cartwright is already in London to be ready on the opening of Parliament to attend to the progress of the Bill thro' the House.

Croudace's object was to get me to bring the subject before the Committee of the Tyne Coal-owners tomorrow. I have therefore kept the letter open for the purpose of informing your Lordship what the opinion of the Tyne gentlemen may be on the subject.

Croudace is much puzzled about the Turnpike scheme, it will cost £6000 and he thinks that Mr Lambton should subscribe £1000 but then 'money is so D—l—ish scarce *with them* that he does not know what to think about it'. I told him when Mr L. has entirely made up his mind as to what he will do, I will then lay the matter before your

---

7   A bill for a railway from the Tees at Billingham to Willington was presented in 1823 but failed on technicalities of parliamentary procedure. A second version was put forward in November 1824. Tomlinson, *North Eastern Railway*, pp. 87–8, 101–2.

8   John Cartwright of Norton, chairman of the committee promoting the Tees to Weardale railway.

Lordship. Croudace however appears to me to be completely on the weigh-scales in the business, and would, if I judge rightly, rather let the matter rest for the present as go on with it.

Newcastle 31st Jan[uar]y 1824

After duly considering the nature and circumstances of the Tees rail-way affair the Committee of the Tyne Coal-owners, do not think that they have any substantive grounds whatever on which to oppose the Bill, and therefore leave Mr Lambton to exercise his own discretion as to the presenting of it.

The whole of the Country is completely Colliery mad at present, and if all the schemes now in embryo, are brought to perfection, we shall in two or three years see the Coal-mining Trade completely over-built, unless indeed by a reduction, or repeal of the Coasting Coal Duty, the market should be proportionately extended.

Beside the speculation in the County of Durham, I hear of 7 or 8 new Collieries about to be opened out on the Tyne. I do not however think that the Collieries of first-rate quality will be materially affected by these new openings but I think the inferior Collieries on both Rivers will be rendered of no value whatever.

The Dean & Chapter are boring below the top seams at Ferry-hill, in hopes of finding our Hutton seam there.

Mr Lambton is also boring at Nun-stainton; but Croudace tells me they are going to sell the Estate, and are boring to see if it contains Coal, in which case the value will be greatly increased.

Bakers joining the Hetton Co.[9] seems to have given fresh vigour to the concern. They are as far as I can see, making the most active preparations for extending their Vend after the 30th June. And from what has recently occurred between Capt. Cochrane & Mr Lambton & Baker being also a particular friend of Mr Lambton, it is not to be expected that he will again attend a Chester meeting, to beat the Hetton Co. down. I don't therefore calculate on a continuance of the regulation after 30th June next, even if a parliamentary investigation should not be a bar to it. It will therefore be prudent to conduct all our measures in the mean time, in anticipation of an open Trade after the 30th June.

With this view I should submit to your Lordship the keeping up of our Workings to the *fullest pitch*, even if we should lay up the Coals in the mean time, so that we might have the power of making a

---

9   George Baker joined the Hetton Co. in early 1824.

rush in the Vend after the expiration of the present regulation should circumstances call for such an effort.

After that period we shall be very well off for Pit room, as both the Adventure and Meadows west pit, will be in a working state by that time.

I have had much trouble with Anthony Taylor[10] for a month past about the renewal of his Way-leave Lease. Our Waggon-way passes through his ground from Sedge-letch Bridge to Chilton-moor. The old Lease expires next Martinmass. We pay him £45 a year to cover Way-leave and damage of ground under the present Lease. For a new lease he demands £150 a year rent, with an allowance of fire-Coal and I have only been able to beat him down to £130. I have agreed with General Maxwell's[11] Agent for £60 a year being an increase of £10, but until I could agree with Taylor, I did not think it worth while to go to Byers and Story.

Not being willing to submit to Taylor's obstinate demand I have looked at the matter in every point of view, and have found out a better line, than either Mr Lambton's, or our own Way. It will go through Lambton's ground (which we have a right to do by the Convention) in an intermediate line, between our present Line and Mr Lambton's. The only Way-leave we shall have to pay will be to the Bishop of Durham for passing thro' Mr Lambton's Lease-hold Estate of Murton which joins Chilton-moor. I have applied to Faber[12] the Bishop's Agent for a lease. He will refer the matter to Th. Fenwick and I have no doubt but we shall get the lease on fair terms.

As soon as I get an Agreement with the Bishop's Agents, I would join our Waggon-way with Mr Lambton's, and lead our Coals with Horses down his line during the summer.

I would at the same time be removing the Cast Iron Rails from our old way to the new Line, which I should have completed by next Martinmas with it's machinery. I would then quit Mr Lambton's way and sell off our Waggon Horses.

When your Lordship comes to England I shall be glad to point all this out to you on the ground.

On coming here this morning I found a very civil Letter from John Pemberton the eldest Son of our friend old Richard offering your

---

10   Anthony Taylor, local landowner.
11   Sir William Maxwell, landowner, Newbottle.
12   Thomas Henry Faber, 1779–1833, secretary to Bishop Barrington. *ODNB, s.n.*
      Frederick William Faber.

Lordship the accommodation of Way-leave through their property. I enclose the Letter in another cover.

I wrote a polite answer & will breakfast with him on Monday morning on my way to Sunderland to talk the matter over. Mr John Hopper also called upon me a short time ago, and offered the like accommodation through his Grounds. He deported himself on this occasion in the most gentleman-like manner, and said it would give him the greatest pleasure to accommodate your Lordship. He is in treaty to sell part of his property near Wearmouth, but will reserve a Way-leave for your Lordship's accommodation.

So far this is all very well, but we shall be better able to measure the extent of these gentlemen's friendship when we come to the actual negotiation of *Terms*.

On Monday I have to see Gen. Aylmer's[13] Agent again, he is a keen little fellow & I doubt I shall have some trouble with him. I wish if possible to secure the Way-leaves on the same principle as the Daldon Line viz. not to pay any rent until we actually lead Coals. In this case the holding of the privilege will cost us nothing.

On Monday 2nd February will be our receipt. I shall then see Friend Edward and learn if the Hetton affair with them is concluded.

The Coal Trade still continues as dull as possible, our Walls-ends are down to 41/6 & 42/. and others in proportion. We shall however get about 80,000 Ch. this month which will be the best January Vend we ever knew. It is said that both Hetton & Newbottle is [sic] freighting ship at 16/6 per London Ch. which will occasion a most enormous loss. The School master at W. Rainton died lately. A great number of applications have been made for the place. I send your Lordship two of the most likely. Lesh from being connected with a great Clan of Durham Freemen (the Hoppers) & his father being also a Freeman is perhaps the most proper but your Lordship will please to decide.[14] The salary from the Colliery is £8.8.0 a year.

The Marquess of Londonderry	I have the Honor [&c.]
Mount Stewart	Jno Buddle

---

13 Lt.-Gen. Arthur Aylmer, 1772–1832, of Walworth Castle, Co. Durham.

14 On appointing Buddle as colliery manager, Lord Stewart expressed a wish that Durham freemen should as far as possible be employed: D/Lo/C267, 9, 10 Jan. 1819. The freemen were the electorate for the City parliamentary seats.

34.

D/Lo/C142/8   27 Norfolk St Strand London
                                              Saturday evening 6th Mar[ch] 1824

My Lord

I arrived here last Thursday morning and have ever since been incessantly occupied partly with Mr Russell's business & partly with the affair of the Coal duty.[15] With the latter I have much labour in collecting & arranging information against our audience with the Chancellor of the Exchequer[16] which we expect will take place next Wednesday.

The Coal-buyers and factors, as well as the Ship-owners here view the proposed measure of reduction on the Canal Coal Duty with alarm, but seem *cowed* & spiritless, and cannot make up their minds to take any active part in opposing it.

On the other hand the canal proprietors & inland Coal-masters are quite alive to the prospects of advantage which it holds out to them. The canal proprietors are meditating a reduction on their tonnage dues, and have made some proposition or other, to the Coal-masters on the subject, but I am not yet informed of it's nature.

We are mustering all our forces here and hope to make out so good a case, that if we cannot prevail with the Chancellor of the Exchequer to place the Canal Coals on the same scale of Duty, as the Sea-borne Coal, we expect that we shall at least, be able to induce him to modify the scale he has proposed.[17]

My colleague Mr R.W. Brandling and myself have seen or communicated with all the Members now in Town, who are interested in this question, and we find them all very much alive to it. Mr Lambton has not yet come to Town, but will be up on Monday.

I have seen Sir H. Hardinge, who from the press of official & parliamentary business under which he is now labouring it would

---

15 On 28 February the Tyne coal owners committee decided to send Buddle to London, with R.W. Brandling, chairman of the committee, and John Clayton, the Town Clerk of Newcastle, to lobby the government about a proposal to reduce the duty on coal brought to London by canal: Northumberland Archives (hereafter NRO) 263/A1/9.

16 Frederick John Robinson, Viscount Goderich, Earl of Ripon, Chancellor of the Exchequer 1823–4, Prime Minister 1827–8. *ODNB*.

17 The North East coal owners joined with those of South Wales in a campaign for the reduction or abolition of the heavy duties on sea-borne coal, which nearly doubled the price of coal between Newcastle and London. On this occasion they were not successful. Flinn, *Coal Industry*, pp. 283–5.

be cruel to draw out to run after this business but he will afford us all assistance by talking to Mr Robinson about it quietly in private.

I was informed today, that a principal Coal-buyer here, had tried a sample of the Forest of Dean Coals, and found them equal to Stewart's W[alls]end. This must be an exaggeration. It is most desirable that the business should be set at rest in one way or other without delay, as the present state of suspense has completely paralysed the trade.

With the exception of getting a peep at Holderness House I have not been able to look after any of your Lordship's commissions; but the moment I am disentangled from this Coal Duty affair I shall attend to them. Wyatt seems to be attending closely to the business at the House, which seems a very serious job indeed; but I will write more fully after I have had time to examine it. That it must cost a large sum of money is however quite evident.

I have written to Mowbray, but as the subject will require the grave consideration of the whole Co. I don't expect an answer for some time. Our proposition is a likely thing to strike Arthur's fancy; but others of the Co. may pause upon it.

The Marquess of Londonderry   I have the Honor [&c.]
Mount Stewart   J^{no} Buddle

35.

D/Lo/C142/8   27 Norfolk St Strand London
                                        Thursday evening 11th Mar[ch] 1824

My Lord

We had our audience of Mr Robinson this morning. He gave us a fair and candid hearing, and whatever may be the result of our representations we left him with feelings of highest respect.

To avoid repetition I enclose a copy of the minutes of what passed at our interview, which will best inform your Lordship on the subject.

All my previous labour on the estimates of expence of delivering Coals from various places & by various modes to London, extracts from Acts of Parliament relative to the imposition, repeals and alterations in the Coal Duties &c. &c. was never called for, as all the arguments employed on the occasion, were grounded almost entirely on Mr Robinson's *own principles of free trade*.

The discussion afforded us an opportunity of directing Mr Robinson's attention to the Oversea duties on Small and round Coals, and he did not seem to be disinclined to make such modifications as might on due consideration be deemed generally beneficial. We therefore think of laying our heads together to see if we can suggest any plan for his consideration on this branch of the Trade.

With respect to the immediate object of the deputation, I think stripping it of all incumbrance it terminated in the following short proposition to Mr Robinson.

If you will consent to tax the Canal & Sea-borne Coals equally in the London market, we will not ask for any limitation of quantity upon the Canal Coals as has hitherto been the case.

Mr Robinson did not commit himself as to what he would do, but we think that he rather thought favourably, than otherwise of our proposition, and we do hope, if he does not go to the full extent of our wishes, he will at least make the disparity in the Tax much less than what he talked of in the first instance.

We certainly gained one satisfactory point of information from him, viz. that he does not blame the Coal-owners of the North for any measures, or regulations which they may adopt, to benefit themselves. He has not therefore any wish to bring us before Parliament so that on that score we have nothing to fear, except from Alderman Wood,[18] or some such meddling fool.

Those most obtuse of all blockheads, the N. Country Ship-owners still talk of sending an address to Mr Robinson to thank him for reducing the Duty on canal Coals – the deplorable Idiots. They are also, my letters from home state, deliberating on the propriety of petitioning the Common Council here to assist them in putting down the Combination of Coal-owners on the Tyne & Wear!!! But what is it that such a set of wrong heads won't do – they seem determined to run a muck.

I hope my stay here will not now be long. It is expected that the Chancellor of the Exchequer will bring the Coal Duty affair to a conclusion in the House very soon and my Colleagues won't let me go 'till the event is seen.

The Marquess pf Londonderry   I have the Honor [&c.]
Mount Stewart   J^no Buddle

---

18 Matthew Wood, 1768–1843, Lord Mayor of London 1815–16, 1816–17, MP for the City of London 1817–43, radical politician. *ODNB*; *Hist. Parl. 1820–32*, vii, 886–94.

36.

D/Lo/C142/8   Walls-end 24th May 1824

My Lord

I have this morning had the honor to receive your Lordship's Letter & packets of the 22nd Inst. and will reply to the several points of your Lordship's in the order they occur and first as to the

Rental. The ideas of the Chapter are I hear from all quarters so outrageous as to our profits, that I almost despair of being able to bring them to look at any thing like a moderate & reasonable fine. The principle which they adopted on the last renewal was both novel and unfair; they estimated on *profit* instead of *Rental*, as had been usual from time immemorial. At the former Renewal of Rainton Lease, which was made at the end of the first 7 years of the term, the annual rental of the mine was estimated at £2000, and according to their *then* established custom the Fine was set at 1¼ years rent, or £2500. There was some reason in this way of proceeding; but it is quite a different affair when they go upon the Profit.

They have lately charged 1½ years rent as the Fine at the end of 7 years to fill up the term to 21 years on Land, Houses, &c.

Now to go on this principle with Rainton Colliery the matter would stand as follows. The annual rental according to the present Tentale might be stated at £10,000.

Add ½ year   <u>5000</u>

                                          £15000   Fine for 7 years, or
£34,285.14.8 for filling up 4 years.

This would be quite outrageous, and I conceive, under existing circumstances, entirely out of our reach, either to pay by instalments, or otherwise. If therefore any such notion is persisted in by the Chapter, we must give up the idea of renewal by Fine – *run* the Lease to take the chance of some more favourable time, or circumstances, and if better cannot be done at last, we, or our successors, must endeavour to renew on the simple plan of an annual and tentale Rent, in the manner they now let the most of their Collieries. Being in possession of the stock, we could always afford to give a better tentale than any body else.

Before we stir at all in this affair, I must get Tommy Fenwick to come and look at all our difficulties, and furnish him, with substantial proof, that our profits from the Dean & Chapter division of our Colliery operations, are enormously *over rated*. This I conceive is the right way to go to work in the first instance. I will therefore dismiss the subject for the present 'till I can bring *Tommy's* mind to bear upon it.[19]

Pay Bills are unusually high from the following causes. 1st Holding back Tradesmen's Bills during the spring months of 1823, owing to the scanty Vends during those months. 2nd The increased price of Horse-Corn & Hay. 3rd. The great expence of sinking pits, now going on, to place the Collieries in a situation to supply the required Vend, and to reduce the Number of underground Horses. 4. Keeping the Workings and leadings up to the fullest pitch, altho' the Vend is limited – the object and policy of this measure has been explained in former Letters.

In addition to No. 3 I must remark that we are going on with measures for the renovation of Pensher Colliery so as to bring it into *full play* in case of *need*, and to render it capable of bringing Biddick, the Baronet's and D. Lambton's Coal into play also. It will also be made a stepping stone to *other* objects which I have in view, as I shall explain to your Lordship at a future opportunity.

It is unfortunate that all this cause of increased expenditure should occur at this juncture; but delay would involve greater mischief, and three months will put us through our troubles.

Regulation. This affair is in my opinion in the most unsatisfactory state possible at present. I believe the Hetton Co. will go on, to the extent of their 50,000 *full* at least, while we are going on, over our allowed quantity, as if *by stealth*, and thereby incurring censure. I really think it would be much more consistent with propriety to come at once to a distinct understanding on the point, The arbitration of the Hetton question has been shuffled past; would it not therefore be better to state distinctly, that if the Hetton Co, will not confine themselves to the *Basis*, that your Lordship will consider the Regulation at an end. I think it would be well if your Lordship could see Mr Lambton on this subject, and communicate those sentiments. You might say that you should expect the point with regard to Hetton, to be settled

19   The Rainton lease was not renewed in 1824, but on 20 Nov. of that year Lord Londonderry acquired the right to make outstrokes from Rainton into the coal he now owned under adjoining land at East Rainton and Hetton. DCM, B/BA/ 102, fols 36v–45r.

against the end of May, or that you cannot be longer bound. By this your Lordship would elicit Mr L—'s feelings as to Hetton &c. As to our *power of working* I would not state it at more than 120,000 Ch. *Fitters' Coals* yearly; this is as much I think as we can work with *safety and certainty.*

All that we have to fear in an open Trade is a reduction of price. As to quantity there is little doubt of vending it, at some price, or other. If the regulation continues the Wear best Coals must either be *raised*, or the Tyne lowered, as the latter are now too high compared to the price of the latter [*sic* ?former] at the London market. As soon as the regulation ceases, the price on the Tyne will fall 2/- to 4/- We shall then see, whether our *Turn coat* friends will send their Ships to the Tyne, or load them at Sunderland, where I am sure they will not find any difficulty in getting a *return.*

How we might *fend* under an open trade is altogether a matter of speculation; for a month, or two, I have no doubt but we should make more money; but if the price of Coals fall 2/- to 4/- per Ch. we shall unquestionably make much less profit at the end of the year. I however beg your Lordship to exercise your own judgment on this important point; as to myself individually, it is a matter of indifference which way the scale turns. But I will most readily enter into your Lordship's views whatever they maybe.

Seaham. With respect to Ravenshaw & the treaty with Forster & Co.[20] I scarcely find it necessary to say anything further at present, until the result of the measures stated in my Letter of yesterday is decided.

The sale of the Coal is the plan to be adopted if possible, and nothing but necessity should drive us to the partnership. I will therefore push the Division by all possible means, the instant Stobart gives me an opening.

Finances. The remittances shall be attended to as directed, and I have written Coutts and Drummond under other covers agreeably to your Lordship's wishes.

Parker. I have been in correspondence with Hawkes on this affair, and we must manage it some how, or other, so as to keep clear of the *Law.*

---

20 Perceval Forster, land agent to Col. Bradyll.

Dent.[21] I hardly know what to think on the information communicated by the Doctor on this affair. As *no money whatever* of your Lordship's comes thro' Dent's fingers at present, nor for a long time past, he has not the opportunity, even supposing him to be rogue enough for it, to purloin anything. Indeed no money, except the receipt of the Landsale Coal money, from the heap inspectors at the different pits, ever came into his grasp, since I came into the concern, and he has not received that, since before his late illness. When he fell ill Hunter took the receipt of the Landsale money and has since kept it. I have thought it right to hold Hunter solely responsible for all our Coal transactions, as it is much more easy to check all matters in the hands of one person, than in the hands of several.

As to the system of *rapid Fortune-making* of which the Doctor speaks, I really am not aware of it. If the Doctor's criterion for forming his judgment, is the respectable appearance of your Lordship's Agents, in their respective stations, I think he has some grounds; as I certainly must say, & I say it with satisfaction, that none of them, with the exception of one (old Legg) dissipate their means in the publick Houses, but apply them to the reasonable & decent enjoyment of the comforts of Life. If however the Doctor calculates on the same date in this case, as he has done on the saving to be made by vending the Coals by Agency instead of Fitting them, I don't at all wonder at his applying the adjective *rapid*. But as he is quite as ignorant of the circumstances and nature of the fitting system, as he is of the *fact*, that the experiment of *vending by Agency* has already been *tried & failed*, we must leave him to pursue his own speculations *quietly* on this occasion. To go into the subject fully at present, would draw me too much out at length, but I shall have great pleasure in giving full information upon it, whenever your Lordship may require it.

I remarked with high satisfaction that my Lady was the most brilliant Constellation at the Drawing Room; but found my spirits rather damped, on not finding your Lordship's name in the List – his Majesty's apostrophe[22] has however dispelled my cloud. The compliment was justly due, his *tried* friend and *gallant* Soldier, and the sentiments

---

21 Unidentified.

22 Lord Londonderry had been censured by the Commander in Chief, the Duke of York, for accepting a challenge from a Lt. Battier, a former cornet in his regiment, after the Duke had issued an order that neither he nor any other officer of the regiment should take notice of statements made by Battier to the press. At the royal Drawing Room on 20 April the king received Lord Londonderry with particular graciousness. *The Journal of Mrs Arbuthnot 1820–*

expressed in it, are in unison with the feelings of every man in the Kingdom, worthy of bearing the name of one of His subjects.

Through all this Country the *cause of the reproof to the Soldier*, has elevated the character of *'the Man'* beyond all description and has completely retrieved the character of the 10th. It has absolutely torn the Tongue of Slander up by the roots, and has inspired feelings of respect for the whole Corps. It has produced a striking example of the effect of the *Head* over all the members of the Body. The regiment owes more to your Lordship than it is possible to tell, and I hope from the highest to the lowest they will be fully sensible of the obligation. As to the odious Ruffian, the tables are completely turned upon him, and he must rapidly sink into his native dirt, & insignificance. I have not yet seen Sir H. Harding's statement. I am grieved that he should be brought into collision with such a Sweep.

The Marquess of Londonderry   I have the Honor [&c.]
London   Jno Buddle

The Wind is still North, scarcely any light Ships have arrived, the vend is nearly at a stand, and I am almost in despair.

37.

D/Lo/C142/8   Newcastle 19th June 1824

My Lord

The die is cast, and now comes the tug of war. Our meeting[23] was but short this morning, as the general feeling was for an open trade, at all hazards, rather than submit to the clandestine conduct of the Hetton Co. It was therefore unanimously resolved that the regulation was no longer in force – Of course every one is now left to vend as he can, either as to price, or quantity. A general reduction of prices is expected to follow shortly – particularly on the inferior Coals, and the best will not maintain their position very long I doubt; however we must take our chance on this, and do the best we can – a short time will shew how matters will work.

I have agreed with Croudace for the 45 acres of Coal – subject

---

1832, ed. James Banham and the Duke of Wellingtron (2 vols, London, 1950), i, 313.

23 NRO 263/A1/9.

to Musgrave's approbation, to whom he is to write tomorrow. He seems greatly afraid that Musgrave should think he has shewn any partiality to us in the treaty. His fears are however vain, and I hope the return of the post will bring the ratification.

Arthur [Mowbray] is expected home in a few days, when I hope we may get a beginning made with the Division,[24] but I fear it is too great an undertaking to be accomplished, and the Coal brought to sale in time to meet the engagements of next month. And if we are obliged to hurry, and press, the matter unduly, and of necessity, we are sure to lose by it – this consideration makes me very anxious and unhappy about it.

If your Lordship cannot plan matters so, as to provide the ways and means for carrying us through next month I cannot see how we are to avoid going to Edward, and to endeavour to make the best terms with him, we can; either on the participation plan, or a sale. He may however boggle till the division is actually made, but I think his scruples on this point may be got over too. The breaking up of the regulation will also serve as a hook to hang up his scruples & fears upon; and will give us at least a couple of *days works*, additional – nibbling & quibbling, and consulting friends at Darlington.

I have received your Lordship's two letters of the 17th Inst. with their enclosures. Coutt's letter is civil enough, altho' they look to the main chance; – if we only can but have sufficient time, to *train our little black horse* & bring him fairly up to the post, we shall soon be out of the reach of all these gentlemen; and leave all pecuniary pressure far behind – nothing can exceed my anxiety on this point, it presses incessantly upon my mind and engages all my thoughts.

As to Sir T. Charges,[25] we must give him full credit for his good intentions, but he little knows his man – 'the Staffordshire Viewer'. If he had witnessed 1/100th part of the impudence, ignorance & knavery of that character, which I have done, he would no longer blame me for being his *enemy*; nor wonder at it, knowing my absolute detestation of every species of quackery.

It would be well if Sir Thomas would inform your Lordship, what Collieries the 'great genius' has had the management of, for the last 9 years, and by whom he is employed? Surely every body cannot have been so blind to his merits & *their own interest*, as we – poor

---

24 Of the portion of the Hetton coal. See letter No. 27, n. 3.
25 Unidentified.

benighted creatures, the Coal-owners of Durham & Northumberland have been.

The Marquess of Londonderry   I have the honor [&c.]
Holderness House   J^{no} Buddle
London

I am much concerned to learn that my Lady continues so poorly, altho' your Lordship says she is rather better.

38.

D/Lo/C142/9   Pensher Colliery 16th July 1824

My Lord

I have this morning received your Lordship's private letter of the 14th Inst. My letter of yesterday enclosing Croudace's will exonerate him from the suspicion of shuffling us with respect to Musgrave's Coal but at the same time I don't think we can entirely acquit him of the charge of *trifling*; but it is his way.

The other subject of your Lordship's letter perplexes & distresses me the most; as I am at my wits end how to get our next Colliery Pay made at the end of the month. To aid in the accomplishment of this I am obliged to hold back everything that can possibly be held back, and after all I shall not be able to effect it without considerable aid from Edward, and I am really almost afraid to go to him about it. Not to pay our workmen on the *usual pay* day will cause a mutiny and incur the most imminent risk of having our Works stopped altogether; besides the very death blow which it would give to our character and credit. The apprehension of the bare possibility of such an occurrence almost makes me ill – with the exception of a stoppage of the bank, nothing half so disastrous could happen to us. And what does not at all contribute to my comfort on the occasion is, that the very necessity, is I believe the only ground which I can take to induce, or rather to compel Edward to grant the requisite assistance for making our next pay. I feel that reasoning and argument is about at an end with him, and as a last resource in this case, I apprehend that I shall have to employ *terror*, as I feel confident that he *dare not* risk the consequences of the pitmen striking work for want of their wages. But I feel equally confident that he *will not* advance £5 for any other purpose. I don't therefore see my way at all how to continue to afford pecuniary assistance to your Lordship, and this I cannot conceal from your Lordship makes me consummately miserable.

It seems quite indispensable for your Lordship's comfort, & I must candidly confess to your Lordship that I feel it indispensable to my own, that this incessant financial pressure & difficulty should be relieved by the obtaining of a large sum of money. And it is to the sale of Hetton Coal that I look for this relief. My anxious wish therefore night & day is, that we may get it speedily accomplished, but at the same time I am incessantly tormented, with the fear 1st that, old miscreant may contrive to shuffle & procrastinate the time for getting the division effected, and 2nd that Edward (from whom I am afraid it will be impossible to conceal our difficulties) will compel us to let him have it on *his own* terms. Would but any of your Lordship's opulent friends accommodate your Lordship with a temporary loan of £20,000 until we could get this all accomplished, and keep us out of the fangs of the *Jews*, it is impossible to estimate the benefit which might result from it.

I am sorry I cannot throw a more agreeable shade on this affair – finance; but as it now occupies my attention almost to the exclusion of every other object, I may perhaps stumble upon something to penetrate the black cloud that o'erspreads me at the moment. And most happy shall I be if I can discover a beam of sunshine through it. I implore your Lordship's indulgence for this free epistle. I have written it without the slightest disguise, or exaggeration of my feelings. Sincerely hoping that circumstances will e'er long enable me to write more cheerfully,

The Marquess of Londonderry   I have the honor [&c.]
London   J^{no} Buddle

39.

D/Lo/C142/9   Greens Hotel Seele St
Lincoln's Inn Fields
29th Dec[ember] 1824

My Lord

I met Mr Russell at J. Gregson's at 2 o'clock & have bro[ugh]t the Hetton affair to a close as near as possible under circumstances. He was very timid about coming to the point of payment, and was only reconciled to it by Gregson's provisoe of security – see the memorandum under another cover. All the points stated for legal arrangements may be speedily accomplished on my arrival at home – only let us keep out of the hands of London solicitors. The whole may be done and the money paid within a month with an attorney who will not *twaddle*. I have as usual been kept bothering with lawyers 'till I have not time left for writing satisfactorily – suffice it to say that notwithstanding the number of things which yet seem to be required I consider them all superable and think I have an expedient which will meet the required point of security. I cannot now explain it & it is the less necessary as I shall start by the Mail tomorrow, evening or the Highflyer on Friday morning, & hope on Sunday to explain all fully, viva voce, to your Lordship.

Groom has just called & bothered me for ½ an hour when I the least wanted him – tomorrow he says he will complete the purchase of 2/3rd of the baronet's Herrington. He wants immediate payment of the interest money up to *this day*. He wishes me to go to Murray with him tomorrow when he settles this affair – having to see Gregson & also to go to Drummonds with Cowburn[26] I cannot accompany Groom, but have to meet him at R[ussell] square at 4 o'clock, to hear all about this & other affairs. I sincerely hope we shall soon get thro' all difficulties & Law *bother*. I have had so much of the latter since I came here, that I am quite qualified for a *village lawyer*.

It was well I rec[eive]d a copy of your Lordship's letter to Mr R. this morning as he had not rec[eive]d the original nor may not receive it for some days to come. I have had sev[era]l interviews with Morrall & have got quite *thick* with him – he is a near neighbour. I think I have got the *old Fox* & the legal *prig* into a see-saw which will prevent the Eppleton lease from being signed, or any Coal wrought out of it for 6 months at least – this may operate as a diversion in our favor at the present crisis & if possible it must be known at the meeting of the Committee next Tuesd[a]y. I wish writing was a rapid as talking & y[ou]r Lordship should have an amusing history. I w[oul]d also say a good deal about Lambton's 2/- per Ch. letter. Your Lordship has with your usual gallantry, seized the proper position in this affair. I think we shall *hammer* out something at the proposed Congress at Durham, but my colleague has too little tact & too much *bow-wow* for an affair of this kind. We will *talk* of all this.

The Marquess of Londonderry   I have the honor [&c.]
Seaham   J[no] Buddle

---

26 William Cowburn, London solicitor.

40.

D/Lo/C142/10   Walls-end 13th Mar[ch] 1825

My Lord

I have this morning rec[eive]d y[ou]r Lordship's dispatches from Tadcaster of the 12th Inst. and shall attend to all the various objects they contain, as circumstances will allow; but on the eve of *binding* time I am most terribly beset & worried with all sorts of people wanting changes of situation, and 'till after the 19th will be hunted like a Badger. I meant to have written a sort of brief on the Railway affair & had set this morning apart for the job; but I am so surrounded and worried that I cannot get any thing done.

As to going before the Committ[ee][1] I can only state facts & give my opinion on such facts, in doing which I don't see how any thing should be elicited, that would be injurious to the interest of any of my immediate connexions or friends. The discrepance which exists, as to the character of the Auckland Ferry-hill &c. Coals, may be reconciled. They are good says one party, – they are bad says another. Now they are *both good and bad*, according to the situation or market to which they are sent. They are good in quality, generally speaking, but not hard: and are therefore, for home consumption i.e. where ever they can be carried in carts &c. without being more than once turned over, *good* Coals. But for a market, which they can only reach by sea carriage, they must sink into an inferior Coal, owing to their not being hard enough to bear the hardship of shipping, unloading & all the tumbling about which they must unavoidably endure before they come into the cellars of the consumers. Hence it is, that I conclude they would not answer as 'Housekeepers' Coals' but must fall into the class of what is called in London 'Consumers Coals' of which there is already *an over supply*. Witness the several Collieries on the Tyne & Wear which could supply an unlimited quantity of that sort of Coal, but from the want of demand at any price, are either *laid in*, or are working on the most reduced scale possible. Quality &

---

1   A fresh version of the bill for a railway from Haverton Hill to Willington, with a branch to Sedgefield, was submitted to Parliament in November 1824. It was opposed by the Stockton and Darlington Railway, Lord Londonderry, and others; a petition against it was presented by Sir Matthew White Ridley. The bill was rejected in Committee. Tomlinson, *North Eastern Railway*, pp. 101–2.

hardness must be combined, to make a good House Keepers Coal. Of the Newcastle Coals, the East Percy Cowpen & Hartly are the *hard* Coals which are deficient in quality. The Pontops, Bates Walls-end, Garesfield &c. are the *soft* Coals of excellent quality. The 1st class of Walls-end &c. are those which combine hardness & quality. The shades of gradation from the latter medium to both extremes are innumerable.

On Tuesday morning I will see Edward and will act as circumstances may require.

Boyd[2] gave me a call yesterday, to say that their house would enter into the arrangement I had named, on having security. I repeated that the idea was my own unsanctioned by your Lordship & that if it went no further, I hope they w[oul]d not think anything of it; and that I might probably have occasion to renew it at a future time. He said he w[oul]d consider it in that point of view, so that we have an opening in that quarter, if we cannot do better. I hope the Committ[ee] will not sit 'till after Easter, as to come to Town before then, would be most inconvenient (I don't mean personally) to me. I have various matters of importance at y[ou]r Lordship's Coll[ierie]s to get put under way which require *personal* attention, and from which it has, by other occupation been for some time past too much abstracted.

The Marquess of Londonderry   I have the honor [&c.]
Holdernesse House   Jno Buddle
London

41.

D/Lo/C142/10   Pensher Barracks 23rd Mar[ch] 1825

My Lord

I now have leisure to reply to your letter of the 21st Inst. Nothing can be more proper than the remarks your Lordship has made to J. Gregson in reply to his two points, on which he thought your Lordship might require my advice. The security Coal is in the first instance to be wrought by the Hazard pit, and ultimately, if necessary by a *new pit* to be sunk by Mr Russell. The allotment as marked out, cannot

---

2   William Boyd, partner in the Old Bank, Newcastle. Phillips, *History of Banks*, pp. 174–95.

certainly be wrought so conveniently by the Dunwell and Hazard pits, as that marked out when Gregson was here; but the allotment last marked out was proposed by *Morriss*,[3] who contemplates the sinking of a new pit; in preference to occupying the Dunwell Pit. If he makes any more difficulties on this point your Lordship may communicate the above and refer him to Morriss, who can explain the affair. My Letter of yesterday is a reply to his schedule of Documents. Nos. 2,3,4,5,6,7 may all be completed without difficulty, as they mainly depend upon himself. Nos. 8,9,10,11, are sufficiently noticed in my letter of yesterday. But No. 1 cannot be supplied, until the Quakers are satisfied, and this your Lordship will have to manage according to the means which may arise out of the purchase money from Russell, & from what may spring out of your negotiations with John Hutchinson.[4]

I don't much like the appearance of this gentleman's delay, in presenting himself to your Lordship. As it seems, as if our account was *too heavy* for them, without the assistance of some London house; and I conjecture, that he has gone to Town, for the very purpose, of seeking for an alliance, with some great house or other, to enable him to undertake it. This sort of seeking will necessarily excite enquiry & if he stumbles upon the same channel, as Backhouse's first alarms, sprang from, the business will be at an end. I can only hope that my apprehensions on this subject may be groundless.

I had my conversation with Mewburn & Ord,[5] this morning, and think we have made out a pretty strong case. I advised them to alter a sentence in the petition, which was too strongly expressed, as to the quality of the Ferry-hill Coal. This prevented the petition being sent off to Sir H. Hardinge by this day's mail. I have also had the Way-leave Agreement with Mr Lambton, discussed with Ward & Croudace, Gregson being my Coadjutor. I think I made more play on the merits than Gregson did on the Law of the case; but the grand leaver was the *independent Line* – towards the close of the debate this Gun was brought to bear with great effect, and prevented a defeat on our part. From all that passed I think the legal argument is against us; but the *turning of the corner* has entirely taken the *sting*

---

3   Thomas Morriss, North Hetton colliery.
4   John Hutchinson, Tees Bank, Stockton.
5   Francis Mewburn, Darlington, solicitor to the Stockton and Darlington Railway. See *The Larchfield Diary: Extracts from the Diary of the late Mr Mewburn, first railway solicitor* (London, 1876); John Charles Ord, subscriber to the South Durham Railway.

out of Croudace, and he thinks that as it is only for a short time, that Russell may want to use Mr Lambton's way, it is hardly worth while his (Mr L.'s) thinking about charging any way-leave: as on this affair Mr L. has always expressed the most *liberal sentiments*. I would not concede the point of right, as our Law men could not agree upon it, but proposed that Croudace should first fix with Mr Lambton the amount of Way-leave he would charge, on the *supposition* that your Lordship could not assign; and then if your Lordship did not approve of it, that we should submit a joint case to some eminent Councillor to decide the point; and that of course your Lordship's decision on the latter alternative would be entirely governed by the view which Mr Lambton would take of the subject. If he were moderate in his ideas, your Lordship might not probably think it worth while to take a legal opinion upon it – considering the *very short time* that Russell would find it necessary to come thro' Mr Lambton's property *at all* with his Coals.

Croudace and I dined together, jogged home to the Barracks together, cheek by jowl, and got more kind and confidential, than we have been since the Hetton affair was blabbed. He is to write Lambton tomorrow on the affair and is *sure* he will act *liberally* with your Lordship, as it has always *been his wish to do*. He is more convinced than ever, that we ought to carry on our affairs on amicable terms, and have a perfect understanding on our Way-leave affairs. He is desirous that we should meet quietly ourselves and see if we cannot come to an understanding on liberal principles. We to grant them the liberty of going thro' Herrington to Sunderland. They to grant us the use of some of their spouts &c. &c. This is just what I expected we should come to, after the plan of the independent line was understood. Croudace's *wax* is nearly soft enough to be moulded according to our wishes; and I think it likely that his master will, with an air of liberality say to your Lordship, that Russell may bring the Hetton Coals down his way, *rent free*, until the new line is ready. Upon the whole I think this way-leave affair in as good a train as we could wish – turning the *little corner*, has turned the cards in our favour.

Our binding has not gone on quite so smooth, as usual, a great number of men have left us, and we have got a number of Strangers. We have got as many as will make us safe, but yet I should like to have about 30 more *Hewers*; and have no doubt we shall pick them up before the Binding affair is entirely settled. We have not for many years had so much shifting from place to place amongst the pitmen as has occurred this year. There has been the strongest possible inclination amongst them, to stop for an increase of Wages, but circum-stances have not favoured their views – otherwise we should have had a troublesome business with them. they are combining for an increase, and I am apprehensive, that to a certain extent, we will be obliged to comply with their demands.

The *Hettonians* have made almost a clean sweep of the best of Lambton's families of pitmen from Newbottle, and nearly deprived him of the *putter* Boys. They have also carried off a great many from us. Report says they have bound 100 Hewers more than their former complement. Their two new sinking pits will employ about 40 addi-tional men, but still it is clear that they mean to work every chaldron of Coals they can possibly raise; and they will sell them too, at any price they can get. I am apprehensive that they are interfering with the vend of Eden-main considerably by underselling our Fitters, as the vend of Eden-main is very slack at present. We are however, notwithstanding doing better than Lambton.

I am apprehensive that Mewburn will not dispense with my evidence before the R-way Committee. Not that I care about it, in any way except its taking me from home at a time, not the most convenient for my concerns here. I must however make the best of it I can, and certainly shall not flee from the Witness Box, as some of my friends have done. What a 'Kettle of Fish' it is to be sure; I am really sorry for it.

Croudace is coming to see me tomorrow evening again to have a good gossip, he is in *grief* about so many of his Newbottle *troops* having gone over to the Enemy.

The Marquess of Londonderry	I have the honor [&c.]
London	J^{no} Buddle

42.

D/Lo/C142/10	Newcastle 25th Mar[ch] 1825

My Lord

I had the honor to receive your Lordship's letter of the 22nd & that of the 23rd both at the same time this morning at Pensher; but I have been so fully occupied all day, that I was obliged to give up the idea of writing to your Lordship until I could sit quietly down here this evening.

The chief business of the day has been the Chester meeting: – the following parties were present

Mr W. Lorain	for Lambton
Croudace	
Wade	himself
Lamb	Lambton's tenants
Stobart	ditto
John Smith	J.M. Davison
Tommy Elliott	Lord Ravensworth
Mowbray	Hetton Co.
And myself	

We had a great deal of conversation about a regulation of Vends, and Arthur fought shy; but in the end he stated, that the Co. would join in any measures that might be considered for the general benefit of the Trade (not that they were desirous of any regulation of Vends on their own account) provided they could be placed upon such a basis, as their growing consequence in the trade might fairly entitle them to expect.

He was pressed to say what quantity the Co. would expect on the Basis; but this he declined to do, on the grounds, that the Co. were entirely unprepared to name a quantity, as the subject of regulation had *never been named* amongst them since the last discussions in 'this room' which were not of a pleasant nature. He undertook however to lay the matter before the Co. at their next monthly meeting on Tuesday the 5th April and on the following day we are to meet again to name quantity. So rests the affair of regulation 'till the 6th April.

Billy [Lorain] and Croudace appeared cowed & very shy about naming quantity, and there was a general timidity and shyness on this point. Billy paid considerable court to Arthur & as I thought pressed him beyond the point of due discretion to name his quantity. I kept myself perfectly quiet and showed no anxiety on the subject.

Croudace is very anxious and fidgety on all the affairs of the trade, and is anxious to *cotton* with me. He did not get to me last night but came this morning. We had a long prose & rode to Chester together. He is very anxious for *moderation* in quantities, he thinks that if we could stand at the same quantities (120,000) as we had last Regulation and support, or improve, our present prices, we ought to be perfectly satisfied. He has a great horror of a reduction of prices now, when the prices of every article of Colliery consumption & of wages are rising so rapidly. I found his object was to sound me as to your Lordship's ideas of quantity & I thought it best to set his mind *at ease* on the subject. I therefore told him 140,000 was *our* quantity & that I should demand 30,000 for Russell. He looked very serious upon it & said, he thought 120,000 & 30,000, making 150,000 in all would be very fair. I told him I had no authority to go lower, but if others shewed great moderation, your Lordship might probably be induced to relax *a little*, if such relaxation would be the means of attaining the objects we had in view. He is very low upon it, as he thinks a reduction of prices inevitable. His vend is going on very slowly indeed, the Hetton Co. pick up most of the *free* ships as they come straggling in, and his Fitters are not sufficiently numerous & powerful in Shipping to carry off his Coals – so as to keep pace with his neighbours; and if matters keep much longer in their present state, I really think Mr Lambton will be obliged to reduce his prices, which will of course bring all the rest down. Croudace is doing all he can to struggle with his difficulties, by making a very limited quantity of Walls-end & making them *very good*. He is also mixing Primrose with Nesham, all of which manoeuvres amount virtually to a reduction in price; but he is anxious to avert a *direct* reduction as long as he can. All this however is entirely *entre nous*; and must not on any account come to the ears of 'Our Squire'[6] through *us at least*.

The D[raf]t of a petition against the Stockton Rail-way was submitted to the Meet[in]g and after being corrected was committed for engrossment. The claims of our Carpenters, Smiths &c. &c. were considered, and an advance of 1/. per week, on their wages was agreed upon. This all arises out of *the union* System, now making its Way amongst all the labouring Classes. The Pitmen are arranging it, and as soon as circumstances favour their views, it will break out. In Scotland the system is completely organized, a Letter from that country yesterday informs me that the Duke of Hamilton's Collieries are nearly *laid in*, his Colliers having dispersed, and quartered themselves, on the *Brotherhood* of Colliers, all over the Country. And subscriptions from the Colliers in England are expected to be sent for their support, until they carry their point against the Duke. In the end this will become a serious grievance to the Country. The carpenters & Sailors, at Sunderland &c. have succeeded in this System.

To return to my conversation with Croudace. He has written to Mr Lambton on our Durham discussions of the Way-leave affair. And what is *odd* enough, Mr L. seems to have been strongly acted upon by *sympathy*, as *Croudace has just rec[eive]d a letter* from him, expressing the most liberal sentiments on the subject. With your Lordship, & as between your Lordship & Mr Lambton £200 or £300 a year on

6   William Russell.

the affair of Way-leave, can be no object, & Mr L. is anxious for an amicable arrangement as he can accommodate y[ou]r L[or]d[shi]p with *some of his Spouts* and y[ou]r L[or]d[shi]p can accommodate him with Way-leave thro' Herrington & the Baronet's to Sunderland; the payment of Rents to each other seems merely a matter of moon shine; our interests being so nearly balanced that he (Croudace) thinks we might just as well afford each other free & reciprocal accommodation. Mr Lambton writes Croudace, that he understands I am to be in Town on the Stockton Rail-way affair & *if any thing is to be said on* Way-leave business, he *thinks* Croudace might as well run up at the same time, & let us have the thing settled in London, where if necessary y[ou]r Lordship and Mr Lambton might have personal intercourse. And as to Croudace himself he does not feel that he would have any objection to a journey to the Metropolis at this time. – Oh! These little *independent Corners*, what wonders canst thou work!!!

I have no doubt we shall get all Way-leave matters settled to satisfaction – a new and extended treaty on liberal terms may be formed; and it is only for us to look sharp *about us*, to see what our future views & plans may be, so as to secure privileges accordingly.

The Lynn Fleet has appeared I am glad to say; and their [*sic*] is a bustle at the Staith, though not such a *rush* as I should have liked to have seen – enough however to lengthen Croudace's chin considerably, as his Fitters have not got a single Ship of them. We have had above 60 Keels both yesterday and today, and if all goes on well I still hope we shall run off about 10,000 Ch. to the Fitters this month.

I cannot get Ships to carry the Stones to London; but am led to expect that in a month or so, they will be more plentiful, i.e. small craft fit for the purpose, and every exertion is using at the Quarry to get Stones ready.

Amongst other advances we have been obliged to advance the Wynyard Waggon[me]n 2/- per ton on the Stone leading – they therefore will now have 18/- per ton, their original price was 14/- but I don't think the increase is more than in proportion to the increase in the price of Forage &c.

I will take a fresh sheet for other matter.

The Marq[ues]s of Londonderry   I have the Honor [&c.]
London   J^no Buddle

43.

D/Lo/C142/10   Walls-end 5[th] June 1825

My Lord

I have this morning had the honor to receive your Lordship's Letter of the 3[rd] Inst. and hasten to explain that it is *only* the Newbottle Coals that Croudace is freighting and *not the Lambton Coals*. His object he says, is, to inflict the greater loss on the Hetton people. This freighting arises entirely from the want of a sufficient number of Fitters, who *themselves have shipping to carry off the Coals*. The loss by this system is frightful, and if we adopt it, it will be at a loss of 5/- or 6/- per Ch. at least, as by urging more Coals into the Market, prices must still come lower. The affair of freighting, at the Hetton spouts stands thus. The price of their Walls-end Coals to the Ships is 34/- per Ch. or per London Ch. 17s 0d.

They are paying 15/- to 15/9 per Ch. freight but say 15. 6d

Duty, Coast Lights &c. 9..0

Cost of Coals in the pool 41. 6

But the selling price is only 38. 0

Loss per Ch. to the freighter 3. 6 which is *7/- per Newcastle Ch.*

If therefore the Co. use the freighters, the price of their Coals is reduced as much per Chal[dro]n as the loss by freighting amounts to. If the Fitters are the Freighters then the loss falls upon them. Darnell's[7] Clerk states that they (for their share) have already lost £5000 by freighting.

With respect to Newbottle Fawcett's main the matter will stand as follows

I think the price is 28/6, by spout, but am not certain. I will however assume it to be so, which is per London Ch. 14.3

Freight say only 15.0 Duty, Lights &c. 9.0

Cost in the Pool per London Ch. 28.3

I have not a Coal List by me, but I don't think Fawcett's main will fetch more than 31/- or 32/- in the market, at present, but say 32.0

Lost per London Ch for the Coals 3.9

Or per Newcastle Ch. 7.6

---

7   Robert Darnell, Grange, Sunderland, partner in the Hetton Co.

Price at the spout, say 28.6

Loss by freighting 21.0 per Ch.

If therefore Mr Lambton is really freighting these Coals, as Croudace states, it must be at a loss of 20/. to a Guinea per Ch. and I think it quite out of the question to suppose that any Fitter can stand such a loss. And with all deference to Croudace's judgment, I much question the soundness of his policy in running the race of ruin, with the Hetton Co. or their Fitters, as the case may be.

With respect to our own case the matter stands thus

We charge our Fitters for the W[alls].end Tub Coals 30/- per N. Castle Ch. or per London Ch. 15.0.

They pay Keel-dues & runn[in]g Fitters Wages	1.6
They have Fittage	0.6
Duty, Coast Lights &c.	9.0
Cost of carrying the Coals in their own Ships	26.0
The Coals sell for, in the Pool	38.0
Leaves for Freight	12.0

The Fitters are therefore making 3/- per London Ch. or 6/- per Newcastle Ch. less by carrying the Coals in *their own* Ships, than the independent Ship-owners are doing by carrying Mr Lambton's Newbottle, & the Hetton Coals, at 15/- per Ch. freight. Several of our own Fitters are sending the Coals in freighted Ships, however in a quiet way I believe, Hubbard[8] has 2 vessels carrying on freight. As long as our Fitters can get off 10,000 Ch. or so a month, or even *less* I would earnestly recommend your Lordship not to think of freighting; as I feel confident that we should lose 5/- to 7/- per Ch. on every Chald[ro]n so vended. It would be better at once to reduce the price 3/- or 4/- per Ch. but even this ruinous as it w[oul]d be, would not I really believe enable us to vend any more Coals, as all the rest would come down in proportion, or still continue freighting, until they are ruined.

I consider the Hetton Co. just now, as a pack of madmen, with swords in their hands slashing about them on all sides – ruthless of consequences. A[rthu]r [Mowbray] has always been so in any concern he has had the manag[emen]t off – his Lead-mines, Bank, & the Collieries, as far as he was able, all prove the restlessness of his

8   John Hubbard & Co, Sunderland fitter.

spirit, & if possible he will never stop until he involves the whole Coal mining interest of this Country in one general ruin.

I however think the worst part of this year is now about over; and that we shall shortly derive great assistance from our Lynn and their coasting friends. The only thing we have to dread, is the rivalry of some of the *cheap* on the Tyne. These Coals being now almost entirely driven out of the London market, their proprietors are using every possible exertion to get them introduced into Lynn & the other *bye* markets, and are increasing their sales in that way. The chief hold we have, is in the long credit given by our Fitters to the merchants. Some of the Tyne Coal-owners are offering to give six month's credit.

Our meeting took place at Newcastle yesterday,[9] but no body appeared to represent the Hetton Co. & of course no progress could be made towards the completion of the object of the meet[in]g. A resolution to this effect was passed & a copy ordered to be sent to the Hetton Co. A meeting of the Wear representatives was also ordered, at Chester next Thursday, for the purpose of giving an official answer, as *a body*, to the Tyne, to say whether they will join us in a general Regulation, or not. A notice to this effect has been sent to the H. Co. – if they don't send any representative to the meeting there will be an end to the business. If they do attend, we shall hear what they have to say at least. William Brandling[10] stated at the meeting yesterday that Mowbray declared to him, that he w[oul]d not be satisfied with less than 3/4ths of Lord Londonderry's & Mr Lambton's quantity, and that he thought they might be satisfied with 120,000 Ch. each & him with 90,000 – particularly Lord Londonderry he s[ai]d who had sold off a part of his Collieries for which there was an additional claim for 30,000, making his Lordship 150,000 in all, at 120,000 for the old Coll[ierie]s.

I really don't know what is best to be done, under all the embarrassing circumstances of the Trade & having those pig-headed D—ls to deal with. Even to turn them a side in the least degree, is difficult, but to stop them is impracticable, we must either fight them greatly to our own loss, or carry them along with us; and I am inclined to consider the latter, the most prudent. We shall decidedly make more profit at present prices, on a large reduction of quantity, than we can possibly do under a large reduction of price, at any rate of Vend we could with the utmost exertion raise. And, again when we consider

9   Minutes in NRO 263, A1/10.
10   William Brandling, 1795–1843, brother of Robert William Brandling.

that the D[ean] & Chapter's tentale above 60,000 yearly, takes place on 20th July, it is obvious that working a large quantity at little, or no profit, would merely be putting the money into their pockets.

As it appears, that matters are fast approaching a crisis, when we must either sacrifice price or quantity, I shall feel obliged by y[ou]r Lordship's giving the subject your best considerat[io]n and, directing me how to act for the best.

Matters having arrived at such a pitch, were I to follow the impulse of my own feelings, I would allow them to go on & find their own level, coute que coute; but on the other hand prudence suggests this question – are we in a situation to do so? The point therefore for y[ou]r Lordship's decision is, whether to adhere to our demand of 140,000 or 130,000 (the latter they seem inclined to give) *inflexibly*, or to temporize and get as near that mark as we can, but not by being too tenacious, to be the cause of knocking up the hopes of a Regulation, and thereby render a reduction of prices, almost inevitable. It might perhaps be well if your Lordship could confer with Mr Lambton, as to the course, it may be most prudent to take as respects the Hetton Co. next Thursd[a]y, as I feel & I conceive that Croudace must also feel, that acting from our own discretion alone on such an important occasion, is incurring an heavy responsibility – the making or losing of many Thousands a year may hinge upon the result of this meeting. Croudace will have the benefit of Lorain's assistance, I must rely on the advice I receive from y[ou]r Lordship. A Letter addressed to the post office Chester-le-Street, will find me there on Thursd[a]y morn[in]g next. Your Lordship may rely on my best exertions in whatever way affairs may turn.

The idea of your Lordship being so teazed by Wyatt's Tradesmen, makes me sombre. £17000 to £18000 is a tremendous Sum yet to have to provide, after all that has been done, but it is a great consolation, that there is now an end of this source of expenditure. I have sent the list of payments under another cover, not having room in this. I hope my Lady continues as well as is to be expected, under circumstances.

The Marqu[es]s of Londonderry   I have the honor [&c.]
London   Jno Buddle

44.

D/Lo/C142/10   Newcastle 25th June 1825

My Lord

The memorandum enclosed in your Lordship's Letter of the 23rd
Inst. tended in a considerable degree to tranquillize our meeting
this morn[in]g, and a general meeting of the Tyne Delegates is
convened next Wed[nesday] to endeavour to perfect the Scheme of
regulat[io]n on the Tyne. I presume Mr Lambton will have made a
similar communication to Croudace as your Lordship has done to
myself, which I feel imposes a difficult task upon me. In the temper
Croudace is in, as to having the same quantity on the Basis as us, I
am satisfied, that I cannot beat him down a single Chald[ro]n. I must
therefore either consent to take the same quantity, say 124,000 (as
proposed yesterday) or we shall remain in statu-quo 'till doomsday.
I am however very unwilling to quit my position, or even give in
at all, without your Lordship's entire sanction. At the same time I
cannot but feel that by adhering too pertinaciously to our principles
I should run great risk of injuring your Lordship most materially,
if a reduction of prices should ensue. Under all these conflicting
considerations, I am sure your Lordship will make due allowance
for the degree of embarrassment, which I feel in the present state
of affairs. To take a single Ch. less on the Basis than I think we are
fairly entitled to, would be gall to me, and by standing out for that
right, and incurring a frightful loss, would complete my misery. Had
our Treasury been in a more flourishing state my plan w[oul]d have
been, to have had an entire compliance with the Reference plan, or to
have left matters to take their own course. I shall however be glad to
adopt, any line that may be deemed most expedient under existing
circumstances. Without actually going to extremities I don't think
either Lambton or the Hetton Co. can be beaten from the ground
they have taken.

I apprehend some difficulties on the Tyne, the people are all in
very bad humour & seem quite ready to worry each other, and
unless the feelings of distress are stronger than those of vexation
and obstinacy at the meet[in]g on Wed[nesday] I do not expect much
good to be done.

A large Fleet of light Ships has at last arrived – the greater part
for Sunderland. It is reported here, that the Sunderland Fitters have
been cruising in Steam Boats, and freighting the *Ships at Sea*!!! This
is quite new, and if persisted in for any length of time must inevitably bring on their ruin. With Fitters & *Bankers* I foresee a gloomy

meet[in]g at Sunderland next Friday. I sincerely wish matters were in a more settled state, as I am quite worked to *an ail* with all the worry of the present state of affairs. *Union amongst the Workmen*, and dissention amongst the Masters throws every thing completely out of joint, and renders the management of great concerns very troublesome.

The representation made to Mr Lambton of what I stated at the Coal meet[in]g here respecting Hetton Coll[ier[y is inflated. I have written a separate letter in explanation in delicate terms which if your Lordship thinks right you may shew to Mr L. *King Crou[dace]* and his *butty Billy* [Lorain] w[oul]d I daresay be glad enough in their present humour 'to pick a hole in my Coat'. I however will deal with them in all charity & make due allowance for their cause of excitement at the present moment.

The Marqu[es]s of Londonderry   I have the Honor [&c.]
London   J[no] Buddle

45.

D/Lo/C142/11   Durham 21[st] July 1825

My Lord

I am happy to inform your Lordship that the N. Pittington affair is concluded.[11] The 1[st] Instalment is paid, the Bonds are given, and I have got the heads of an Agreement for the lease sanctioned by some of the members of the Body signed by Tho[ma]s Fenwick.

This has not however been accomplished without the most desperate *Skirmish* I ever had with the *flying parties* of the Body. In conformity to a Standing clause in their Colliery leases, *Tommy* had put down, that we sh[oul]d only be allowed every 2 years of the term to make up short working. I objected to this insisting that we had purchased the quantity of 30,000 Ch. a year & that it never could be the intention of the Body to abridge your Lordship of that limited quantity, which as the Colliery is not yet won, must obviously be the case if I allowed this Clause to stand. I convinced Tommy as well as Griffith[12] of the equity of my demand, but neither of them *durst*

---

11   The lease by the Dean and Chapter to Lord Londonderry of the coal of North Pittington was signed on 28 Sep. 1825. Lord Londonderry was to pay a fixed rent of £10 for up to 6666 2/3 tens, plus a tentale rent for quantities above that total. DCM, B/BA/ 102, fols 57v–69v.

12   Thomas Griffith, Durham solicitor, deputy clerk to the Halmote Court.

without the consent of the Body modify the clause so as to meet my wishes. It was therefore agreed that Tommy should submit the Clause in my own writing to Durell[13] for his sanction. In a short time Tommy returned in the greatest dismay, with a petted [sic]message from Durell to say, 'that as I had not paid the money yesterday, there was an end to the contract & he had nothing more to say on the subject'.

I told Tommy it was impossible for me to rest satisfied with such a comm[unicatio]n and that I must at all events see him, or the Dean, or some of them, to have such a strange line of conduct explained, as he Tommy knew that I had been sitting all day with the greater part of the money in my pocket, merely waiting their decision on the terms of the Agree[men]t. I therefore, insisted on Tommy going with me to the College to have an expla[natio]n with Durell.

This Tommy absolutely *durst* not do, but said he w[oul]d go & introduce me to the Dean with whom I might work my way as well as I could. I could only prevail on Tommy to go to the Dean on the score of introducing me, as I did not know him personally. Off we set to the College, but the Dean had walked out, Tommy wished me to wait his return, but I insisted on his going in search of him with me, as he probably might not return for 2 or 3 Hours. Fortunately in crossing the College area we met Durell & Ogle.[14] The former looked like a Volcano on the eve of an eruption – I said I was sorry to find that some mistake had occurred as to the pay[men]t of the money. We understood that you were not prepared to pay it yesterday & were the more inclined to think it, from your not coming to the Chapter Room to tender the money, was his reply. I said I had waited in my Inn from 8 in the morn[in]g 'till after *four* in the afternoon, with the money in my pocket, expecting any minute to receive a message to wait upon them. He replied you knew the Chapter house was the place of business & you ought to have presented yourself there & not left it to us to seek you out. I thought it more respectful, said I, to announce to the Body through their confidential agent, that I was waiting their convenience, than to obtrude myself upon them, at a time, when they had so much business on their hands, and appealed to Tommy for the correctness of my assertions. We carried on this sort of conversation until I entirely convinced him, that they had acted under a false impression, and that no blame whatever was

13 David Durell, 1763–1852, prebendary of Durham 1801–52.
14 John Savage Ogle, 1767–1853, prebendary of Durham 1820–53.

imputable to me. During our conversation the *new Dean* joined us, and expressed himself perfectly satisfied with my explanation; and my making a sort of unpremeditated display of Russell's cheque for £2000 and the Bonds which I happened to have in my pocket, dissipated all the gloom from Durell's countenance, and we began to get on as smoothly as I could wish. From the manner in which Tommy hung his ears during this interview I am convinced that the misunderstanding had entirely arisen from some blunder of his, in communicating between the Body & myself, and all the apology he can make to me is, that they so *bamboozled* him, with various enquiries & calculations & kept him trotting about so that he was half bewildered. This I really believe to be the case, and if they don't shew him a little more *quarter*, they will in a short time, drive the wits entirely out of him I think.

Having got friends made again with Durell & his Colleagues, I said that I really felt much hurt at the idea of having been the innocent cause of probably drawing upon your Lordship the imputation of unpunctuality from the Revd. Body, & which I was sure would excite painful feelings in your Lordship's mind, should it come to your knowledge, and begged of them to do me the favor of explaining the matter to the Gentl[eme]n who left Town last night under the false impression. This they cheerfully undertook to do, and Durell said they must now just consider the 21st of July in point of completing the purchase as the 20th. I then took the opportunity of explaining my wishes with respect to the principle of making up Shorts, and after a slight struggle carried my point. I read the clause as I had written it, which poor Tommy had not dared to shew before, and obtained the sanction of the *Triumvirate* to it; and lost no time in getting Tommy's signature to it.

I then went to Leybourn[15] their Treasurer & settled the payment with him – all these transactions has given me a full day's work, but I consider it a conclusive & satisfactory one, as it has got this affair settled.

I am sorry for my friend Tommy who seems utterly incapable of maintaining a just and reasonable opinion amongst his inquisitorial employers. Dr Gray left Town last night, so that I have not had an opportunity of explaining matters to him.

I received Cowburn's Letter on the £10,000 loan affair, and have written in reply that under all circumstances I preferred the orig-

---

15 John Leybourne.

inal arrangement, to a fresh loan. Besides I plainly perceive that we sh[oul]d have a great bother and expence about making out the Title.

I am going to Pensher this evening & to Chester – meeting tomorrow.

The Marq[ues]s of Londonderry   I have the honor [&c.]
London   J^{no} Buddle

46.

D/Lo/C142/11   Pensher Colliery 4th Nov[ember] 1825

My Lord

T. Fenwick & Dunn[16] were here yesterday, at the request of the 'proprietory' (what a fine name) of the N. Hetton Coll[ier]y, to advise, as to the sinking of a new pit &c. Dunn I presume will have to be consulted on the value of the Security Coal, but I suggested to Morriss that it would not be prudent to take Tommy's opinion, on account of his connexion with the Dean & Chapter.

I took the opportunity of making an official app[licatio]n to the Chapter for Way-leave from Belmont, and expect to learn their terms on the 20th Inst. which is a 'grand Chapter'. This being done, I can at once make my offer to Pemberton, with whom I have nearly about established the principle of a Certain yearly and tentale Rent, as being more expedient under our present circumstances than a *lump sum*; and I can keep him in play well enough until I know the Chapter's terms. It would be a good job if we can secure this, and throw it into the Quaker's Chops, instead of N. Pittington; but more on all this affair in the course of two, or three days.

Our Vend up to last night is as under viz.

Walls-end	Ch. 440	
Eden-main	1136	
		1576
Splint	8	
Small	16	
		1604

---

16 Matthias Dunn, viewer at North Hetton, author of *An Historical, Geological and Descriptive View of the Coal Trade of the North of England* (Newcastle upon Tyne, 1844) and *A Treatise on the Winning and Working of Collieries* (Newcastle upon Tyne, 1848).

This from the few Ships which got in on the 1st, but it has blown from the North since & we have not had a single arrival. We shall therefore be out of Ships again unless we have an immediate change of Wind – this uncertainty in the arrival of the Ships is tantalizing beyond measure. We are getting cram full of Coals, which is a great loss and inconvenience to us, yet in the ticklish humour, in which the pitmen are, I think it prudent, to keep up the Workings, so, as not to run our stock of Coals too low. At Jarrow Colliery, where we have been fighting the United Pitmen for upwards of 4 months, I think a victory is going to declare for us, which will greatly weaken the rascally compact.

One of the Newbottle Pits is put hors de combat for an indefinite period. The compressed inflamm[able] air is forcing the Water up out of the Hutton, into the work[ing]s of the Maudlin (Fawcett-main) Seam, and the danger of a Water blast is so imminent, that we could not feel justified in risking the men's lives, by keeping the pit at work. The case is similar to that at our North pit, in Dec[ember] 1819, arising from bad management in the first instance. The new Sinking Pit at Houghton is also in a bad way and requires decisive, and expensive measures to be promptly carried into effect, to make it fit for it's object. Croudace & his Staff are in consequence of all this, in a very low key. I am happy to say that we have no such difficulties in hand. We only wait a supply of light Ships to make us quite comfortable.

I have rec[eive]d the Counter part of the N. Pittington Lease, and have sent it to Bowlby by Th. Fenwick this m[ornin]g.

The Marq[ues]s of Londonderry   I have the Honor [&c.]
Mount Stewart   Jno Buddle

47.

D/Lo/C142/12   In continuation   Pensher 2d Jan[uar]y 1826

My Lord

It was just as I expected with Edw[ar]d when his pressing message caused me to leave off my former letter.[1] I found him in the greatest *stew* imaginable; he had discovered that from the short vend in Dec[ember] the House would be between £9000 and £10,000 in advance *uncovered*, *if they* make our Pay next Friday, and the following pay on the 20th Inst – after both the receipt of this day & the Fitters' acceptances for the Vend of December were paid in. He therefore 'took leave' to inform me that the Ho[use] would not advance us any more money unless your Lordship gave them some sort of *available* security, to indemnify and cover them, to the *full extent* of whatever advance they might have to make, observing at the same time that the House could not think of the Bal[an]ce ranging so high again as it has hitherto done. After a long and painful discussion, all that I could make of him was, that he will advance money for our pay next Friday, on my pledging my honor and personal responsibility that no charges sh[oul]d be made in the Bill, except such as were bona fide Coll[ier]y payments, and that he sh[oul]d have the Fitters' acceptances for the vend of the present Mo[nth] put into his hands on the 1st Feb[ruary]. As having communication with your Lordship at this juncture was impracticable and thinking anything better than actually *stopping payment* next Friday, nothing was left for me but to accede to this arrangem[en]t.

He observed that he had always relied on my word of honor that I w[oul]d not charge any sums in the Pay Bills which did not strictly belong to the Coll[ierie]s but if he could have reason to think other-wise, 'I would take leave to ask thy permission to look at the pay Bill'!!! It would be painful to go into a detail of a hundredth part of what passed on this occasion, but the exposure of our Acc[oun]t at Hutchinson's[2] has done irreparable mischief, and Ed[war]d shewed a

---

1   D/Lo/C142/12. January. Buddle had had to break off the earlier letter after discussing Londonderry's debts.
2   The Tees Bank at Stockton had recently failed. Lord Londonderry had evidently borrowed from them (see p. 34) although his main banker in the North was Backhouse's.

knowledge of the embarrassed state of our Finances both in London
& here which quite surprised me. He is going over to Darlington
tonight to consult 'the House' as to what they will do with respect to
our acc[oun]t and he has promised to write me the result. I however
don't expect it to be at all satisfactory, for if even they consent to
make our pay next Friday, I am *sure*, if they follow Ed[ward']s advice
they will not make the pay on the 20th without having ample security. We are therefore at this point – either to satisfy them with security, to provide money elsewhere, or to *stop payment* on the 20th. It
is most painful to me to have this to communicate to your Lordship, but it is really the precise position in which circumstances
have unfortunately placed us. I shudder at the consequences of not
having the means of making our pay on the 20th. It would alarm all
the Coll[ier]y tradesmen, as well as other creditors – they would all
rush on with legal proceedings, and we should be completely upset.
Ed[war]d pressed for the N. Pittington Lease in security, but when I
intimated that it w[oul]d not be forthcoming without an additional
advance, he *shoved off his Boat again*. Something decisive & efficient
must however be done, or we shall inevitably be *shipwrecked* and I
can only crave your Lordship's directions and advice for my government; and nothing shall be wanting on my part to the utmost exertion of my judgment & power. We must face our difficulties manfully
& hope for the best.

Altho' Ed[war]d has frequently told me that he cons[idere]d
y[ou]r Lordship's Pro[missory] Notes as mere waste paper yet *Cuddy*[3]
tells me that he offered them to him as security for the Co[unting]
Ho[use] money, & also to another person in security for a deposit of
money lodged with them – they were not however accepted in either
case. – This is too bad – it is acting the *double distilled* Jew.

Croudace seems much out of spirits, or perhaps the depression
of my own makes me think so. Mr Lambton is very poorly – if he is
well enough, he is to set off for Lond[o]n on Wed[nesday]. Public
report has him dying of Consump[tio]n already, and an anticipation
of the election of a member to succeed him.

Hawkes expects y[ou]r Lord[shi]p to start on the 5th Inst. for
Wyn[yar]d. I shall look most anxiously for y[ou]r Lordship's arrival
& wishing you all a safe journey

The Marq[uess]s of Londonderry   I remain [&c.]
Mount Stewart   J^{no} Buddle

---

3   Sir Cuthbert Sharp.

48.

D/Lo/C142/12   Newcastle 25[th] Feb[ruary] 1826

My Lord

After all that *unsoncy* beast Blab[4] has not made good his p[aymen]t of the £5000, as appears by the enclosed. This fellow's *uniform* irregularity really haunts us like an evil Spirit, he seems to be regular in nothing but his irregularity. Edward's Letter however which I also enclose is in better humour that I sh[oul]d have expected on the occasion.

I have had a long conversation with Boyd & young Bigge[5] to day on taking our Acc[oun]t. At any other time they w[oul]d have been glad to have done it, but at present they dare not venture to let their 20/- Notes go out, as they are run upon with them immediately & have to give Sovereigns in exchange. They will however consult their partners on the subject & will give me their ans[we]r on Monday or Tuesday next. I have however little expectation of their complying with our wishes.

This conversation has let me into the present state of the banking concerns of our neighbourhood, a good deal. The whole of them have a quiet but heavy run upon them. Ridley's are running out sov[ereign]s or B[ank] of England £1 notes at the rate of £1000 a day and the others in proportion. Since the beginning of Dec[ember] the Banks in this Town have p[ai]d away upwards of £200,000 Sovereigns, scarcely one of which have returned; and the general opinion, is that the run will not cease as long as a single £1 note is out.

The bankers are in consequence in the greatest embarrassment, and apprehend, unless a favourable change takes place shortly, that they will all have to decline business entirely. They are now curtailing their Discounts in such a manner, that no money can be had for home Bills & the consequence is that Tradesmen of every description are getting into the utmost difficulties. In short every thing & every body is looking as sombre & bad as possible and it is difficult to say what the end of it will be.

The pitmen's Union is going on with great vigour & there is scarcely a doubt but we shall have a general turn-out about the 24th Mar[ch]. The Coal-owners must seriously turn their attention to

4   Gregson, who had committed an indiscretion about Lord Londonderry's affairs. See also below, p. 137.

5   William Boyd, Charles John Bigge, partners in Bell, Cookson, Carr, and Avery, the Old Bank, of Newcastle. Phillips, *History of Banks*, pp. 174–95.

the subject and make preparations to resist this combination. I will endeavour to call their attent[io]n to it here as soon as the bustle of the Election is over.[6]

It is a hard heat at Alnwick.[7] Bell was only 8 a head last night. Beaumont's force is to be bro[ugh]t up to day in support of Liddell, which is expected to give him a majority – Against this, Bell has some London Voters to bring, but the general opinion here to day is that Liddell will win the day. Party spirit runs high & money is spending freely. It is not true that the Duke has been stopping at Ravensworth – this is merely an Election *lie*; he has remained quietly at Alnwick & takes no interest in the Poll. Some of his Agents have voted for Bell & some for Liddell.

I hope your Lordship has not suffered any serious inconvenience from your fall. I return the pitmen's 'Appeal' which if y[ou]r Lordship think proper it might be well to send to Mr Peel.[8] The regular organization of such a large body of half civilized men, ought not to be regarded with indifference by Govern[men]t. Coupled with the present embarrassed state of the finances of the Country there is no little hazard of it's leading to the most frightful consequences.

I have the honor [&c]
J[no] Buddle

49.

D/Lo/C142/12   Newcastle 8[th] April 1826

My Lord

Correspondence between Messrs Cowburn & Chisholm

I have shewn this Correspondence to Donkin.[9] He is in daily expectation of receiving the D[ra]fts of the conveyances of Col. Reed's[10] estates, down from London, to enable him to complete the Sales

---

6   A general election was due in June. See below, p. 146.

7   For the Northumberland election of 1826, see Peter Borroughs, 'The Northumberland County Election of 1826', *Parliamentary History*, x, part 1 (1991), pp. 78–104.

8   Robert Peel, 1788–1850, Home Secretary 1822–7, 1828–30, Prime Minister 1834–5, 1841–6. *ODNB*.

9   Henry Donkin, Durham solicitor, County Clerk.

10   Unidentified.

of them, which will enable him to get Sir E. Banks[11] his mortgage money, upon them p[ai]d off. On this affair he expects shortly to be in London and, advises in the mean time, that Mr Cowburn should keep Chisholm[12] as easy as possible – perhaps the less communication he has with him the better, & when Donkin comes to Town he is not without hopes, that he may be able to get Sir E. Banks through Chisholm satisfied.

Settlement of Security Coal purchase

I am happy to inform your Lordship that this affair is now on the point of being settled. I have satisfied Morriss on all Gregson's points of the D[ean] & C[hapter]'s acc[oun]t of the quantity of Coal sold, without giving him an *Inch* more & so, I think, as to convince Gregson that he was wrong. I have allowed him an equivalent quantity for the Coal lost in the N. Pittington Barrier, next Elemore & N. Hetton, which is only fair.

In another Cover I enclose you 8 Bills for £500 each for the remaining £4000 of Russell's purchase money of which for £2000 are drawn at three & the remainder at six months. They are not dated, but this your Lordship will please to do when you sign the Deeds. Gregson will then take them to Russell for acceptance. The only unpleasant feeling which I have on this occasion, is, the idea of bringing Gregson in contact with your Lordship, which I foresee will take place. I know that he is anxious to know how your Lordship feels towards him, as to whether you have forgiven him for the *blabbing affair*. He thinks not, as your Lordship *he says* w[oul]d not see him when he called at the House last year, as *he heard* y[ou]r Lordship tell the Servant, that you were not at home. He is not at his ease on this point, as he does not like the notion that your Lordship has *cut him*; and I fully expect he will call with the deeds for execution himself & take the Bills for acceptance. In this case your Lordship will receive him as you may think most proper, but it will be best not to make any allusions to the Skirmishing I have had with him, to get this affair closed; as it need not be supposed that your Lordship knows all that has passed during our negotiation.

---

11 Sir Edward Banks, 1770–1835, builder and contractor for public works of an engineering character. *ODNB*.
12 Unidentified.

The Coal Trade

Both Loraine and Croudace attended our meeting to day, nothing decisive was done as the circumstances and prospects of the trade are most embarrassing and gloomy. Although every one admits that great irregularities are going on under the regulation, yet all are afraid, boldly to declare it to be at an end, and are disposed to cling to it, as affording the only chance of preventing an immediate and ruinous reduction of prices. All cry out for a great reduction of Vend, & in this cry Billy & Croudace join most cordially, as holding out the only chance of enabling them to get their Coals vended. But this does not suit our case, and I have been obliged to resist this cry; it was 1st for 40 & then for 50 per Thou[an]d on the basis, for the Vend in April – the former w[oul]d have given us 5000 – the latter 6250 Ch. for the month. This would have unquestionably have been the best step that could be taken to bring the trade to a healthy state, and enable us to support our prices: but how could we exist upon such an allowance? I therefore fought for a larger quantity and at last the Comm[itt]ee fixed on 60 to the Thousand, which upon our basis of 120 Th[ousan]d will give us 7500, to which may be added the Shorts up to the end of Mar[ch] – probably 2000 – making 9500 Ch. in all for the Vend of April. This will do pretty well, provided we can maintaiin our prices. Of this however there are great doubts, and the general expectation that further reductions will have to be made both on the part of the Ship & Coal-owners, is such, that the Committee have decided to convene a meeting of the whole trade, on the 18th Inst. to take this and other matters into the most serious consideration. The price of Coals has fallen at all the bie-ports as well as in London & the general cry is that the Coal-owners must reduce their prices and I am sadly afraid that we shall shortly be obliged to do so.

The Union men still hold out at some of the Collieries, and will not allow Strangers to be bound, nor will they quit their houses. In some places they have proceeded to violence, and have mobbed & ill treated the Strangers who have bound; but in a few places this must be put down, altho' probably not without some broken heads.

I will write again shortly and have the honor [&c.]

Jno Buddle

50.

D/Lo/C142/12   Pensher Colliery 4th May 1826

My Lord

I scarcely had a minute left, to save post when I wrote my *Bulletin* from Sunderland yesterday, and was therefore obliged to give your Lordship a very short and imperfect account of the transactions of the meeting.

We had a full attendance, Loraine and Croudace, Mowbray & Darnell, and Wade, Stobart &c. &c. single handed.

Croudace said little, as Billy [Loraine] seems to have taken the lead of him in the business of the meetings; Arthur [Mowbray] was *as eloquent* as usual, and talked, *balderdash* without measure. The sole object of this man, in which Loraine joined him, was to continue the regulation on the Wear; and to support the price, *nominally*. I say nominally, because it is notorious that the Hetton Co. give extra measure to the extent of 1 in 10 say 3/6 per Ch. on their W[alls]-end, and 3/3 on the Lyon's main, which is tantamount to a direct reduction of price to the same amo[un]t. Besides this, they have freighted upwards of 30 Vessels, as stated in a former letter, so that the more they can keep us back, by any sort of manoeuvring, or chicanery, the less will be their loss on their freighted ships.

Loraine joins Arthur in the cry of restriction & keeping up of prices, as affording him the only chance of vending Mr Lambton's quantity. I can only therefore see the matter in this light, that if we comply with the wishes of these parties, we shall most certainly become the victims, or dupes of the one's indiscretion, and the other's cupidity. I could not therefore consent, to tie your Lordship up to a strict observance of the rules of the regulation 'till the end of July, *knowing* that those who are the most anxious for the measure, are slily breaking those rules, daily. It was then proposed that we should keep up prices 'till the adjourned meeting on the 11th. This led to a long discussion, in which I stated the impossibility of our doing so, while others undersold us by freighting & giving great measure. Arthur advises me to do the same. I told him, we could not do so by keels; he replied, but *you may charge the Fitters a keel or so less for each Ship*. It is not worth while to pursue a dialogue of this description further, but the end of it was, that the meeting broke up without coming to any resolution, and we separated under the impression that every one was to do the best he could for himself. Only Loraine said he could not make any alteration in the price of his Coals, until he communicated with Mr Lambton.

Our Fitters were waiting the result of their meeting, as none of their Customers will load with them, unless they can be supplied, on the same terms as at the Spouts, and the consequence has been that we have stood stock still all this week. Under the circumstances I felt great embarrassment and after much discussion with the Fitters, and giving the subject the best consideration in my power, I thought it most expedient to take off the advance of price laid on 1st Aug[us]t viz. 2/- on the W[alls]-end, and 1/- on E[den]-main. The Fitters are not however to announce this as a direct reduction of price, until it receives your Lordship's sanction, but are to pass it off, to the Captains, as a bonus given in lieu of the large 'content' they get at the Spouts.

It is with great reluctance, that I have taken this line; but at the same time I have adopted it, under the absolute conviction, that it was the best, & most expedient course to pursue, at this time for your Lordship's interest. Without it, I am satisfied your Coals might have lain at the pits, the loss attending which, is more than equal to the reduction made. I am aware that Loraine & the Hettonians will raise the hue & cry against me on this occasion, particularly as our Vend last month so far exceeded our allowance; and I should not be surprised if your Lordship receives a communication from Mr Lambton, in the shape of remonstrance or complaint. I trust however that I shall be justified in your Lordship's estimation; as whatever may be your Lordship's inclination to act in concert with Mr Lambton, the plan which he has adopted of vending his Coals, render any thing like an alliance, or co-operation, almost impracticable. And the truth is, that we have to conduct our business, between the pressure of his necessities, on the one hand, and the desperate fortune of the Hetton Co. on the other.

Under these considerations I have thought it most politick at our late meetings, to assume a firm aspect, and not to *trim* or crouch, to any party; nor seem to dread the result of a free trade & fall of prices, as I am satisfied, in the end, that such a line of conduct, knowing the temper & *trims* of those we have to deal with, will be most beneficial. All these underhand tricks in my opinion ought to be boldly combated by a direct reduction of price, as the best & speediest means of bring[ing] them to a steady point. And this ought to be promptly done between now & 20th July. We have free scope at Rainton; if in the mean time we shew determination, ten to one but a *truce* may be made by then, much to our advantage. Loraine, I regret to observer trims & crouches far too much, to Arthur under existing circumstances – but this *entre nous*. I have thus stated freely to your Lordship my sentiments on the affairs of the C[oal] Trade of the Wear; but at the same time, beg to assure your Lordship that I do so with the utmost deference. It is my anxious desire, to act at all times strictly according to your Lordship's wishes, and directions, & in the absence of the latter to exercise my best judgment & discretion. The state of the trade & times is very difficult & critical, and with the best intentions we may err.

I hope we shall now get on again with our Vend – a brisk vend being the only mode of compensating for the reduction of price. Our fitters are exceedingly low & dispirited in consequence of the losses they have sustained & many of their best friends having gone past them. Hubbard delivered upwards of 900 Ch. into London by his own Ships last mo[nth] by which he has lost more than £200 and they have all lost less or more according to the quantities they have vended. As vend is now our object I don't see why we sh[oul]d confine ourselves to *our own* fitters if they are not able to carry off all our Coals. I therefore think, with your Lordship's approbation, of letting any of Lambton's old fitters have Coals, provided they can satisfy me as to the payment. I met with one of them (Tom Cropton) yesterday, and agreed with him to load his own Ships with Eden-main, at our current selling price, he *to pay for them at the end of the month in cash*, on being allowed discount – say 3d per Ch. This I think much better than giving credit, and having to pay the discount on the Bills at the Bank. Introducing a stranger or two in this way may also put our old fitters on the alert. Cropton has a good connexion at Wisbeach in Norfolk, which he has hitherto supplied with Lambton's Primrose, and is satisfied that they will like E[den]-main equally well – they have not yet had a taste of them.

Our pay Bills are unavoidably running high, the increase of Work, and the arrears from holding back, during Jan[uar]y, Feb[ruary], and March, so much, compels us to large payments now.

I have the Honor [&c.]
J^{no} Buddle

51.

D/Lo/C142/12 *Confidential*   Pensher Colliery 19th May 1826

My dear Lord

I have this day rec[eive]d your Lordship's very serious, and important Letter of the 17th Inst. and altho' I cannot but consider it

as being of a melancholy nature, yet I entirely approve of the conclusion your Lordship has drawn, and feel my mind greatly relieved by
the judicious view which your Lordship has taken of the state of your
affairs, as I think the plan you have suggested, is the most rational,
at least, if not the only one, which can place your Lordship in that
state of ease and comfort, which, from every consideration, of proper
feeling, you are so justly entitled to enjoy, after all the noble exertions, both public & private, which you have made, to attain what
every great and generous mind ought to aspire to – the establishing
of a noble family, on such a foundation as may ensure it's welfare
and consequence, down to the latest posterity. There is however a
limit to the exertions, for the attainment of this object, beyond which
prudence forbids us to go; and it ought to be borne in mind, that it
is the *productiveness* and not the extent of property, which is the most
conducive to this end. The Estates which have been purchased on
credit, have increased the extent of territory, without increasing the
revenue – but the contrary, as the Interest p[ai]d on the purchase
money exceeds the income derived from them. They are therefore
not only unproductive, but are a dead weight, and drain on the other
property. Land under the present, and probable future state of the
Country, cannot ever be expected to retrieve itself, out of *it's own
resources*, if mortgaged any way near to it's full value. This being
the case, with the most of your Lordship's late purchases, it follows,
that selling, to such an extent as may be necessary is, in every point
of view, the most advisable, as well as the most legitimate mode of
obtaining effectual relief.

This point being established, it is next to be considered, what part
of the property ought to be sold, and which ought to be retained
– bearing in mind the most judicious combination of present and
future benefit.

As to Storey's Property, we now have no material object, in
retaining it. It might therefore (the land I mean) be sold to pay off
Storey, Wooler, &c. as far as it w[oul]d go; but these people cannot
be expected to relinquish their security on the property, unless the
whole of their money is p[ai]d off. The easiest way of getting quit
of this w[oul]d be to prevail upon 'the Proprietory' to take it off our
hands at once, & let them arrange matters with the mortgagees.

I am not sufficiently acquainted with the locality & circumstances
of Redmarshal,[13] to form an adequate opinion, as to whether it, may

---

13 Near Wynyard, agricultural land.

be best to sell, or retain it, in preference to D. Lambton's Herrington property. The latter I consider to be a very improvable property, and even essential to the maintenance of the power & consequence of the family in the Coal-trade. With the Baronet's it forms an extensive, independent Freehold Coal Territory, with *free access* to the water – perfectly independent of D[ean] & Chapter, or any other person, or party, which may keep the family in the Coal Trade, without any bother, of Lease taking, for a Century to come. Indeed by the time Lord Seaham comes of age, I should consider it to be the most valuable Tract of *virgin* Coal, on the Wear. My present feeling is, therefore strongly in favor of keeping it in preference to Redmarshal. I have however written to Hawkes to meet me at Sunderland next Monday, to give me information as to Redmarshal, after which I shall be better able to give an opinion.

I hope Hawkes may be able to close with Gregson on satisfactory terms. I will give the subject of your Lordship's letter my best cons[ideratio]n & if anything occurs to me upon it, will write without reserve.

Nothing can exceed my anxiety to see your Lordship placed in comfortable & easy circumstances, & to enjoy life, as you are really fairly entitled to do, after such a large portion of it has been spent in such active and arduous service.

I have the honor [&c.]
My dear Lord
Your most devoted and
faithful Servant
J^{no} Buddle

I am happy to say that we have a *Swarm* of keels up this morn[in]g. The *Flotilla* has got into port, & in 2 or 3 days I hope to be able to give a good account of our Vend. Our Fitters are as much upon the qui vive as possible, and will not I daresay stick at trifles to secure their customers.

52.

D/Lo/C142/12   Pensher Colliery 31st May 1826

My Lord

I was yesterday called upon to witness one of those horrible scenes which too frequently occur in Coal-mining; – it did not, thank

God, happen in any of our own concerns – it was at the Twenty-main Coll[ier]y on the Tyne *above Bridge*. I was called professionally. The men were going to their Work at 3 o'clock A.M. The first of them must have nearly reached their working places in the interior of the Mine & the last five were descending the Shaft, when the pit exploded, & blew the latter out of the pit high in the air – they fell behind the *Pully-frame* still attached to the Rope, & what is extraordinary two of them were still alive. As soon as the machinery could be put in order again, the Viewer went down, & with difficulty extracted 4 individuals from amongst the Wreck at the bottom of the Shaft; but could not proceed further. These 4 men much hurt, one had a leg & one arm broken and another died in a few minutes – 2 or 3 mangled and mutilated Carcases were also found at the bottom of the Shaft. On arriving at the pit, I made every arrangement that the resources of the place w[oul]d allow of, to give a chance of saving life, altho' my hopes were slender. And I soon discovered, that all who were down, must inevitably have perished. At the end of 15 Hours from the time the accident happened, I was not able with the utmost exertion, to advance more than about 150 yds. from the bottom of the pit, and only recovered the dead bodies of two Boys. I then made all the arrangements for restoring the Ventilation, so as to enable the parties, interested, to make an effectual search for the dead Bodies, and returned here last night, considerably exhausted with the breathing of the bad air, & my head is still swimming.

The no. of lives lost on this occasion is not yet known but it is upwards of 30 probably near 40. The scene amongst the relatives of the Sufferers is most heart rending. It is not known how this accident happened, as there is not much inflammable air in this Colliery; but there is no doubt of it's having arisen from neglect. The system of ventilation practised was sufficient for it's object, if duly attended to. The two overmen are killed so that no information can be gained as to the immediate previous state of the pit. Hoping that we may long keep clear of anything of a similar nature.

The Marq[ues]s of Londonderry   I have the honor [&c.]
London   J[no] Buddle

53.

D/Lo/C142/12   Newcastle 10th June 1826

My Lord

I received your Lordship's Letter of the 7th Inst. and respecting Backhouse, do not know how to proceed, as I am quite satisfied that he will not grant any further accommodation. I have totally failed in *inducing* him to do so, and I dare not *menace* him, as by so doing I should most assuredly incur the risk of having our present engagement, for supplying, on the accept[an]ces, the Coll[ier[y pay money, broken. He knows too well that he has the whip-hand of us, and is neither to be led, nor driven out of his *own way*.

He has never disputed your Lordship's word, but their principle is, not to advance money except on negotiable Bills: and he is not to be driven from this. I cannot therefore get anything from him for Dawson. After what has passed between us I feel confident that he would not pay my cheque to Ryle[14] for any sum I might draw it for. This is the only way in which I could pay Ryle anything, and Backhouse would immediately know, that it was not for the Coll[ier]y pay. I am therefore entirely nonplussed, not having the command of a single pound. A good vend is our only hope.

We cannot sell Storey's Land, unless your Lordship could pay the difference between what it w[oul]d sell for & the amo[un]t of the mortgage – this would be about £2000 I should think; consequently we should lose Ground by the transaction. The only way in which we could have got quit of it on eligible terms w[oul]d have been for Russell to have taken the Land with the Coal & to have satisfied the Mortgagees. Gregson is not now in the humour for this, but may probably change his mind, when he comes to see that it is a favorable situation for building pitmen's &c. Houses on.

We held our adjourned meet[in]g here this m[ornin]g. Arthur was anxious to have something done to benefit the trade, but until the North[umberlan]d Election is over nothing can be done, as the Tyne people, are too much occupied with that affair to attend to any thing else. In the mean time, prices will still go lower on the Tyne, and I am not sure, that they will not drag the Wear down with them. Billy did not attend & Croudace came late, he says they are not getting on well with their Vend; but still thinks it maybe as well to let the trade take it's own course for a while longer, before any measures are taken to

---

14 Unidentified.

mend it. The general opinion is, that whenever another regulation may be attempted, the question of quantities should be submitted to disinterested persons, and that a sum of money sh[oul]d be deposited by each Coll[ier]y as security for the faithful performance of it's engagements.

I hear that the Election went off smooth at Durham,[15] yesterday, as it did here. Things are however very different in Northumberl[an]d. Lambton's attack on Beaumont has caused a great sensation, and a stormy meet[in]g is expected in consequence at Morpeth on Tuesday. The general opinion here is that Lambton's interference, will greatly injure Lord Howick's interest.[16]

I have the Honor [&c.]
J[no] Buddle

Vend up to last night

Walls-end	924 Ch.	
Eden-main	<u>2831</u>	3755
Small		<u>328</u>
		4093

54.

D/Lo/C142/13   *Private*   Pensher Colliery 10[th] Aug[us]t 1826

My Lord

I have this morning rec[eive]d your Lordship's secret dispatch; and am sorry to learn that your Lordship is still so pressed. I will

---

15 In the City of Durham Sir Henry Hardinge and Michael Angelo Taylor were returned unopposed. In Durham County also there was no contest, Lambton and the Hon. William Powlett being returned unopposed. *Hist. Parl. 1820–32*, ii, 353, 356, 362, 364–5.

16 In Northumberland there were personal animosities among the candidates and their backers. Lambton campaigned for his brother-in-law Lord Howick, son of Earl Grey, against another Whig candidate, the sitting MP T.W. Beaumont. The latter accused Lambton of making personal attacks and, at a meeting at Alnwick, of prompting the inexperienced Howick. Lambton challenged Beaumont to a duel, which took place on the sands at Bamburgh. Shots were exchanged, but neither party was hit. Both Howick and Beaumont were defeated. H.T. Liddell and Matthew Bell were elected. *Hist. Parl. 1820–32*, ii, 768–70; New, *Lord Durham*, pp. 87–91.

however do the best I can by endeavouring to get *Edw[ar]d* to remit the £1000 to Coutts's instead of sending it to Hawkes. I left him without having received a flat negative to my request to pay the £1000 on the 24th and my plan was to write an order for it against that time without going near, or tampering with him any more about it; so that I might not run the risk of a refusal from any caprice or misgiving of his mind. And this is the line which I still think it best to pursue, and I have little doubt of it's success against the 24th, but how to accomplish it sooner is the difficulty. I really don't know how to set about it, as I see great danger of losing my object by going to him sooner. He would find no difficulty in telling me that I wanted to be at the old game again; and that if he had given me a decided negative as to my application for the 24th I would not have troubled him *now*. He always reproaches me for want of proper feeling towards him, saying that the more accommodation he is disposed to grant, the more I press him, which is not *becoming* and *delicate*. I must therefore consider well what I am about before I approach him.

I have written to Hawkes on this affair in the way your Lordship wishes.

In other covers I have written to S[i]r Henry on the Pittington &c. affair.

The Surveyor of the Crown Lands applied to me the other day, to ask me in case the Comm[issio]n should decide on having an Inspection in the Forest of Dean if I w[oul]d undertake it. I said I should be glad to undertake it, provided I could have my own time for it. Altho' I have declined business of this sort generally, I should rather like to see a mining Country which is entirely new to me, if I could find a convenient opportunity of doing so. It is always adding to one's stock of professional experience. I should not bother myself with making any actual Survey, as that might be done by any competent practical person. I should merely take the Reporting, Estimates &c.¹⁷ Mr Arbuthnot¹⁸ & another of the Comm[issio]n are to be down at Newcastle shortly when the business will probably be decided,

17 Buddle was appointed to the position, and made annual visits to the Forest of Dean in the following years. See his Place Books in NEIMME, NRO 3410, Bud/60, 1–15.

18 Charles Arbuthnot, 1767–1850, diplomat, MP for Orford 1812–18, St Germans 1818–27, St Ives 1827–30, Allerton 1830–1, Commissioner for Woods, Forests and Land Revenues 1823–8, Chancellor of the Duchy of Lancaster 1828–30. *Hist. Parl. 1820–32*, iv, 71–85.

and if I find it a business that may be accomplished in ten days I should like to do it.

The Marq[ues]s of Londonderry	I have the honor [&c.]
Holderness House	J[no] Buddle

55.

D/Lo/C142/13   Pensher Coll[ier]y 6[th] Oct[ober] 1826

My Lord

We are making great progress in our great work, but at the same time I see clearly that it is impossible to bring it to a satisfactory conclusion, within any thing like the time which Robertson[19] had proposed to allow himself. I have therefore prevailed with him to stay with me over Sunday – indeed to stay 'till we can entirely complete our discussions in all their ramifications. We are now (having nearly about finished the harbour) discussing the affair of the Town. He seems to have discovered that he has, in the first instance been too liberal in his ideas of the Gro[un]d rent, and now proposes the following modification.

Instead of commencing the payment of the *full* Ground Rent of £100 per ann[um] on 100 acres – minus the quantity to be occupied by the Streets &c. at the end of two years, he now proposes to take the 100 acres including all Ground to the very margin of the Cliffs, only reserving the necessary approaches i.e. the Gro[un]d requisite for the rail-ways &c. to, & from the Harbour, but *not reserving the Gro[un]d to be occupied* by the Streets. The ground rent to be paid as follows viz

At the end of the 2[nd] year of the Term,

That is for the 3[rd] year to pay	£2000
For the 4[th] ditto	4000
Ditto 5[th] ditto	6000
Ditto 6[th] ditto	8000
Ditto 7[th] ditto & every succeeding year of the term	10000

---

19 Alexander Robertson. By an agreement dated 6 October 1826 Robertson was to build the harbour at Seaham, lay a railway to it, and load and ship coals at a certain price per chaldron, and also to build the town. He professed confidence that he could raise £80,000 to start the work. D/Lo/C595.

The Grass Rent i.e. the farming Rent of the Land to be paid for the whole 100 acres during the first 2 years, and then until the 7th year, on all the Land (that part of it) which shall not be built upon, when the full rent of £10000 per ann[um] shall become payable.

This is the modification of the Ground rent which I have to submit to your Lordship, and if your Lordship approves of it we shall agree. This certainly is *too good* a thing to be missed, and I cannot help acknowledging that it quite staggers me. I find Robertson sagacious, rational, and intelligent, on every subject, but on his ideas of the value of the building ground I must confess that I doubt his *sanity*. On this point he appears to me quite extravagant in his notions, and it is the only part of his plan, which at all shakes my confidence in him. I therefore wish to keep the Harbour & Town as much separate from each other as circumstances will permit, for this plain reason. I consider the harbour to be a feasible undertaking – the Town (according to his notions of it) quite the contrary. And as it is more than probable that some, at least, of his monied men may see the matter in the same light as I do, I am anxious to put matters on such a footing, that if possible, we may get the Harbour *at least*; and by no means to run the risk of *swamping* it, by entangling it with the Town. Let us have both in God's name if we can get them, but don't let us lose the substance, for the Shadow.

I am too much hurried to express my ideas more fully or correctly at present, on this important subject, but I am sure your Lordship will quite comprehend my meaning. Your Lordship will oblige me by a reply, by the messenger, if convenient, or by Post tomorrow, to Newcastle. I presume this will reach your Lordship before my former Dispatch of this morning.

The Marq[ues]s of Londonderry   I have the honor [&c.]
Wynyard   Jno Buddle

I am in *search* of the Timber.

56.

D/Lo/C142/13   Walls-end 15th Oct[ober] 1826

My Lord

By some means or other for which I cannot account your Lordship's Letter of the 12th Inst. did not reach me 'till late last Night. In the first place I exceedingly regret, that from arrangements made out of an entirely different view of my next Week's work, to what I had originally set out; it will not be in my power, to have the honor of dining with your Lordship tomorrow. I must be obliged to yield to circumstances, and defer my journey to Wynyard 'till Wed[nesday] with S[i]r Henry as stated in my Letter of yesterday.

By Gregson's letter it seems we are committed with Hildyard[20] for the increased Interest next payment. It is certainly no great matter, but yet it is something, & every *feather* in this way adds to the general Load.

The answering of your Lordship's enquiry respecting Robertson puzzles me much. I really don't know what to think, or say, of him, further than that he is, decidedly a man of talent and *practical experience* in the erection as well as in the planning of great Works. I saw enough of him during our late discussions of the Harbour &c. to satisfy me, that his *Scull* is furnished with the organs of arrangement, and combination for all matters of that nature. We have however known many people of this stamp fail, in their undertakings, from causes over which they could have no control, and I am willing to hope that this will turn out to have been the case with him. We have heard of his having been broken down in circumstances, it is true; but not the most distant hint as to any *crack or flaw* in his Character, which is a great point.

Robertson the Historian[21] was his Grandfather. His father was a Scotchman & he had, or has a Brother bro[ugh]t up to the same profession as himself – a Builder. This is all I know of his history at present, but as he is well known to Renny,[22] Telford,[23] Banks &c. we shall e'er long learn more of him.

It is probable that he may be employed as a sort of *Jackall* to some *Coterie* of monied men, to hunt out *prey* for them; but it is not to be expected that they will, at once pounce upon his scent, & seize open mouthed, without first *harking back* a little. I therefore reckon on his *project* being subjected to the cool deliberation of some eminent *Chamber Council* in the Engineering Line, before we hear from him

20 Rev. Henry Hildyard, 1772–1832, from whom Lord Londonderry had bought the manor of Seaham. He was a director of the Clarence Railway, lived at Stokesley and did not hold a benefice. J.A. Venn, *Alumni Cantabrigenses*, pt 2, vol. 3 (Cambridge, 1947), p. 365.

21 William Robertson, 1721–93, Principal of Edinburgh University, author of *History of Scotland during the Reigns of Queen Mary and James VI. ODNB*.

22 Sir John Rennie, 1794–1874, civil engineer. *ODNB*.

23 Thomas Telford, 1757–1834, civil engineer. *ODNB*.

again. And unless he can make his Ground sure under some such tribunal I have little hopes of his bringing up his men to the *scratch*.

The Harbour project is feasible, but that of the Town, I mean the enormous ground Rent which he offers, staggers me, & I'm afraid may produce a staggering effect on his monied friends – on this branch of the subject I think him quite wild. The harbour however is our object, and if we can but secure *this Bird*, even if the other escapes, we ought to be satisfied for the present at least.

I have very much to say on all these matters when I have the honor to see your Lordship. I have thought it best to send this in a packet, with Robertson's agree[men]t, a copy of which I have kept, and the monthly return & last Pay Bills. Pray don't be alarmed at the retrograding of the Bal[an]ce in the last return – the 1st Oct[ober] Receipt will appear in the next & will make it up.

I have the honor [&c.]
J[no] Buddle

I hope to give your Lordship a satisfactory account of the Timber on Wednesday.

57.

D/Lo/C142/13   Walls-end 25th Dec[ember]. 1826

My Lord

I last Night received your Lordship's packet, covering your Letters official & private, on the subject of the Coal trade meeting – Regulation.

I am really sorry to find that I have committed an indiscretion, in stating at the Newcastle meeting, that your Lordship was favorable to regulation, on the principle of an arbitration of claims, for quantity on the basis, between the Committee & individuals. In doing this, I assure your Lordship, that I acted under the entire conviction, that I was representing your Lordship's wishes and sentiments on the subject. I trust your Lordship will not consider me guilty of *blabbing* table talk, after Dinner, in this instance, when I call to your Lordship's recollection, that you have in all our late conversations on the general state of the Coal-trade, expressed your sentiments uniformly to the above effect.

The extent to which I committed myself at the Newcastle meeting was, that your Lordship was favorable to Regulation founded on the principle of a reference, in case of a difference of opinion as to the claims for quantity between Individuals and the Committee. This is the extent to which I am committed, and your Lordship will please to consider, that the copy of the resolutions which I sent, are the resolutions of the *Tyne* – the Wear being no further committed by them than as to the proportion of the 3/5ths & 2/5ths and this is for the reconsideration of the Wear meeting tomorrow.

The Newcastle meeting was in fact nothing more than the preparatory meeting to ascertain whether the trade of both Rivers was disposed to regulate, or not. But all the details of the rules &c. of the Regulation for each River, have to be gone into at the private meeting of the Committees of each River. The only thing, that the general meet[in]g could do, was to fix the proportions between the Rivers: but this has nothing to do with the distribution of the basis on each River – this distribution will be the business of the respective Committees. And it by no means follows that any one is to stand on the same basis as in 1825. This could not be the case, on either River – particularly on the Wear, where new Coll[ierie]s are coming in & old ones going out. Lambton's Fatfield 24,000 Ch. on the basis has gone out, in consequence of Lamb's failure & his Leefield, J. Humble 12,000 on the Basis, will also be out before April, so that 36,000 will be to add to others.

Now as to the proportions between the two Rivers I am of opinion that the Tyne will gain on the Wear this year. From the Co[mittee] House acc[oun]ts it is said the Tyne Vend this year will be 800,000 Ch. which will require the Wear to be 533,000 to be up to it's proportion of 2/5ths which in my opinion it will not be. I therefore anticipate, that a comparison of the quantities vended by each River, will be *against* the claim of the Wear for it's 2/5ths – this fact will however be ascertained at the Committee at Sund[erlan]d on the 20th Jan[uar]y.

I shall now advert to some remarks in your Lordship's private letter.

The conferences after *Dinner* are disposed of already in a former part of this Letter.

As to the additional profit this year of £7000 to £8,000 – this is merely a cash bal[anc]e the real increase or decrease in profit can only be known, by a Balance of the Books – shewing whether we have increased, or decreased our stock in Trade & Book Debts. I however hope, that the bona fides profit is more than last year, but I attribute it entirely to the working of Pensher Colliery, which has both increased the quantity and work, cheaper than Rainton. I am *sure* that no increase of vend which we have obtained from Rainton in consequence of the Regulation having been broken up, has at all compensated for the reduction of 4/- on W[alls]end and of 1/- on Eden. The reduction of the 4/- alone, will next year am[oun]t to £7000, or £8000. That is for the *same expence* of working, our profit will be less by that sum than it w[oul]d be if the Coals were sold at their former price. And the 1/-on Eden-main in the same way, will amo[un]t to £6000, so that if under regulation we could obtain only the same Vend, we shall get this year; our Expences w[oul]d if anything be diminished, while our Receipts w[oul]d be increased £13000 to £14000.

Your Lordship says it is evidently the distress of the Trade on the Tyne that forces regulation. I really do not know that the present attempt to effect a Regulat[io]n has originated with the Tyne. I think it has originated with Mowbray, who has for long been using all his endeavours to bring it about. He has written a series of papers on the subject & sent copies to both Ship & Coal-owners. Your Lordship saw his first essay on the subject written on the 13th May last & you approved generally of it. The idea that the Hetton Co. w[oul]d regulate *at all*, has had great influence in bringing the Tyne into the measure & your Lordship's communication to Mr W. Brandling[24] on the same subject, has also had it's effect.

My own opinion is, that Regulation is equally necessary to the Wear, as the Tyne, as I feel confident, that with Bewickes Walls-end *free on B[oar]d* at 26/. the Walls-end on the Wear cannot fetch 34/-. And that with Northumberland, Killingworth &c. at 21/- or 22/- that Eden-main, Primrose & Lyon's cannot obtain 28/6. If things continue in this state on the Tyne Prices will inevitably be pulled down on the Wear. On this point we ought not to deceive ourselves; in the contemplation of such an event, every one ought to consider his own position. In our own, it is evident that a general reduction – I mean a further reduction of about 3/6 per Ch. would entirely deprive us of profit, let the extent of vend be what it might. A further reduction would incur a *Loss* then the more Vend the greater the Loss. This is my serious and unbiased opinion.

I shall now remark on my own feelings about the trade, in which your Lordship thinks I have difficult cards to play. I can with truth assure your Lordship, that the greatest anxiety which I feel, is in the earnest wish to play your Lordship's cards well. Our stake is so great, that I consider it almost, a sort of Life & Death affair. For if

24 Footnote in original: At a personal interview in London I believe.

once such an enormous establishment takes a retrograde movement, or even *halts*, we need not ask 'what will be the consequences'. Could we act independently of the trade, and sell our Coals at a superior price & in larger quantities than others, it w[oul]d be ridiculous to think of regulation & I should never think of advising your Lordship to enter into anything of the kind, if you could make more money by keeping out of it. But I am at this moment of a contrary opinion, as I do not think, with or without Fitters, that we could sell our Coals at a penny a Chald[ron] more price than either Hetton, or Lambton – that is Coals of like quality, as it is plain that our Coals have no preference in London. We could therefore only force a large vend by underselling them, and can we afford to do so? We must recollect that we are now saddled with 1/- Dean & Chapter's rent on Rainton Coals.

With respect to the utility of Fitters, with or without regulation, I don't see that I can add anything to what I have said on the subject on former occasions. It has already been proved that they cannot vend the Coals when undersold by others. Neither could we do so, under similar circumstances. I shall only intreat of your Lordship to understand most distinctly, that although I do feel it to be my duty, to state my opinions freely, and without reserve on all points which I consider to be of great importance to your Lordship's interest; and although those opinions may occasionally not accord with your Lordship's sentiments, yet I do also feel it to be my duty, not to support my own opinions pertinaciously but to obey your decisions, and to carry your Lordship's wishes and orders into effect, to the best of my ability.

As regards the business of the meeting tomorrow, I feel that I stand committed on the point of reference, on which it seems I have misunderstood your Lordship: but at the same time if better cannot be done, however uncomfortable the circumstance, I must state it to the meeting – lay your Lordship's official Letter before the meeting, and state that I have no discretionary power.

In the first place however I will push *Billy* home upon the extent of his powers; and if they do not go to the full recognition of the plan of reference, I shall at once be relieved from my difficulties, and then we shall all be fairly at Sea again. For the sake of my own feelings this is the result which I must evidently wish for. And let matters turn as they may, I shall take care not to risk placing myself in such a position again.

I think your Lordship has omitted to send a sheet of your private Letter, as it ends at the end of the 4[th] page, with the word – If I was.

Then follows a note at he bottom of the page to say that S[i]r H. Browne has just returned.

The only *bit* of comfort which I feel this good Christmas day in the morn[in]g is that he has succeeded in his object, which will I trust be the means of placing your Lordship in a situation to meet all pressing Engagements: for it is but too clear that the Collieries will not be able for some months to do more than maintain themselves, and it is even questionable whether for Jan[uar]y & Feb[ruary] they may be able to do that.

I will see Donkin in the morning on my way to Sunderland, on Banks's affair – I do not like the tenor of Chisholm's letter at all.

No Letter from Robertson this morn[in]g but as we have two deliveries of letters a day, it is possible I may receive one in the Ev[enin]g in which case I will send to Wyn[yar]d a Messenger from Sunderland *after* the meeting. I then go to Pensher, where I have asked Stobart to take a Bed to be ready for our ride to Sherburn next morning.

The Marq[ues]s of Londonderry   I have the honor [&c.]
Wynyard Park   J^no Buddle

58.

D/Lo/C142/14   Sunderland 24th J[a]n[uar]y 1827

My Lord

I have had a full day's work with Robertson, to day and have barely time left to save post. His Harbour project seems to have assumed an entirely different character, from his first design. *He* is, it seems, to be the *sole proprietor*, now to take the contract-deed with your Lordship in security, for the payment of 5 per cent, on their advances, and the redemption of the capital, to be paid out of the earning of the rail-way, and harbour. He to be allowed a reasonable ann[ua]l Sum for his maintenance, until the capital is redeemed. The plan is feasible, no doubt, and if he has managed to satisfy the people who have come forward to support him, it is not for us to throw difficulties in his way.[1]

He estimates the whole Cost of the Harbour & rail-way, with all the establishment of Engines & Machinery &c. at £165,000, and *he says* that he has got persons to advance from £85,000 to £90,000 in Money, and materials (only about £25,000 in cash) leaving a deficiency of £65,000 of *Cash*.

This he *fully expects* to obtain from Bradyll, but if he does not succeed with him (of which however, he has not the least doubt) he is *sure of obtaining* it elsewhere. He has gone to Durham this Evening to meet Bradyll's Solicitor, to accompany him to Ulviston, to see Bradyll, and if he succeeds in his object, the business will be completed, and he is to write me direct; so that I may lose no time in treating for the way-leaves, of the new Line. He has already informed your Lordship of his having made an Ally of Bradyll, and giving the *coup de grace* to the Hawthorn-hive scheme.

Of the £200,000 trust money which Bradyll has the command of for the opening of his Collieries &c. if he succeeds to expectations with Bradyll, he *promises*, in one month from this time to commence, with from 300 to 400 men. This all looks like being in earnest certainly, but at the same time I shall not place implicit confidence in him until I see a little further. He is quite *mum* on the subject of the Town. I therefore

---

1   A further agreement with Robertson, on the terms outlined above, was signed on 30 March 1827. D/Lo/C595.

conclude that he does not see his way in it. It is of the less importance however now, the Harbour is everything to us; and if we only get this, the Town will follow as a matter of course. He fully calculates on being in London, next Sat[ur]d[a]y week, the 3rd Feb[ruary] and to see your Lordship there. I have talked to him on obtaining a Loan of £30,000 to £40,000 on the Irish Estates – also a Loan of £20,000 to £25,000 on Pittington. The former he thinks he cannot accomplish; but the latter he thinks he can, and he will explain his views on these points to your Lordship when he comes to Town. I shall do what I can to keep *Blab* [Gregson] quiet about his Indemnity.

The Mortgage on Pensher requires a different sort of valuation to be made for Chisholm. The estate must be included with the Coal. I am going into it tomorrow, but have not now time to explain.

There is mischief in the *Hive* at Hetton, but I no [sic] nothing further at present for *certain*, than that I. Dunn is for being out, if possible.

A heavy fall of snow has stopped our pits, and loading today – only 4 keels *in all* up – alas!

The Marq[ues]s of Londonderry   I have the Honor [&c.]
London   J^{no} Buddle

59.

D/Lo/C142/14   Pensher Colliery 21st Feb[ruary] 1827

My Lord

I cannot be [sic] feel that Robertson's Letter of the 7th Inst. is satisfactory. I think with S[i]r Henry Browne that the poor creature is doing his best, and considering, that he has *Trustees*, and 'yellow Breeches', with all the cast of Lawyers which 'sails in their Wake' – we need not wonder at his encountering, *delays*. Giving the poor animal, therefore, credit for doing *its* best, it would be cruel to whip & spur it, beyond it's power. This consideration has prevented my writing to him again, as I feel that it will be infinitely better, to wait, with patience, 'till he can get his foundation stone *firmly laid*, than by pushing him on, to a premature commencement, thereby risk some hitch, or difficulty, which might retard the work in its progress, or eventually stop it altogether.

I feel intense interest & anxiety in this affair, as I am of opinion that, it (the Harbour) is the only thing we can look to, to enable us to keep at the head of the trade of the Wear, for any length of time to come. I am therefore most desirous to see it's speedy & successful commencement, – but at the same time I have made up my mind to wait patiently until all is fully prepared for an effectual commencement. The Harbour once in operation – frosts, Snows, and Floods need have no terrors for us.

Your Lordship observes, we have 'plenty of frost & Snow now'. We have a super-abundance, as we are completely blocked up, and are all as dead, as ditch-water, – neither Keel, nor Waggon stirring. We have however this consolation, that it is preparing the way for future good. It is now beginning to thaw, and if it continues, the flood will soon carry the Ice out of the River, and we may even yet get our vend for the month up.

Tommy Fenwick promised me to be here tomorrow, to look at Rainton affairs, and to talk over the Sherburn Hospital business.[2]

Poor Croudace I am sorry to say is reported to be in a very dangerous state – the Imposthume has gathered again in his ear, and threatens to affect his brain. His loss to Mr Lambton would be great, but to his large family it would be quite irretrievable.[3]

As a publick loss, that of Lord Liverpool's services, at this juncture, is most unfortunate – the Corn Bill – free trade, the Catholick question & the war, with other important business, all before Govern[men]t make a change of Administration, particularly unfortunate at such a crisis.[4] I have a great horror of a Whig administration and should be sorry to see that party prevail. A messenger has this instant arrived from Ravensworth with dispatches – to be forwarded. I therefore send my dispatches forward with them.

I regret that the C[ommitte]e meeting is put off tomorrow as it prevents me the pleasure of seeing your Lordship so soon as I expected, but I can come to Wyn[yar]d the day after our Receipt – Friday, or on the Sund[a]y morning as may be most convenient to your Lordship.

The Marq[ues]s of Londonderry   I have the Honor [&c.]

                                         J^{no} Budddle

---

2   Buddle was investigating the possibility of leasing the coal of Sherburn from the Bishop of Durham. The project did not come off.

3   Croudace died shortly after this date.

4   Lord Liverpool suffered a stroke in February 1827 and resigned office. He was succeeded by an administration under George Canning, who also took the office of Chancellor of the Exchequer.

60.

D/Lo/C142/14   Pensher Colliery 11th Ap[ril] 1827

My Lord

I have had a full day's work to day in examining the Country from N. Pittington to Seaham, for the purpose of setting out a Line of rail-way to the harbour. I have marked out two Lines – one of the N. side of Hetton-le-Hole, the other on the S. side of it. The latter is the most eligible, both as to distance & level, but it throws us through a greater number of different properties than the former. Whether it may be the line which we shall adopt must therefore depend upon the terms we can make for way-leave.

The Line past the N. side of Hetton-le-Hole, passes through Lyon & Marshall's property *only*, into Gregson's and so on immediately to our original Line. That on the S. side of the Village, passes through property belonging to the following parties viz. Robertson, Lyon, S[i]r Jas. Musgrave, Lyon again, Pemberton, Fox, Sheppardson, & Ranson, into Gregson and then into Seaham. By the Line on the N. side of the Village we should avoid Hutton, Ironside & Hutchinson £571 a year together, to enable us to pay Lyon and Marshall. By the Line on the S. side of the Village we should evade Brough & Carr, as well as the above named parties £701 in all, to meet, or at least to go in relief of the demands of Robinson, Lyon, Musgrave, Pemberton, Fox, Sheppardson and Ranson. Robinson & Ranson might be avoided, but the Line would be more complete by passing through them.

I have marked out those Lines and Longstaff[5] will commence the actual survey without delay. Until the Survey is finished and the plan made, I cannot enter into negotiation, very well, with the parties for the Way-leaves, but I can apprise them of my probable intention of having to do so shortly.

On looking over the country from the Eppleton heights, and referring to the Map of the County, I cannot help thinking that our harbour, will at no distant period, become the Shipping place for all the lead from Weardale – the Rail-way may be easily extended, by Durham into that District. By referring to the Map of the Co[unty] your Lordship will see that it is a much shorter Line, than the Darlington Way from the heart of the County, and that it would certainly *take the Shine out* of that Concern.

If Robertson performs his promise of coming to Seaham next

---

5   William Longstaff, viewer at Pittington.

Wed[nesday] I will do all that lies in my power to expedite *his commencement*, as of all things I sh[oul]d like the actual commencement, to preceed the *report* of it. There is not yet a whisper of it, but our going over the Line of way, will naturally draw the attention of the publick to the subject.

At N. Pittington every thing is going on very well – the waggonway is now laid as far as the Village of Pittington from the Alexandrina branch and I think there is no doubt of the whole line being completed by the middle of June.

By the middle of May, I sh[oul]d hope that Robertson will be *blasting* the Rocks, and that our Line of Way will be decided on; and I should be glad indeed if your Lordship could contrive to run down, if it was but for 2 or 3 days, to see how we are going on – it would give effect and spirit to all operations.

The Harbour fills my head with so many new notions & speculations – it's advantages to the property will be so vast, that I really dare scarcely yet venture to yield to the entire conviction of its *reality*.

I have the honor [&c.]
J^no Buddle

61.

D/Lo/C142/14   Pensher Colliery 15th May 1827

My Lord

In consequence of the miserable state of the London Market the Committees durst not venture to issue a larger quantity for the last fortnight of the present month 35 per Thous[an]d than was issued for the first fortnight – making 70 per thousand in all being the same as was issued last month.

The Ship-owners are making terrible lamentations – an official Letter was received by the meeting of the Committees this morning from the Ship-owners of Shields; imploring them to give out a short vend, in order to get the prices up in London, or they will be compelled to lay up their ships.

The Committees have, in compliance with the wishes of many individuals convened a general meeting of the Trade at Newcastle, next Sat[urda]y for the purpose of drawing up a memorial to the Treasury praying to have the duties on Coals exported to foreign parts, reduced to the same scale as the Coast Duties, that is to say, the duty on round Coals to be reduced from 17/- to 12/- and the small from 4/6 to 2/- per Ch. This it is expected would give great relief to the trade. I have no idea however that the *new* Chancellor of the Exchequer[6] will do anything for us.

The trade is in a most deplorable state, limited as our quantity is this month, we shall have difficulty in getting it vended – particularly the Walls-end – we have been actually leaving them on the staith both yesterday and today from the want of ships. The bad market of last Wed[nesday] and Friday has so frightened the Ship-owners that they are afraid to load on their own account, and are hanging off for freights. We have therefore only the Fitters' *own ships* to depend on. Loraine says he only sent 3000 Ch. to London last month, his Vend was made up by his Coasting Coals. This is all very bad and embarrassing – to find difficulty in vending the limited quantity slowed by a Regulation, at this time of the year is what I never before knew.

No intelligence whatever respecting Robertson's movements!!!

I shall go to Wynyard tomorrow Evening to be ready for meeting the Assignees next morning at Stockton.

I have the honor [&c.]
J^{no} Buddle

62.

D/Lo/C142/14   Pensher Colliery 13th June 1827

My Lord

The pacific result of your conference, and our prospect of coasting vend here brightening a little, has relieved my mind greatly, and has place me in a state of more comfortable feeling than I have for long experienced. Although there has been a great scarcity of Ships in Sunderland, for a Week past, owing to contrary Winds, yet the License granted by the Comm[itt]ee for allowing Vessels, not exceeding 10 Keels, to load freely for the Coast, has enabled our Fitters up to last night to push off 3656 Ch. of Eden-main, and 1056 of Walls-end – 4712 Ch. in all, exclusive of 504 of Small. This is very well considering the want of Ships, but as the first favorable change of Wind, is expected to bring a fleet of Lynn men, I hope we shall make a good month's work coastwise. One of our great buyers (Bigg) of Lynn, is reported to be dead, but I expect that Hubbard, Scurfield,

---

6   Canning.

& Co. will look sharp, and keep his *connexion* attached to our Eden-main.

The *Quaker* [Backhouse] is quite impracticable. I inclose the answer he has given to my application for Hildyard's Int[eres]t which is all he will say upon it. It is quite impossible either to lead, or drive, these preventive leather backs, out of their own track. Their plan seems to be, only to assist a man when he does not require their liberality, but to be sure to hold back, when he really requires their assistance. I trust however that your Lordship will be enabled, by receiving the Irish money to satisfy Hildyard, which seems now to be the most pressing demand.

I am amused with Mr Lambton's *news*. He has no doubt received his information through the same *authentic channel* by which he received *such accurate information* of my being a partner in the N. Hetton Colliery. This however is great news to me, as I have not before heard a syllable of it. All that I have heard respecting myself, of late is, that I was going to Hetton. Then it seems that our *friends* & neighbours know very much better than ourselves, what we are *going* to do. It is said here that Mr Lambton is not coming down to the North before he returns to the Continent.[7]

Old Banks giving up the taking of Stones is a nuisance, and I wish we could get another Customer. If Wyatt was to be depended on, in anything like ordinary business, I think he might find us out a Market for the same sort of article as Banks took.

I have not heard anything more from Robertson, altho' he promised to write me from Ulviston last Sat[urda]y when he got his £3000. He also assured me, he would be in London yesterday, and that he would call on Sir Henry this day.

The Marq[ues]s of Londonderry   I have the Honor [&c.]
London   J^no Buddle

63.

D/Lo/C142/15   Newcastle 11th Sep[tember] 1827

My Lord
    I am glad to learn by your Lordship's Letter of yesterday that the Duke has made his final arrangements for being at Wyn[yar]d

---

7   Lambton had spent the winter of 1826–7 in Italy for the sake of his health: New, *Lord Durham*, pp. 31–2.

on the 24th.[8] Nothing that we can accomplish shall be wanting to give him the sort of reception which your Lordship would wish. We shall be able to muster a little Troop of Horse, from the Collieries to join the Tenantry, to greet him on entering the County. I will be at Wynyard on Sa[turday] the 22nd without fail, to have every thing finally arranged with your Lordship. If the band's coming on Sunday will answer instead of Sat[urda]y it will save expence.

The waggon &c. will all be ready – will Ships' Colours do? Silk ones will be very expensive.

Scarcely a yard of Ribbon of any kind is to be had here – the Lilac & Yellow can only be had from London, and it will require a Week to obtain it after the order is sent, and all that is ordered *must be taken*, as the Shops don't keep any stock of the article. It would therefore probably be best for your Lordship to order the required quantity direct from London, being the readiest way of getting the article.

In case however you should decide to have it from hence, I send patterns of the colours for my Lady to choose. The pattern of the Colours approved may be returned, specifying the breadth of the ribbon and No. of yards required, and I will see that the order is sent off – only I am sadly afraid of bother, or disappointment happening. The price I understand will be from 9d to 1/- per yard depending on the breadth, and whether the ribbon is silk, or satin – the silk being about 1d per yard cheaper than the satin. I find *one yard* of each sort of ribbon on Bell's Election cockades i.e. 2 yards in each – this may probably be some guide for estimating the quantity of Ribbon required – they seem to be quite large enough for the tenants at least.

This place is quite on wheels to day in consequence of your Lordship's dispatch to the Mayor last night. His worship set off with four horses (an unusual thing) this morning to call upon your Lordship. They talk of erecting a Triumphal Arch, on the Bridge against the Duke comes. There is a great cry for *Cuddy*[9] at Sunderland I hear, to

---

8　The Duke of Wellington visited North East England in September–October 1827. In Co. Durham he stayed at Wynyard Park and among other places visited Penshaw, where Buddle provided a cold collation. See Alan Heesom, 'The Duke of Wellington's Visit to the North-East of England, September–October 1827', *Durham County Local History Society Bulletin*, no. 60 (Nov. 1999), pp. 3–35. Accounts in Richardson, *Local Historian's Table Book*, iii, 358–63; John Sykes, *Local Records, or Historical Register of Remarkable Events*, 2nd edn (Newcastle upon Tyne, 1866), ii, 209–12.

9　Sir Cuthbert Sharp.

assist in the arrangements of the King and Constitution Club – they must bring him from Harrogate.

The issue on our new basis this Mo[nth] will give us decent bundle of acceptances on the 1st October – this will put me in *pluck* for receiving our great Visitor.

I am really sorry for poor Billy, he is quite chapfallen – the vend allowed them by the new award – deducting their *overs* cannot possibly raise money to make their pay. What am I to do, says poor Billy? I hear that Lord Grey, and Mr Ellison[10] are the Trustees for Lambton's affairs, and that Stephenson[11] acts under them

The Marq[ues]s of Londonderry   I have the honor [&c.]
Wynyard Park   J^{no} Buddle

---

10 Cuthbert Ellison, 1783–1860, MP for Newcastle 1812–30. *Hist. Parl. 1820–32*, v, 46–7.
11 George Stephenson, Sunderland solicitor.

64.

D/Lo/C142/16   Sunderland 7th Jan[uar]y 1828

My Lord

   We have had a long and rather stormy meeting here, to day, and have separated without coming to any definite result. The difficulty is, in a great degree, if not wholly with the inferior Coll[ierie]s – Stobart excepted, who agrees to take the quantity allotted to him by the last award. I have not moved from the ground which your Lordship pointed out to me & have therefore been little more than a spectator in the fray; but towards the close of the business, I perceived an inclination on the part of the most exorbitant claimants Wade & Davison's Agent, to make concessions, and the meeting is adjourned to 10 o'clock on Frid[a]y morning, when after due reflection, I think the refractory parties will come to reason. Hill[1] I perceive, has now the entire direction of Lambton's Coll[ier]y affairs, and seems, as Cochrane does, very much inclined to meet your Lordship's wishes, as far as circumstances will permit. The meeting at Newcastle, on Friday, will I think, bring the affair of the Regulation nearly about to a close, and enable us to judge, whether we shall have peace, or War. In the event of the latter, an immediate reduction of prices, will take place, and your Lordship, will please to consider whether, it will be most prudent to take the lead on this, or to follow the current, and instruct me accordingly. At present there are few Ships in the Harbour, and scarcely any demand for Coals, so that pushing the vend, is impracticable.

   I called on *Edw[ar]d* [Backhouse] to sound him as to the payment of the D[ean] & C[hapter[Install[men]t on the 20th Inst. But he won't do it, unless he gets the Lease; but he seems inclined to stand to his former offer of advancing £10,000 upon it. It is uncertain however how long he may continue in this – Sanders[2] is *cleared out* & retires to the Country to live with his father. Edw[ar]d was his surety & may probably have had to help him, to make his pays, which may have soured his temper a little.

   There is a good deal of talk here about the representation of

1   George Hill, Lambton's colliery manager.
2   Unidentified.

the County;[3] Capt. Cochrane says that Sir H. Williamson, is fully expected to *stand*; and that Gen. Aylmer, Sir Rob[er]t Eden,[4] Mr Davison of Beamish,[5] and Mr R.E.D. Shafto,[6] are getting up a requisition for a Co[unty] meeting, to consider of a proper person to represent the County. Morriss tells me, that Tennyson[7] & Gregson were to leave Brancepeth for London, yesterday, or to day, and that they don't expect any opposition. Gibbon,[8] Sir H. Williamson's Agent here, is giving it out, I am informed, that Sir H. will stand, & that he is immediately expected in the Country. This is all I hear about electioneering.

I have not yet received a Letter from your Lordship, since you left Wyn[yar]d but I hope you have arrived safe at Belvoir and that my communications reach y[ou]r Lordship. I have received your Lordship's check for £500 from Sir H. B[rowne] last Sa[turday] morning and sent it, by that day's post to Hen[r]y Donkin. I think of calling upon Sir Henry, at Gosforth, in the morning if nothing occurs to prevent me. I got your Lordship's last pro[missory] Note from Ed[war]d (the £5000 note I mean) to day, and now return it. He does not now hold any sort of Bill, or a Note whatever of your Lordship's, which is a great comfort

The Marq[ues]s of Londonderry   I have the Honor [&c.]
Belvoir Castle   J[no] Buddle

65.

D/Lo/C142/164   Walls-end 20[th] Feb[ruar]y 1828

My Lord
I have this morning received your Lordship's Dispatches of the 18[th] Inst. In reply to your Lordship's remarks on the 'cash Bal[anc]e

---

3   Lambton was raised to the peerage on 28 January 1828 as Baron Durham (Earl of Durham 1833). In consequence a by-election for the County seat became necessary. In the end William Russell was returned unopposed. *Hist. Parl. 1820–32*, ii, 357–8.
4   Sir Robert Eden Bt, 1774–1844, Windlestone Hall.
5   John Davison, Beamish Hall.
6   Robert Duncombe Shafto, Whitworth Park.
7   Charles Tennyson, 1784–1861, uncle of William Russell, MP for Grimsby 1818–26, Bletchingley 1826–31, Stamford 1831–2, Lambeth 1832–52, *Hist. Parl. 1820–32*, vii, 402–18.
8   Thomas Gibbon.

Sheet' for last year, I have to observe 1st with respect to the payments on account of the estates, that this will depend upon the extent of the Work your Lordship intends to do at the Building, park Wall &c. &c. The Supplies at present ordered are £375 per mon[th] or £4500, which with hay & Corn, Sheep cattle &c. may be stated at £5000, If Timber & other materials are req[uire]d or Stone loads sh[oul]d be wanted, the Cost will be so much the more. And at any rate we have Fletcher[9] & the Stockton Tradesmen to pay in Coals or cash, over & above the £5000, so that it w[oul]d not perhaps be prudent, to reckon on less, than £6000 for the supplies of Wynyard & the estates this year.

2nd I cannot just now state what amount will be required by N. Pittington Winning, but the winn[in]g charge will cease in July. I will estimate the expenditure between this, and that time, in a few days.

3. About £800 now remains to be paid to Davison – the last Instalment, will be paid on the 1st October.

God knows what this year may turn out; so far, it has been most inauspicious, and the prospect at present, is as gloomy as possible.

It is no doubt desirable to oppose the measures of improvement, for shipping Coals from being carried into effect at Stockton &c. but at present I don't see what grounds of opposition we can take. The injury which this plan may do to the Tyne & Wear, will not avail us, as that sort of competition, is the very thing the public wish for, and will support, and encourage. Unless, therefore, it can be made out, that their plans will interfere with private property, I don't at present see, on what other ground, we could oppose them. By the Common Law, of the land, any body has a right to ship Coals where they please, on paying the Duties, and as the Tyne and Wear don't enjoy any exclusive privileges, there is no strong point to lay hold of, for grounding an opposition to the Stockton Schemes.[10]

I will however endeavour to gain some information on the subject, to see if something can be found out to put a spoke in their Wheel.

---

9   Unidentified.

10   Proposals for shipping coal from the Tees were under consideration from 1825. Since Stockton itself was not able to handle large amounts of shipping, because of difficulties in navigation, the directors of the Stockton and Darlington Railway were contemplating a new port either at Middlesbrough on the south bank or at Haverton Hill on the north bank of the river. A bill to extend the railway to Middlesbrough was approved by Parliament in May 1828. See William Lillie, *The History of Middlesbrough: an Illustration of the Evolution of English Industry* (Middlesbrough, 1968), pp. 46–56.

The Coal-owners, on both Rivers, are very anxious, to have the Oversea Duties on Coals put on the same footing, as the Coast Duties viz. 12/- on Round & 2/- per Ch. on Small – the Newcastle Ch. At present the Oversea Duty on Round, is 17/6 & on Small 6/- per Newcastle Ch.

The general opinion is, that if the Oversea Duty was thus reduced, the revenue would be greatly benefited, by the increased vend, which would ensue; and that both the Coal, & Ship-owners would be greatly relieved. It is likely that some plan for approaching Gover[nmen]t on this affair, will shortly be fixed upon by the Coal-owners, The Oversea Duty rec[ieve]d at present by Gov[ernmen]t is only about £15000 a year. It w[oul]d be no great risk for the trade to farm the Duty, or guarantee the above sum to Gov[ernmen]t & to run the risk of the reduced Duty.

The Marq[ues]s of Londonderry   I have the honor [&c.]
London   J[no] Buddle

P.S. I have just heard from Hunter that he has got £400 on acc[oun]t of the Stone sent to Sunderland Chap [sic]. Mr King[11] requires time to examine into the Way-leave accc[oun]t which L[or]d Durham's people think is not correct & that the Bal[anc]e will be in *their* favour! This however cannot I expect be the case & will get the matter cleared up. But as this may require a little time I w[oul]d submit to your Lordship, that the £400 sh[oul]d be p[ai]d to D. Lambton on acc[oun]t of the £500 Int[eres]t & I may be able, by some means to get him the remaining £100 on the 1st Mar[ch] – this may keep him quiet.

66.

D/Lo/C142/16   Newcastle 10th June 1828

My Lord
        The excitement occasioned by the Elect[io]n[12] having now nearly

---

11 Undetified.

12 There were two by-elections in Durham City in 1828 in consequence of Sir Henry Hardinge being, firstly, re-appointed Clerk of the Ordnance and, secondly, appointed Secretary of War. In the first election, in February, Hardinge was opposed by Alexander Robertson but was returned by a large majority. In the second election, in June, William Chaytor declared himself

subsided, the mind is left at liberty, to return to the calm consideration of matters of business.

Our Vend is going on steadily, but tamely, the present state of the
markets not being such, as to encourage, a pressing demand. This
being the case, I do not look for any stir this month, beyond the ordinary jog-trot routine of business, and that nothing can be effected by
any extra exertions, either mental, or bodily.

The most immediate point for consideration, in the affairs of the
Coal-trade of the Wear, is Lord Durham's *overs*.

Nothing can be more proper than your Lordship's official Letter,
and I think it is quite as far as it is necessary for your Lordship to go
in the matter, at present. Your Lordship having gone so far, it is now
for the Comm[itt]ee to take it up, and to pursue it, to a decision, in
one way or other. The onus of the affair will, however, I think rest
with Col. Grey, and myself, as from the supineness of the Hetton
Co. and the perfect apathy of others (who probably calculate, on
skreening their own misdoings, under the shadow of Lord D[ur]-
ham's *great black wing*) little support is to be expected from them.
It is not my wish to give your Lordship any unnecessary trouble in
this affair, and I will exercise my best discretion in pursuing it in the
Comm[itt]ee. But as it will not, I am sure, be moved in at all, until I
stir it up, the sole consideration, now before your Lordship, is, as to
the *time* for moving on it.

The Election is now fairly over and if consideration, connected
with that affair, no longer operates on your Lordship's mind, in reference to the business of the overs, the sooner it is brought before the
Committee the better, as the year is spending, and the longer it is
under consideration, the more difficult it will be to settle.

As to the Election. Notwithstanding the late, and former opposition, caused much trouble, and anxiety, at the moment, I am satisfied
from all that I have heard and observed, that the effect of them has
been, to strengthen our interest in the City, infinitely more, than if no
such opposition had occurred. And I am under the conviction, that
the money which has been spent in consequence, has been laid out to
advantage, as I am of opinion, that the future benefit, to result from
it, will do much more, than compensate for the present outlay

I am not yet able to estimate the cost of this Election, but it will
not be considerable and I hope it will not prevent your Lordship

a candidate but withdrew on the day before the poll. *Hist.Parl. 1820–32*, ii,
364–6; Heesom, *Durham City and its MPs*, pp. 42–3.

making a remittance on acc[oun]t of the Biddick Int[eres]t at least. The Herrington Interest, G.D. Lambton having filed his Bill, and done *his worst*, need not perhaps be so immediately attended to, but I leave all this entirely for your Lordship's consideration.

The Marq[ues]s of Londonderry   I have the Honor [&c.]
London   J[no] Buddle

67.

D/Lo/C142/17 (12)   Newcastle 19[th] Aug[us]t 1828

My Lord

I received your Lordship's packet of yesterday, on my arrival at Pensher, with Sykes[13] last night, after 9 o'clock. I feel exceedingly obliged by your Lordship's invitation, to drive over, but if I had even received your card in time I could not have accomplished it, as I am circumstanced.

I have shewn Sykes all my plans, and estimates relative to the harbour, and although naturally a torpid sort of character, my explanations have put him more upon the qui vice than I expected. He now even expresses anxiety to get a start made, as soon as possible. He has gone to Gregson to day, to discuss the legal form of the leases from your Lordship, to Bradyll, and I am to breakfast with them at Durham in the morn[in]g at 8 o'clock, for the purpose of endeavouring to get the business brought to a conclusion. Sykes is acting quite independently of Robertson, who, poor creature, is, in consequence, in a state of mind bordering on distraction. He complains bitterly of the injustice of depriving him of his ultimate interest in the concern.

I have written to the *Cub*[14] to say, that on acc[oun]t of our 3 Pays this mo[nth] I could not make the stipulated remittance to the Trust

---

13 Bradyll's agent. By the end of 1827 Robertson had failed to produce any of the money he had said he was confident of raising to build the harbour and railway at Seaham. Lord Londonderry and Bradyll agreed to terminate the agreement with Robertson on grounds of non-performance. The bill for the harbour passed Parliament in July 1828. In September, in the absence of a new agreement with Bradyll, Lord Londonderry decided to proceed with the work on his own. D/Lo/C595.

14 Frederick William Robert Stewart, 1805–72, Lord Castlereagh, Lord Londonderry's son by his first marriage, fourth Marquess of Londonderry 1854.

Fund, but hope to do it out of the receipt on the 1st Sep[tember]. We must be punctual in this, or they will be upon us like vultures.

The deferring of the Colliery pay, next week is impracticable, it would be considered as an act of Bankruptcy, and would occasion a complete uproar – 1500 people being disappointed in the receipt of their wages, on the accustomed day w[oul]d make them furious. Pray, my dear Lord, don't think of it, we must, at all costs avoid such an expedient. It would most certainly produce some catastrophe.

I came here, to attend the Comm[itt]ee meet[in]g this morning, and rec[eive]d the enclosed from Geo[rge] Hill, conveying Lord Durham's sentiments thro' Stephenson, in reply to your Lordship's Manifesto. He seems to shew *fight*, but what does Hill's wish to see me, mean? Unless he has authority, under private orders, to offer some sort of terms why should he want to see me? However we shall see, and I will act under your Lordship's superior diplomacy.

I will send from Walls-end a copy of your Lordship's Manifesto by post this Evening to refresh your Lordship's memory of the subject.

In the course of next week, I will come over to Wynyard, to confer with your Lordship on financial affairs, and the *then* aspect of the trade &c.

Sykes has seen Wyatt, he went to the Priory, but Col. Bradyll would not see him.

He cannot imagine what he has done to offend both Lord Londonderry, and Col. Bradyll to such a degree, that they won't even see him!!!

The Marq[ues]s of Londonderry	I have the honor [&c.]
Wynyard Park	J^{no} Buddle

68.

D/Lo/C142/17 (41)   Walls-end 5th Oct[ober] 1828

My Lord

We had a meeting of the Committee of the two Rivers yesterday, to fix the issue of vend for the month of October. It was fixed at 95 per Th[ousan]d for the Tyne and 80 for the Wear – the difference 15 per Thousand, being allowed in liquidation of the surplus vend of the Wear, which at the end of Sep[tember] was 37 per Thousand and will of course at the end of October, be reduced to 22 per Thous[an]d if the vend of both Rivers goes on as calculated.

I do not yet know what the precise quantity for the month will be for us, as the calculations for the adjustment of the overs, and Shorts, on the Wear is not yet made.

On entering the meeting, Billy gave me his hand, apparently, with the utmost cordiality, and during the whole time of the meeting, treated me with the greatest attention, and politeness. So I suppose, there is now a *truce* between us, and that we shall go on in our usual way again.

Hunter learnt from Crawford[15] when the latter was at Pittington last Week, as mentioned in a former Letter, that they (Lord Durham's people) are waiting the result of a boring to explore the Hutton Seam, at Shadforth, before they decide on the Winning of Little Town. If these borings turn out favorable, their present notion is, to make a grand Winning, at Shadforth, and to bring the Coals from it, in a direct line over the Hills, by a rail-way to join Russell's at Moorsley, and to connect it with their Sunderland Line at the Houghton New Pit. This is a magnificent scheme, but by no means the most beneficial for Lord Durham, I conceive. I think I can manage, through Hill, to learn the bottom of this, and suggest to him a better plan, in the benefit of which we may participate.

It seems that Billy is restored to office, but not to it's original extent, as old King retains the Chancellorship of the Exchequer.

Houghton Feast commences to day, and our Pitmen will keep holy-day Monday, Tuesday, Wednesday. During these 3 days, as the Waggons will be off, we must make a rush with all the carts that can be mustered, to lead Stones, Coals, and Materials of every sort to the harbour, with the Waggon horses.

I have the honor [&c.]
J^{no} Buddle

69.

D/Lo/C142/17 (66)   Newcastle 29th Nov[ember] 1828

My Lord
    After seeing the sudden change of the Weather this morning, and contrasting the gloom of this day with the sun-shine of yesterday,[16]

---

15 Thomas Crawford, viewer to Lord Durham.
16 The foundation stone of Seaham Harbour was laid on 28 November 1828. An account of the event, with a description of the harbour and the plan for the town, was included in E. Mackenzie and M. Ross, *Historical, Topographical and*

who can doubt that my Lady has been born under a lucky planet? Every thing connected with our great work has hitherto flourished, and will I trust continue to prosper under *her* auspicious patronage. Since we commenced there has not been a single *kink* in our Chain, and all our Wheels have run so smooth as oil – God grant they may continue to do so, to the end of our journey.

I hope you all got safe home, but I thought my Lady appeared fatigued from the exertion of such an immense day's work, and I fear she may suffer from it.

My chief object in writing at present is to request the favor of your Lordship to send me, by my Messenger, to Sunderl[an]d on Monday morning, Chapman's Speech and a Sketch of your Lordship's reply to my Speech, and Cuddy's[17] address. My object in this, is to enable us, to get something like a correct statem[en]t of the day's proceedings drawn up for insertion in the news papers. None of the newspaper reporters attended except Humble,[18] and he had not been able to collect a single sentence, and at best he seems to be but a *Leather headed* sort of chap. Your Lordship will also please to say which of the London papers you would have the article appear in, and Grieveson[19] their *Collector* in Newcastle, will have it inserted accordingly.

The Committee of the two Rivers I find, are to meet on Tuesday next to fix the Vend for December, and I feel I ought to attend. My plan will therefore be to stay at Sunderland on Monday Night, to visit Seaham, on Tuesday morn[in]g then go to Newcastle to the meeting, and return to Pensher in the Evening. As the great meeting takes place, on Friday at N[ew]castle, our meeting with Gregson, at Durham, will under circumstances, have therefore, to be, either on Wed[nesday] or Thursday.

Could your Lordship continue to take Durham, and Pensher, on your line of march to Newcastle, for the meeting? That is to say, to meet Gregson at Durham on Thursday morning – dine and *bivouac* at Pensher – take a peep at the quarry on Friday morning, and then go on to the meeting at Newcastle. At Pensher I will promise your

Descriptive View of the County Palatine of Durham (Newcastle upon Tyne, 1834), pp. 374–80. See also Sykes, *Local Records*, ii, 231–4; Richardson, *Local Historian's Table Book*, iii, 405–9.

17 Sir Cuthbert Sharp published his address in a pamphlet which was reprinted on the centenary in 1928 under the title *Seaham and Seaham Harbour.*

18 Francis Humble, newspaper publisher.

19 Thomas Grieveson, journalist.

Lordship better quarters, than you often had, in Galicia on Sir John Moore's retreat.[20]

Whatever plan your Lordship may decide on, for meeting Gregson, you had better write direct to him, to fix the appointment, and I will be punctual.

My friend Burden Sanderson[21] was just on the point of leaving Pensher last night as I arrived – he had left the enclosed on my table, and as I think his Latin inscription pretty, I send it for your Lordship's perusal.

I have the Honor [&c.]
J^{no} Buddle

70.

D/Lo/C142/17 (135)   Walls-end 21st Dec[embe]r 1828

My Lord

I have perused your Lordship's Letter of yesterday which came in the packet with the *botheration* clauses for the lease &c. and will get forward with all that is required, with all diligence. All this *stuff* and *bother*, is only to be got through by the exertion of invincible patience, and perseverance. I shall therefore prepare myself, to start to it, with a clear head, and firm resolution, in the morning, and will not leave my *hole*, 'till it is done. Tomorrow, therefore, I shall be *invisible*.

The appointment of the Trustee, owing to the glorious complication of our laws, with respect to *real* property is quite essential for your Lordship's security and protection, against any meddling, or interference of the trustees under the Settlement,[22] and is the only method by which the harbour and it's appurtenances can be secured to you as a *personal* property, and by which your Lordship can be enabled to deal with it, independently of them. I will see Sir Henry when I can, and talk to him, on all this in the way your Lordship wishes.

With respect to the watching of the Clarence rail-way Bill,[23] I

---

20 Lord Londonderry commanded a cavalry brigade in the corps sent to Portugal under Sir John Moore 1808–9.

21 J.B. Sanderson, Newcastle lawyer, Jesmond.

22 The Londonderrys' marriage settlement.

23 A bill to allow the building of a railway from Haverton Hill to Simpasture,

hardly know what to advise. Let us go to whatever Law-man we may, it is only a choice of evils – it is neither more nor less, than going from the frying Pan, to the Fire; and there is no keeping them in humour, unless every one is allowed to have his way and run off with his share of the prey. And I feel we shall never get rid of this infliction, until we get into that situation, to which I have often alluded – *out of Debt*, and I am under the conviction that the attainment of it, is worth any immediate, and temporary sacrifice whatever. I am always led from my subject, and am apt to *rave* on this to me distressing subject; and I had almost forgot the watching of the Clarence rail-way Bill. Whitton & Gregson,[24] are Gregson's agents in London I believe, and I don't think any one more competent than *John*, to a job of this kind, if your Lordship does not feel objections to him.

Groom seems, from his Letter, disposed to be civil – would it be politick, to employ *my son*,[25] as *Sentinel* on this occasion?

Your Lordship will have seen Gregson, on the Biddick Chancery Bill and I have nothing to remark upon it further, than that it seems requisite to face it, at once, and get it disposed of in one way, or other, I will try if I can work Neddy out of any thing on the Life Policy. As Bankers they *will not* make any permanent Loans on Mortgage, or otherwise, as it does not bring in Commission, &c. plus of Interest. But he may possibly know some individual who may be disposed to lend on dead security at 5 per cent,

I don't think that Sykes, and Bradyll *cotton* together cordially, and I don't qujte like the notion of Phi[lip] Wyatt going chattering about amongst parties. His twattle is much more likely to set people by the ears together, than to preserve peace.

I have the Honor [&c.]
J^{no} Buddle

---

with branches, was passed in May 1828, but work did not start. After a number of changes to the line a new bill was presented, and passed on 1 June 1829. Tomlinson, *North Eastern Railway*, pp. 174–82.

24 John Gregson jr.

25 This must mean Groom's son: Buddle was childless.

71.

My Lord

I have the honor to acknowledge the receipt of your Lordship's most excellent letter of last night.

The able exertions which your Lordship has made to avert the catastrophe in the trade, which is about to ensue, is well known, and duly appreciated and praised by every sensible man in, or *out* of the trade. Indeed it is the universal topick of conversation. I still maintain my opinion, in favor of regulation, but I am not so blinded by my passion for it, as to sacrifice every feeling of honor and propriety for the sake of maintaining the system. No, I am for regulation, only, when it can be established on principles of honor and fair dealing, as so clearly laid down by your Lordship.[1]

Altho' I detest War, yet when it becomes necessary, for the support of a just cause, I will be found at my post, and however averse I may be to go into it, I will never shrink from it; and I must say, that if ever there was a just cause, for making War, in the Coal trade – the present one, in my judgment, is it.

I learn from *good authority* that, Stephenson is at the bottom of this business, and pushes Lord D. on to it, with all his might.

Can it be the plan of this fellow to embarrass his L[or]d[shi]p still farther by setting him by the ears with the trade, with the view of keeping him longer in his grasp? And as he can *lose nothing* at any rate, may he not entertain an expectation, that by getting the *great powers* to cut each other in pieces – he may in the end come in for a larger share of the plunder? He at any rate is playing a safe game. He finds the sweets of a *Receivership* from one Peer of the realm, and why may he not have his eye, on another victim? I have so very

---

1   A joint meeting of the committees for the Tyne and the Wear on 5 December 1828 (NRO 263/A2) agreed to consider a court of appeal for disputes between the two rivers on the bases of regulation. Lord Durham objected on the ground that it would leave the Wear wholly dependent on the Tyne. Further meetings were inconclusive. Buddle to Londonderry, 16 Dec. 1828, D/Lo/ C142/17; Paul Sweezy, *Monopoly and Competition in the English Coal Trade 1550–1850* (Cambridge, MA, 1938), pp. 88–90.

much to say to your Lordship on all matters connected with this important affair, that I find it impossible to put it on paper, at least, in any reasonable compass. I shall therefore be happy to see your Lordship, as early on Tuesday as may be convenient – to have a *good long morning*. I will either come to your Lordship at Durham, be happy to see you at Pensher, on your way to Seaham, or meet you at Seaham, as your Lordship will please to signify by a note, by the Boy. It is not in my power to get to the ball at Durham on Mond[a]y Evening.

The frost continues as obstinate as ever, and is greatly against us in opening the campaign. We must anxiously look forward for being placed in a *better position*, on the Sea Coast, for carrying on War, as one independent Power, at no very distant period – I have little reliance on the co-operation of the naval power alluded to – only it is well to keep on good terms, as long as may seem right.

I have the honor [&c.]
J^{no} Buddle

72.

D/Lo/C142/18 (23)   Pensher Tuesday Evening
3rd Feb[ruary] 1829

My Lord

After all the Tyne meeting has not thought it prudent to draw the sword to day,[2] but has resolved, once more to try the chance of a pacific appeal to the trade of the Wear – that is to say, to Lord Durham.

After much debating, and chopping and changing, the resolutions of which I enclose a copy were concocted, and a Meeting of the Wear, will most likely be convened next Friday, but ten to one, that Loraine, and Hill will [?not] feel themselves authorized, even to undertake to support the present price of their Coals, until they can receive Lord Durham's opinion & directions, respecting the proposition conveyed in the resolutions of this day; as there does not seem to be any sort of cordial communication between Lord D. and Loraine. For altho' his L[or]d[shi]p stayed two or three days at Biddick last week, he neither saw Loraine, nor had any communication with him!!!

As Mr R.W. Brandling will see your Lordship tomorrow I must

---

2   Minutes in NRO 263/A2.

refer your Lordship to him for the details of the business of the meeting, which may enable your Lordship to make up your mind, and to send such orders as you may think right, for my government, at the Wear meeting on Friday. I gave it as my opinion, that I did not think your Lordship would take a less quantity on the basis than Lord Durham, unless it should be so awarded by a referee. And I presume your Lordship would not consent to act upon the old Basis, until the plan of reference can be arranged, unless the period, for such arrangement is *limited* to a *reasonable* time and that the award shall take effect from the 31st Dec[embe]r 1828. These I think are the only conditions on which your Lordship can after all that has passed, entertain this *new* view of the subject.

I must own that I expected to see the meeting of this day, act very differently but after so much bluster & bravado, I never saw a meeting more tame, every one, almost, seemed to be horrified, and appalled at the idea of a complete rupture. I shall go to Sunderland tomorrow to see our Committee of Fitters and to spur them on. I have not heard of any irregularities whatever, having yet been committed at L[or]d Durham's Fitting office; but Cochrane[3] says *they* have freighted 4 ships for the year, for which he is *very sorry*, and will put a stop to any thing more being done in that way, 'till the decision of the Wear, on the Tyne resol[ution]s of this day is known. I told him that such transactions would lead inevitably to a reduction of prices.

If our Fitters continue as they have commenced the month, we shall have nothing to complain of. I send the Staith Bulletin of this evening, to shew your Lordship the first two days' works, which, considering the ship-owners are lying off for *cheap* Coals, are very fair.

I return the bank Book (Coutt's). Ed[war]d charges neither dis[coun]t nor Commission on the Bills sent to Coutts & Co. and their *average* dates do not subject your Lorship to the paym[en]t of a greater am[oun]t in disc[oun]t to Coutt's than Ed[war]d's Commission w[oul]d amount to, if he remitted cash. Your Lordship will be aware that the £10,000 calculated for the pays in Feb[ruay] covers the payments in both Jan[uar]y and Feb[ruary] as we have had no pay since the 9th Jan[ua]r[y], which was the closing pay for the last year. If our Vend should not happen to go on so well as might be wished this month, it might be well to give Forster[4] notice, that we should

---

3   Archibald Cochrane, partner in the Hetton Co.
4   Perceval Forster, Bradyll's land agent.

want some money for the Harbour, in the latter end of March; but I should if convenient prefer waiting 'till May, or June, and then call upon him, for the means of enabling us to make a *rush* with the piers, in the summer months. I would rather call for the money when the *Season* demands it, than give them reason to think that our *necessities* require it.

Capt. Maling[5] came to me yesterday, just as I was going to the bank, and I made an appointment with him at 2 o'clock; but saw no more of him, so that I had no opportunity of learning any thing more of the grand new Scheme, from himself; but I hear, from other quarters, that old Arthur is in it, if not at the bottom of it.

I enclose a letter from Oliver on the subject of his expences, the gross amount of which does not appear to me to be out of the way, but as I don't recollect your Lordship giving me any specifick directions on this point, I think it right to lay the acc[oun]t before your Lordship in the first place.

I should have been happy to have accepted your Lordship's invitation if I had found myself quite a free agent; but under the menacing aspect of affairs, with A. Robertson Way-leave acc[oun]t Staith case, harbour, &c. &c. on hand, I do not feel I could be at such a distance from my post, with any sort of comfort. After we see distinctly *which way the cat will jump,* and get our vessel trimmed accordingly, I shall be happy to come to Wynyard, to receive your Lordship's very kind and valuable present.

I beg to thank your Lordship for your very kind offer, in *another affair*, but I feel, that I cannot embark in any new affair until the harbour is finished – it will not do to have *too many* irons in the fire at once, and I find, that I have quite a sufficient quantity in hand at present.

I am glad to find the *Squire* is with you, and hope soon to see all matters run quite smooth in that quarter. I wrote him a Bulletin of this day's meeting, by post to Brancepeth, but which he will not of course receive for a day, or two. Your Lordship will therefore, please to shew him the resolutions, and Mr R.W. Brandling will explain the proceedings of the meeting.

I am glad to learn that our friend Sir Henry[6] is going to Wyn[ya]rd with the Brandlings tomorrow.

The *on dit* of the day is, that Lord D-ham's debts are £400,000 and

5   John Maling, Inspector of the River Wear and Quay.
6   Sir Henry Browne.

that his ann[ua]l allowance is £14,000 – if there is anything of the truth in the am[oun]t of the Debt, it is frightful.

I have the honor [&c.]

J^{no} Buddle

73.

D/Lo/C142/18 (38)   Sunderland 11th Mar[ch] 1829

My Lord

I am much concerned to learn by your Lordship's Letter of the 8th Inst. that you are indisposed, and so much out of spirits, the more especially, as I have nothing cheering to communicate at this time.

After seeing Gregson this morn[in]g I came on here to see Edw[ar]d but found him as repulsive as ever. I tried him on every tack, and all I can possibly make of him is, that, if towards the end of the month our vend is in such a state, as to enable me to *assure him* that it will leave a sufficient surplus, on the 1st April, he will on such assurance, remit £600 to Coutt's for the trust fund.

On arriving here I met Tanner just going to put the enclosed letter[7] into the post, with a duplicate addressed to me at Walls-end. It contains a correct account of the present state of affairs, and I am quite certain that the Fitters cannot continue to contend successfully with the fearful odds which are against them.

The Hetton Co. are vending exclusively by freighting, at the loss already stated to your Lordship. Lambton's are vending their Primrose *slily* by giving great measure to those ports, where they are the favourite Coal; but cannot get off any quantity in this way. One day the orders, at the office are, to freight freely – next day, orders come, that not a single Ship is to be freighted, on any acc[oun]t whatever, and thus they keep blundering on. On Monday their pits were idle for want of trade. Yesterday orders were given to freight; 3 Ships were accordingly freighted and loaden; but to day they are not freighting & are in consequence standing *stock still*. The fact is, that by freighting they are sacrificing 10/- or 12/- per Ch. and it is *quite certain* that *they cannot stand it*. The report is, that they were

---

7   In this letter Tanner wrote that he would require a guarantee that a regulation, if adopted, would be adhered to, since six of the Wear owners had exceeded their quantities.

obliged to freight the 3 Ships yesterday, to enable them to make their Colliery Pay, by drawing for the am[oun]t of their cargoes, on the factor. But enough of them, let us now look at our own position. By this freighting system, the price of Hetton Coals, both W[alls]-End & Lyon's are virtually reduced full 10/- per Ch. We have reduced 4/- It is not, therefore, to be expected that any Ship owner will take a single Ch. of our Coals, seeing that they rarely beat Hetton price at market & that seldom more than 3. Our sole dependence therefore is on the Shipping of our Fitters, which altho' powerful, cannot possibly take off the quantity, which we must either obtain, or knock under to the Hetton Co. It is impossible to maintain our price at 6/- above them, and obtain Vend also. Matters have therefore arrived at this point, that we *must* either reduce our prices, or be satisfied with a very limited vend. Whether then, are we to pursue a temporizing and timid policy, and be satisfied with what our Fitters can do for a *while* (as at the tremendous loss they are now going on at, *not many* of them can go on long) or are we to shew our Rivals, by a further reduction, that we are determined, at any rate, not to die of a *lingering consumption*. I have given the subject my best and deliberate consideration, and I am most decidedly of opinion, that reducing Eden-main, without reducing Walls-end at the same time, will not answer our purpose, but on the contrary be greatly against us. By keeping up the W[alls]end & reducing Eden, we might increase the vend of Eden, but W[alls]end would *stick*. The consequence w[oul]d be, that we should have to make a considerable quantity of W[alls] end into Eden, for if we could not vend the Coals, as W[alls]end we have no alternative but to make them into Eden-main, and thus lose 7/- per Ch. on every Chald[ro]n converted.

If we are to obtain a vend and keep up with the Hetton Co. we must inevitably make a further reduction of 2/- generally *at least*; and this reduction must take place from the 1st of the mo[nth] as the Fitters have been going on, upon the faith of it. It will be better not to reduce at all than not to reduce from the beginning of the mo[nth]. This reduction I am persuaded would check the freighting very materially, and enable us the more easily to bring the Hetton Co. to an understanding when Cochrane returns. As to Lord Durham, it is evident that he must *strike his colours*. The game is a desperate one, but it appears to me, that it must and ought to be played. We are fairly in for it, and we must fight bravely – the more desperate the fight, the sooner the battle must be over.

I give your Lordship my free, and candid opinion, without bias, in one way or other, leaving your Lordship to the full exercise of your own independent and excellent judgement, and beg to assure you, that whatever your Lordship's decision may be, you will find me ready to act upon it, to the very best of my ability. The reduction of 2/- more w[oul]d give fresh vigour to our Fitters and strike our rivals with dismay, and would also I think enable us to negotiate better terms, in case of a *Truce*.

Our vend up to last night is good, but we shall now slacken, as our Fitters have got thro' most of their own Ships. It is as follows

Walls-end	1816	
Eden	1762	3578
Vane's	154	
Nuts	180	
Small	440	774
		4352

Tomorrow I will write the result of what occurred on the perusal of Robertson's Bill with Gregson this morning.

I shall anxiously wait in hope of a more favourable account of your Lordship's health. I most sincerely wish it to be as good as my own at this time. I really don't think I ever was in such *high feather*, as I have been since the war broke out. The worry & turmoil, as a Comm[ittee]man, in endeavouring to get people to do what was *best* for their own Interest, under a regulation, was a thousand times more wearing & irksome to me than any event that war can produce will be. As far therefore as *personal feeling* goes I *vote* for a continuance of war. At the same time I am ready and willing to do my best to bring about peace.

I have the honor [&c.]
J[no] Buddle

74.

D/Lo/C142 18 (74)   Walls-end 29th Mar[ch] 1829

My Lord

I have the honor to acknowledge the receipt of your Lordship's dispatches of the 27th Inst. this morning; by which I am glad to learn that you will not require my presence in London, 'till after the

Cath[olic] Question is disposed of;[8] but if not 'till after the Easter recess, so much the better, as it will allow more time for preparation. I think however, that I have all my materials pretty ready. I don't think our points can be better arranged, than in the manner your Lordship suggests. The following heads will all require investigation, but it is for your Lordship to decide whether you will bring them *all*, or what part of them forward in the *opening* of the Trenches.[9] Your Lordship is best able to decide which to bring into action, and which to keep in reserve, to be brought into action, as the exigencies of the service may require.

1. The difficulty of sinking and establishment of a Colliery, in all it's details, with it's establishment of Stock & investment of capital.

2. The great risk & uncertainty of Coal-mining, from Accidents by *Creep*, Explosion, and water.

3. The Uncertainty of the profits from the fluctuations of prices.

4. The great expence, and deficiency of produce, by working Pillars.

5. The great loss by Skreening, to make the Coals large enough to suit the taste of the Consumers.

6. The progressive increase of Mine and way-leave Rents.

7. The high rate of labour, and other Charges at the ports of delivery, as compared with the wages and salaries paid by the Coal-owners.

8. The very high Government, and local Duties imposed upon the sea-borne Coal – the very oppressive Tax levied by the Government on Coals both for home, and foreign Markets being from 600 to 800 per cent on the prime cost of the article paid to the proprietor of the Mine.

9. The poor rate on Mine, and Way-leave.
This is a delicate point to notice, as the Collieries do not maintain their own poor. They only pay with the lands, according to their rental for the time being, and when they cease to work, they leave

---

8   The bill for Catholic emancipation passed both houses of Parliament in April 1829. Catholics were now entitled to vote and sit in Parliament, and to hold any public office except those of Lord Chancellor and Lord Lieutenant of Ireland. The Tories were divided on the issue. Lord Londonderry voted for the bill. *Parl. Deb.*, new ser., xxi, col. 694.

9   On 24 March Lord Londonderry moved in the House of Lords for a committee of enquiry into the coal trade, citing in particular the high levels of duties. The Duke of Wellington said that he had no objection to a committee, but the revenues were necessary. *Parl. Deb.*, new ser., xx, cols 1409–13.

the Lands &c. burthened with the *whole* load of Paupers, they have created. I therefore submit that your Lordship should not touch upon this point.

I enclose the most accurate statement of the Charges on the Shipment and delivery of Coals, I can make out, and believe it to be very near the Mark.

I also return the Duke's note and on the whole, think the Comm[ittee][10] a very fair one, altho' I should have preferred it if it had been composed of persons, with all of whom your Lordship had been on terms of perfect amity.

Nothing further occurs to me at present on this subject, but whenever any thing strikes me which I may think worth communication, your Lordship shall hear from me, without reserve, as I am determined to support my Chief, to the utmost of my power in this as well as in all other matters. God knows we have difficulties enough in all quarters, and it require that every man should do his duty – to bring our Bark fairly through the Breakers.

I have the honor [&c.]
J[no] Buddle

75.

D/Lo/C142/18 (117)   Walls-end 31st May 1829

My Lord

I have this morning received your Lordship's letter of the 29th Inst. which explains the plan of your Lordship's diplomacy at the meeting of the 28th and which claims to your Lordship the Victory, as it is quite clear, let him put it in what shape he may, or gloss it over, as he will, that Lord D[urham] has been the first to cry out 'enough'. It cannot be doubted that we have gained the Victory, but the fruits of Victory are, an advantageous and permanent peace. This is the object of our hard fought field, and the attainment of it, on satisfactory terms, is now open to your Lordship's able diplomacy. The main object of the Wear (compelling our great rival to recognize the principle of equitable reference) being attained, the sooner the

---

10 The committee met in May–June 1829. Buddle gave evidence on 6, 8, 11, 15 and 25 May. The report was published as *Report of the Select Committee of the House of Lords appointed to inquire into the state of the Coal Trade*, Parliamentary Papers 1830, VIII (663).

principle can be reduced to practice the better, as it can answer no useful purpose to continue the fight, especially as it is now but too evident that it cannot be longer continued, without a greater sacrifice than any object to be obtained by it can justify.

After writing yesterday I learnt from what I think good authority, that the Hetton Co. are so sick of freighting that they are determined to put their Coals down to a selling price; and if they cannot get Ships at 26/- for their Walls-end their determination is to put them down to 22/- In short they are so annoyed at our Fitters that they are resolved to put their Coals on board of Ship, at the same price we charge our Fitters. I however consider this mere rodomontade & bluster, but I do think it probable, that they may reduce their W[alls]-end to 24/- and Lyons to 18/- or 19/- In this case we cannot compete with them but to a certain & positive loss. We cannot come lower than the prices stated in my Letter of yesterday. There we must take our stand, and just take such Vend as we can get at those prices. Or stand still, as if we go lower our sales will not raise money to make the Colliery Pays.

I tremble for my meeting with Edw[ar]d on Tuesday morning. 'Brother Richardson' – the Fitter,[11] is a great sufferer, by his Vend of April, and May, and Edward will know all about it. He had called (Richardson I mean) a meeting of the Fitters to memorialize your Lordship, on the state of the trade, and to pray for relief and assistance, under the heavy losses they are sustaining. Under the circumstances, especially if the receipt on Tuesday will not cover the pays in June, my chance of obtaining a remittance is very poor indeed. And I feel satisfied, if the *war* is continued, that we must give up the expectation of any surplus receipts – it will be well if we can hold our ground, without assistance.

Some coal-owners are already beginning to make advances, as the bankers from the state of the Currency, & prospects of trade, *will not advance*. I long for your Lordship's orders on Wed[nedsay] m[ornin]g. If a fleet arrives in the mean time & I am not prepared to meet the Hetton reduction, it will I fear be construed into a defeat.

The Wind is still contrary.

I have the honor [&c.]
J^{no} Buddle

---

11 Thomas Richardson, a Sunderland fitter, Quaker, related to the Backhouses.

76.

D/Lo/C142/18 (120)   Sunderland 1st June 1829

My Lord

I have this morning received your Lordship's Letter of the 29th June [*sic*] and am vexed to think that the conduct of the Hetton *Clan* should have so annoyed your Lordship. I feel however, almost confident that they are merely *coquetting* with the trade in hope of driving a bargain & I think when I have an opportunity of talking to some of the partners, which will be shortly, that I shall convince them of the folly of such a line of policy and that they very much mistake their men, indeed, if they imagine, by pursuing it, to compel us to knock under. Nothing can be more impertinent, or more absurd, than for them to presume to fix their own quantity, and also the *maximum* price of coals for the whole trade. Also to demur about signing the articles of the 5th Dec[embe]r at Newcastle – upon which the articles they now boggle at signing, were bottomed. They will I have little doubt conform to these articles by-and-by, but then the D—l of it is, that we are losing the best of the season, in the mean time.

Our vend for June is in all 14,500 Ch. which for the short time we have had to do it in, is very great but owing to the low prices, the receipt is *miserable*. It is for

The Fitters acceptances	£10,662.	18.	3
Wynyard tradesmen &c.	667.	12.	3
Colliery ditto	823.	4.	1½
	£12,113.	14.	7½

I will send the particulars tomorrow. The Fitters acceptances will do nothing more than find the £375 for Wynyard and make the pays this month. I met with Ed[war]d at the meeting of the Commissioners & went to the bank with him to have a gossip, and to see if I could find out how he might feel towards a remittance tomorrow.

The banking trade like all others is getting worse & worse, the discontinuing of the £1 notes is lessening the circulation of the *Fives* also, and the Fives are no sooner issued than they are back again for Gold, and the demand for Sovereigns is in consequence enormous.[12] Bankers must therefore have an extra Commission for all

---

12 An Act of 1826 prohibited the issue in England of bank notes under the value of £5. The re-issue of existing notes was allowed until 1829, but then ceased. John Clapham, *The Bank of England*, vol. 2 (Cambridge, 1944), pp. 106–7.

their issues in Gold, otherwise their trade will not be worth carrying on. Edward's prudence has led him to 'take time by the forelock' and he is actually charging a Comm[ission] of ¼ per cent (5/- per £100) on all the Sover[eign]s he issues. Thus it is clear that *paper money* is already at a discount of ¼ per cent, from which we may infer that we shall shortly have two prices – a money price & a paper price. It also shews the profound ignorance of the Chancellor of the Exchequer, in asserting that the place of the £1 notes w[oul]d be supplied by a greater issue of *Fives*. This affair of the currency is now coming home to every man's fire side, and the immediate effect upon our own affairs is, that our banker cannot, or will not, in the day of need make a little effort for us. I did not come to a clear point with Ed[war]d on a remittance, as I shall leave that for tomorrow, but made out enough to induce me to expect that he *will not* do any thing for us. 'An advance of £10,000 now, is a much greater object to Bankers, than £20,000 has been in other times & under other circumstances'.

As to the renewal.[13] I have talked the matter fully over with Tommy & think he is disposed to be reasonable, but this is all *under the rose*, as it is on his part *Treason*. I think I shall get him to adopt a principle in the estimating of the Fine which will leave an opening to us for negotiation. Tommy means to act correctly, but my apprehension is, that he has not firmness, and moral courage enough to maintain his own opinion, against the rapacity of the *Rooks*. In a short time he will make his calculations & shew them to me *privately*, when if I see, that they are such as I can approve in principle, as I expect they will be, from what has already passed between us, the next step will be to write a Letter, to the Body stating your Lordship's desire to renew. Your Lordship will then be requested to send in your offer, and Tommy will be ordered to estimate the Fine.

As soon as I see Tommy's calculation of the Fine, I will communicate it, with my own strictures thereon; and if a personal communication with your Lordship should then be deemed necessary, previously to writing the letter, of application, for the renewal; I will come to your Lordship anywhere, that may be most convenient to you; as a little extra exertion, entirely ceases to be an object of consideration, when such a *very important* point is to be gained. It is in all probability the last renewal of Rainton, we shall have to negotiate in

13 Of the Rainton lease. The negotiations in 1829 were not successful; the lease was not renewed until 1832: DCM, B/AA/103.

our time, we must not, therefore, stick at a little trouble, or exertion to accomplish it.

Shakey[14] came *hopping* up to me, at the Committee meeting, as gay as a Jack-daw, to enquire what 'friend Thompson'[15] was doing about the rail-way, and expressed great satisfaction when I told him that Thompson was on the point of commencing.

The fire at Newbottle colliery still gains strength – there seems to be a great want of union and exertion in the Viewing department. And as misfortunes seldom come alone, it seems that a very formidable feeder of Water has broken into the Cocken Colliery supposed to have communication with the Wear, which has the appearance at present of laying off one of the pits at least.

A good deal of work is, therefore, cut out for Lord D[urham] when he comes down, to *manage his own concerns.*

I will write again tomorrow, and have the Honor [&c.]

J[no] Buddle

77.

D/Lo/C142/18 (139)   Walls-end 29[th] June 1829

My Lord

I have this morning received your Lordship's note with Bradyll's Letter of the 25[th] Inst. But I have not yet rec[eive]d any intelligence from Durham of the arrival there of the money. If it comes to day, I am certain that Forster will inform me of it by tomorrow's Post. I do not however, much like the complexion of this letter, as Sykes' story, about not having sufficient notice, is palpable shuffling. The fact is, he called upon me in Newcastle, shortly after the payment of the first £1000 on the 2[nd] April, and volunteered to pay the remaining £6000 of the £7000 for the present year, into Backhouse's Bank at Durham immediately on his return, to Ulverston, which he s[ai]d would save him trouble. I then told him, my wish was, to draw £1000 regularly every month to assist in making the harbour pay, and that I would want £1000 on the 15[th] May for that purpose. No money, nor any latter from him, however, came to hand, before I started for London,

---

14 Shakespear Reed, JP, Thornhill House, Sunderland, backer of T.E. Harrison, railway engineer.
15 Benjamin Thompson, engineer of the Seaham railway.

on the 2nd May. I then saw Mr Forster several times in London, who I know wrote him very strongly on the subject, & enclosed a note, or two, which I had written to him pressing for the money. All this however produced nothing, not even a letter to Forster, & when I returned to the North on the 31st may I wrote him again pressing for £1500 on the 11th June & £500 on the 25th or (to allow him still more time) to send the £2000 on the 25th June, & not on the 29th as he has told Mr Bradyll. His story of want of sufficient notice, is therefore, shuffling and nonsense, and entirely shakes my confidence in his punctuality, as to money transactions, at least. As soon as I receive the money I will replace the £1000 to the privy purse, by an immediate remittance to Coutts & Co. But I hope Bradyll will come up with his £2000 of arrears for May & June, & also with £1000 for our pay on the 9th July, or at any rate on the 23rd at latest.

All idea of regulation seems to be relinquished for the present, but as we are on the point of opening a negotiation with the D[ean] & C[hapter] for the renewal of the Rainton Lease, I the less regret it, as I think, it will furnish us, with arguments for stemming the rapacity of the *Rooks*, which I could not avail myself of, if all was going – smooth as oil in the Trade. And I am now inclined to think, it will be quite as well for us, if the regulation should not take place before the 1st Aug[us]t or Sep[tember]. We may suffer a temporary loss, and inconvenience from this; but we must bear it in mind that the renewal of the Lease is a *regulation for 21 years*; and that to make it a good one, is worth a temporary sacrifice. The present low price of Coals will enable me to oppose Tommy Fenwick's statements of great profits, and also to prove the great uncertainty & precarious nature of the trade. Under these considerations the present may be considered, a favourable time for negotiating our renewal.

I shall be anxious to send your Lordship an Acc[oun]t of our receipt &c. as soon as possible, but I don't think it will be in my power to make a Statement before Thursday, so that your Lordship cannot have it before Saturday. I am however, very *flat* about it, as I fear, the acc[oun]t will be any thing but a flourishing one, and that Edward will be impracticable. Our Newcastle bankers, especially Lambton's, are curtailing their Discounts very much, and lessening their accommodation. Like all other trades, they seem to be afraid of doing business, and are *pulling up* as fast as they can; and I am expecting to find that Edward is following their example. Indeed business of every kind, is getting the longer the worse, and the affairs of the Country seem to be drawing towards some great crisis.

The lessee's (Fawcett's) Viewer, of the Newbottle Colliery, has called upon me this morn[in]g to consult me on behalf of Fawcett on the state of that concern. He says, that the attempt to drown out the Fire, in the Dorothea pit, last Sat[urda]y failed, from the want of Water – the Tubs in the Shaft being dry, and that the fire has greatly increased. They are, this morning, covering up the pits, to smother it out, and he thinks *all the* Pits, except the new one, at Houghton, will have to be closed up. In this event, it will be a troublesome, and expensive affair.

Thompson has all his contractors for the Cuts and embankments &c. on the new Line, this morning, to Seaham, to let the Contracts for the Work, and he means to commence *immediately* with the utmost vigour, so that I hope a *Scratch*, at least, will be made by the time your Lordship comes down. He has the utmost confidence in the success of the Harbour.

> I have the Honor [&c]
> J^{no} Buddle

I would not have your Lordship communicate the observations on Sykes' conduct, contained in the former part of this Letter, to Bradyll – Sykes' shuffling may be a convenience & possibly connived in by his master. Shewing him up, cannot therefore be of use to us, it is enough, that we *know our men*, and must deal with them accordingly. If we can but get the *stuff* tied from them, it may be as well not to *squeeze* them too hard.

78.

D/Lo/C142/19 (27)   Pensher 22nd July 1829

My Lord

The renewal has been running in my head, ever since my gossip with Tommy yesterday – morning, and I find that I can have no repose, until my mind is unburthened of it. I therefore, send in another cover, a Sketch of a proposal, for your Lordship's considera-tion. If your Lordship approves of the principle of this Sketch, you can make such alterations in the wording of it, as may appear to Your Lordship to be requisite. I then submit, that your Lordship should sign a fair copy (Cowburn might get it made for you) and send it direct to the Body, under cover, to Chaytor[16] their 'Register' – this

16 William Charles Chaytor, Durham lawyer, registrar to the Dean and Chapter, MP for Durham City 1831–4, *Hist. Parl. 1820–32*, iv, 636–7.

is his title; and your Lordship might accompany the proposal by a Letter, couched in such terms, in support of it, as your Lordship's superior diplomacy might suggest, at the moment. The prudence of allowing that part of the proposal (marked with pencil in the margin) to stand, in which I have glanced at the effect of the change in the state of the Currency &c. is for your Lordship's consideration. It is thrown in, by way of giving them a little *food* for reflection. With respect to the assertion, that Coals will not again reach the prices they recently sold for, I am *quite in earnest*, it being my grave opinion, that the various causes enumerated in the proposal, will have the effect therein stated, & that we certainly shall not again see Coals – especially the 2nd Class, at the prices they had attained under the late regulation. I have not loaded the proposal, with all the reasons I could give, in support of a reduction of tentale, lest it should have the appearance of wishing to *cram them* too much. I have, therefore, left a few 'good shot in the Locker' to be used in future negotiation, as circumstances may require.

Nothing but a good fine will tempt them; and our object is, to get as large a quantity for it as we can. I have, therefore, put the tentale at 22/- which for the £15099. 15 Fine will give us an ann[ua]l vend of 1000,000 Ch. This is about the tentale paid by the Hetton Co. (exclusive of their outstrokes) and by Bradyll. These are recent examples, and may be referred to as precedents.

In the event of your Lordship deciding to send the proposal, direct to the Body, pray don't send it 'till after next Monday the 27th Inst., as in order to give a little time, for considering the affair, I prevailed on Tommy not to announce his having seen me to the Body, 'till next Saturday.

Our vend is accruing from 80 to 90 Keels a day.

I have the Honor[&c.]
J^{no} Buddle

I have not dated the Sketch of the proposal, your Lordship will do that on sending it. I feel satisfied that the proposal will produce a stronger impression, if sent by your Lordship, than if it was presented by me.

79.

D/Lo/C142/19 (73)   Walls-end 6th Sep[tember] 1829

My Lord

I have this morning received your Lordship's Letter of yesterday, with the Copy of your Lordship's letter to Col. Bradyll, than which nothing can be more proper.

The devising of any plan, likely to meet Stephenson's Chancery suit, puzzles me beyond measure, as he has repeatedly told me, it is the *Title*[17] they want. Any plan, therefore, of procrastinated payment, of giving of Coal, is not likely to meet his wishes. The way-leave rent, would not do, as the amo[un]t of it, will scarcely pay the Interest of the £16000 – much less redeem the principal. And even admitting, that we had any Coal, that we could transfer to him, & that he would accept it, would it be prudent to act upon such a plan, considering the difficulty we have in dealing with the Dean & Chapter – and the uncertainty of our position with them, in respect to all that we must look for the future support, and aggrandizement of our Family, as it is but too clear, that the land, never can extricate itself from the Load of mortgages, with which it is saddled, nor can the *state* of Wynyard be supported, without the assistance of *the Coal*. We ought, therefore, to be circumspect, in the *highest degree*, as to parting with a single acre, or admitting a *subtile rival* to get a footing in any sort of way, in even the most remote corner, of our *Black inheritance*. We ought really to look upon it as our very 'Flesh & Blood', and ought therefore to strain every nerve for it's conservation, accordingly. The only feasible plan, by which we might allow Lord D—m to *work out* the Biddick £16000, would perhaps be, by accommodating him, with our harbour for the Shipment of a part of his Coals, say from Little-town, or Shadforth, in the event of the borings there proving successful. But then, even this is a remote object, as it could not (I mean, the winning of a Colliery at Shadforth) be accomplished in less than two years, and at a Cost of from £30,000 to £50,000, and how is L[or]d D. to accomplish this, in the present embarrassed state of his affairs?

All these considerations bother me exceedingly, and I don't at all see my way through them. The true and legitimate way of surmounting

---

17 To that part of Biddick which Lord Durham was buying from Lord Londonderry. The whole property was still subject to a mortgage. See below, p 197.

this, as well as every other pecuniary difficulty, is by suspending all *extraneous* expenditure, and by paying off, out of savings. My plan would be, instantly to dismiss every mason, Carpenter, &c. to the *bare living establishment,* and cease to spend a single shilling in building, except at the harbour, either in improvements in gardens, Grounds, or any thing else. One single year steadily persevered in, in this way w[oul]d do much towards extricating us from all difficulties, but *two* would certainly accomplish it. And the object to be attained is surely worth the sacrifice. In that time, the Harbour instead of being a drain, would cause something handsome to flow into the Exchequer. But good God! If by carrying too much sail, we should be upset, before we can accomplish this object, – who can foresee what the consequences may be?

Pondering over all this, sometimes makes me quite low, and unhappy.

I think I hear your Lordship say 'yes, it is all very well, for an old bachelor to talk thus, who does not understand, nor cannot enter into the feelings of a family Man, and more especially into the feelings and views of a person in my sphere in Society'. Granted, but my reply would be, that the sacrifice is only temporary, and for the attainment of a most important object. I also feel, that this sacrifice would fall heaviest on my Lady; but I also know what her excellent mind is equal to, on a great occasion. And I feel, that if she was so deeply impressed, with the prudence, if not the necessity, of adopting such a plan, as I am, she would be the first to carry it into effect.

I am sure your Lordship will not be angry, nor think me impertinent, for offering my sentiments thus freely on so delicate a subject, as I have done in the sincerity of my heart – in the earnest wish for the prosperity and welfare of your Lordship's family, a wish, which had ever been uppermost with me, since I have had the honor to be attached to your Lordship.

In ten days I will if possible bring Morton[18] to a point, about the way-leave acc[oun]t but will not seriously menace him with the alternative of stopping the waggons, without further instructions, from your Lordship. I told him yesterday that I could not admit of any connexion whatever between the way-leave acc[oun]t and the Staith affair, the latter being quite a distinct matter.

---

18 Henry Morton, Lord Durham's managing agent.

I omitted on Thursday to mention Brook & Penny's,[19] that is to say Hancock & Rixon's[20] affair to your Lordship. They take a cargo of Coals in payment of their acc[oun]t once a month. The vessel may possibly be down in a few days; and the question is, is she to be loaden. This Vessel is freighted for the year by Hancock, and if we don't load her, it will likely make them clamorous. We had, therefore, perhaps better load her. She does not, I believe, take in quite 100 Ch. of Eden-main

> I have the Honor [&c.]
> J[no] Buddle

80.

D/Lo/C142/19 (76)   Pensher 15[th] Sep[tembe]r 1829

My Lord

I received your Lordship's very kind letter of the 7[th] just at the instant I was setting out for Scotland, and I have not since had time to reply to it, as it deserved. I am exceedingly grateful to your Lordship, and my Lady, for the very kind and indulgent manner, in which you bear, with the sombre effusions of my thinking, and serious fits. I think, however, that I have not made myself sufficiently understood, on some points, as I never contemplated the paying off of mortgages, out of income, and the stopping of Buildings, all at once. What I meant to convey, was, the propriety of forming prudential arrangements, for accomplishing, *all*, progressively – finishing the most important first. But this is all for discussion, in the *Cabinet*, and I shall not, therefore, now trouble your Lordship further, on the subject, at a time when I hope my Lady, & your Lordship, are enjoying the gaiety of Doncaster, & this fine Weather, which must greatly contribute to it.

The Dean & Chapter's reply to your Lordship's letter, through Chaytor, is a curious production – the *murder* is, at length out. They want to share in the profit, without incurring any risk of loss!!! This is quite a novel, and unprecedented feature, in the annals of Colliery letting, and none, but a Junta of Christian (Jew) Parsons could, I think, ever have had the hardihood to have broached it. When the proper time comes, they must be *handled* upon it, but let us wait for

19 Unidentified.
20 Unidentified.

the promised *projet* of the Fine, on 60,000 Ch. ann[ua]l Vend, and the estimated scale of profit, which these learned Doctors are to calculate for us. On all this there is great scope for discussion.

I saw Redhead[21] in coming thro' Newcastle to day. He says the referees for setting the Wear quantities are to meet next Monday. This w[oul]d appear premature, as the proportions between the Rivers ought first, by rights, to be settled; but Mr R.W. Brandling, whom no doubt your Lordship will meet at Doncaster, will inform you all about it. Redhead seems to despair of establishing the scale of prices, we have commenced with, and thinks we ought to reduce the best to 30/. This would, however, I think be quite absurd as I have no doubt, we shall carry it, by the end of the month completely. He says also, that the Coasters have flocked to Stockton, where more Coals have been shipped, since the 1st of this mo[nth] than had been shipped from the beginning of the year, up to that time. I however doubt the accuracy of this account, and I am for steady perseverance, in the plan we have adopted.

At Newcastle, the Ship-owners, are struggling for freights, and resisting the advance of prices. Still most Collieries are getting more, or less to do. Walls-end, & Bewicks, have ships to take off their quantities for the month. The Ship-owners are sticking placards in Newcastle – the following is a specimen

'Ship-owners, great and small
Freight your Ships be up-held
Or, don't go at all'

It seems that the Common Council of the City of London are shewing their teeth, and snarling at us; but this is what might be expected, they will not readily forget, or forgive, the Bridge approaches affair.

I enclose a letter from William Bell[22] our Fitter – formerly Lord Durham's principal Fitter, from which it appears that his L[ord] s[hi]p is going to re-let the Collieries now occupied by W[illia]m Stobart who is insane, and the leases of which expire this back end. This I think is a mistaken line of policy, on the part of his Lordship. Nothing but the renewal of the regulation would have induced the parties named, to embark in these Concerns – that alone can enable

---

21 William Readhead, partner in the Hetton Coal Co., director of the Hartlepool Dock and Railway Co.
22 William Bell, Sunderland fitter.

them to make money, and it would be strange indeed, if under regulation the Coal being chiefly Lord Durham's own property, if under his own management, he could not have made more profit, than any amount of rent the new lessees can afford to pay him.

The mischief of letting of Coll[ierie]s in this way is, that it introduces more parties, and more difficulties into the trade. I only hope his Lordship will take care, to bind up his tenants so, in this case, that they will not have it in their power to play 'Matty Atkinson' over again in the trade.

I enclose a note from Mr Burdon,[23] which is very civil and attentive, & shews kind feeling, and I have written him accordingly. I don't however see how we can be benefited by having our Road to the harbour included in the Stockton Road Act,[24] as in that case, it would be chargeable with Toll, and put under the control of commissioners, and I don't immediately see what good would arise to your Lordship from all this. The matter may, however, be viewed, and considered in all it's bearings when your Lordship next visits Seaham.

I have your Lordship's note written at the moment you were setting out for Doncaster. Rest assured my dear Lord, that nothing shall be wanting as far as in my power lies to accomplish your Lordship's wishes with respect to vend receipt & remittances, for next Mo[nth].

Our Vend is now quite a *jog-trot*, regular daily business, as the Fitters are taking off all the Coals, we are allowed to send them.

I returned from Scotland last Even[in]g having been detained all Sunday at Edinburgh for want of a conveyance. *Sawney* won't allow any coaches to travel on the Sundays, except the Mail, but I could not get a place in it. So I went to *kirk*, and heard a capital sermon of half an hour long.

I am glad to say, that if my directions are accurately carried into effect the conflagration in L[or]d Mansfield's Coll[ier]y will be stopped. I have seldom seen my way so clear, in so difficult a case.

> I have the Honor [&c.]
> J[no] Buddle

---

23 Rowland Burdon of Castle Eden.

24 A new Act for maintaining the turnpike road from Catterick Bridge to Durham via Stockton was passed on 8 Apr. 1829: Thomas Richard, *Local Records of Stockton and the Neighbourhood* (Stockton and London, 1868), p. 157.

81.

D/Lo/C142/19 (130)   Newcastle 21st Nov[ember] 1829

My Lord

Since I saw your Lordship at Seaham, I have been turning in my mind, how to turn Martin's[25] Bills, am[oun]t £1451. 16.3 to the best acc[oun]t with Henry Donkin for the arrears of the Herrington, and Biddick interest. I have ascertained that 'the House' will discount these Bills although they are made p[aya]ble at Lambton's bank here. This being the case, I submit to your Lordship that it would be more creditable, and have the best effect, to discount them and pay Donkin £1000 *in money* on acc[oun]t of Biddick. I would make it out thus

The Bills, amount to	£1451.16.3
Deduct Discount	19.3.4
Amount when turned into cash	1432.12.11
Amount of Bills, when cashed	1432.12.11
Cash to be charged to the Coll[ier]y Pay Bill	67.7.1
	£1500.0.0

That is to say, a cash payment of £67.7.1 will make up an even payment of £1500, which I should hope, would keep Donkin quiet, till we can get him another payment made. If your Lordship approves of this, I will, on receiving orders to that effect, act accordingly

I have seen Morton, and talked to him, about the Biddick *Title*. Stephenson is to be down next mo[nth] when he would be glad to promote any arrangement, that might tend to bring this uncomfortable affair, to an amicable arrangement, if Stephenson can be brought into it. But he thinks, it lies between your Lordship and D. Lambton's Trustees, and has little doubt, but Stephenson would sanction any arrangement your Lordship will make with them for attaining the title to that part purchased by lord Durham.

I have seen Tommy Fenwick also, to day, and have not been a little amused, at the high diplomacy, which he has practiced upon me, and which my *counter* diplomacy led me to *affect*, not to see through. In short, my diplomacy was, to act the part of 'Billy green' and not to seem to see through his little *harmless ruse*.

He was at Durham yesterday – saw, indeed got a copy of my letter

---

25 Unidentified.

to your Lordship on the D[ean] & C[hapters]'s offer for the terms of the renewal. Deplores that such a difference as to the am[oun]t of Fine, should exist. Thinks it most desirable, that your Lordship, and the Revd. Body should come to an agreement. Asked me, if I thought your Lordship would make an addition to the sum offered. Had little doubt but £39,000 would be accepted. Offered to *venture* to make any accommodation I might think proper, to entrust him with *privately* to *some* of the members, with whom he is most intimate, & mentioned the dean. Offered, to use his best endeavours, to bring about a renewal of the treaty, if I would sanction his doing so, but begged, that the whole affair might be considered as strictly *entre nous*.

I told him, I could not authorize him to make any communication on the subject, as I was not myself authorized to do so, by your Lordship; but I had not the least doubt, your Lordship would always be ready, to renew the treaty upon fair, and honourable principles. But that I never could advise your Lordship to offer a random sum like bidding a fancy price for a Horse. At the same time I did not suppose, that your Lordship was not, to be induced to amend your offer, as to the amo[un]t of the Fine; provided you obtained an equivalent, or something like it, in an extension of ann[ua]l quantity, or an abatement of tentale. In short, I *laid it into him*, as well as I could, and left it, to his discretion, to communicate these *unauthorized* observations of mine, as he might think it prudent to his *intimates* in the Body.

Now, from Tommy's manner, of introducing this subject, and of talking about it, I feel quite sure, that he was sent, for the express purpose of sounding me, as to the probability of renewing the negotiation, with the Body. I saw, that he had received his orders to this effect, at the Chapter meeting yesterday, as clearly as I saw the nose on his face. And I have not the least doubt, but that there is a complete schism between the *old* & *young* Rooks, as to the policy of taking a Fine, or renewing the lease. Let them *caw*, & worry one another, for a while – let us *open our Door*, but not bow & *scrape* them into our house, and relying, on the *Allies* – age & greediness, which we have, in their camp, we may fairly reckon, in carrying our point, by hook or by crook, in due time – probably by next July. Prudence, and patience, must be the order of the day, with us, and our *faithful Allies*, above named, will work wonders for us, The difference between the 'Bird in the hand', and the 'Bird in the Bush' will become every day more and more conspicuous *in College*.

Our speculations, however, on this subject, must be carefully kept to ourselves. The slightest whisper, of our ideas on the subject might do infinite mischief. And in any communication your Lordship may happen to have with any of the individuals of the Body, any allusion to my intimacy and conversations with Tommy must be *carefully avoided*.

I have the Honor [&c.]
J^no Buddle

82.

D/Lo/C142/19 (158)   Pensher Colliery 23rd Dec[ember] 1829

My Lord

I have this morning rec[eive]d your Lordship's Letter of the 21st Inst. returning Gregson's and others. My letter of the 21st from Durham will have informed your Lordship fully, of the position which Gregson has taken, and unless your Lordship can soothe him, I feel satisfied, that he will not give up the D[raf]t of the 99 years' Lease to *John*, until the £326.8.0 which he has paid for the expences of the Act &c. is paid him. How mortifying it is, to be opposed at every step, by this infernal Law-entanglement; but it will ever continue to be so, until, by economy and management, we can get out of debt, and then, all these Law-Leeches, would fall off like the withered Leaves in Autumn. It is really grievous to think, that the fruits of our best exertions during the best parts of our lives, is to be continually swallowed up, by Mortgages & lawyers – besides the pain and sacrifice of feeling, to be endured from their insolence. It is impossible to enjoy either comfort, happiness. or tranquillity, until the current is made to flow, in the opposite direction. Your Lordship will please to pardon me, but I really feel *nettled*, at the communication made to me at Durham on Monday. At the same time it seems the best policy, to let it pass quietly, as Gregson's open hostility might be injurious to us, in our present position, of entanglement, with Chancery suits &c. And under all circumstances I don't think your Lordship can possibly do, without an Attorney in the Country.

I enclose, in another cover, a letter from Spearman[26] – written in the style of a Gentleman I think, and as the valuation of his Coal, has been actually made, I don't see any objection to his being furnished with the Shadforth boring. And if we can make a friend of him, by

26 Henry Spearman, Recorder of Durham.

letting him have the Kelloe boring, under the restrictions proposed, it may at a future date lead to the winning of Kelloe, and his Thornley Coal, in one grand Colliery, for Seaham, in your Lordship's Family – *quite independent* of the Dean & Ch[apter].

Kelloe contains 1340 a[cres], 1 r[od], 7 p[erches] and Spearman's upwards of 1700 – making a tract of upwards of 3000 acres or 3/4th as much as Rainton. I don't know, if the *Church* lies between Kelloe and Seaham; but still, this is an object for the family to keep it's eye upon. And as an act of Policy, I sh[oul]d think it might be advisable, to continue the Kelloe Boring next summer in search of the Hutton Seam.

I hear under the rose, that there is a considerable *fistling* & cawing in 'the Rookery' at the result of our late negotiation for the renewal; and apprehensions are entertained, that we may have other schemes, & that they may, not only, lose the Golden Egg, but also *kill the goose*. This is the ground for us to push, by all means as the only chance of bringing them to reasonable terms. And a demonstration, by boring at Kelloe, and talking *knowingly* about the harbour, being within 8 or 9 miles of it, will at any rate do no harm. It the Coal should prove of good quality, to the South of Elemore, it is clear that the Theatre, of the Coal trade, will in a few years approach Kelloe.

The refusal of the Common Council, to recommend the City, to advance Money to Blanchard & Co.[27] will, I should expect, seal the doom, of the Clarence rail-way. These Common Council, and Coal, and Corn Committee fellows, are getting very impudent, and when Gregson is down I think the Committees of the two Rivers, ought to take it into consideration, whether we should take any steps with them. It is also for consideration, what is to be done, in the Committee of the Lords, when parliament meets.

The Weather, here, is now very severe, but we expect, to finish our year's vend, tomorrow, and to lay off the pits, as stated in a former letter. We shall, however, keep the Harbour workings going, at a moderate rate, as from what I gather, the stopping of them altogether, would have a bad effect, in shaking the confidence of the builders &c.

---

27   Henry Blanchard was one of the promoters of the Clarence Railway. After further difficulties in raising the capital for the line, he asked the corporation of the City of London for assistance, promising to supply coal at a cheaper rate. Although the Corporation approved of the railway, it refused the request on the ground that it would not be a proper use of the City's money. Tomlinson, *North Eastern Railway*, pp. 174–82.

I found the Brancepeth Squire in good health, but a little out of sorts, at the state of the times. The N. Hetton concern is turning out *very badly*, and his Hardwicke, Thorp &c. Tenants, have given notice to quite their Farms, in a body, if he does not make a large abatement of rent. This he has made up his mind to do, as he does not like the notion of changing his Tenantry; but to what extent, or in what way, he will reduce the rents he has not quite determined. He seems to think of 15 per cent 'till May, and then to have a valuation, like Mr Beaumont. The farmers are getting into a sad state – in one of the Newcastle papers of last Sat[urda]y 42 farms were advertised to be let.

Both at Collieries, and Harbour, we are in as good a state as possible.

I expect to see J^{no} Gregson at Newcastle on Saturday. I have not heard any thing more of Sykes. If we can obtain a Loan of £15000 through J. Gregson it would only serve B---ll right, to throw him overboard, and let him forfeit his £4000. His shuffling conduct, has been quite scandalous. If he makes, an effort, with some small payment & a *promise of more – to save his distance*, against the 31st Inst., we must not be *gulled*. We ought either to have the full £4000, or no bargain. We must not submit to another year's humbugging. I shall feel obliged by your Lordship's opinion for my govern[men]t on this point.

I have the honor [&c.]
J^{no} Buddle

I trust your Lordship's health, is still improving.

1830

83.

D/Lo/C142/20 (26)   Walls-end 13[th] Feb[ruar]y 1830

My Lord

I am delighted to learn by your Lordship's dispatches of the 12[th] Inst. that you have returned from Brighton, in such good health, and that you found my Lady and the little Stranger[1] doing so well.

I am happy to observe, that your Lordship found yourself, in such force for opening the *Coal Campaign* in the Lords.[2] I don't understand your Lordship to say, that my coming to Town again 'next Monday sennight' – tomorrow Week, the 22nd Inst. is requisite. I shall, however, hold myself in readiness; but if my attendance could be dispensed with 'till after our receipt, on the 2nd March, it would be much better, as I should have more leisure, and opportunity to get all my arrangements completed with Edward. The first Witness to be examined, I conceive, will be Dickson the Comptroller of the Coal Duties – in continuation, as his examination, was not completed last year.

Our case, I conceive, was fully made out, and what we now have to do, is to call upon Ship-owners, or captains, to prove the extravagant charges of delivering the Coals, in the port of London – as compared with the delivering at other places. Coal-meters – Water, & Land – as well as Coal factors, Buyers, bargemen, &c. should also be called upon to shew, in the same unreserved manner, as we have done, *if they can*, that their charges, are no more than reasonable, and fair. Or to disprove our statements respecting the enormous charges of delivery. In short all the parties concerned, in the delivering department of the trade, ought to be called upon, to explain the nature of their respective branches of the work, to enable the public, by having a full view, of every branch of the trade, from the digging of the Coals, in the Mine, to their delivery, into the Cellar, to judge where and in what particular department, abuses exist; and in what way they are to be remedied. Or at least, to be satisfied that

---

1   The Londonderrys' sixth child, Adelaide Emelina Caroline Vane, was born on 31 Jan. 1830.

2   On 11 February Lord Londonderry moved in the House of Lords for the renewal of the committee on the coal trade: *Parl. Deb.*, new ser., xxii, cols 392–4.

there are *no abuses*, and that no reforms, in the management, of any branch of the trade are necessary. Without such an examination into the *delivering* part of the trade, the public *ought not* to rest satisfied.

I will thank your Lordship to inform me by return, if you can, when I should be in Town, that I may arrange accordingly – and if my journey can be delayed, 'till after the 2nd Mar[ch] so much the better.

I hope nothing will occur to prevent our accomplishing the Loan, with Amory,[3] as it will be the foundation stone to a great *relieving* arrangement.

Gregson has seen Per[cival] Forster, who informed him, he now had no doubt, of Bradyll's advance to the Harbour being regularly made.

I have the Honor [&c.]

J^{no} Buddle

Your Lordship had better direct your ans[we]r to *this* to Pensher, where I shall receive it early on Thursday morning.

84.

D/Lo/C142/20 (41)   Pensher 1st Mar[ch] 1830

My Lord

I had the honor to receive your Lordship's Dispatches of the 27th Inst. [*sic*] this morning, before I called upon Edw[ar]d. I found him in the most sombre mood I have ever seen him in, since the panic of Dec[ember] 1825, and very much disposed to shuffle, and back out of the promise to support my plans with remittances as communicated in my former Letters to your Lordship. By bit, and by bit, I made out the cause to originate, in a confidential communication received from London this morning, of a very alarming nature, as to the state of the Currency & money affairs of the Country, at large – especially the Bank of England. He *read* some passages to me. One stated that the Bank of England had 20,000,000 of paper in circulation, and held 7,000,000 of deposits. That the whole quantity of Gold in the Bank, & in circulation in the *Kingdom*, was only 25,000,000. Consequently if a run sh[oul]d take place on the Bank of England, it would be

---

3   Samuel Amory, a London creditor.

minus 2,000,000 if it could even command the *whole* of the Sovereigns, now in the Kingdom – without leaving the Country Bankers a single sovereign to meet any run upon them. Altho' I cannot but think this is an exaggerated acc[oun]t it has *cut Edward's* comb, and he is evidently under feelings of great anxiety, and apprehension on the occasion. This communication recommends also, in the strongest terms, that they should not invest money, in any of the public securities, whatever, and adds, that the state of affairs are such, that the whole structure of our money system, may be blown to the Winds any day.

This untoward communication, has *cowed* Edward so much, and made him pull in his horns so, that I am really apprehensive of his *backsliding*, as to his former promise of support. He will not now bind himself for more than *one month* – to go on, from month to month at his option. This has of course, as your Lordship will naturally conclude, launched me into a sea of anxiety, as nothing can be more uncomfortable, than to have all our arrangements hanging by so uncertain a *twig*. I have found it expedient to temporize, for I perceived clearly, that if I had gone straight forward, at him, to *pin* him, to his former promise, he would have *bolted*.

He has consented, to make the remittances this month; but will not promise any thing for the next; and I am to make him an estimate of our payments, & receipts of all sorts, for the next six months, to enable him to judge, to what extent he may be called upon to advance. This is both a difficult, and disagreeable job, but I cannot avoid it, & must comply. I'm afraid, according to the present prospects of the trade, we shall require very heavy advances. For this estimate it is requisite that I should know the probable am[oun]t of all the Irish rents – to which Mr Andrew's[4] Letter, & statement does not extend.

I will order your Lordship's £1000 tomorrow, & £100 to Cowburn to stop his mouth for the present. Lord Castlereagh's £500 will be sent to Drummonds, to be *there*, when due on the 12th, and all the rest accordingly. I don't like to send these remittances, before they are due, because we lose so many days Interest by it. I am quite aware that Hildyard's Interest is not due 'till May, and have taken if off the remittances for this mo[nth] – notwithstanding which, they amount to £3789.10.4.

---

4   Unidentified.

As to any thing for Phillips,[5] or Sir H[enry] H[ardinge] the mere hinting at it, almost threw Edw[ar]d in to a cold sweat – I could not approach him at all upon it. At the moment, therefore, I see no other chance for these objects but trying Amory on the Policy. It really grieves me to think that I cannot accomplish the means of extricating your Lordship from all dealings, with this very low fellow. I would not advise your Lordship to make any changes in the remittances for this month, in obtaining the renewal of Dowbiggins[6] &c. Bills. This w[oul]d not afford efficient relief, and is attended with expence, & inconvenience in deranging our plans. Besides, Ed[war]d knows the List, and making changes would shake his confidence, as he is naturally very jealous.

Edward is very uneasy, about the prospects of the Coal-trade, he says he is sure, the people cannot afford to buy them, under the present *distressed*, and *alarming* state of the Country, and is therefore sure that our Vends will be very *moderate*. I really fear he may be too prophetic in this. If there is really any ground for Edw[ar]d's alarm, as to the critical state of the money machinery of the Country, I should imagine, that it must also be known in other quarters, and that your Lordship will be hearing something of it. He says, the people, *they find*, have got a *taste for Gold*, and that the circulation of their £5 notes, is diminishing. I send Letters, on other matters, under other covers.

The Marq[ues]s of Londonderry	I have the Honor [&c.]
Holderness Ho[use]	J^{no} Buddle
London	

85.

D/Lo/C142/21 (5)   Sunderland 2nd July 1830

My Lord

Electioneering

I have had Gregson, and Watson,[7] here, to day consulting on, and arranging all matters, for opening the Campaign at Durham tomorrow.

---

5   Unidentified.
6   Unidentified.
7   Unidentified.

All is arranged for bringing Sir Roger[8] into the Town, with eclat, tomorrow. Watson, and Hunter, will meet him at Darlington in the morning, and Gregson, and myself, will receive him at Durham. The advance Guard, will stop him at Darlington, to canvass the Freemen, in that neighbourhood; and we shall have the main body of the Household Troops, assembled, with the band, &c. to usher him into the City. On Monday and Tuesday he will be occupied in canvassing Durham – Wednesday, Sunderland, and Newcastle; and on Thursday, Shields, and the Outposts. *Neddy*, through *spite*, I believe, to *Taty*,[9] has promised us, all possible assistance, in every thing, & in every way possible, save *Money* and of this indispensable article, he won't consent to advance a *single penny*. It is, therefore, fortunate, that your Lordship has got £5000 nearly, and if Sir Roger is not bringing £1500 or £2000 of it, down with him, your Lordship will please to remit that amount, *immediately*, as the ready is *absolutely indispensable*. It might probably be best, to remit the money to the Durham Bank on your Lordship's *Electioneering* acc[oun]t and Hunter might be made treasurer, and be authorized to draw the Cheques.

Our own Inn, the Crown and Thistle, in the Market place, is to be head-quarters, it is a capital situation.

I cannot find that *Taty* has made a successful canvass, notwith-standing the noise and sputter that has been made about it; and I have no reason to doubt our ultimate success. Yet this *greasy beast*, is by no means an Enemy to be despised, and we must take the field with vigour. The notice is short, yet I hope, we shall make a good muster tomorrow – from the Collieries, and Seaham, I expect, we shall muster about 115 rank and file, of the Household troops, besides the garrison troops in the City, and the detachments from the outposts which will be brought in, on the occasion. Our attack must be brisk and firm, as by putting a good countenance upon it, and shewing a bold front, the Campaign may be soon ended, by our antagonist beating a retreat, as he did before. But the *Sinews* of War must *positively* be forthcoming. An idea prevails, that we are *poor*, and our opponent builds upon it. This makes it the more necessary to have the *ready-money* in hand, to put down this notion, as much as possible. The growling of the Durham, Stockton &c. tradesmen does us much mischief in this respect.

---

8 Sir Roger Gresley, 1799–1837, Tory candidate for Durham City. *Hist. Parl. 1820–32*, v, 417–20; *ODNB*.

9 William Chaytor of Witton Castle, Bt 1831, banker, partner in Sir William Chaytor & Co Bank, Newcastle upon Tyne, nicknamed 'Tatie Willie' on account of his grubby appearance. He came third in the election of 1830.

Gregson is in high good humour, and zealous, and seems determined to do his best, and Watson is sanguine, in his hope of Victory.

The Marq[ues]s of Londonderry   I have the Honor [&c.]
London   J^no Buddle

86.

D/Lo/C142/21 (16)   Walls-end 15th July 1830

My Lord

I have to acknowledge the receipt of your Lordship's letter of the 12th Inst., also your Lordship's order, with a letter from Amory, for providing the means of paying the Int[eres]t on the £5000 lent by him, on the Life policy – the pay[men]t of the premium on the Policy, and the repayment of the Loan by Instalments. The payment of the first £1000 which falls due, on the 2nd Jan[uar]y next will be quite out of the question, as our receipts at that time, are always very small. It is, therefore very well, that your Lordship has come to the understanding with Amory that he is *not to press* for the punctual payment of the Instalments as stated in the Agreement.

I find that *Tatie* is pushing his canvass *personally*, with the utmost diligence in all quarters and in every Village where ever a freeman is to be found – he gives them plenty to eat, and drink, is quite familiar with them, and is certainly gaining ground amongst them in the County. I don't, however, think, from the information, I at present possess, that he is doing so well, amongst the distant Voters. I think we have the *lead* amongst them; but then, the expence of bringing them up to the Poll, will be tremendous. If matters go to the extreme, I don't think £5000 will do any thing like covering the cost, the expence of bringing in the distant voters from all quarters will be so great. I have this morning received a promise of a plumper, from a Freeman in Dundee, whom I wrote to last Sa[turday]. The bringing of this man, if necessary, will cost as much, as bringing a voter from London – say £25. A *Thousand* Pounds will therefore only bring 40 of those fellows and supposing that we should have only 200 of them to bring in, it will swallow up our £5000 at once. I merely mention this, to shew the prudence of looking out for further supplies of Money, in case of need. Mr Taylor[10] has been very diligent in his canvass,

---

10 Michael Angelo Taylor, 1767–1834, MP for Durham City 1800–17. 1818–31,

his old friends stick steadily to him, but I do not learn, that he has increased his strength materially, by enlisting many new recruits, and I should think, the issue of the Contest will be against him.

I am preparing myself for a meeting with Edw[ar]d. I have made up my mind, to work out the security on the Pensher lease, if possible. The harbour must be kept out of his view, as it is by no means improbable, according to the present state of our affairs, that we may be driven to the necessity of raising Money, if we can, on the harbour, to enable us to finish it. This great work has now arrived at the most critical period possible. To enable us to place it in a state fit for opening, against this time next year, with reasonable hopes of success requires, that the work should be pushed, for four Months to come, at a scale of expenditure, that even with Bradyll's Instalments, we cannot afford, and at the same time meet our other engagements. And to relax in the works, let alone suspending them, would be injurious, to our Interests, and prospects, in this undertaking, in the highest degree. What is best to be done, under these embarrassing circumstances, requires the most serious consideration. I am, therefore, most anxious to see your Lordship on the spot, to consult on the course we are to pursue.

The Marq[ues]s of Londonderry   I have the honor [&c.]
London   J[no] Buddle

87.

D/Lo//C142/21 (17)   Walls-end 18[th] July 1830

My Lord

Since my return from London[11] I have very often had occasion to see *Tommy Fenwick* on different matters, and he has often thrown himself in my way, and never failed, on these occasions, to bring the subject of the renewal of the Rainton Lease into discussion. As I could not, however, make out, that Tommy was authorized by the Body, to *sound* me, I in a great measure considered it as mere

---

married to Frances Anne Vane, only daughter of Revd Sir Henry Vane, Bt, and thus aunt to Lady Londonderry. *Hist. Parl. 1820–32*, vi, 373–8.

11 Buddle had appeared before the select committee of the House of Commons on the state of the coal trade on 13, 18 and 20 May. The committee's report was published as *Report of the Select Committee on the State of the Coal Trade*, Parliamentary Papers 1830, VIII (9).

twattle, and did not think it worth while to mention it to your Lordship. He yesterday came to me again, to shew me, his statement of the Rainton, and North Pittington Tentale acc[oun]ts and I am quite delighted, to observe, that we have no *surplus* workings, to pay for *this* year – thanks to the 'Meadow Engine'. Next year, they will certainly catch us, but 'sufficient for the day is the evil thereof'. Tommy grumbled about this, talked about our application for Way-leave from Grange and Sherburn &c. and then entered again, on the old subject of the renewal. We soon got *very confidential*, and as I felt my way with him, I asked him, if he really knew, any thing of the sentiments and feelings of his *Maisters*, on this matter, or that his frequent expressions of a desire, that your Lordship should renew, arose, merely from his own good wishes, to serve the interests of both parties. Tommy exercised his best *diplomacy*, and after many injunctions, as to prudence, and secrecy, on what he could communicate to me, and as to what might pass between us, as old Friends, I think I elicited the following points, with tolerable accuracy, which throw considerable light, on the present position of affairs between us, and the reverend Body.

Our application for way-leave, from the Grange and Sherburn, have filled them with alarm as they suspect, that we have some Scheme on hand, for guarding ourselves, against the contingency, of not renewing the Rainton lease. The policy, therefore, of granting the way-leaves required, is under the most serious discussion, of the learned & Rev[eren]d Body, and the minds of those *Divines*, are sorely agitated, by the conflicting feelings of hope, fear, and interest. A desperate Schism, however prevails, between the old, & younger members. The *older*, which I shall call the *Liberals*, being for renewal, and granting way-leave &c. Licenses, while the younger members, are decidedly against these measures. Tommy thinks, the *Liberals* are the stronger party, and will in the end prevail. He is, therefore, of opinion, that the renewal of the lease is still to be accomplished.

I told him that your Lordship was always ready to meet them, on fair & liberal grounds, but as their last offer had more than doubled, both his own, and my estimate of the Fine, I was really *afraid*, to approach them again, on the subject; adding, that it was only from his own suggestions, that I had, with your Lordship's permission, made our late offer; and that, if I could have imagined, that their ideas would have been so extravagant, I certainly would not have recommended your Lordship to have made the application at all. I further observed, that if they still continued in the same mind, and were not disposed to relax, greatly in their former demands, that our further discussing the matter would only be a waste of time. I wound up this part of our conversation, by observing that, if the Revd. Body really wished to renew the lease, on fair, and equitable terms, I had no hesitation in saying, that your Lordship, would cheerfully meet them, in the same spirit. Many collateral points were alluded to, in this conversation. I told Tommy, that the Revd. Body ought gravely to consider, what would be the ultimate effect, upon themselves, if they *set their* market, by exacting too extravagant terms, in the renewal of Rainton, when they saw new, and powerful Rivals, springing up daily, on every side. And he knew very well, that the new Collieries, were all taken on more moderate terms by far, than they wished to exact. Tommy admitted all this.

He said, they wished us very much to purchase the Meadows Engine, which they would sell us very cheap. I replied that we would be disposed to meet their wishes, in any reasonable proposition, but at the same time, I did not see, what good could result from entering into treaty, for secondary objects, if the accomplishment of the great one, of the Renewal, was not seriously contemplated, as if we went into this, it would of course embrace every other.

I find that the Dean,[12] is at the head of the *Liberals*, and it is for your Lordship to consider, the policy of approaching him, through some channel or other, on this important affair – only be most cautious, in keeping Tommy out of *sight*, because, if by any accident he should be *shewn up*. It might close the only channel through which I can gain intelligence of what is going on, in the Enemy camp.

I have no doubt, but *Tommy* will communicate the substance of our conversation to the *Conclave*, next Tuesday, and it is by no means improbable, that it may lead to a renewal of our treaty. If any thing occurs, your Lordship shall hear from me without delay.

I hope soon to hear of your Lordship returning to the North, but it would be desirable, before your Lordship leaves Town, if you could get Banks's affair with Amory settled. August is at hand, and unless this point is arranged, the old man will be furious. Chisholme positively calculates on a settlement in August, and it will be impossible to keep him longer quiet without a payment.

The Marq[ues]s of Londonderry   I have the Honor [&c.]
London   J^{no} Buddle

---

12 John Banks Jenkinson, 1781–1840, Dean of Durham 1827–40, Bishop of St David's 1825–40. *ODNB.*

88.

D/Lo/C142/21 (19)   Newcastle 11th Aug[us]t 1830

My Lord

I was delighted to receive your Lordship's Letter of the 8th Inst. this mor[nin]g altho' I am rather disappointed to find that y]ou]r Lordship is not further advanced on your journey; and which I think accounts for your Lordship's want of intelligence. By the written statement of your Lordship's route sent to myself and Gregson, your Lordship is 4 days behind your time. You say Kendal the 7th, Carlisle 8th, Castle Douglas 9th, P[ort] Patrick 10th, Mount Stewart 11th, and our Letters are directed accordingly. Indeed I have written very few, as Gregson charged himself with forwarding the state of the poll, with all the Electioneering intelligence, every night, to meet your Lordship on the Road, according to the route you sent.

Our battle was a hard fought one, but our victory was complete.[13] Every man did his duty, and no exertion nor pains were spared. In 2 or 3 instances of the *Household troops*, we experienced the basest ingratitude, and desertion; but on the whole, they behaved well. This campaign has, however, shewn me some errors in our system of management, which must be corrected; but this is a subject for discussion in the cabinet. It was fortunate that we acted so decisively in sending for the distant Voters from all quarters – without their aid, I really believe, we should have lost the battle. But the expence of bringing them, paying for their lost time, and sending them home again – all to be done by money paid on the nail, is quite terriffick. I have not yet received a statement of our Expences from Gregson, but fear they will run near to £7000 altho' he told me he thought £6000 would cover them; but *odds & ends*, are tumbling in, without end, daily. And the thought of such a waste of money, at such a time, with other worry, has inflicted a bilious attack upon me, & I cannot get time, to lay myself up for a day or two, to get it shaken off.

Gregson's not receiving a remittance, as I mentioned to your Lordship, in a Letter to Kendal, threw us into the greatest embarrassment, on the afternoon of the day of the Election. Without money, we neither could get the Army *paid off* & disbanded, nor maintain our

---

13   Taylor (Lib.) and Gresley (Con.) were elected, Chaytor (Lib.) coming third; but Gresley was later unseated on a petition, for bribery and treating. *Hist. Parl. 1820–32*, ii, 366–8; Heesom, *Durham City and its MPs*, p. 43. See below, p. 220.

credit in the eyes of the public which was a matter of the greatest importance. Under the pressing necessity of the case, we agreed, that Sir Roger should draw 3 Bills, at short dates, on your Lordship which I was to use my endeavours with Edw[ar]d to give us the cash for – the amount being £2500. next morning, early, I went to Sunderland, and prevailed upon Edward to discount these Bills; but he would only do so, on my pledging my *honor*, that I knew your Lordship was provided with the money, to redeem this Loan in a few days, and that I believed your Lordship's remittance had not reached Gregson, in consequence of some break, in the correspondence from your Lordship being on the Road to Ireland. I am sure your Lordship will see the positive necessity of sending the money, to save my word, & honor – I shall, therefore, say no more on the subject. Gregson was exceedingly sulky on this affair, as he fully reckoned on receiving the £2500 from your Lordship – I never saw him in worse humour nor more disposed to pick a quarrel with us. I should scarcely think *Tatie*, will come again, after the *basting* he has got this time.

The Marq[ues]s of Londonderry	I have the Honor [&c.]
Mount Stewart	J[no] Buddle

89.

D/Lo/C142/21 (49)   Newcastle 21[st] Aug[us]t 1830

My Lord

I received your Lordship's Dispatches of the 18[th] Inst. last night. On Ben Wyatt's,[14] and Cowburn's letters I have thought it best, to write distinctly, under separate cover.

The City Election is, I fear, going to turn out, to be much more onerous, in point of expence, than your Lordship calculated. If the expences in London, are really £1,300 to £1,400 as your Lordship states, the cost, in all, will be full £9000 or better. But I should hope, when the acc[oun]t of particulars is rendered, a considerable sum, will be left, out of the above – otherwise, considering the number of Voters, the expences, in London, have far exceeded those in every other place. I have had no communication with Rawlings,[15] nor do I know if he has yet handed an acc[oun]t of particulars to Sir Roger,

---

14 Unidentified.
15 Unidentified.

or your Lordship; but I think it would be well to have the acc[oun]t to enable us to see, what the whole cost has been

At any rate, however, the amount, is quite terrible considering the exhausted state of the Exchequer. And I cannot but feel myself placed in a critical situation with Edward, as to the retiring of Sir Roger's Bills. I will do all I can, with him to gain time; but when put to the pinch to raise money, to support our credit, in Durham the day after the Election, relying on the £7000 to be supplied by your Lordship, and hoping that the expence, would not, in all, exceed that amo[un]t I pledged *my honor*, to induce him, to discount the Bills, that your Lordship had provided the money, and that the Bills would be paid without calling upon him, to advance any thing out of the general acc[oun]t. If therefore, I should, unfortunately, be under the necessity of going to him, to say that there is no other way of providing for the Bills than out of the general acc[oun]t, he will say, that I have deceived him, and I need never again, apply to him for assistance, on any pledge of my own. I therefore feel very uncomfortable, until I can see my way through this.

This system of representation, is now becoming so terribly expensive, that we need not wonder at what would have happened in Yorkshire, and Middlesex &c. No individual, be his fortune what it may, can stand those repeated contests, without ruining his family. The spirit of Liberalism is spreading most rapidly, and the late affair in France,[16] has given it an immense, and accelerated impulse. Brougham,[17] it is said, is endeavouring to form a party, to turn out the Duke. Should he succeed, we may possibly have another Election & another contest for the City, at no distant period. My only hope is, that after the signal defeat given to *Tatie*, it will be difficult to get any one to step forward, to *wrestle* with our Interest.

I have not time, to day, to say any thing on Coal-trade matters. Tommy Fenwick is better, & will, I hope, come round again. As soon as he is able to do business, I will see him & your Lordship may be assured, I will do all I can to forward the object of the Renewal.

The Marq[ues]s of Londonderry   I have the Honor [&c.]
Mount Stewart   J[no] Buddle

---

16 In July 1830 a rising in Paris against reactionary royal ordinances forced the flight of Charles X. He was succeeded by his cousin Louis Philippe, King of the French 1830–48.

17 Henry Brougham, 1778–1868, Whig lawyer and politician, Lord Chancellor in Grey's government of 1830. *ODNB*; *Hist. Parl. 1790–1820*, iii, 265–76.

Aug[us]t 21ˢᵗ 1830

I was at Seaham yesterday – a tremendous sea on, which had washed off 200 to 300 tons of Blocks off the unfinished end of the S. Arm of the N. Pier – there never was such a season. In every other respect, every thing is going on well – House building going on briskly.

I visited my young friends, at the Hall,[18] and was treated with my promised Duett – 'Sweet Home' – very nicely played. But poor Lady Frances has had an attack of tooth-ache. It was much better while I was there & I tried to *conjure* it away. Lord Adolphus[19] is in high spirits, but looking rather pale, as if he had not *romping* enough in the open air. By your Lordship's permission, I will take him to the harbour with me, next time I go, if the Weather is suitable. We are great allies, and every possible care will be taken. In Shaw's absence I really think some steady, decent, sort of man, beside the old gardener, ought to sleep in the House, as there are many loose fellows going about the Country at present.

90.

D/Lo/C142/21 (105) 5   Newcastle 6ᵗʰ Nov[ember] 1830

My Lord

I am much annoyed to learn that your Lordship is detained in Town waiting for the Tyne petition[20] – the more so, as there has been great apathy, and negligence, on the part of the Coal-owners, in signing it. Altho' highly approved, many have not taken the trouble, to come to the office, to sign it, 'till this day, and I have had Gills running about the Town all day to obtain signatures, and after all, some will not be got. I have requested him to send it off, by the Mail, at all events to night, to obtain the signatures of the parties resident in London, and to have it given to your Lordship without delay. I expect Brandling will write to your Lordship officially upon it.

I most sincerely wish, I could write something cheering to your Lordship; but to do so, and tell the truth, at the same time, is impossible. I really never knew affairs, either political, or private, look more gloomy. Oliver has been with me, as low as possible, about the

---

18 i.e. Londonderry's children, at Seaham Hall.
19 Adolphus Frederick Charles William Vane, born 2 Jul. 1825.
20 A petition for the repeal of duties on coal sent to London by sea was presented on 14 December 1830: *Parl. Deb.*, 3rd ser., i, cols 1115–17.

receipt of the Rents, which he says, he is sure will be the worst, by far he ever had. He has sold off, two of the Longnewton tenants, but has got little, and is sure, that many of the tenants in other parts of the estates are not solvent. He is to receive, at Wyn[yar]d on Tuesday next, and at Pensher on Wed[nesda]y. Many of the Wyn[yard]d creditors are urgent for their money, at the rent day, but I have told Oliver, to pay all his receipt into the Bank, and leave me to settle, with the Creditors, as well as I can. I fear *Edw[ar]d* will be greatly disappointed at the receipt of the Rents, and I shall have difficulty in getting him to believe, that they are not applied to some other purpose. I trust I shall have a better account from Mr Andrews of the Irish rents. The people here, are very busy about the rail-way from Durham to the Tyne[21] – I am asked to attend a meeting on the subject next Friday, when the prospectus is to be exhibited. The notion seems to be, that the line should run by Old Durham, Pittington, Rainton Bridge, Herrington, Grindon, and to cross the Wear at Ford – thence by Boldon to the Tyne at So. Shields. The distance is estimated at 16 to 18 miles – I think it is more. The money, they say, will be subscribed immediately. This will startle the *rooks* exceedingly, and will greatly paralyze the Clarence line, as it would suit the Sherburn *Circle*, much better than the Clarence. Whatever may be the result of this project I consider it to be our policy, to countenance it in the outset – it never can injure our Harbour, but eventually, may benefit it. This is all for discussion, and deliberate consideration, *in the cabinet*. The subject cannot be brought before parliament this session at any rate.

With respect to politics we are in a state of great excitement. The King's Speech in the first place, and then the Duke's, has caused the greatest disappointment imaginable, and dissatisfaction amounting to disgust.[22] The Duke's popularity has vanished in an instant, and the mildest epithet bestowed upon him, is 'military despot'. The Liberals.are delighted, but the timid are alarmed – both parties being satisfied, that the Duke's *apparent* ignorance, of the wishes, and feelings, of the great majority of the people, will soon bring matters to a Crisis.

21 The Durham Junction Railway. See below, pp. 256–7.
22 The new Parliament met on 2 November. The Speech from the Throne promised financial economies but said nothing on parliamentary reform. In the course of the debate Wellington, the Prime Minister, declared his intention of resisting any measure to that end. *Parl. Deb.*, 3rd ser., i, cols 52–3. The government was defeated on 15 November. Wellington resigned and was replaced by Lord Grey.

I have received a *Dunn* from Groom for Thorold's Interest, and Sir J. Beckett's Trust pay[men]t. Wilkinson of Stockton is anything but satisfied with the reply given to his application for pay[men]t.

The Marq[ues]s of Londonderry   I have the honor [&c.]
London   J[no] Buddle

91.

D/Lo/C142/21 (127)   Newcastle 11[th] Dec[embe]r 1830

My Lord

I received your Lordship's packet, last evening – enclosing My Lord P[rivy] S[eal]s[23] private & confidential note to your Lordship, with copy of his note to the Lord Lieut[enan]t, both of which I herewith return.

The new Ministry seem quite in a *stickle* to get yeomanry Corps raised, but I must own, for the reasons I have already stated to your Lordship I do not think the plan a good one. If it should become necessary to employ the military, in the event of riot, in the Country – let them be *regulars*. I have frequently seen the military called out, in our Pitmen's & Keelmen's *strikes* – both yeomanry, & regular cavalry. The former, ere generally a laughing stock to the mob, while the latter, were always feared & respected. I would rather go against a mob, with a dozen regular dragoons, than with a whole troop of yeomanry. The same men, as mounted special constables, would be equally efficient, and less expensive, and less *odious*, in the eyes of the mob. A *painted* staff, with G.R. upon it, is more awful, in the hand of a special constable, than a sabre w[oul]d be in the hand of the same individual, as a yeomanry man.

Morton called upon me, last Thursd[a]y morning, *privately*, on this subject, and I gave him my opinion, in favor of a well organized special Constabulary, and I think he fell in with my views, of the matter; but I strongly deprecated any *open* measures being taken, as it would shew a want of confidence, and apprehension, on our part, which would at once, set the pitmen, to think of mischief, if even they should not have had the least notion of it before. In this, I think he did not quite agree with me, but lest he should not have distinctly understood my meaning, I wrote him a *private* letter

---

23 In Grey's new government Lord Durham received the office of Lord Privy Seal with a seat in the Cabinet.

yesterday morn[in]g to explain my notions of the way in which he should proceed. And it was my intention to have stated the whole affair to your Lordship this Evening. I enclose a copy of my letter to Morton – he will probably communicate it to Lord D[urham] and your Lordship may perhaps collect something from it, to enable you to *pass-by* his L[or]d[shi]p's application for *Recruits* to serve in his Corps *at present*.

I offer my opinion on all this, with great deference, as I am confident your Lordship is much more competent to judge than I am, as to what is best to be done, in the present state of affairs – all one would wish, would be, to act for the best if one only knew how.

It may perhaps be best for your Lordship to keep the matter *alive*, without committing yourself with my Lord P[rivy] S[eal] until you are enabled to decide the course which you may adopt on the other more important affair. This matter is of great importance, and many reasons may be urged, both for, and against accepting – it requires great consideration, and ought not to be hastily decided – in the end I have no doubt your Lordship will under all the complicated circumstances of the case, decide correctly. In the event of your Lordship deciding to accept office, then I presume, the raising of a *Troop* would follow, as a matter of course, altho' under the circumstances of your Lordship's bare establishment of over-worked agents it would be difficult to obtain much personal assistance from them.

Should your Lordship decide, in the *negative* – I submit, that we ought not to go beyond, the Corps of Special Constables.

The Marq[ues]s of Londonderry	I have the Honor [&c.]
Seaham	J[no] Budddle

92.

D/Lo/C142/21 (130)   Newcastle 17[th] Dec[embe]r 1830

My Lord

I received your Lordship's packet of yesterday, but deferred replying to it 'till this Evening, to take the chance of communicating any thing that might turn up to day.

Cowburn certainly possesses the art of ingeniously tormenting, in an eminent degree, and of making 'much ado, about nothing', All that I can make out of his long *Brief*, is, that he *knocks under* to Boxer,[24]

---

24 Unidentified.

and *trusts* that he will abandon his order nisi, amend his Bill, and proceed. Corresponding with this man, on this subject seems to be quite as endless, as it is hopeless. He cannot be put out of his mill-horse track, and I don't see how your Lordship, is to elicit any thing satisfactory from him, on Robertson's business, unless you can do it, by personal communication when you go to Town.

The best part of his communication is that relating to Sir H[enry] H[ardinge]'s £4000. We need not hesitate to promise the regular payment of the Interest – this must be done coute que coute. It will be a great point to get your Lordship's mind set at ease on this point, and as you justly observe, it is not *increasing debt*.

I have some misgivings about Rawlings's ability to get the Bill cashed – tomorrow or next day will, I hope, bring something more satisfactory from him on this affair.

The Lord P[rivy] S[eal] has certainly given in, but I think the latter part of his note a *little crusty*. I expect to see Morton tomorrow, and may learn something more.

We have had a long meeting to day, on regulating the Tyne, but made slow progress – we adjourned to Tuesday next. The affair of the Coal-duties, seems to be assuming a brighter aspect. Tomorrow we shall write to Mr Spring Rice[25] to move for returns, of the cost to the Govern[men]t of Coals, in every way. They state the gross amount of the Coast-duty, at some way about £900,000, but then this includes the duty paid on all Coals, consumed in the navy, barrack garrisons, Dock-yards, Post office steam packets &c. &c. all of which amounts to a large abatement of the Duty. Then again there is the expence of all the Custom-house establishments, to be taken off the full amount of the Duty, so that it is questionable, if the real bal[an]ce paid into the treasury, amounts to £600,000. Lord Grey, I think, from his speech, the night before last, must be *regretting* a little, as I cannot doubt of his real wish, and intention to be the abrogation of the Coal-duties. The taking off, of the House, and Window Tax, would not benefit the labouring classes, who are *not subject* to those taxes. But every man from the Peer to the peasant will be benefited by the abolition of the Coal-duties – especially the latter class, as besides giving them fuel, cheaper for domestic purposes, it would be the means of creating more objects of employment for them.

---

25 Thomas Spring Rice, 1790–1866, MP for Limerick 1820–32, Cambridge 1832–9, Baron Monteagle 1839, Secretary to the Treasury 1830–3. *ODNB*; *Hist. Parl. 1820–32*, vi, 244–57.

The people here are all crazy about reform – the Mayor has given notice of a meeting at the Guild-hall, next Tuesday, to take the subject into consideration.

I shall be at Pensher tomorrow Evening and will be with your Lordship in good time, on Sunday morning.

The Marq[ues]s of Londonderry   I have the Honor [&c.]
Seaham Hall   J[no] Buddle

It is reported that Phillpotts is to have a Stall at Durham, and that Darnell is to have the living of Stanhope!!![26] This is not to my *taste* – I wish they had[27]

---

26 Henry Phillpotts (see p. 13) resigned his stall at Durham in 1820 on being made Rector of Stanhope, the second richest living in England. In 1830 he was made Bishop of Exeter, but said that he could not afford to accept unless he could continue to hold Stanhope *in commendam*. Amid pressures for Church reform this caused controversy; the new Government (members of which Phillpotts had attacked personally) refused to issue the instrument allowing the *commendam*, but acknowledged that he had been given a promise and undertook to compensate him with the first available Crown appointment that did not involve the cure of souls. The problem was solved by an exchange at Durham. William Darnell moved to Stanhope and Phillpotts took Darnell's stall, the sixth. See Anne Orde, 'Beetles in the Holes and Crevices: the Cathedral and Reform, 1820–1830', in *Conflict and Disaster at Durham: Four Talks delivered to the Friends of Durham Cathedral* (Durham, 2003), pp. 56–7.

27 The bottom of the page is frayed, so that the text here is incomplete.

93.

D/Lo/C142/22 (29)   Walls-end 7th March 1831

My Lord

The information which I have this day received respecting the machinations of the pitmen, induces me to think, that it is quite as likely, we may have a general stop, about the 20th Inst. as not.

All their plans are arranged, and the point which remains to be determined, is, whether the result of a general stop, is likely to compel the Coal-owners to *give in* – and whether it is worth a month's stop, to try the experiment. Great difference of opinion exists on this point, as at many Collieries – particularly on the Tyne, the men are satisfied with the prices for their work, if they could only have constant employment. It is chiefly the rise in the price of provisions, which has excited the spirit of discontent.

The whole affair will have the deliberate attention of the trade, next Saturday. I however, think it would be prudent to increase the work, at your Lordship's Collieries, and get a few Coals before hand, at the pits & staith, in the mean time – in case of the worst happening.

I have been endeavouring to draw every circumstance relative to the Durham Election[1] to my recollection – to try to make out what Letter of mine, it can be, which Chaytor's myrmidons have got hold of.

The only probable circumstance, which I can call to mind, is, that of a ragamuffin who called upon me, here, one Sunday morning about the time of the Election. He said he was a mason, had worked at Brancepeth Castle – voted at Russell's[2] Election – had come last from Carlisle – wanted work, & came to me, to ask for employment, as he knew my father very well, & if I would employ him, he would vote for whom I pleased. I gave him 5/- & directed him to Hunter & to remain at Pensher 'till I went there on the Tuesday following. He urged me to give him a line to Hunter, as he did not know either

---

1   Sir Roger Gresley had been unseated on petition, for treating and bribery. See p. 211, n. 13. In the ensuing election Chaytor's son William Richard Chaytor was elected with the Hon. Arthur Trevor. Chaytor, 1805–71, MP for Durham City 1831–4, *Hist. Parl. 1820–32*, iv, 636–7. For Trevor, see below, p. 231, n. 32.

2   William Russell, 1798–1850, MP for Co. Durham 1828–32, owner of Wallsend Colliery and Brancepeth Castle. *Hist. Parl. 1820–32*, vi, 1077–9.

him, or any body else at Pensher. I accordingly gave him a line, but do not recollect that I s[ai]d any thing more in it, than telling Hunter that he was a freeman & requesting Hunter to employ him.

When I went to Pensher on the Tuesday & inquired for my *friend*, he had not appeared, & I never heard, or saw any thing of him afterwards. It is, therefore, by no means improbable that this fellow, might be a Spy of Chaytor's, and that this was a scheme, laid to take me in – yet I cannot think, that what I might say in the letter I gave him, can be construed into an act of bribery, as I was not an authorized agent of Sir Roger's. I openly avowed, that I was a friend of Sir Roger's, and that I would do every thing in my power, to have him returned, but I disavowed being his *agent*.

I am very *fidgety* about this affair and shall hope to have a good account of it on Wed[nesday] morning.

I am aware how much your Lordship's time must be occupied at this juncture and will not, therefore, trouble you with much writing, nor will expect your Lordship to notice my communications in regular course.

The Marq[ues]s of Londonderry   I have the honor [&c.]
London   J^{no} Buddle

94.

D/Lo/C142/22 (41)   Pensher 29th Mar[ch] 1831

My Lord

I had the honor to receive your Lordship's Letter of the 26th Inst. yesterday morning, but the business of the Coal-trade meeting and other matters prevented me from writing your Lordship by last night's post.

If the remittance of the £1000 is not made on the 2nd April, it will be the same thing as your Lordship sending a £1000 out of the Irish money – the one must therefore stand for the other, until we can look about us a little, to see what is best to be done.

The spirit of the resolutions entered into at the meeting yesterday, was not to give in to the claims of the pitmen – particularly not to suffer them to work after the 5th April, unless they will hire as usual. This will bring matters to a crisis – they will either give in, or stop after this day week. They are by no means unanimous, & I do not, therefore, expect an obstinate stand to be made. The Hetton men are the chief instigators of the mischief, and but for them, I believe, that all the men in the Trade would hire, and go peaceably to work. They have already committed some acts of violence, and threaten vengeance against the men of any neighbouring Colliery, who may hire, without having obtained their full demands.[3]

We have a meeting of the Wear, at Chester, next Thursday, to resolve on such measures, as may be deemed expedient under existing circumstances, and I mean to propose, that we should have a Troop or two, of Cavalry, & two Companies of Infantry, stationed at Houghton. The pitmen have got it into their heads, that there are no soldiers in the Country, and that they my therefore, do as they please. The sight of a few soldiers at Houghton will, I am sure, produce the most salutary effect.

I have been to the Harbour to day, & find every thing going on satisfactorily, as far as the weather will permit. But the late gales of wind raised the sea, so as to break over the Dam & retard the completion 'till the middle of May. The mischief of this is, that it will prevent the opening of our Lime-trade, 'till the latter end of May, which is much to be regretted. Spence[4] has returned from Scotland, from his Lime-trade tour, which has been most successful, & if we could have taken the dam out of the entrance into the Basin, we should have had twenty sail of Lime vessels into the Harbour, to load immediately.

I saw Lord Elgin's[5] agent in Newcastle last Friday – he had been to see our Lime-works, & Harbour, and was quite *crest-fallen*. He says he is sure from the superior quality of the Lime, & the convenience of the Harbour, that we will rob them of their trade entirely – it is quite impossible that they can have any chance to compete with us. This quite confirms Spence's statement, and is very gratifying.

This will probably be the last letter your Lordship will receive from me, before you leave London – tomorrow or Thursday I shall

3 For the miners' strike of 1831 see E. Welbourne, *The Miners' Unions of Northumberland and Durham* (Cambridge, 1923), pp. 27–32. Cf. Carol Jones, 'Experiences of a Strike: the North-East Coalowners and the Pitmen, 1831–1832', in R.W. Sturgess (ed.), *Pitmen, Viewers and Coalmasters: Essays in North-East Coal Mining in the Nineteenth Century* (Newcastle upon Tyne, 1986), pp. 27–54.

4 William Spence, general agent, lime fitter and pilot master at Seaham Harbour.

5 Thomas Bruce, 1766–1841, seventh Earl of Elgin, soldier and diplomat. In addition to acquiring the Elgin Marbles, he devoted attention to developing the lime quarries and mines of his estates in Fife. *ODNB*.

probably hear from your Lordship, as to your route & when, and where I am to have the pleasure of meeting your Lordship.

A brisk canvass is going on in South Shields by J^{no} Brandling,[6] Ingham[7] & Ogle,[8] in case a member is to be returned for that place.[9] The Newcastle & North Shields people are furious against Mr Bell[10] for voting against reform, & are determined to throw him out for North[umberlan]d in case of a dissolution before the Bill passes. They won't have Mr Liddell,[11] either. Lord Howick,[12] and Beaumont[13] are the favourites.

The Marq[ues]s of Londonderry	I have the honor [&c.]
London	J^{no} Buddle

95.

D/Lo/C142/22 (49)   Walls-end 10th April 1831

My Lord

I was so fully occupied with the business of the meeting yesterday, which lasted *five* hours, that I could not write your Lordship by the Boy, in time to reach Wynyard by the time your Lordship had ordered him to be there.

It is quite impossible to describe the extent of the mischief, which the advertisement of the Northumberland magistrates has done. It

---

6   John Brandling, 1773–1847, Receiver General of Taxes for Durham and Northumberland, brother of R.W. Brandling.

7   Robert Ingham, Recorder of Berwick upon Tweed 1832, MP for South Shields 1832–41, W.W. Bean, *Parliamentary Representation of the Six Northern Counties of England, 1603–1886* (Hull, 1890), p. 165.

8   Unidentified.

9   South Shields was one of the boroughs proposed for enfranchisement under the first Reform Bill of March 1831, and enfranchised in 1832.

10 Matthew Bell, 1793–1871, MP for Northumberland 1826–31, South Northumberland 1832–52, *Hist. Parl. 1820–32*, iv, 229–31.

11 Hon. Henry Liddell, 1797–1878, MP for Northumberland 1826–30, North Durham 1837–47, *Hist. Parl. 1820–32*, vi, 114–18.

12 Henry George Grey, 1802–94, third Earl Grey 1845. MP for Northumberland 1831–2, North Northumberland 1832–47, *Hist.Parl. 1820–32*, v, 422–32. See also above, p. 146, n. 16.

13 Thomas Wentworth Beaumont, 1792–1848, MP for Northumberland 1818–26, for South Northumberland 1832–37, *Hist. Parl. 1820–32*, iv, 220–4. See also above, p. 146, n. 16.

has given the pitmen fresh courage, and vigour under the impression, that the Coal-owners are *cribling* (crouching to them) and that *they* have applied to the magistrates, to negotiate terms for them, with the pitmen!!!

The injudicious circulation of the advertisement, in the hand bill (copies of which I enclose) from the Coal-trade Office – *without the knowledge or sanction of the Committee* – placed the meeting of yesterday,[14] in an embarrassing situation. It was unanimously resolved, that the magistrates had acted injudiciously, and contrary to the spirit, & letter of Lord Melbourne's circular of the 8th Dec[embe]r last, and that the Coal-owners ought not, therefore, to accept the proffered mediation of the magistrates, nor attend their meeting tomorrow. It was, however, considered, that if this course was adopted, it might give the pitmen cause, to think, that the Coal-owners *dared not* meet them, and that it might also give the public an impression unfavourable to the Coal-owners. All this occasioned much delay, and debating, & besides, there was some difficulty in contriving how to get the proposed meeting of the Viewers, & Hewers, & the meeting of the Magistrates, effected in the same day. In the mean time, Hunter & Tom Forster[15] were sent to the Delegates, at their rendezvous – 'the Cock' – to ask them, if they still adhered to their resolution, of meeting the Viewers. They found the Delegates assembled to the amo[un]t of about 200 all seated at tables, so contrived, as to bring them all, into one large room. Hebburn[16] was chairman, & Dixon (of Cowpen) was secretary – pen, ink and paper was placed at the corner of all the tables. When Hunter & Forster were introduced, by a Backworth delegate, Hebburn was on his legs speaking. After reprimanding the delegate, for having introduced 'the Viewers', so unceremoniously, without first duly announcing them, & stating the object of their visit – they were asked, what they came there for? They replied, to inquire if they adhered to their proposition, of meeting the Viewers, on Monday. The Secretary was ordered to read the resolution, which he did as follows. 'It is resolved, and *unanimously* agreed to, that as the magistrates have taken up the grievances of the pitmen, the delegates shall not be permitted to met the Viewers, as formerly proposed'. They were then asked if they meant to leave all matters in dispute, to the mediation

14 Minutes in NRO 263/A2.
15 Thomas Forster, viewer.
16 Thomas Hepburn, 1796–1864, miners' leader, *ODNB*.

& award of the magistrates? They replied 'certainly not, *by no means* – they only wished to have an opportunity, of debating their case, with the Coal-owners before the magistrates, to convince them, & the public, how far they could beat the Coal-owners, but that they would not suffer the magistrates either to mediate, or arbitrate for them. They were next asked if they intended to stop the pumping Engines – they ans[were]d that they did not mean to stop the draining of the Collieries, but that it *should not be done by power* The next question was, if they intended to persevere, in preventing the Viewers, overmen, Deputies, Shifters, Horsekeepers & Furnace-keepers from going down the pits, to keep them right – this was answered by a general cry, that they had answered far too many questions & Hunter & Forster were ordered out of the room immediately.

On this being reported to the meeting, it was agreed, that a deputation of Coal-owners & Viewers should wait upon the magistrates on Monday – to meet the pitmen-delegates & simply lay the final resolutions of the Coal-owners, as to the terms on which they propose to hire their pitmen, before the magistrates, and to refute the erroneous statements of the pitmen, but by no means, to allow them, to interfere, in the settlement of wages. We shall, however, be prepared at all points – in whatever way matters may turn. My plan would be, merely to prove, to the magistrates, certain acts of violence, & intimidation, & demand protection for the machinery & for such men, as are willing to work, & leave every Coal-owner to agree with his own men. If the magistrates will but act, with due energy & *keep the peace* I will answer for it, the business will be settled in less than ten days. I fear nothing so much, as the supineness, and pusillanimity of the magistrates. The pitmen are all upon the qui vive to day – an immense concourse of people, is expected at the Moot-Hall tomorrow, to hear the Coal-owners *tied up by the pitmen*. I will send your Lordship a *Bulletin*, after our *trial* tomorrow.

The Marq[ues]s of Londonderry   I have the honor [&c.]
Holderness House   J^{no} Buddle
London

96.

D/Lo/C142/22 (55)   Newcastle 13th April 1831

My Lord
    I was occupied all day yesterday in meeting different Bodies of

pitmen, and in talking & reasoning with them. I have made out pretty clearly, the plan of their *Union* – it is in two branches, general, & local. The general Union extends only to 3 points viz. 11 days in the fortnight, 12 Hours for the Boys, and not to be turned out of their houses. The second has been conceded, & they have given up the 3rd. The only remaining point at issue, is to the 11 days work per fortn[igh]t.

The local union, goes to the measure of the Corves,[17] the finding of candles, gunpowder &c. and to certain items of the work, in individual Collieries. On the latter, there will be little or no difficulty – the only point remaining to be settled, is as to the 11 days' work.

We have had a full meeting to day,[18] and after the fullest consideration, it was unanimously resolved, not to depart from the final resolutions of the 28th Ulto., but to stand firmly, and resolutely upon them.

It is deemed infinitely better to stand out, at present, & win *our battle*, at this time, than to concede anything more, which would only strengthen the general union, and lead to perpetual broils, & warfare, with the men. If we stand out firmly, we are sure to *win* in a week, or ten days, and then we shall have a *lasting peace*. It has, therefore, been settled, that we are not to tamper with the men, any further, but to leave them to themselves.

This business has kept me so occupied, since your Lordship left, that I have not been able to attend to anything else. I am going to Pensher this Evening, but do not yet know whether I shall be able to see Gregson this week.

Enclosed is a copy of this day's resolutions, your Lordship has already rec[eived]d a copy of the pitmen's resolutions, as communicated to the adjourned meeting of the magistrates on Monday. The latter gentlemen are quite *huffed* with us, and would I believe, be very tardy in rendering us any assistance sh[oul]d we stand in need.

I have the honor [&c.]
Jno Buddle

---

17 Baskets in which coal was carried underground; measure of capacity varying between 16 and 20 pecks.
18 Minutes in NRO 263/A2.

97.

D/Lo/C142/22 (68)   Newcastle 19[th] Ap[ril] 1831

My Lord

It seems that the resolutions of the meeting of the pitmen's delegates, yesterday, were warlike. They are to hold out to the last – their first object is, to get all the manufactories of glass, iron, &c. stopped for want of small coals, on the two Rivers, by which they calculate on getting the body of manufacturers dissatisfied, and to make common cause with them, as well as Keelmen, Trimmers, Casters, & Sailors in the end. They have drawn the money out of their Boxes (Friendly Societies) which has given them to the am[oun]t of 27/- or 28/- each man, on the average, which they reckon will serve them a fortnight, after which they must *fend* as well as they can.

Percy-main Coll[ier]y on the Tyne, is nearly out of small Coal for working the pumping Engines and it was intended to have drawn a supply out of one of the pits this morning, where there is an ample supply stored below. The pitmen, however, from the neighbouring Collieries, to the amo[un]t of several hundreds, assembled at 4 o'clock in the morning, & drove off the people who were going to draw the Small Coals, and beat many of them barbarously. Unless a supply of Small Coals can be drawn, the Engines must stop to the great injury of the Coll[ier]y. The Body of pitmen, are getting more insolent every hour, they are stopping Waggons &c. and it is quite clear, that they will soon proceed to violence.

A number of Special Constables has been sworn in today on the Tyne, but we are woefully in want of arms. We have nothing but staves & the pitmen are as well provided in that respect as we are – besides which they have a good many fire arms. A few chests of Cutlasses & Pistols, would be of the greatest service, if we knew where, or how, to get them. If our Constables were provided with arms of this sort, they would feel confidence, and keep the peace. Could your Lordship put us in the way of obtaining a supply, from some of the Gov[ernmen]t depots – if from the Tower, they might be down by a steamer, in a few days. The North[umberlan]d Magistrates now seem disposed, to act with more energy than the Houghton gen[tleme]n. They meet at N[ew]castle tomorrow & are to adjourn from day to day, as long as it may be necessary.

I have just returned from Houghton, where Messrs Burdon,[19]

---

19 Rowland Burdon of Castle Eden.

Robinson,[20] Fox,[21] Lorain,[22] Greenwell[23] & Dr Fenwick,[24] formed the bench. Burdon was *worse* than ever, & almost abused the Coal-owners & particularly the Sec[retar]y at War for having sent the Dragoons to Houghton – without consulting the Magistrates. Thanks to the good sense, & energy, of Dr Fenwick. It was at length resolved, that application sh[oul]d be made to the Commander of the District for more troops, and that we should have (if we can get them) Infantry, from Sunderland stationed as follows: 40 at Lumley, 40 at Chilton-moor, 40 at Bowers, 40 at Fatfield & 40 at Hetton. But as the troops cannot act, except in the presence of a magistrate, some one, or two of the Body, must be got to stay at Houghton. When I left, they were talking of Loraine, and Daile,[25] for this duty.

The pitmen are to hold a grand meeting on the Ballast-hills at Jarrow, next Thursday. These hills are situated on the S. Side of the Tyne, about a mile & half below my house at Walls-end. They have chosen this position, on account of its not being assailable by cavalry, & also, if necessary, they can easily cross the river, to the Hawden Ballast Hills – out of the jurisdiction of the Durham magistrates. I have little doubt of their proceeding to mischief, after this meeting, unless they are restrained by force. The best thing would be, to prevent the meeting, but it does not appear that the magistrates think they have any right to prevent it. The circumstance described in the enclosed paper, is true – but worse than described – the Corves were thrown down the pit, then fire, to set them, & the pit on fire; but two men, happening to be down, prevented the fire from taking effect. They threaten to do this, with all pits, where *any sort* of work is attempted. I have not time for more – matters are drawing to a crisis.

The Marq[ues]s of Londonderry   I have the honor [&c.]
London   J^no Buddle

---

20 George Robinson, Hendon Lodge, Sunderland.
21 George Fox, Westoe.
22 William Loraine.
23 William T. Greenwell, Greenwell Ford, Durham.
24 Dr Ralph Fenwick, Durham.
25 E. Dale, Ryhope.

98.

D/Lo/C142/22 (70)   Walls-end 21ˢᵗ Ap[ril] 1831

My Lord

I received information from time to time during the last 3 or 4 days that the Hetton men were to cross the River, after the meeting to day, with the North of Tyne men, to *rase* my House and that of the resident Agent, here, to the Ground, and to murder us.

Our pits, in the event of any men going down, to keep them in order were to be attacked last night, by the Killingworth men, *whose turn it was for duty*. As the plan of our magistrates is not to give us protection, 'till after mischief has *actually been done*, I did not think it prudent, to risk the *shafters* going to work, but armed the Special Constables as well as I could, to protect the Store-houses, granaries &c.

During the night, our patrols observed the Enemies' scouts prowling about; but as they did not find anything stirring about the pits, the party destined for the attack, did not approach.

Having rec[ieve]d further information, as to the attack upon myself, from the Hetton men – for the purpose of killing, or *frightening me out of the Country*; both of which I determined to avoid if possible, I decided on preparing myself for a desperate resistance, in the event of being attack[ed]. I had 64 special Constables – upwards of 20 of them my old Rifle-men[26] – one artillery, 3 Infantry, and two men of war Penshioners, besides the Agents & Overmen &c. who I know would stand by me to the last. During the early morning I got two six pounder Ship Guns dug out of a ballast-heap, had them mounted on temporary carriages, and all fit for service by 7 o'clock. The pitmen at the different Collieries were then mustering and the *scaling* of my two guns, announced that I was ready for them. I put my House & offices, in the best state of defence I could, armed my old Riflemen with the muskets, and gave the Guns in charge of the artillerymen and old sailors. I then went to Mr Clark,[27] & Mr Sanderson,[28] two magistrates – told them what I had done, & declared that I was determined to defend myself to the last extremity coute que coute, whether the magistrates would support me with the military or not.

---

26 Buddle commanded the Wallsend Rifle Corps raised by William Russell, like other similar bodies of volunteers, to meet the threat of French invasion in 1803.

27 William Clarke, Benton House, Newcastle.

28 R.B. Sanderson, Jesmond Dene.

These gen[tleme]n entered fully & cordially into my plan, & declared that they would use their utmost exertions to induce the magistrates, at the adjourned Sessions, to send some cavalry to support me, if any hostile movement should be made against me from the meeting, and I was directed to send an express to them, when the meeting began to dissolve. The meeting began to assemble between *ten* and 11 o'clock, but was not fully formed 'till twelve. The position was taken up by the different Colliery Battalions, with military precision – the men marching 3 abreast, with a sergeant to every nine, & a *Capt[ain]* to every twenty. The meeting continued in deliberation for an hour, the different battalions filing off in good order, several embarked in Keels, steam & small boats, & crossed, or went up, or down the River. I immediately sent this information to the magistrates, & in less than two hours, Messrs Clarke, Sanderson and Bigge[29] senior arrived with a Troop of the 3rd Light Dragoons, at my post – just as the last of the pitmen had left the ballast Hills. The Deputy Lieutenants had ordered out Bells yeomanry this morning – to assemble in Newcastle. The different Battalions of the pitmen marched home, & *towards* home, in the most peaceable manner – and all that I have yet heard is, that they resolved to be *firm* but peaceable. If this is the fact I attribute it mainly, to the shewing of the military power as they had got it into their heads, that there were only 15 Dragoons in the Barracks at Newcastle, & I am certain, that the *shewing* of the troops to day will be attended with the most beneficial results. The keeping of the Troops shut up in the Barracks has hitherto, done incalculable mischief. This night, & tomorrow, will prove whether the pitmen have resolved to remain quiet, as should this be the case, they will not interrupt the drawing of Small Coals for the use of the Steam Engines any longer, and should this be the case, the combination will break down very soon.

The Wear has been deserted by the pitmen to day, and tranquil, but the Hetton Constables could not execute 8 Warrants yesterday. It is clear that petty tradesmen, & publicans are subscribing to support the pitmen. Our patrol, in this small place, picked up a list of subscriptions last night, which had been dropped by one of the delegates – a Butcher, & a Publican had each subscribed £5 – others £1 & 10/- 5/- 1/6 & even 6d – to the amo[un]t of nearly £20. This is, however, triflling & must soon have an end.

---

29 Charles William Bigge.

The Marq[ues]s of Londonderry   I have the honor [&c.]
London   J^{no} Buddle

99.

D/Lo/C142/22 (81)   Newcastle 4th May 1831

My Lord

   I enclose your Lordship a copy of the Resolutions of this day's meeting,[30] and hope that Mr H. Brandling's interview with your Lordship will lead to a better understanding between the trade & your Lordship. Unanimity was never more necessary to the welfare of the Trade, than at the present moment. An attempt is to be made to shake the frightful power of the Union by all the working Collieries, supporting the *ten* who are not at work. Against the arbitrary dictation of this *Hydra* – God knows whether it may succeed or not. If the power of this *Monster* cannot be checked, we shall have another stop in a couple of months. In short there is no certainty of any Colliery continuing in work for a month.

   Ed[war]d has got home. I will see him in a day, or two.

   The *March of intellect* has reached the Auckland country. The Black Boy Coll[ier]y[31] has stopped & the men, are *uniting*. What will Brother Jonathan say to this?

                                                   I have the honor [&c.]
                                                   J^{no} Buddle

100.

D/Lo/C142/22 (85)   Newcastle 9th May 1831

My Lord

   Mr Trevor[32] wrote your Lordship from Pensher, the result of our meeting with the delegates of that Coll[ier]y – those from Rainton & Pittington did not look near us. Our line was short, merely to offer them all they had asked on hewing, narrow work &c. amounting

---

30 Minutes in NRO 263/A2.
31 The Black Boy Colliery near Bishop Auckland was owned by members of the Backhouse family.
32 Hon. Arthur Hill Trevor, 1798–1862, MP for Durham City 1831–43, *Hist. Parl. 1820–32*, v, 628–31.

to about £3000 a year. We pressed them to go to work immediately, and quit the Union, but this they very civilly, but firmly refused to do, unless they obtained the permission of the *united Delegates*. I asked them, as they had now got all they asked for, if they would be permitted to go to work, before all the rest of the Collieries went to work. They replied that they could not answer this question, 'till after they consult the united delegates, tomorrow, when they will inform us what they will be permitted to do.

I learn, however, that their [*sic*] is to be a meeting of Delegates at Houghton this Evening, when I can scarcely doubt that a general break up will take place, and that all the men on the Wear, will bind tomorrow, or on Wed[nesday], as Redhead has just come from Hetton, and informs me, that their men have struck their Colours, *without having gained any concessions at all*, except the 30/- per Fortnight. And the Lambton men have done the same, so that your Lordship's men are the only gainers by the stop.

We got our pits, Walls-end, Willington and Percy-main, to work on the Tyne this morning, and as the Wear men will follow in a day, or two, without obtaining their demands on Hewing &c. At any rate the Tyne Owners, will not give up this point, nor anything else, except what has been already conceded, as the pitmen are sure to give in, during the week – the firm and decisive answer of the Coal-owners last Saturday broke their spirit, and the setting the pits to work under protection, has confirmed the determination of the Coal-owners. If this had been done at first, the stop would not have lasted a fortnight. I am desperately low at the thoughts of our being the only beaten party, in the trade, and that our pay Bills should be increased £250 a mo[nth] more than our Neighbours.

The Marq[ues]s of Londonderry   I have the honor [&c.]
Mount Stewart   J^no Buddle

101.

D/LO/C142/22 (92)   Newcastle 14th May 1831

My Lord

The requisite complement of men is now bound at your Lordship's Coll[ierie]s & we fully expect they will resume work on Monday – especially as Lord Durham's men after holding out all the week for an advance on the Hewing &c. similar to your Lordship's, have given up the point, and began to bind generally this morning. All is not yet, however, quite certain, as the *Union* is not broken and the Hetton men still stand out in hopes of forcing their masters to give the same advances, as your Lordship has done. The Comm[itt]ee are to meet on Mond[a]y to take this point into consideration & my notion is that they will give in & that the pitmen will shout 'Victory' as they have done at Rainton.

There has been another meeting to day of the Coal owners, at Newcastle – all very uncomfortable as your Lordship's handbill is considered a breach of faith. The Tyne people are determined to hold out, to the last, and my belief is, that they will succeed, before another week passes over – On Monday coercive measures are to be taken, against the bound men. The bound men, at the three Western coll[ierie]s Tanfield-moor, Beamish and Pontop, have decided to start on Monday, in defiance of the Union.

I have this instant received your Lordship's Letter of the 11th and am glad to learn, that your Lordship will be here, next week, as a meeting with Edw[ar]d before he starts for London, on financial matters, is quite indispensable. I hope Lord Castlereagh's efforts will be crowned with success, & that the contest will not be a very expensive one.[33] Hoping soon to have the pleasure of seeing your Lordship at Seaham again I have the honor [&c.]

J^{no} Buddle

Hunter has been here, he was obliged to make a great abatement in the fines, as well as to give 1d per day additional on the driving, before the pitmen would bind.

The Marq[ues]s of Londonderry
Mount Stewart

102.

D/Lo/C142/22 (123)   Pensher 9th June 1831

My Lord

I am glad to inform your Lordship that our pitmen are all steadily at work to day and are *minding their hands* a little so that if no new

33 Lord Castlereagh was MP for Co. Down 1826–52. *Hist. Parl. 1820–32*, vii, 276–9.

freak comes into their heads, I hope we may get a better month's work than we at first supposed – but they won't stand the spurs at all. We must just let them jogg on, in their own way.

Hunter has shewn me your Lordship's Letter to the pitmen, and as your Lordship leaves me a discretionary power, as to communicating it to them, I submit that under the disposition which they are now shewing, to settle into something like their former habits, it is better not to communicate the letter to them. It might risk the exciting of them, to some fresh claim – as they think they made some omissions in their petition, & might have got more, if they had asked it. This is my opinion, but I don't press it against your Lordship's wishes.

The Hetton men are standing again, until the Co. dismiss some lead miners, they had employed during the Stop, and I have no doubt but they will carry the point. Some more of the Tyne Collieries have agreed with their men, having submitted to the most degrading and humiliating terms.

Morton has not yet got Newbottle to work – he has fought a noble battle, but will be overpowered, and must yield.

I return Lord Durham's note. I cannot perceive any analogy between the state of political affairs, and the pitmen's stop – but I have made up my mind, not to interfere in politics in any way. I will leave the affairs of state to the rulers thereof. I have far more than enough, to do with other affairs, without troubling myself with public matters. I have included the Harbour in our pay Bill to day, and expect Edw[ar]]d will send the money, altho' I have some doubts about it. We had a very narrow escape from fire, at the Londonderry Pit on Sunday Evening. By some means or other the Timber at the bottom of the Shaft had been set on fire – this set fire to the Coal just at the moment it was discovered. Fortunately it was extinguished, or the consequences would have been *most serious*.

The Marq[ues]s of Londonderry	I have the honor [&c.]
London	J^no Buddle

103.

D/Lo/C142/22 (133)   Newcastle 13th June 1831

My Lord

I have this morning received your Lordship's letter of the 10th Inst. *frank wrong dated – double postage.*

It strikes me, that it would be better that Rawling's should treat with Amory for Bills at long dates, than that I should negotiate with him by letter. It would give us a better chance of gaining time, and save trouble.

I am glad to learn that your Lordship's discussion with 'the Chairman' was of an amicable tendency, but at the same time I apprehend, that if the talking about amicable arrangements, or positive engagements is deferred, the opportunity may be lost – indeed I think the affairs of the trade, generally, are looking blacker, & blacker.

There has been a meeting, here, to day[34] to consider, what was best to be done, for the relief & support of the *proscribed* Collieries. The meeting was badly attended, & little disposition was shewn, to give any assistance to the Collieries, which are marked, as the victims of the Union. After some time the representatives of these Collieries, seeing that they were likely to be left to their fate – those who have agreed with their own men, seeming to think, that they were totally safe, came in self-defence, to a determination, if they could do no better, to offer a Bounty of 10 Gui[nea]s per man for Hewers. This startled the Gentlemen who had agreed with their men, as was this measure acted upon, their [sic] is no doubt, but it would excite a fresh commotion immediately & that another stop w[oul]d take place. This led to the passing of the resolution, a copy of which accompanies this. I much question, however, that the resolution will be acted upon, as the representative of Callerton[35] left the room, declaring that he would take his own course, and Col. Mills agreed with me, that we sh[oul]d do the same for W[alls]End. I will, however, wait 'till Friday, before the *Rocket* is fired, but if Crawhall fires the train, I question that I can hold back, as I cannot again place myself in *the gap*.

The deputy Overmen, Wastemen, Sinkers, &c. have this morning begun to enter the Union, & will in a few days claim an advance on their wages, equal to what the Hewers have got. The other classes mentioned in my Letter of yesterday, are discussing matters, & will not, it is thought, be long before they present their petition. Their demands *must* be complied with, or they will stop, which they know, from what the pitmen have done, will soon force the Coal-owners into compliance.

---

34 Minutes in NRO 263/A2.
35 Note in text: Jas. Crawshall.

I will forward some copies of the *rules* of the Union, to your Lordship, as soon as they are printed

I hear, from good authority, that the Hetton men, have stinted
themselves to such a scale of work, as will not raise by 20 Keels a
day, the regular Vend of the Colliery. *This is regulation*!!!

If there was anything like unanimity in the trade, there would be
no difficulty in advancing Coals 2/- on the 1st July which w[oul]d
indemnify the Coal-owners, for the advance they have given the
pitmen, and also for what increase they will soon have to give to
other classes. This however is impracticable in the present disorgan-
ized state of the Trade.

The Marq[ues]s of Londonderry   I have the honor [&c.]
London   Jno Buddle

104.

D/Lo/C142/22 (144)   Walls-end 27th June 1831

My Lord
I am happy to learn from you Lordship's Letter of the 25th Inst.
that you entertain the expectation of being able to run down, in
the Mail, to be present at the loading of the first Coals at the new
Harbour.[36] Your Lordship's presence, on the occasion, although it is
to be as *quiet* as possible, will give countenance & a degree of *éclat*
to the commencement of this important concern, which it would not
otherwise possess.

The 'Lord Seaham'[37] will take in the first Cargo of Coals. She is
a fine Ship, is in great forwardness – will be launched on Sat[ur]-
d[a]y the 9th July – will be rigged on the 11th & 12th, will be taken
round from the Tyne, to the Harbour, by a Steam Boat on Tuesday the
12th and will be loaden on the 13th Wednesday. This is our plan, at
present, and I hope nothing will occur to interrupt it. If the Weather
is favorable I purpose to go round in the L[or]d Seaham, with Spence
& a few friends, from Jarrow Quay to the Harbour.

How happy should I be, if this was the only object to which my
mind had to be directed, or to which I had to draw your Lordship's

36 The first coals were shipped from Seaham on 25 July, without ceremony. An
     account is given in Mackenzie and Ross, *Historical View of the County Palatine
     of Durham*, i, 376.
37 A collier owned by Buddle.

attention – the picture would be a pleasing one. Necessity, however, unfortunately compels me to be incessantly drawing your Lordship's attention to matters of a very different character, and against which it is impossible to shut one's eyes or be silent. I need scarcely say that I allude, to the present most distressing & pressing state of our pecuniary affairs. I feel that they are hurrying on, with daily acceleration to a crisis, and that speedy relief must be had, to the extent of at least £20,000, or we shall be driven to a *capitulation* with our Creditors. To keep ourselves afloat, by the renewal of Bills, is according to my conviction, impracticable, as the expence of such a system, for stamps, & discount, even supposing that the Creditors, could be prevailed with, to go on, in this way, would soon swallow up all income, & leave no surplus for liquidation. The most of the Colliery tradesmen have been called upon to renew their *long-winded* Bills, once and some twice, which has caused considerable uneasiness – bordering on alarm, and to have to go to them again will destroy their confidence in our Credit. The following is a list of the Coll[ier]y Tradesmen's Bills, which have been renewed, in the course of the last 3 pays, and which ought to be paid on the pay-days as under.

Pay ending July 8th ----	£411.	15.	0
22	950.	7.	10
Augt 5	1531.	13.	2
19	1437.	7.	10
Sep. 2	2140.	0.	0
16	2345.	16.	8
30			

These are independent of your Lordship's Tradesmen's Bills, and other payments. As the Colliery & Harbour Pays, in July, for *Wages alone*, will absorb the whole of the Fitters' Bills, to be received on the 2nd, and as Edw[ar]d will be called upon, to remit something to your Lordship, I don't think he will pay any of the tradesmen's Bills falling due in July, which will expose us to the consequences of legal measures, should they be compelled by their own necessities to take them.

Assuming that our Vend in July may be about the same as this mo[nth] suppose £15000 receipt, we shall have probably £4000 surplus after paying *Wages*, on the 2nd Aug[us]t but then the *3 pays* fall in Sept[ember], which will absorb all again. I really do not know what to do, or how to turn myself, in the midst of all this pressure, as I cannot see my way, at all, to the only mode that is open to us, viz. the raising of a large sum, by sale, or otherwise, for relief. All property is so entangled under settlement &c. that it cannot be rendered available for such a purpose.

The Marq[ues]s of Londonderry   I have the Honor [&c.]
London   J^no Buddle

If your Lordship could run down, as you propose, to see the Lord Seaham loaded probably something might be divised for relief with Gregson. Indeed your Lordship's presence in the North seems almost indispensable, as some decisive steps must of necessity 'eer long be taken. To carry on our concerns, under such circumstances, much longer, does not seem practicable.

105.

D/Lo/C142/22 (146)   Walls-end 29th June 1831

My Lord

I have received your Lordship's long and serious Letter of the 27th Inst. I have thought on the various suggestions, which your Lordship has thrown out, for obtaining relief, with all the attention I possess – until I am almost bewildered, but cannot as yet see my way, or bring my mind steadily to bear on, anything like a feasible plan for affording efficient relief. I will endeavour to follow your Lordship's suggestions in the order they occur, and remark upon them as I go on. Your Lordship says 'I do trust, by commencing that great nostrum of *reform* in our expenditure, in every thing, so fatal a blow to the family may be avoided.' No doubt, retrenchment, is the foundation of all prosperity, but then, it *grows* slowly, and requires *time* to ripen it's fruit. But at all costs, it is prudent to adopt it, as it cannot fail to produce the most beneficial results.

'We are sure of our means before November.' I do not know to what means your Lordship alludes. 'As soon as the Harbour can *ship* Coals, I would stop all the finishings for appearance &c. till next year'. It is not intended to do anything in this way – the expenditure will be reduced, but still it will be considerable as the work at the N. pier-head, and the S. Breakwater *must be* carried on.

'I have written to propose to stop every thing he possibly can at Wyn[yar]d'. This is prudent, but I cannot help recollecting that your

Lordship promised me the same thing in Sep[tember] 1828 when we were on the point of commencing the Harbour.

'I will endeavour to retrench & cut down in every way & when we meet after parliament is up, we can see what is to be done'. I fear that circumstances will not permit us to wait 'till Parliament is up, to make an arrangement – they are already *most pressing*.

'Cannot a certain sum be raised on the Harbour works?' Perhaps it might after the shipment of Coals commences – not sooner I think. I will make all the inquiry I can in this Country, & your Lordship would do well to inquire in London.

'Why are we at once to give up the hope of reducing our Debts from income? Surely it is a large one, and time and economy will do very much. There is much in this subject I would say &c.' The chief reason is the want of *time* – payments to a large amo[un]t have now become so pressing, that we cannot obtain time, to allow income to *flow in* to meet them – particularly as we have got into a system of *accommodation* paper, which will cost 12 per cent, or more, in stamps discounts & other expences, to *gain time* even if we could obtain it. Scarcely any amo[un]t of Income, can overtake such an amo[un]t of debt in such circumstances.

Your Lordship says 'you know how entirely I rely upon you – pray consider by what possible sacrifice we can obtain a smoother state of existence & I assure you I am ready to meet whatever you recommend'. I assure you my dear Lord, that I have not spared nor am not sparing, either mental, or bodily exertions, in endeavouring to effect, or devise something for *immediate relief* – as *immediate relief* & nothing short of it, can save our *Bark* – & it is quite impossible for me to describe the distress of mind which I am suffering, at not being, yet, able to see day light through our difficulties. The only consolation I feel is, that I have not been taken by surprise, as I have long already and from time to time expressed my apprehension to your Lordship, on the subject – but *pray my dear Lord, don't for a moment suppose, that I allude to this, at all, in the way of unkindness, or reproach. I name it to explain, that I have not seen the storm approaching, without regarding it, or being quite alive to it's terrible consequences.*

Your Lordship says you will sell Biddick or Herrington Estate – to meet Lord Durham's payment. Neither of them, alas! are saleable commodiities. Upwards of £20,000 has to be paid for each of them, before we can either obtain, or transfer a title to them. We only possess an interest of £6000 at most in Biddick – the remainder being sold to Lord D[urham] and the Land of Herrringon is only worth £12000 and the Coal is worth nothing to any body (that can pay for it) except your Lordship. I cannot therefore see the least chance of gaining any relief from those objects – besides, even if we could make any thing out of them, the time required for negotiations and arrangements, would defeat our object of obtaining *immediate relief.*

Your Lordship's remarks, as to the expenditure of Income for Family objects 'such as House, Harbour &c.' is quite correct. The only particular, in which I have differed with your Lordship, has been as to the *order,* in which those objects have been pursued. The Harbour, in my humble judgment, ought to have come first – it is to produce Income – the other is *dead-weight* but I have I fear, on various occasions said more on this subject, than in strict propriety becomes me. The only apology I can offer, is, that your Lordship's great kindness and consideration, encouraged me, at all times, to express my sentiments, on every subject without reserve.

Your Lordship thinks 'we are not worse off now, than we were many years ago, with infinitely more accomplished'. Admitting that our Debts are not, in the aggregate, more than they were, our facilities for obtaining accommodation, & Credit at Backhouses, are greatly diminished, since the change in the currency & the suppression of the one pound note took place in 1829. Since then, Bankers, like other tradesmen have been obliged to find *real money,* instead of *paper,* to carry on their business, and cannot therefore lend money (paper) so freely as they used to do.

I know one 'House' of not larger Calibre than Backhouse, taking in all their Branches that, within a short period of the £1 being suppressed, had £140,000 in Sovereigns to *advance* into their business.

Your Lordship says 'If we had no Elections, no Stoppages of Collieries, how differently would our situation appear'. This is a melancholy truth. Your Lordship estimated the cost of the Elections at £25000 – then we may state the defalcation of receipts in the two months of pitmen's stop, at £20,000 more, making £45,000 difference – in *nine months*!!! This at once accounts for, and explains the cause of our present difficulties. No stretch of economy, no contrivance, or arrangements, can bear up against such overwhelming shocks as these. The latter especially, was an occurrence, which could not be avoided – I expressed my opinion very freely, on the former, in August last. & shall therefore avoid any allusion to it now. I can only deplore it.

'If you rail at my prodigality, could you get a Loan on a quantity of Coals, to be given to A of B for your Landsale?' No, my dear Lord, it is impossible that I should censure a high spirited and brave man, for his devotion to his principles and party – for although, I might deplore his fall, in the breach, I could not but admire, & reverence his gallantry.

As to a Loan, on a quantity of Landsale Coals, it would be merely receiving pay for them in *advance*, and of course, a large discount would have to be allowed. We cannot attempt any plan of this sort, until we get the Landsale Staith ready, and the Coals led down – this cannot be 'till the beginning of August. We could not sell for 21 years, unless our Coll[ier]y leases were renewed, at any rate.

With respect to the sale of the Lime works, I don't know what to think – we could not sell, but at a great underworth, even if any body would buy. As to Spence, poor fellow, *he has no money* – all this, however, is for future consideration.

I have not heard anything more of the above-ground people, further, than that some Coal-owners have given an advance. Pitmen will never *condescend* to do the above-ground work – a pitman can now make more money in 3 or 4 hours, than the above-gr[oun]d man, can do in *twelve*. Indeed, in some places, their earning is quite shameful – if they would work, the best Hewers would make 10/- per day & the Putter lads 5/- – this is out of all bounds.

The Marq[ues]s of Londonderry   I have the honor [&c.]
London   J[no] Buddle

106.

D/Lo/C142/23 (9)   Newcastle 8[th] July 1831

My Lord

I went my rounds at Rainton & Pittington this morning, & regret to say, that the pitmen at both places, are completely masters of the concerns. They set the Viewers & Overmen at defiance & carry on the work entirely in their own way – threatening to lay off the pits, if every unreasonable demand is not immediately complied with. They won't allow an additional man, to be set on, and insist on all the old, and infirm men, being employed at *shift work* whether they are able to work, or not. They are concerting various new claims, the chief of which is, pay for the *over-plus* measure, which they consider the corves to have carried *all the last year*. The measure they are now sending, is deficient, but they reckon it enough, and they want to be paid for what they *think* they sent to bank,[38] *more* than the present

---

38 Sent to the surface.

measure all the last year. It will be a tedious calculation to ascertain this, but when it is done, they will make their claim. In short, they think they may enforce any demand they please to make, however unreasonable, by threatening to strike work, and we shall never have the least control over them, as long as we continue to vend every Ch[aldron]. of coals, as it is worked Coute que coute, we ought to have a few thousands of Chs. laid up at the pits, or we never can be certain of going on, without some new claims being made, for a single fort[nigh]t. It is the most unsatisfactory state of affairs I ever witnessed, and the increase in the working expences is beyond all calculation.

I met Gregson at Pittington to talk matters over generally – he thinks my plan for Biddick, with Donkin & the Harbour feasible.

I received a note from Edw[ar]d this morning to say, that he would be at Newcastle this afternoon, I therefore pushed on from Pittington to see him. First on the remittances, & second on the Grange coal. From all the *talk* which passed on the 1st point, I can make nothing more out of it, than, that from the load of renewed acceptances staring us in the face, he will not give any definite answer respecting a further present remittance, but if *all goes well*, he may perhaps relax a little, towards the latter end of the mo[nth].

But he has got fresh cause of alarm – his friend Hen[r]y Stobart has told him that your Lordship, it is understood, will not adhere to the regulation. He put the ques[ti]on *plump* to me, and I was obliged to evade a *direct* reply – if I had alluded to your Lordship's letter to the Comm[itt]ee I should not have been able to have got on a single step with him, on any point, as he considers the regulation, at this time, the salvation of the trade. He will only take *his own view* of the subject, and it is of no avail to reason, or argue with him. As to the Grange Coal, I am to draw up a memorandum of agree[men]t for a Lease, for your Lordship's and his approval. When it receives both signatures, he will advance the Pittington mortgage &c. money to Amory, and the remainder of the £10,000 between this and the end of the year for the most pressing calls. I must now, therefore, go to work to get this memorandum drawn up, as soon as I can.

The Marq[ues]s of Londonderry   I have the honor [&c.]
London   J^{no} Buddle

107.

D/Lo/C142/23 (16)   Walls-end 13th July 1831

My Lord

The receipt of your Lordship's Letter of the 11th Inst. this morning, has cheered me, as it holds out the prospect of my having the pleasure of seeing your Lordship so soon. I don't think I ever was so depressed, on any occasion, as when I wrote your Lordship last even[in]g – the inquisitorial *nibbling* which Edw[ar]d had inflicted upon me, for such a length of time, had totally exhausted my animal spirits, and depressed me almost to a state of despondency. I could think of nothing, but the disagreeable circumstances of this inter-view, and deploring out lot, to be placed in such a humiliating situ-ation. I therefore omitted to inform your Lordship, that I had been to the Harbour where the 'falling gate' in the entrance of the No[rth] Basin, was just being hung, and promises to be a complete job – it will make the Basin a sort of wet dock, & does Chapman's ingenuity the greatest credit.

Thompson is ballasting the rail-way & adjusting the machinery – the Lord Seaham will be all complete & will go round into the Harbour, this day week, the 20th Inst. & will be ready to load, as soon as the tides are good enough to float her out – say on Sat[urda]y the 23rd. But as this falls on pay Sat[urda]y the pits will not be at work, and as the best tide falls on Mond[a]y the 25th my notion at present is, that the best plan will be, to load he ready to go to sea, on the 25th at full high water, which will fall about 4 o'clock in the after-noon. I will be able to fix all this more definitely, on the 19th or 20th and will write to meet your Lordship at Wynyard. I shall be most happy to receive your Lordship at the Barracks & to have the *buck* cooked there, on any day your Lordship will please to fix – probably Monday will be best – after the L[or]d Seaham sails – if it sh[oul]d be on Friday, or Sa[urday] it will risk setting the pitmen upon the *ramble* & probably prevent us from getting her loaden for 3 or 4 days.

I must request the favor of your Lordship to furnish me, with the names of those friends your Lordship would like to ask, to meet your Lordship to dinner at Pensher, as they ought to have a few days notice.

I have got an appointment with H. Donkin, to meet him at Durham, on the 19th on his application about the Harbour, and I sent in my proposal for a lease of the Coal, under Carr's 'Hingley-hill Estate' yesterday.

Your Lordship talks of being at Seaham on the 22nd to meet me, on the proposition for the renewal, but I fear I cannot be prepared by that time, as I must see Th. Fenwick and know his opinion on the state of the Colliery, before I can form any calculation. He promised me to view the workings *this week*, but I have not yet heard of his commencing but I will drop him a line to *push* him on. Your Lordship will please to write Hickely about the Buck, and inform me the day you would prefer for dining at Pensher, with a few friends. But I will be happy to receive your Lordship there, any day & to stop as long as may be convenient.

The Marq[ues]s of Londonderry   I have the honor [&c.]
London   J^no Buddle

108.

D/Lo/C142/23 (30)   Jesmond Oct[obe]r 1831[39]

My Lord

I am just beginning to recover the use of my pen, and I feel myself impelled to devote it's first Efforts, to the expression of my profound gratitude for your Lordship's unexampled kindness and more than brotherly solicitude for me during my indisposition – It is all deeply engraven on my heart.

For 6 weeks I have been as competent to the discussion of any subject as ever I was, but unfortunately such a weakness and trembling continued in my hands, that I was not able to write, which was a great distress to me, and even now I feel difficulty in holding the pen.

In the mean time, however, the present menacing aspect of your Lordship's momentous affairs, has greatly occupied my consideration.

It is quite evident that a crisis is approaching, which will require some extraordinary means to meet it.

The Marq[ues]s of Londonderry   I am my dear Lord
                                                          Your Lordship's
                                                          Devoted serv[an]t
                                                          J^no Buddle

---

39 There are no letters between 6 August and this one of October. For Buddle's illness see Introduction, p. xxii.

109.

D/Lo/C142/24 (2)   Newcastle on Tyne 4th January 1832

My Lord

I have recently been in London with a view of setting on foot an opposition to the projected railway from Birmingham to London.[1] This measure had not excited the attention of the Coal trade in the North until it was discovered that some of the Projectors were purchasing fields of Coals in Warwickshire, Leicestershire &c. and that they held out to their subscribers that they would deliver Coals in London to the consumers' cellars at little more than it costs us to deliver them in the Pool, which if true, would be of most serious detriment to the Coal trade of this District. Under these circumstances it was thought that no time should be lost in arranging the best opposition that could be obtained.

Although in the progress of this measure we as Coal-owners should suffer so severely, and we are in a situation to urge the expenditure of large capital upon the faith of the prohibition to the importation of inland Coal to London being continued, it would not do for us as a body to be prominent in the opposition inasmuch as it might be dexterously turned into an argument in favor of the measure, upon the ground that it would go to cheapen the price of Coal to the consumer.

It therefore becomes necessary that we should excite parties who can with more effect appear in front of the Battle, and these parties appear to be the Shipping Interest, as involving the destruction of the coasting trade – the Government, as protectors of the Nursery for Seamen – the Coach proprietors, and Post masters in the line – and the Landed Proprietors through whose grounds the Roads would pass. A communication has been opened with these parties, and there is every reason to hope that the opposition will be formidable and successful. By an account I have received from parties

---

1   A bill to allow the building of a railway from London to Birmingham was presented to Parliament on 20 Feb. 1832. Approved by a small majority in the House of Commons, it was rejected by the House of Lords. A second bill received the royal assent in May 1833: Rex Christiansen, *A Regional History of the Railways of Great Britain, Vol. 7: the West Midlands* (Newton Abbot, 1973), p. 35.

in London I learn that a meeting of landowners is called at great Berkhamstead on the 13[th] January, the Rt. Hon. Richard Ryder[2] in the chair, at Watford on the 14[th] January, Lord Essex[3] in the Chair, & in London on the 21st Jan[uar]y, and the Ship owners and Post masters are in motion.

I saw all the principal Coal-owners in Town, who seemed quite alive to the importance of the subject, particularly Lord Wharncliffe,[4] who requested me to communicate with your Lordship previously to your going South. As I consider the subject is one of paramount importance to the Coal trade of the north, and as I think it highly expedient that your Lordship should be made acquainted with all the facts of the case, I shall be most happy to have the honor of waiting upon your Lordship at any time you may appoint, except Friday first on which day I received notice to attend a meeting of the Committee of the Tyne & Wear at the Coal trade Office here. The Chairman of the Coal trade (Mr R.W. Brandling) has entered so warmly into the question, and is so fully impressed with its importance, that if there be any doubt of your Lordship seeing him before you leave the County, I am quite sure that he would willingly accompany me to any meeting your Lordship may appoint.

I have the honor [&c.]
J[no] Buddle

110.

D/Lo/C142/24 (35)   Newcastle 5[th] May 1832

My Lord

We have had a very full meeting at the Coal-trade Office to day[5] and the whole time & attention of the meeting was taken up with the affairs of the pitmen's war. It was unanimously resolved, that no Colliery should employ any Union men – that 2 per cent on the amo[un]t of sales from each Coll[ier]y should continue to be paid, towards the indemnification of those Collieries which are laid off,

2   Hon. Richard Ryder, 1776–1832, MP for Tiverton 1795–1830. *ODNB*; *Hist. Parl. 1820–32*, vi, 1095.
3   George Capel Coningsby, 1757–1839, fifth Earl of Essex.
4   James Stuart Wortley, Baron Wharncliffe, 1776–1843, coal owner, Lord Privy Seal 1834–5. *ODNB*.
5   Minutes in NRO 263/A2.

and that petition to the Ho[use]s of Lords & Commons should be presented praying for Committees to be appointed, to inquire into the existing state of affairs between the Coal-owners and pitmen. I beg to observe, that I did not commit your Lordship, on any of these points.

I never saw the Coal-owners so unanimous on any point as on this, as they are now fully satisfied, of the necessity of putting a stop to further encroachment, and aggression, on the part of the men. There has been a very large meeting of the delegates at the Cock to day, to consider the expediency of a general stop on Monday – it is rumoured that they cannot agree upon this point, & that the stop will not take place. I hope this account may be true, but there is no certainty about it, & we shall not know certainly what they mean to do 'till Monday morning. They are in a most ticklish state, & the most prudent plan, in my opinion, is, not to meddle with them in any way.

According to the present regulations of the Union, no Coal-owner who has bound his men, is allowed to increase his number – we must not, therefore, at this moment attempt to bind more men, or we shall risk mischief, & an interruption of the work. My opinion is, that we should keep as quiet as possible, & by no means shew any anxiety to increase our workings, at this time.

Building of pitmen's houses at Grange. Our pitmen being bound, & settled in the houses, we have taken for them – we are quite secure in their possession for twelve months at least. Don't. therefore, let us think, of expending money, in build[in]g this year at any rate, when we positively have none to spare. We cannot build by contract without money – if we have the stones & lime – the Contractors *must* have money to pay masons &c. wages, & to pay for the roofing timber, & tiles, &c.

Lime trade at Seaham

This shall have all due attention, agreeably to your Lordship's wishes – and shortly your Lordship shall receive a report on the subject.

The Fullhope tenant

I think I had better write Gregson, & enclose Grey's letter, as I don't think any good will arise from writing to Mills.

Belmont Lease

I can scarcely have a doubt of *working Neddy* out of this, and wish that Gregson may see his way as clearly, for working him out of the

other £5000. I shall have a conference with Gregson, in 2 or 3 days
– before I see Neddy again – to arrange matters for our respective
operations upon him.

The Marq[ues]s of Londonderry	I have the Honor [&c.]
Holdernesse House	J^{no} Buddle

I hope you have had a pleasant & safe journey to town, & that my
Lady continues better.

111.

D/Lo/C142/24 (42)   Newcastle 12th May 1832

My Lord

We have had a long and rather stormy meeting at the Coal-trade
office to day – as apprehensions are entertained that John Brandling
is disposed to depart from the resolutions of last Saturday's meeting
as to not binding any Union men at the So[uth] Shields Colliery –
and betray the trade as he did last year. Should he do so, we shall
have a complete *break up* of regulation & every thing else. The only
chance is that the *Chairman* – his Brother may keep him in order.

The meeting of the Tyne Pitmen last Wed[nesday] resolved, to
hold out a Fort[nigh]t longer[6] – which they say will most certainly
enable them to beat the Coal-owners. They also resolved to petition Parliament to redress their grievances & Hepburn is this day
going through the Collieries, on the North side of the Tyne to get the
petition signed. It is said that Hepburn and other two, are to go to
London with the petition. Notwithstanding all this it is understood
that a majority of the men are tired of the Union.

It is reported, that two Delegates from the political Union at
Manchester, or Birmingham, have been attending the meetings of
the pitmen's delegates, at the Cock this week – to get the pitmen to
join them in a general political union. But I cannot yet answer for the
truth of this report.[7]

---

6   For the strike of 1832 see Welbourne, *Miners' Unions of Northumberland and
    Durham*, pp. 33–43.
7   For the political involvement of the miners, see David Ridley, 'Political and
    Industrial Crisis: the Experience of the Tyne and Wear Pitmen, 1831–32'
    (University of Durham Ph.D. thesis, 1994).

The news of the resignation of Ministers,[8] has occasioned an immense sensation here. Lord Grey is lauded to the skies, & the Conservatives & King, are execrated – the King's popularity is gone for the present. A meeting is convened here next Tuesday – when an immense assembly is expected to take place & strong, if not violent resolutions will be passed. The cry against any Tory administration whatever, is vehement, & the more violent declare, that they would not accept any sort of reform at their hands.

The most violent measures – refusing to pay taxes &c. are talked of, & according to present appearances – unless some most judicious & conciliatory measures are adopted at Westminster – we shall have a political convulsion. Hoping for the best

The Marq[ues]s of Londonderry London

I remain [&c.]
J[no] Buddle

112.

D/Lo/C142/24 (74)   Walls-end 30[th] May 1832

My Lord

I wrote your Lordship from Pensher last night, but was too late for the post – I therefore, embody in this letter what I wrote last night.

At the Boldon fell meeting last Sat[urda]y the pitmen resolved to hold out, in the confident expectation, of wearying out the Coal-owners, by the expence they are put to, in bringing miners &c. and

---

8   The defeat of the second Reform Bill in the House of Lords on 8 October 1831 was followed by riots and disorder. The third bill, introduced in December, received its second reading in the House of Lords on 14 April 1832, but the government was defeated on 7 May on a motion to defer the implementation of certain clauses. William IV, having promised to create enough peers to secure the passage of the bill, now refused to create as many as 50–60, and the government resigned on 9 May. The Tories were in disarray, and Wellington was unable to form a government. He advised the king to recall Grey. The king now acquiesced in the demand to create enough peers, the House of Lords climbed down, and the bill passed its third reading on 4 June, receiving the royal assent on 7 June. Lord Londonderry, who had been vocal in opposition to it, did not take part in the final vote. The Bishop of Durham and the Bishop of Exeter, a Durham prebendary (see p. 219, n. 26) who had voted against the second reading, also abstained. The Dean of Durham (Bishop of St David's) voted in favour. For the whole story, see Michael Brock, *The Great Reform Bill* (London, 1973).

in maintaining such an establishment of military and police – to protect the miners, who they expect either to drive away, or seduce to join the Union. On the other hand the Coal-owners resolved at a general meeting held yesterday[9] – to put down the Union, by every means in their power, and as it seems, that in a little time, an abundant supply of miners, and colliers, can be had from other parts of the kingdom, to supply those Collieries which still want men it was resolved to raise a loan of £10,000 to defray the expence of bringing the requisite supply of strangers – the loan to be repaid by a rate per Ch. on the vend. I w[oul]d just observe that I did not represent your Lordship on this occasion, so that you are not at all committed in the transaction. The meeting was quite unanimous as to the necessity of adopting the most efficacious measures to break the union under the conviction, that if it is not broken – it will not only ruin the Coal-trade but every other trade & finally the whole country will be ruined by it. The pitmen are doing all they can to get other trades to join them & some have joined them.

I understand, that the Coal-owners petition to the two Houses, for committees of enquiry are to be presented forthwith, and I was yesterday told that the pitmen's petition to the Ho[use] of Commons, either was, or would be, presented immediately by Alderman Waithman.[10] *It is said*, that they complain of too hard labour – small wages – working in bad air & above all of the *tyranny* of the Coal-owners!!! They totally forget the tyranny exercised by themselves.

The Meadow-pit men went to work again yesterday – having compelled Robson[11] to do as they pleased – and are working steadily to day. About one half of the Rainton men have put the week up to 4/. – the other half remaining at 3/. But they all agree to contribute 1/3 to the Union Fund – to support the refractory party against the Coal-owners.

The Pittington men, are in bad humour. Longstaff[12] dare not interfere with them in any way – Detachments of strangers are daily marching past them to Hetton, which vexes them, and keeps up the excitement. It is really a most unsatisfactory state of affairs, and is enough to sicken any body of colliery business. Hunter will forward the Seaham acc[oun]t roll &c. to John Gregson – by coach

9   Minutes in NRO 263/A2.
10 Robert Waithman, 1764–1833, MP for the City of London 1818–20, 1826–33, Lord Mayor 1823–4. *ODNB; Hist. Parl. 1820–32*, vii, 592–9.
11 John Robson, viewer at Rainton.
12 William Longstaff, viewer at Pittington.

this evening, and I have *figged* him. I have no doubt he will put his best leg foremost to accomplish his plan, but we must get *Pappy* brought into good humour again, so as to draw kindly with us.

I return Cowburn's Letter – I don't understand Col. Neal's affair – but I hope he will pay Amory's & Cole's costs as we must keep them in good humour if we can.

The Marq[ues]s of Londonderry   I have the honor [&c.]
London   J^{no} Buddle

113.

D/Lo/C142/24 (100)   Pensher 20th June 1832

My dear Lord

I have received your Lordship's dispatches of the 18th with Chaytor & J. Gregson's Letters enclosed. Chaytor's letter is written by Wilkinson and is not I think expressed quite in the way he expressed himself to me or as he meant. He certainly told me that as the Bills would necessarily be returned to them dishonoured they must of necessity provide for them and charge the amo[un]t to the Colliery acco[un]t & this I make no doubt has been done. Tomorrow Hunter will collect what Bills he can to provide for the Pay on Friday and he will then ascertain exactly what has been done about the Bills & give Chaytor your Lordship's Letter.

John Gregson's communication is rather cheering yet I cannot see how under a Law operation for such a large transaction can possibly be completed against the 20th of next Mo[nth] and I tremble for the consequences of delay or failure.

Gregson called here, this morn[in]g and says he has had a inquiry from the D[ean] & C[hapter] Offices to know what progress was making. And he says, he knows – that if we fail to satisfy the Body, by payment – or something tantamount to it – a party are watching and will be ready that *very day*, to step in, and cut us out for ever. This is really alarming, and requires that nothing should be left short to accomplish this object – which is a vital one to the family. Nothing in possession can in point of value and importance, be compared to it both in point of present and prospective value. Houses, Pictures, Plate, Jewels – all may be bought, at any time, for money – but property of this description and *such a property* too, as this, in question not to be replaced for Love or money. My sober opinion, therefore is, that

were I in your Lordship's situation – I would sell off every description of personal property I possessed to raise the means of securing
this source of wealth to the family – rather than risk the losing of it.
I am sure, my dear Lord, you will excuse my thus expressing myself
– I speak honestly, & sincerely – without reserve, as I feel.

The deeds of assignment of the Pensher Coll[ier]y & Way-leave
Leases – to Chaytor which it seems, Neddy must sign, will not be
ready for a few days. Gregson therefore advises, & I think he is right,
that I should not go near him about the Grange affair 'till after these
deeds are executed. He is evidently sulky, and I have not yet heard
from him.

The Biddick affair is to be finally wound up, next Sat[urday] but
this cannot be done, without our paying the Costs of the Chancery
suit which considering that it has been going on for 8 years are
exceedingly moderate – they only amo[un]t to £182.5.3. Still this is
an immediate call on our already too much exhausted means and
helps to keep us under water.

I was mistaken in my Letter of yesterday, in stating inadvertently
that the £1300 was p[ai]d for Herrington Int[eres]t – it was for the
bal[anc]e of the Biddick Interest. The Herrington Int[eres]t alas! still
remains due – up to May last, we owe on this acco[un]t £2129.15.10
which has raised a fresh difficulty as D. Lambton's trustees refuse
to execute the Lease of the Coal to Lord Durham until the arrear of
Interest is fully paid up. Consequently we cannot enjoy the relief
which we are to obtain from the agreem[en]t with Lord Durham
until this money is paid. And by what means it is to be paid, I cannot
at present see.

I have referred the malicious paragraph, which your Lordship
enclosed, to Spence for explanation, as I understand he knows something of its origin.

Gregson says, he has a line from Mr Trevor – to say, he will be at
Durham, this Evening – as Gregson has not received any communication from your Lordship he is at a loss how to act, and we are all
in the same situation here, from the same cause. I dread the expence
of an Election – however trifling it may be, as we are destitute of the
means of meeting any such expence. As to the opposition Mr T. may
be likely to meet with, I have no means of judging & Gregson seems
to be nearly as ignorant on that point, as myself. How the balance
of personal feeling with the Freemen may stand in the City, I cannot
judge, but from what I observe & gather, in the North part of the
Co[unty] of Durham and So[uth] Division of Northumberland there
is very little chance of any Tory members being returned – if Whigs

can be found – indeed at present, the Politics of this Country seem to be exclusively Whiggish.

I have been, and still continue to be so fully occupied with other more pressing matters, that I have not been able to write a word to your Lordship on the Hartlepool Harbour Scheme[13] – I expect shortly to be able to state my ideas on this Scheme to your Lordship.

The Marq[ues]s of Londonderry	I have the honor [&c.]
London	J^no Buddle

114.

D/Lo/C142/24 (125)　　　　　　　　　Walls-end 9th Aug[us]t 1832

My Dear Lord

It was allowed by the general meeting of the Delegates, held here, last night, that matters could not longer continue, to go on in their present state, and that they must be brought to a speedy crisis – the best way of accomplishing which, was to make a *general strike*. This, however, was thought to be too strong a measure for the delegates to carry into effect without the sanction of the pitmen at each, individual Coll[ier]y and it was, therefore, resolved that the Delegates should take the opinion of the men, at their respective Collieries this Evening, and report to a gene[ra]l meeting of Delegates, at the *Cock* tomorrow Evening, when if the Majority should be in favor of a general stop, it will immediately take place & all the Collieries wor[ke]d by Union men will be off work on Monday.

On the other hand, if the majority is for continuing at work – they are to persevere for a while longer, and are in the mean time to endeavour to *wheedle* the Coal-owners into the best terms they can – but still to preserve the spirit & essence of the Union if possible, so as to be able to revive it at a future period, whenever a favorable opportunity may offer. From all I can learn here, the Walls-end men will oppose the stop, and I expect your Lordship's men, will do the same, as well as others, who have positively nothing to complain of, so that I hope *the division* tomorrow evening will negative the motion of *president* Hepburn, for a general stop.

13　A bill providing for the improvement of Hartlepool harbour and for building a railway from Hartlepool to east Durham was passed on 1 Jan. 1832: Tomlinson, *North Eastern Railway*, pp. 212–22. An account of the improvements was published in a supplement to Sir Cuthbert Sharp's *History of Hartlepool*.

If the majority should be for the stop, I have no doubt a fortnight will settle the question for 20 years to come – provided the Coal-owners do but stand firm, and which for *very shame* I think they will do – otherwise they will stamp themselves as the meanest of the mean, and the basest of poltroons.

The Marq[ues]s of Londonderry	I have the honor [&c.]
Wynyard Park	J^{no} Buddle

115.

D/Lo/C142/25 (160)   Walls-end 23rd Sep[tember] 1832

My Dear Lord

I have received your Lordship's letter of yesterday, with Cowburn's & Groom's enclosed – the latter I have forwarded to Gregson, with a request for him to negotiate time with the Rooks. I don't apprehend any mischief from the delay, altho' it is unpleasant – as they retain the farm leases as security, and cannot I think *disturb* the renewal.

I wish I had it in my power to have met your Lordship's wishes with respect to the Harbour[14] – but it is utterly beyond my means. The capital for the Joint Stock bank would have been a *Bagatelle*. I only meant to have taken 50 shares, which would not have required more than £250 *immediate* and £259 at the end of twelve months, which £10 per share is *all* that I should have been called upon to advance. It would by no means have suited me to have made a *large* advance, as what property I have is in land *all free*, in mortgages, and worst of all, in Coll[ierie]s[15] and is not therefore available. I have *nominally* a very fair income, but with the exception of my rents, and *part* mortgage int[eres]t, I really do not get it. Coll[ier]y profits are trifling if any, as I think I lose as much by one Coll[ier]y as I gain by another, and for the last dozen years, I have been obliged, in a great degree, to give up my desultory Viewing & Engineering business

---

14 It would seem that in reply to a gloomy letter of 16 Sep. (D/Lo/C142/25 (156)) about his financial position, Lord Londonderry suggested that Buddle might lend him, for Seaham Harbour, the money that Buddle was proposing to invest in the new Joint Stock Bank of Newcastle: Phillips, *History of Banks*, pp. 330–2.

15 Buddle had shares in several Northumberland collieries – Benwell, Sheriff Hill, Backworth, West Cramlington, Elswick, Crawcrook and Stella. Hiskey, 'John Buddle', ch. 14.

– besides *Salaries* since the Union commenced in 1832 *April* – have
come in so tardily & irregularly, as to have kept my Bank acco[un]t
pretty much in the same state as Cowburn's seems to be in. This with
the exception of a few small sums of which your Lordship is aware,
has kept me in a sort of thread bare state, with respect to disposable
money. Thus the Lord Seaham cost better than £2600 *all paid*, and
Doctors & travelling have cost me upwards of £600 since this time
twelve mo[nth]s so that without *breaking bulk*, which in prudence I
cannot do, I am quite impotent, as to ready money. I am appropri-
ating the Lord Seaham's cargo Bills to the credit of my acco[un]t
with your Lordship but the ship is I fear losing money – she sold
at last Monday's market, and only got 21/3 per ton, which will not
pay her way. I can only, therefore, under these circumstances, aid
your Lordship by my best advice, and exertions and I should be too
happy if I could hit upon any feasible plan for affording the requisite relief, under our present pressing circumstances. I shall be at
Pensher tomorrow afternoon for the Week, and have written to make
an appointment with Lockwood[16] at Sunderland on Wed[nesday]
morning to *sound* him, as to what he may possibly & eventually,
be able or willing to do for us. And shall be able to report progress
on Thursday. Spence writes me, that Chaytors have sent the £250 to
Drummond's for Lord C---h,[17] and expects a harbour full of ships to
day. I wish he may succeed as I *foresee* we shall be greatly interfered
with at Sund[erlan]d, the Hetton Co. being determined not to see us,
and L[or]d Durham run so far ahead of them any longer, have bound
300 of their old pitmen, and are determined to drive away as hard as
they can – a reduction of 6/- per Ch. is talked of – but I presume this
will not take place this Week. It is understood, that the Hetton people
are already *bribing* the cappers and Overseers, *under the rose* to load
with them. I did hope we might have been able to have supported
prices during the remainder of the year, but now almost despair of
it.

The Marq[ues]s of Londonderry   I have the honor [&c.]
Wynyard Park   J[no] Buddle

---

16 George Lockwood, manager of the Joint Stock Bank, Newcastle.
17 Castlereagh.

116.

D/Lo/C142/25 (169)   Newcastle 11[th] Oct[ober] 1832

My Dear Lord

I came here this afternoon to see the Town Clerk, Clayton[18] about advertising the notice for the rail-way in the Durham papers – tomorrow. But on looking through the orders of the Ho[use] he finds that the time for giving the notice has been extended to the end of November – that it to say they are to be 3 times advertised in the provincial papers, before the end of November, which allows us a month longer than he expected.

This is all the better, as it allows more time to consider the matter maturely, as it regards our Harbour. I am glad to learn by your Lordship's letter of the 8th that you approve of Seaham Harbour being included in the notice, as I cannot but think if the plan can be brought to bear, it will prove highly beneficial to the interests of your Lordship's family – by securing *permanent* access to the harbour. We may, however, expect to meet with strong opposition from Gregson & other way-leave proprietors, yet I hope they maybe superable.

I have little doubt but we may manage to obtain £10,000 or £12,000 from the Co. for rail-way machinery and *good will*, but I cannot put the matter into any sort of shape for negotiation, until the Survey, and levellings, are completed so as to enable me to plan the various ascents, descents, and *flats* on the Line, and to estimate the cost, and probable revenue. I have two sets of surveyors at work, and it will take them nearly 3 weeks to finish the survey, plans and sections, on which I have to go to work. It will, therefore, be the 1st week in November, before I can fairly commence the Engineering department, and as I can only devote the intervals of time, which I can spare from other objects to this business – I think it will be nearly about Christmas before I can have all matters fully prepared to submit to your Lordship's consideration. There are not many material difficulties of great consequence on this line – the crossing of the Wear at Barmston is the most formidable. This must be effected by a Bridge, with a single arch of about 180 ft. Span – but whether it will have to be of Wood, Stone, or iron will require me to fill many a sheet of paper with figures, before I can decide. I wish the result

---

18   John Clayton, Newcastle solicitor, town clerk. The Durham Junction Railway bill was passed in April 1834; the line opened in August 1838. The viaduct over the Wear near Low Lambton was a major work. Tomlinson, *North Eastern Railway*, pp. 222–5, 318–19.

of my calculation may be in favour of *Stone*, as in that case it would bring our quarry into fine play.

I fear the *artificial* difficulties we shall have to encounter far more than the natural ones, Without Lord Durham can be induced to countenance, or at least, not to oppose, the plan, it cannot possibly go on. Then we may expect strong opposition from all the Land-owners, who are interested in the present system of Way-leaves. And again we may expect all the opposition the Sunderland *Dock* people, and the Hartlepool projectors can give. So that I do not think it will be an easy matter to get the Bill through Parliam[en]t. The strength of our position in going through parliament is, that we shall neither have new Harbours, nor mere Coal-fields to speculate upon – we merely seek to put established Collieries in communication with *established* harbours by the introduction of the projected rail-ways.

I have filled my paper with this subject, so as not to have left room for any thing else. I have, however, nothing but good to report – the working, and Vend going on full *swing*, and no worrying letters – I have no doubt the pitmen will make up the lost work of Tuesday, before Saturday night.

I hope these equinoctial squalls will be over before my Lady has to cross the Channel.

The Marq[ues]s of Londonderry   I have the honor [&c.]
Eglinton Castle   J[no] Buddle

117.

D/Lo/C142/25 (193)   Walls-end 18[th] Nov[ember] 1832

My Dear Lord

Saturday in Newcastle being a day for *talking*, and not for writing, I could not, in my hasty letter of last night notice the several topicks contained in your Lordship's dispatches of the 13[th] Inst. I shall there-fore, now observe upon them consecutively, as they stand in y[ou]r Lordship's letters – for the sake of clearness. The chief points stand as follows, viz.

1. The South Shields rail-way.
2. The Grange concern.
3. Alienation of the Londonderry pit.
4. Bradyll's Winning.
5. Joint Stock bank.
6. Harbour lease.

7.   Payments to Banks, Coutts, Salvin Amory &c.
8.   Regulation.

The Rail-way – the Survey was only finished yesterday & the plans, and sections, are not yet projected – to set me to work with the estimates. This will be a work of labour, and I feel that I shall not be able to complete it so, as to form a rational opinion on the feasibility of the Scheme before your Lordship's return. Your Lordship will then be fully informed of all I know about the matter, and be enabled to decide accordingly. Your Lordship will see the notice advertised in the Durham papers.

The Grange Lease

My letter of last night will inform your Lordship precisely, the position in which we stand with Backhouse in this affair. Unless we can satisfy him by repayment of the Loan, all our speculations with respect to the Grange, Belmont &c. must fall to the ground, For the accomplishment of our grand Scheme of Colliery extension in this quarter, the Exchequer Loan[19] is indispensable.

Alienation of the Londonderry Pit – to Lord Durham

Would enable Lord D. to bring his Little-town Coal to market 9 mo[nths] sooner than he can obtain it by his own pits – for which he may afford to pay us a handsome bonus. But then it would set him up as a rival 9 mo[nths] sooner. I can mention this as from myself to Morton, and make his chops water. And Geo[rge] Hill & him may puzzle out what bonus they will give for the accommodation – we need not deal with them if we don't like it.

Bradyll's Winning

Is going on most rapidly – the pit is between 120 and 130 fa[thoms] deep – they will have the Main Coal probably by the end of December, and the Hutton seam by June. They will, therefore, be upon our heels presently at the Harbour, which will be a great nuisance, and hindrance to us in the shipment of our Coals 'till the So[uth] Harbour is ready.

Joint Stock Bank

Is *hanging fire* at present. 60 of the most respectable share-holders have forfeited their deposit money & backed out. The other share-

19   An Exchequer loan of £35,000 for Seaham was obtained.

holders insist on retaining them, and *lots* of law suits are likely to ensue. Still they talk of going on, and opening shop, on the 1st Dec[ember]. Wagers are betting that the Shop will never be opened.

Harbour Lease

If we don't succeed with the Exchequer Loan Office I doubt we shall have great difficulty in raising money upon it elsewhere. There is plenty of money in the Country, but people really will not deal with us, we are so blown upon for the irregular payment of Interest.

Payment of Banks, Coutts, Amory, Salvin &c,

Banks I think the most dangerous and first to be attended to, and your Lordship will please to direct what sum is to be remitted to him. Coutts have done their worst by charging the high Interest, and will not I think proceed to extremities. Amory must at all events have the ½ year's Int[eres]t and with respect to Salvin, if we could muster the remaining £300 of the £500, due last Mart[inmas] & give him Bills – in the way we settle the Biddick and Herrington Interest with Green, w[oul]d probably be the best way. I shall wait your Lordship's orders on this point. I am sorry to say, from the present state of prospects of our Vend and Bank Acco[un]t even reckoning the full receipt of rents into the Bargain that none of these remittances can be made 'till after the receipt on the 2nd December. And worst of all Hunter cannot remit my Lady tomorrow when if Vend, and prices continue as at present *rents included*, we may have a surplus of about £3700 – as per rough estimate enclosed.

Regulation

The old regulation is, I think, at an end, and I don't see any reasonable prospect of a new one being formed. I have not attended any Coal-trade meetings lately, but I gather from my friends, that on the Tyne, at least, with the exception of Brandlings & H. Taylor, & 2 or 3 more, that any further attempt to regulate would be unavailing, and the idea of bringing in the Stockton trade, is considered quite hopeless. The cry is as you cannot make a regulation of the two old ports, how are you to regulate *three*. I attended a meeting of the Tyne Comm[ittee] yesterday on financial matters – regulation was only mentioned incidentally, and with the exception of Brandling & one, or two more – there seemed a positive indisposition to regulate.

Great dissatisfaction exists on the Tyne, on acc[oun]t of the excessive vend of the Wear, over it's proportion – the Tyne Coll[ierie]s who are short are determined to vend all the Coals they can and, the price of the best is reduced 3/- and the inferior sorts, no body knows what, as they are freighting, giving away, bribing captains &c.

I left the meeting in the midst of a stormy debate, and don't know the result, but believe that every man will do what he thinks right in his own eyes. I advised the *semblance* of regulation, at least, to be kept up 'till the end of the year – but little attention was paid. Some were for putting the best Coals down to 21/- and others were for reducing only 2/- more, at present and I think the reduction will be 5/- per Ch. I have made up my mind to this, as nothing but a miracle can prevent it, & all we can do is to endeavour to let ourselves down as easily as we can. I anticipate in a few days that we shall feel the effects of this at Seaham by the ship-owners getting laden on better terms elsewhere – and until I can receive your Lordship's orders how to act, I will tell Spence to bribe the capt[ain]s to induce them to load, as we must go on with the vend, at any rate. But I do not like giving a discretionary power to Spence in this way, as it might possibly open a door to fraud. It will be better in case of need to reduce the price 3/- 4/- or 5/- a Ch. Y[ou]r Lordship's Letter has not yet been sent to Martindale, but I don't think it will make any impression on the Wear people as all seem quite careless of consequences.

The Marq[ues]s of Londonderry   I have the honor [&c.]
Mount Stewart   J^no Buddle

118.

D/Lo/C142/25 (228)   Newcastle 24th Dec[ember] 1832

My Dear Lord

I have to acknowledge the receipt of your Lordship's Letter of the 20th Inst. and feel obliged by your Lordship's kind consideration as to my writing, and assure your Lordship that a corresponding feeling has of late restrained me from writing so much as I might otherwise have done – more especially as my Letters must have been of a very sombre cast.

The Durham City election[20] is undoubtedly a most vexatious and annoying affair, but it has I am satisfied arisen from unavoid-

---

20 In the election for Durham City of 11–12 Dec. 1832, W.C. Harland and Chaytor (Libs) were elected, with Trevor (Con.) third: Heesom, *Durham City and its MPs*, p. 43.

able causes viz. the disqualification of so many of the Household troops,[21] and the hostile coalition. I don't however, think this (the coalition) would have given the victory to our opponents any more than in Bradyll's case – except for the active part taken by the clergy. The system has become so decidedly obnoxious that as far as I am able to judge, as a quiet looker on I would say, that whatever side the Clergy take must lose, in all situations where any thing like freedom of election really prevails. It was this same feeling which nearly ousted Hodgson[22] at this place and it was entirely owing to the *Saints* who took it into their heads that Attwood[23] was an Atheist which prevented his being returned. Hodgson lost all hold of the town, and if any man of respectability – of moderation in politics had offered himself, whether Tory or Whig, it is believed Hodgson would have lost his election. It was my neighbour old Osterby[24] I am sorry to say, who proposed Attwood and why and wherefore I don't know as I have heard him frequently condemn Attwood's ultra radical principles. Mr Bell[25] succeeded but he certainly has not got the most desirable colleague of the two, for moderation and cool judgment in these most difficult times – than which none in the history of the Country ever required more good sense dispassionate feeling and talent. Whether the collective wisdom of the new Parliament may possess these requisites remains to be seen if the parliament house is to continue, like a cockpit or to be the mere arena of factious wrangling instead of dispassionate discussion and judicious legislation, suited to the state of the Country & the temper of the times. Then indeed matters will soon arrive at an awful crisis, and it will be 'sauve qui peut'. Let us, however, hope for better things for altho' a few violent & desperate men of all parties may have been returned, yet it is to be hoped there will be a preponderance of good sense, honesty and moderation. The Whig Ministry is certainly not

21 The franchise in Durham City was confined to freemen of the borough. In 1761, on the eve of a general election, the corporation created 200 'occasional' freemen to add to the existing 1050. This particularly blatant piece of vote-rigging led to an Act (the Durham Act) being passed under which freemen would have to hold the position for at least twelve months before being able to vote. *Hist. Parl. 1754–1790*, i, 274. The 'household troops' were employees or clients of Lord Londonderry's concerns who were freemen.

22 John Hodgson, later Hinde, 1806–69, MP for Newcastle 1830–4, 1836–47. *Hist. Parl. 1820–32*, v, 669–72.

23 Charles Attwood, came third in the election for Newcastle in 1832.

24 Unidentified.

25 Matthew Bell.

quite in such high estimation here, as they were – their sincerity as reformers is beginning to be doubted – as they are accused of not having used any influence whatever, with the Greenwich Hosp[ital] tenants &c. in the late Election – but left them entirely to the management of the receiver & it is said that they have mostly voted for Mr Bell. I beg to apologize for this political effusion – it is entirely out of my line, and is a subject in which I never did, nor ever will meddle. I never attended a political meeting in my life but one, & that was on catholic Emancipation. To return to the Durham affair – I do not learn that any of our Freemen, who have been employed, under your Lordship deserted the cause, which is certainly very creditable to them. If even bribery could be proven against the Clown – Bartt[26] in prospect we cannot attack him. Unless we can find another Shop – which considering the position of the D—ham affair seems to be getting every day more desirable.

I have not a word of Coal-trade news – the gen[era]l meeting will take place on the 26th[27] but I shall not attend – the chief subject of discussion will be your L[or]ds[hip]'s affair, and I would rather not be present. If your Lordship can only meet other calls by any means, and leave the Collieries to fight their own battle we shall in the end gain an honourable peace, but it will be a long & severe struggle. It is said that Bradyll's have sunk thro' the High main & found it *magnificent – new seams are generally so* at first. If this is true, it will be mischief to us, as they will greatly interfere with and impede our shipments, 'till the Harbour is finished. I wish I had a bit of good news – to enable y[ou]r L[or]d[shi]p to keep Co[mpany] with B[rady]ll in this – at any rate it augurs well for our Seaton *space*, and if the Downs pit answers on the opposite flank we may surely be able to turn the penny, in some way of other, with the Seaton concern. I sincerely congratulate y[ou]r L[or]d[shi]p on Lord C—rgh's return[28] – but how have you contrived to accomplish an Irish Elect[io]n for £100? It is capital, but almost incredible. I trust I shall soon have the pleasure of seeing y[ou]r L[or]d[shi]p on this side of the Water – as there are many very important matters for discussion. I therefore wish you a safe & as comfortable voyage, as the Season will permit, and remain your Lordship's most sincere & faithful servant.

Jno Buddle

---

26   Unidentified.

27   Minutes in NRO 263/A2.

28   For Co. Down.

119.

D/Lo/C142/25 (230)(230)   December 25th 1832

My Lady

I have the honor to acknowledge the receipt of your Ladyship's letter of the 20th Inst. And altho' I am deeply grieved that any circumstance should have occurred to give your Ladyship reason to suppose that my opinions, in these most stressful times should be inimical to my Lord and your Ladyship's wishes, yet I am greatly obliged by the opportunity which your Ladyship has afforded me of explaining myself and of expressing my thanks for the candid, kind, and Lady-like manner in which your Ladyship has been pleased to express your sentiments on this vexatious affair.

In the first place, I have to assure your Ladyship, that in principle I am neither Whig, nor radical – altho' Mr Bell has chosen, without my permission, to make me a *Whig*. I am however, a reforming Tory – a rational one I hope, as I have long been convinced, that certain reforms are necessary, and that if they are not made prudently, by timely concession, they will in the end be enforced, in which case matters would in all probability be carried into the opposite extreme. One point of reform which I think indispensable to the peace, and welfare, of the Country is the Church, as I am under the conviction that its affairs, as at present administered are any thing but Christian, and in conformity to the principles which its supporters profess – its practice being in open contradiction to their principles. Hence my declining to vote for those candidates who intend to perpetuate the system. But altho' I have not voted individually for such candidates, I have not used any the least influence with others to prevent their doing so, but have left every one to do according to their own views & interests. I have acted strictly on the principle of doing by others as I would wish to be done by, and therefore several of my friends & connexions, as well as my tenants, have voted for Mr Bradyll & Mr Bell.

Then as to Mr Trevor, I assure your Ladyship that I was most anxious for his return, knowing how much it was an object with your Ladyship and the great expence, the retaining of this seat has been to the family. And I declare without fear of contradiction, that I have always acted as closely on my Lord's orders, as to dealing with, and employing freemen, as possible – they have always had a decided preference in every thing.

Prudential considerations have prevented me on this, as on former occasions, from taking an open decided course, as our banking affairs with Chaytor placed me in a ticklish situation, and rendered it neces-

sary, under existing circumstances, that we should not take a decidedly hostile part against him. And he durst not coalesce with us, lest
he should injure his own popularity & interest. I tried the ground
confidentially with Sir W[illia]m with a view to serve the cause &
save expence, but as I found it would not do, I never named the
matter to any one – not even to my Lord – as the Baronet was in a
desperate stew, lest any suspicions should be excited of such a plan
being contemplated. If there had been any opening in this way, I
should have communicated it immediately to my Lord, but as there
was not, I never mentioned it.

I really cannot agree with your Ladyship in thinking that the Election was lost from the want of due exertion on the part of the Agents
as I have reason to believe that they exerted themselves to the utmost
to ensure success – in my opinion our failure arose from two uncon-
trollable causes. First and chiefly, if not solely, from such a number
of our freemen not having been resident within the prescribed limits
of the Borough for a sufficient length of time, to entitle them to vote.
And secondly from the coalition of our adversaries.

In conclusion, I beg, after again assuring your Ladyship, how
deeply sensible I am of the kind & indulgent manner, in which you
have been pleased to express your sentiments, with respect to myself
individually, on this occasion, that altho' I may venture to claim the
privilege of a Freeholder in the Co[unty] of Durham, yet as regards
the City, in which I have no property whatever, I shall consider
myself in precisely the same situation, as the lowest of the Agents,
and will be equally answerable to your Ladyship's wishes. My
anxious wish is for the affairs of the Country to be speedily placed
on such a footing of just & equitable legislation, by the amelioration
of vindictive party spirit, as will produce good understanding and
better feeling amongst all classes. And I fully rely on the good sense
of the community prevailing over violent party feeling, and in the
end, that we shall see all matters work well, and that respect for
the higher classes, and cordiality amongst the middle & lower, will
supersede those angry and excited feelings which at present prevail.

I beg to apologize for troubling your Ladyship at such length, and
begging to assure you of my inviolable attachment to your Ladyship's family, I have the honor to remain

The Marchioness of Londonderry   with profound respect
Mount Stewart   your Ladyship's most obedient
                                            faithful servant
                                            J[no] Buddle

120.

D/Lo/C142/26 (20)   Walls-end 20[th] Jan[uar]y 1833

My Dear Lord

I was so completely jaded & worn out with the transactions of yesterday, and detained so late with Batson, Carr[1] & Lockwood[2] that I neither had time, nor sufficient spirits left to write in detail last night.

Since my interview with the directors last Tuesd[a]y their minds have been poisoned to the highest degree with all sorts of stories, as to the desperate state of your Lordship's affairs – and they stated their absolute *fear* of connecting themselves with us – lest they should by so doing, involve themselves in difficulties. They had been told frightful stories of the extent of your Lordship's personal debts – that *all* the Collieries were settled property, and that they were mortgaged to the last shilling of their value, that mortg[ag]e payments were largely in arrear – that your Lordship was living largely beyond your income, & that in short you were a ruined man. All this I was obliged to hear, and the only way by which I could rebut such falsehood, was by telling the truth – as far as was prudent or necessary.

Their horror, that in the event of their taking the Acc[oun]t that an *execution* for some large debt might be served on the stock &c. and that they might be called on to pay such debt, to keep the Coll[ierie]s going, even for the sake of themselves – which might compel them to make much greater advances than they ever calculated upon, or that could even be in their power to make. I said all I could, to remove this impression, but I found it expedient to state that neither Pittington nor Lambton's Pensher Coll[ierie]s were in settlement, & were therefore entirely at y[ou]r Lordship's disposal – that as to Pensher

---

1   Thomas Carr of Carr & Jobling, Newcastle solicitors, solicitors to the Joint Stock Bank.

2   Thomas Batson, joint managing director of the Joint Stock Bank of Newcastle; John Carr and George Lockwood, directors. At the end of 1831 Lord Londonderry's bank account was transferred from Backhouse's to Chaytor's Bank of Newcastle; but this arrangement only lasted one year because that bank was not strong enough to stand the risk. Buddle was now negotiating with the new Joint Stock Bank, and an agreement was reached under which Lord Londonderry's overdraft was to be limited to £35,000. The limit was soon exceeded. Hiskey, 'John Buddle', ch. 8.

Chaytor's Mortg[ag]e was all it owed, and that Amory's £22000 and Backhouse's 2nd Mortg[ag]e for £10000 as a collateral security to the Grange Lease, was the full extent of the encumbrances upon it. The next question was – What is Pittington Coll[ier]y worth? I s[ai]d Jno Watson had valued it at £90,000 two years ago. But what is it worth now? I replied, that even under the present unfavourable aspect of the Trade I w[oul]d give £60,000 for it. This satisfied them, on this point, but then Back[house]s 2nd Mortgage was in the way – I told them I hoped to get this liberated by granting Back[house]s a Lease of the Grange Coal. I was then sent to Donkin to enquire how this would be, and to have it explained, as Carr doubted Backhouses giving it up. I went to Donkin, & he went to Jonathan Richardson[3] – but as the negotiation for the lease was with Uncle Ed[war]d & John Buddle, Jonathan declines giving an ans[we]r but refers the matter to Uncle Edw[ar]d. He is, however, of opinion that the Lease alone is not valid security for the £10,000, and that they must either retain the Pittington Mortg[ag]e or have some other collateral security, as your Lordship cannot ensure the pay[men]t of the Coll[ier]y rent beyond the period of your natural Life. Or if my Lady joins in the Lease, it will ensure the pay[men]t of the rent in liquidation of the £10,000 during your joint lives. All this is communicated to Carr & Batson, and after a long consultation with Lockwood – they come to the conclusion that the only terms on which they can recommend the directors to take the Acc[oun]t under all the *new* circumstances which have come to their knowledge, is, in addition to the other securities to take a mortgage on Pittington Coll[ier]y – getting as much out of Backhouse's hands as they can. And in this case they will dispense with the new Life Insurance – further than may be necessary to make up any deficiency between what Back[hous]e may hold, and the full value the Coll[ier]y will give. This will be a cheaper plan for your Lordship than the Life policy.

My first business, tomorrow, therefore will be, to see what can be made of Edw[ar]d to get the mortgage for the £10,000 out of his hands – if not wholly, as much of it as possible so as to render the security on Pittington as respectable for the Joint Stock bank, as possible. They have fixed with Nich[olas] Wood (Lord Ravensworth & Co.'s Viewer)[4] a respectable man, with whom I am on the best

---

3   Jonathan Richardson, manager of the Newcastle branch of Backhouse's Bank.
4   Nicholas Wood, agent to Lord Ravensworth. Earlier in his career he had been viewer at Penshaw.

terms, to value Pensher Coll[ier]y. But in the event of their taking security on 2nd or 3rd Mortgage of Pittington, I hope I may be able to induce them to waive the valuation of Pensher – for altho' I am sure I can induce Nich[olas] Wood to take as liberal view of the subject as his conscience will permit, yet under the prospects of the Coal-trade it will be most difficult at this time, to shew that Pensher Coll[ier]y is of any value whatever.

Your Lordship will perceive from the foregoing statement in what a very difficult & critical position we are placed, and what a difficult negotiation I shall have tomorrow to get matters arranged with the Joint Stock – they are most anxious & well disposed to do all they can and would wish to do more –but they are *positively afraid* of being drawn out of their depths by engaging with us. And Batson told me privately that some of the directors are decidedly hostile and opposed to their taking the acc[oun]t at all, so that those who are favourable to us, are incurring a serious responsibility. *Pay day* is however fast approaching, and I must by hook or by crook bring matters to a close with them tomorrow, or we shall be *done up* on Friday.

As to the Coal-trade I am quite puzzled about it – scarcely any two men you meet are of the same opinion, as to what should be done with it. Some are for having Stockton into regulation –some are not for regulating unless the 3 great Collieries are first reduced to 100,000 each on the Basis, and others are not for regulating at all. The Owners of seve[ra]l of the inferior Coll[ierie]s have turned very bold during last week, from the circumstance of a steady *little* demand to the Coast for their Coals, at a reduction of only 2/- per Ch. and from the extraordinary circumstance of some of them approaching so very near to the price of the best Wear Coals in the London Market, that in fact they are *better* Coals to the Ship-owners, than any of the Wear Walls-ends. This has raised the hope and spirits of the Owners of those Collieries, and they flatter themselves that a change has taken place in the public opinion, as to the great superiority of the Wear Walls-end Coals, and that they are losing the preference which they have hitherto maintained. I pay little respect to all this, but it has produced the effect of rendering the accomplishment of any arrangement for bettering the condition of the trade more distant, and more difficult. Henry Stobart a partner with W[illia]m Bell in Lord Durham's Harraton & Fatfield Coll[ierie]s and an owner also of the Etherley Coll[ier]y from which the Coals are shipped at Stockton, has been sent by the party who wish to bring Stockton into the regulation – to sound the Stockton Coal-owners on the subject.

His mission is not, as far as I know, authorized by the trade of the Tyne & Wear, and will not be recognized by many – I for one should protest against it, as I can see nothing but an increase of difficulties and mischief from any such alliance. The Stockton Collieries have been living upon our distresses and to take them up now would only be nourishing a serpent in our bosom to sting us to death when brought to maturity. To make allies of the Stockton people at this time, would convince them, that we are afraid, and *cannot do without them*. And are we to suppose that our *meek* friend Jonathan & others won't take due advantage of this feeling? As to Stobart he has an especial interest to serve by bringing about this alliance – without it *Etherley* Colliery *must cease* to be a *sea-sale*.

On talking to Morton yesterday we agreed in consequence of the slippery conduct of Redhead with respect to the sub-regulation – that it is better for us not to *seek* him, but to leave him to himself and shew no anxiety for the measure, until he seeks it. Indeed it is probable that he will be turned out of office next Thursday when the Co. are to meet to appoint a new manager.

Your Lordship will conceive how anxiously I look forward to the result of my meet[in]g with *Neddy* – and the bank people tomorrow, which I will communicate by post. I will hold y[ou]r Lordship's letter to Chaytor 'till after I conclude with Batson & Co. as we don't know yet what we may be forced to do.

The Marq[ues]s of Londonderry   I have the honor [&c.]
Wynyard   J^no Buddle

121.

D/Lo/C142/26 (26)   Newcastle 26th Jan[uar]y 1833

My Dear Lord

Our Coal-trade meeting to day was very short. Redhead handed in the resolution of the general meeting of the Hetton Co. which stated briefly that they *would not regulate* at present. This of course put a stop to all further proceedings, and the Tyne Committee absolved themselves from all further connexion with the Wear – until the Wear Committee can come forward, and say, that they are fully prepared to negotiate the terms of a general regulation. Thus we are completely at sea, and at the mercy of the Winds & Waves as possible. And every man is entirely at liberty to do the best he can for himself – and I am sure, that will be bad enough.

Morton had got a hint last night of the decision of the Hetton Co. and instead of going to Durham this morn[in]g as he intended he came here, to confer with me, on the occasion. He has no doubt from what he has heard, but that this resolution of the Hetton Co. is a blow levelled at y[ou]r Lordship, and Lord Durham – as they have it reported that you are both, as Coal-owners, on the very verge of Bankruptcy, and that by carrying on the game of destruction for a while they will put you both down, and have the game in their own hands. Morton is exceedingly anxious that we should put our shoulders together, and unite in any measures we can devise for mutual defence. Dunn for N. Hetton has also taken the alarm, and is anxious to join us. I scarcely know what to devise, but will turn it in my mind and instruct Hunter, how to act in my absence.

I received your Lordship's letter of yesterday, enclosing Hunter's – this morning. Hunter's Letter contains nothing new – but is only a different version in blacker terms than I have stated the actual state of our affairs. But the truth is, Hunter has lost all nerve, and is completely done up. The arrival of the Post sets him a-trembling every Morning, and he continues in a state of constant nervous excitement, and I am apprehensive, that unless we get into smoother water soon he will positively break down – he really has not nerve to support the worry much longer.

I will give the best directions I can as to pushing our Vend, but we cannot *force* it without *freighting*, and this cannot be done without a *d*ead loss of 2/- or 3/- per Ch. so that the more we force, the more we shall lose, and the sooner be bro[ugh]t to a *dead stand*. We positively must strike out some plan to get better prices for the Coals, or it will be impossible to keep the Collieries going, and to attempt to carry them on by raising money on the estates, or out of any private Funds whatever, would be *certain ruin*. It they cannot be made to carry themselves on, they must stand still. Yet I feel that so many must be in as bad a state as ourselves – that some effort must, and will be made before Binding-time to put matters on a better footing. I understand *Gully*[5] has struck this *knock-down blow* in the Hetton meeting.

As to what is with the London Tradesmen & others, I am utterly at a loss to know – as I am sure they are not to be quieted by more promises, or small payments. We shall not have either peace or safety, unless we can propose some general & clear plan of meeting

5   John Gully, partner in the Hetton Coal Co. and the Thornley Coal Co.

all demands – by instalments, in a given period. And this cannot be done, without a considerable sum of money – or a guarantee and where to look for either the one, or the other I do not know. We can only obtain money by the Exchequer Bills, or a loan on the Harbour Lease, and the negotiation of either will I doubt be a work of time. My mind is incessantly occupied on the subject, but as yet I don't see my way. I have had Gregson to day arranging with Carr & Donkin about the securities for the Joint Stock – more Law alas!

The Marq[ues]s of Londonderry	I have the honor [&c.]
Holdernesse House	J^{no} Buddle
London	

122.

D/Lo/C142/26 (44)   Newcastle 23rd Feb[ruar]y 1833

My Dear Lord

It is strange enough that in his Letter of the 20th Spence entirely *blinks* the damage done to the Shipping in the So. Harbour, while it is 'gratifying' to him the Ships in the inner harbour, lie as *easily* as in the best *Dock*. There is nothing new nor extraordinary in this, & I give him credit for endeavouring to make the best of it – yet he ought to have put your Lordship in possession of the facts, instead of allowing you to be alarmed by the exaggerated statements which are sure to appear in the public papers. I suspected Spence would not tell you about this affair in full detail, and therefore, wrote from the first impression I received.

It is surprising what a noise, and sensation this affair has occasioned here, and it was well that I saw the extent of the mischief with my own eyes, yesterday, as Batson & Grace,[6] had received the most alarming acco[un]ts – the latter in particular was in a state of the greatest alarm – the Coal-trade in such a state and the Harbour *washed away*. I however had little difficulty in allaying their fears as to the Harbour – but they are far from being at their ease with respect to the Coal-trade, as they suspect what I fear is too true – that if we are not working to loss, we are certainly not making any profit.

---

6   Nathaniel Grace, joint (with Batson) managing director of the Joint Stock Bank.

Young,[7] the owner of two of the injured Ships in our Harbour, came to me this morn[in]g. One of them must, he says, go into Dock, and has suffered £200 of damage. He endeavours to make it out that y[ou]r Lordship will be liable to this damage from Spence not having taken the Ship into the N. Basin in her due turn. I don't, however, think he will be able to substantiate this.

We have had a long meeting to day[8] on the Binding business, and some resolutions have been passed, of which I will send your Lordship a copy next week, but they are not of material consequence, as every one is left to take his own line. Some will bind their men, and some won't. It is however generally admitted that Wages must be reduced, and the upholding of certain Wages abolished. This meeting was as uncomfortable a one, as I ever attended – every body peevish, and out of humour, and disposed to quarrel & worry each other. Nothing said about regulation, nor any disposition shown for endeavouring to mend matters, but rather the contrary. Some observed peevishly that it was better matters should go on for a few months longer, and then those who had done the mischief would feel the effects of their imprudence and folly.

After the meeting I got a quiet word with Brandling, Hugh Taylor, and another or two reasonable people. It was agreed that unless the mischief can be moderated in the beginning of next month, it cannot be done this year – but how to set about getting any thing done, is the difficulty. Until the Hetton Co. appoint a representative to attend the meetings, and evince a disposition to treat, nothing can be done. It does not appear that John Wood[9] has yet got full powers but there is to be a committee meeting at the Colliery next Thursday, when I think it probable they will see the propriety of putting themselves in communication with the trade again. If even, however, this should take place, and the trade should all at once resolve to regulate, it is quite clear to me that no advance of prices can take place here until the prices in London advance, and this most assuredly will not take place unless we pull up and lessen our shipments, as it is quite out of the question to expect prices to rise while our unrestrained vend is going on, by freighting, and upholding prices, &c. If therefore we expect to advance our prices, we *must positively* be prepared to contract our Vend – this is as clear to me, as the Sun at noon day.

7   James Young, ship owner, South Shields.
8   Minutes in NRO 263/A2.
9   John Wood, viewer at Hetton.

As Hunter will be with your Lordship tomorrow I need not write on the distribution of the Loan he has obtained from the Fitters – nor on the *profitless* state of our trade, as he will be able to shew your Lordship from the papers he has prepared.

The Marq[ues]s of Londonderry   I am [&c.]
Wynyard Park   J^no Buddle

123.

D/Lo/C142/26 (58)   Walls-end 17th March 1833

My Dear Lord

I have received your Lordship's letter of yesterday, and beg to congratulate your Lordship on the favorable result of the binding yesterday of which your Lordship will have been informed by Hunter's report. *All* the Collieries in this neighbourhood who intend to hire any men, have bound without difficulty, at even lower prices than they contemplated – as the pitmen are panic struck lest they should not get employment, and in the end I believe those Collieries, who have not bound any men will fare best – as they will be supplied with the best workmen, on very reduced wages. It seems now clear that Hepburn's late endeavour to re-organize the Union has failed – he applied at Backworth Colliery last Thursday to be employed as a Shifter or Stone-workman – but was told, that we only employed Hewers there. I hope we are now fairly freed from the *curse* of this Union, but it will be long before the trade recovers from the mischief which it has inflicted – if ever it does. This humbled state of the pitmen is a great point gained for the inferior Collieries, and will make them much more saucy to deal with in settling the preliminaries of a regulation.

In reference to what passed the other day at Seaham – believe me my dear Lord, it is not thro' an arrogant or captious spirit that I may some times in the warmth of discussion, urge my opinions with more than becoming vehemence – I am very sensible of my failing in this respect & can only plead the sincerity of my intentions in mitigation. The unparalleled difficulties of our position, as between your Lordship's pressures and what is fair and reasonable to be done, in reference to the affairs of the Coal trade place me in a very difficult situation, as it is impossibly [*sic*] at all times to make the general measures of the trade *cotton* with what may be due to your Lordship's private and pressing objects. And all that I desire, is not to be placed in a situation which may compel me to compromise my integrity.

I have locked myself up to day which with the ease of yesterday afternoon has put my leg in the way of mends, and if I can give it rest tomorrow, and Tuesday, it will get well. I shall therefore be ready to start for London if necessary by this day Week – but I should first hear from Brickwood[10] which I should think there is little fear of my doing before that time – if even no board should be held before next Thursd[a]y.

I have had a letter from John Gregson on the *Squire's* Coll[ier]y affairs, in which he mentions the Vice Chancellor having dismissed Robertson's suit with costs.[11] I have not seen an account of this in any of the provincial papers (I scarcely ever read a London paper) but which I think ought to appear. If it has not already been done I think your Lordship should get Gregson to put it in the Durham papers from which it would find its way into those of Newcastle.

It would seem that *regulation* is as much wanted at Downing Street as in the Coal trade. I wish this party squabbling was at an end and that something like public virtue, good feeling and good sense would take the lead at Westminster. If the fight for the ascendancy between Conservatives and Wigs [*sic*] continues – it is but too clear that the radicals will run away with the bone.

The Marq[uess] of Londonderry   I have the honor [&c.]
Wynyard Park   J^no Buddle

124.

D/Lo/C142/26 (88)   Walls-end 19th May 1833

My Dear Lord

I am happy to learn by y[ou]r Lordship's Letter of the 10th Inst. that my Lady's and Lady Frances' attack of measles has been so mild, and I hope they are by this restored to perfect health. I am also happy to observe that your Lordship is benefited by and enjoying the salubrious air of Paris not willing to admit that it can exceed at this season our own at *Seaham*. I wished exceedingly that your Lordship

---

10 Unidentified.
11 Alexander Robertson had sued Lord Londonderry for breaking his contract to build Seaham Harbour. See above, p. 170, n.13.

had been there, last Thursday – the beauty of the day – the bustle of the place, and the Sea prospect, presented altogether, one of the most imposing scenes imaginable. The Hall really looked delightful – being at a proper distance from the bustling scene of the Harbour; I could not help wishing, that head-quarters had been established there during this delightful part of the year. I really consider Seaham to be the *Montpellier* of the North, at this Season, and can only regret that it is so solitary. But to business – for after all there is no doing without it – and in these times one can hardly do with it.

The Harbour

The Works are resumed with great vigour – the building of the So. Breakwater has commenced at both ends, to get the *gap* closed up with the greatest expedition. The So. Harbour is now very useful in fine weather. 13 light Ships were in it on Thursday last. When the *gap* is closed light vessels will lie there safe, in all Weathers.

After all Telford & Macneil[12] *took the cow* about finishing the end of the N. Pier with wood, and declined giving a plan for it. Macneil frightened himself about the foundations & then frightened Telford. The latter therefore, desired me to make a plan of the piling &c. for him to revise and correct as he may think best.

I have had the Foundation bored, and find it *so good*, that Nicholson[13] & Thomson, concur with me in opinion, that with our Sheet iron Cassoon, we can lay the foundation and build the Pier-head more effectually, and quite as cheap with stone, as with piling & *Concrete* and there is no doubt but it will be a stronger and more permanent piece of work. I have T. Nicholson in hand with the drawings & sections, and when finished I will report upon & send them to Telford. In this we shall adhere as closely to poor Chapman's original design as circumstances will permit, as every thing he planned has answered so completely that we have implicit confidence in his designs.

The Quarry too is in full activity, and we are building Barrack Stables for 20 Horses on the Bank to the So. of the Harb[ou]r. This is better than keeping the Horses at the Farm Stables – being more conveni[ien]t, keeping our own Forage quite separate, and preserving the manure to our own uses. We have bought 8 Horses for the use of the Harbour – one was killed at the Works on Friday & 5 men

12   Unidentified.
13   Thomas Nicholson, engineer at Seaham Harbour.

had a narrow escape by the breaking of the tackle, in hoisting some framing on the Break Water. It would no doubt be a capital job if we could accomplish the purchase of the Rail-way – but in the present state of the trade and our Finances it seems quite hopeless. We shall pay Thompson £20000 or £130000 this year for leading!!!

State of the Coal-trade

Your Lordship will see by the papers the prices in London. It has now become quite evident, that the London Market, is completely glutted and over-done with best Coals, and prices cannot rally again, unless the supply is shortened. To persist in cramming our full quantity into the market by upholding freights would be ruinous. Our daily work of W[alls-]end are about 50 keels, but on due consideration of the best mode of carrying on the War, and maintaining the Fight, we have thought it best to reduce the quantity of W[alls-]End to about 25 keels, and to send the remainder coastwise as Eden-main, *masking* the screens so, as to reduce them by an additional admixture of Small – to the *standard of Eden-main*. By this scheme we shall obtain 5 or 6 keels a day more Eden, from the *same quantity of workings*. This is to operate merely as a regulator, or *safety valve* – for as soon as the prices in London rise again, so as to make the Walls-end leave as good a price as Eden-main, we shall then increase the quantity in London.

Up to this time, it seems, as nearly as can be ascertained that we have averaged from the commence[men]t of the year 22/- for Walls-end. This would not have happened but for the good prices in April. Now however, the case is altered, and we can only calculate on 15/- to 18/- or 19/- It is therefore better to sell to the coast for 21/3 as long as we can get it. But from others acting in the same way, as far as they can, such an extra quantity is now being sent to the coast, that notwithstanding the extra demand from the low prices – a glut & reduction of prices must soon I think take place to the Coast also, and it is by no means unlikely that a further reduction of 3/- or 4/- on the Coast Coals may take place shortly – as every body seems determined to vend Coals, come what may, even if they *give them away*.

It is very difficult to know what we are really getting for our Coals, as we cannot learn what the freighted Ships leave until the Factors' Acco[un]ts are received, which is not less than a month after the sales. But as nearly as I can *guess*, and it is little better than a guess, we are on the general average of Sunderl[an]d & Seaham, & for W[alls-]end, and Eden-main, netting about 20/. and under the reduction of prices at the late Binding they will cost about 16/3 so that on a large quantity 3/9 per Ch. profit may be about the mark. So that on 160,000 Ch. Vend a profit of £30,000 would be left. This in reference to the Coll[ierie]s in the Abstract is a fair profit, but it must be borne in mind that we are slacking away a valuable article – the *substance of the Family* for an *inadequate profit*. When Lord Seaham comes to years of maturity, and finds that the *Kernel* has not been duly preserved, and nothing but the Shell left – what will he say of our administration – this thought torments me, as we cannot but admit the fact, that we might, if we could, so manage as to obtain as much or *more* profit, at a vast less sacrifice of the Inheritance of the Family.

Joint Stock Bank

I am in negotiation with the Directors to get them to pay one of Hunter's £2000 acceptances to Chaytor's, and to obtain me the Rose-bank[14] deeds. I hope to accomplish this in a few days.

Matters are becoming so serious in every branch of trade, from the depressed state of the Coal-trade, and all the Bankers are so pressed, and timid from the unpromising state and aspect of affairs – that unless our Vend will leave larger surpluses over the pays, so as to keep the Bal[anc]e within the prescribed limit the Directors will not advance further. They as well as all the rest of the Bankers are positively alarmed at the hopeless state of the trade – and they *dare not* be liberal beyond their engagement.

Backhouse

Neddy is in London, and won't be at home again for 3 Weeks, but I have talked to Jonathan Richardson. I first arranged with the Joint Stock Directors, that they would pay the £10,000 in a Bank Bill at 2 mo[nths]. I then went to Jonathan, and sounded him, & made out that the chief obstacle in Neddy's mind, from Hunter's communication was that some quirk or trick was intended to humbug them, & shuffle the paym[en]t of the £10,000, but when I told him I was prepared to pay the £10,000 by a Banker's Bill his countenance brightened up, and he s[ai]d he thought there w[oul]d be no difficulty if Mr Bell did not object, and undertook to write Uncle, by last night's post. The condition is that Neddy shall give up the Pittington Mort-

---

14 A villa on the Thames at Hammersmith, bought by Lord Londonderry.

gage, & the Grange Lease, with all claims whatever against your Lordship, on receiving the Bank Bill for his £10,000.

The Marq[ues]s of Londonderry   I have the honor [&c.]
Paris   J^{no} Buddle

125.

D/Lo/C142/26 (92)   Walls-end 2nd June 1833

My Dear Lord

I am happy to learn by your Lordship's Letter of the 24th Ulto. that you are enjoying yourself so entirely, and wish most sincerely that matters were running so smooth here, as not to render it necessary for me to trouble your Lordship, or disturb your enjoyment, and tranquillity with a single word on business. This however is impossible under existing circumstances – overwhelmed with debt, on one hand, and carrying on the most inveterate warfare, in our staple trade on the other, that was ever known.

Wade's failure[15] has caused a great sensation, and has thrown a degree of discredit on the whole trade. He was brought to a stand by Lambton's Bank refusing to advance the money for his Coll[ier]y pay – the Acco[un]t being over-drawn £6000. The bankers are now becoming the longer the more timid and cautious, and neither can nor will supply the Coal-owners with money to carry on a fighting trade. This is the determination of our bankers, and we are getting into difficulties with them – as they will not advance beyond the £35,000, and the £10,000 to Backhouse – come what may – we therefore know the length of our *Tedder*, and must keep within bounds accordingly. It is impossible to conceal from them the extent of our renewed Bill transactions, which alarms them, as they consider it, as it really is, ruinous. They consider that we are paying 30/- in the pound on this floating debt, which no Income nor business can stand.

Chaytors positively refuse to give up the Rosebank Deeds, unless the full amo[un]t of the estimated value of the property £3400 is paid. This, in the present state of the Acc[oun]t the J[oint] S[tock] will not pay, so I am completely non-plussed with Banks. Lock-

---

15   Thomas Wade, Hylton Castle, owner of Springwell Colliery. He went bankrupt in 1833.

wood has been twice at Sunderland this week to see Wilkinson, and notwithstanding Wright did all he could to induce the latter to accept a pay[men]t of £2800 for one of Hunter's Bills, and to give up the Deeds, he would not budge. It is impossible for me to describe all the trouble and turmoil this affair has occasioned. In yesterday I proposed that they should remit £2000, which they had agreed to pay to Chaytor's, to Banks, to keep him quiet – they seem to entertain this proposition, but will wait the result of our receipt tomorrow, as the pay of last Friday has greatly over-drawn the Acco[un]t and made them very *skittish*. Banks and Chisholme will be furious at this disappointment as I had written Chisholme, in reply to an angry Letter, that I fully expected to be able to put the R[ose] B[ank] Deeds into his hands, as yesterday. I should have been in utter despair if your Lordship's letter to Hunter, announcing the arrang[emen]t with Lord Castlereagh to have been completed – by which you will be able to raise £20,000 – had not come to hand on Thursday morn[in]g. I took advantage of this, right or wrong, God knows, to shield us from Banks' wrath, by writing Chisholme, to apprize him of such arrangement, by which I trusted your Lordship would be able to satisfy Sir E. Banks' wishes. I hope, and trust, no hitch will occur to delay this arrangement, as I positively think our situation depends upon it. However objectionable in principle, the pressure of circumstances at this time renders it expedient – high as the Int[eres]t & Lord C---'s allowance is, it is better than raising money by accommodation paper as we are doing, and which I am convinced cannot be much longer continued, without destruction – particularly if our trade is not made more profitable, as the surpluses left, notwithstanding the largeness of the Vend, are utterly inadequate to meet our engagements, and we *must not calculate* on further aid from the Bank. Hunter will write your Lordship more in detail on money matters after the receipt tomorrow.

The Coal-trade

I agree with your Lordship, generally in the view you take of the state of the Trade. We have I am firmly persuaded the best of it at present – but still we must take into consideration, the uncertainty and casualties of warfare – even a Napoleon was foiled in his attempt to conquer the Russian Empire, after having actually got possession of Moscow. My notion is, that we should not reject negotiation, while we have the vantage ground. It is the Coast-trade *alone* which enables us to maintain our superiority at present – as in the London market we are only *second best*. As I stated in my last, our competitors are commencing an attack upon us in the Coast markets, and if they succeed, as they have done at London, they will knock us up, as well as themselves, and we shall then have to start again on *equal grounds*. If therefore the opportunity occurs before this happens, I would try negotiation – we could not be worse if it failed. John Wood has written to the Coal-trade office to say, that he is willing on the part of the Hetton Co. to meet the representatives of the other Coll[ierie]s of the Wear to discuss their relative powers &c. Nothing however, can be done in consequence of Morton's absence – he will not return for a Fortn[igh]t or 3 Weeks. He was by no means favorable to a meeting of this sort, & I think he wishes to keep aloof 'till the Little Town is ready to come into play. But as it will be some months before this can take place, he may probably change his mind, after consulting Lord Durham and Stephenson.

In a Fortnight Bradyll's Pit will be at the Hutton seam – his fortune will therefore soon be told. Perc[eva]l Forster met me at the Harbour last Wed[nesday] to see about the arrangements for the shipping of their Coals. He is willing to have the thing done in any way we will point out – but I clearly foresee, that we cannot, until the South Harb[ou]r is finished, do their business in any way without curtailing our own, to the extent of one third. Which if the War continues will be highly detrimental to us – there is, however, no help for it, 'till we get more Harbour room.

I made my voyage of observation, along the Coast to Hartlepool, and Middlesborough last Wed[nesday] and I must say it was a very satisfactory one, as it has convinced me, that neither of those *great lions* have any chance to compete, with our *gentle Lamb* at Seaham. As to Middlesborough, it is the most complete piece of *Baby-house* work I ever saw, much ado about nothing, and more scream than wool.[16] Two 20-horse Engines are employed to lift the Waggons 18 ft perp[endicular] to the platform – to supply the spouts drops each about 80 ft distance from the platform. The teeming of the Wagg[on]s is therefore so inconvenient as to require 16 men and a pony upon the platform exclusive of Engine-men, Hooker-on &c. to carry on the work. The drops are all on Chapman's plan, and I did not discover

16 An extension of the Stockton and Darlington Railway to Middlesbrough was opened in December 1830, by which time staiths for loading coal had been constructed and building of the town had begun. The first coals were shipped on 31 Jan. 1831. In 1832–3 336,000 tons were shipped. Docks were opened in 1842. Tomlinson, *North Eastern Railway*, pp. 187–90, 437; Lillie, *History of Middlesbrough*, pp. 52–3, 55.

any thing whatever, out of the old beaten path, except the cast iron Turn-rails, or Turnabouts on the Platform. The perpendicular lifting of the Waggons is an imaginative application of the power of the Engines, for this sort of business. Inclined Planes ought to have been tried. The difficult navigation of the Tees, is greatly against the shipment of Coals at this place, and the best part of my *view* was, that I saw only *one Ship* at the 6 Spouts – in the rear of the Spouts the loaden Waggons were standing for a mile in length waiting for Ships. At Hartlepool, they seem to be building an immense mansion, without a door to it. They have put in an immense Coffer Dam to shut out the Sea 'till they excavate two Docks –one 8 the other 12 acres – which will hold between 400 & 500 sail of Ships, if *ever they are completed*. How they are to get Ships into, or out of those Docks – unless they mean to carry them over the sands on a *Rail-way*, I don't know. If they calculate on making a Channel thro' the Sand to the Harbour, & keeping it open by *scouring* with the back Water of the light vessel Part of the Harbour – they will most assuredly find themselves mistaken. The grand defect of Hartlepool Harbour, is the want of an entrance, and I cannot find out that they even contemplated the right way of going to work to make one – indeed if they were, it would take twice the sum of money which is estimated to complete the harbour, to make a proper entrance to it. If their Docks were completed tomorrow they will not be able to get Vessels of more than 10 or 12 ft. Water into them – for Vessels of a larger size I am decidedly of opinion the undertaking will prove a complete failure. Indeed I can hardly persuade myself that the thing can go on, unless the subscribers suffer themselves to be duped, by a few wrong-headed interested persons – I consider it altogether a *Quixotic* scheme. And I should not be at all surprised, if the *rush* we are making at Seaham, gives it its death-blow. When our So[uth] Harbour with the Dock is completed – neither Middlesborough, nor Hartlepool, can possibly compete with it, and I cannot doubt but it will become the general shipping place for Coals from the adjacent country, to the full extent of its powers

The Marq[ues]s of Londonderry   I have the honor [&c.]
Paris   J[no] Buddle

126.

D/Lo/C142/27 (9)   Seaham Harbour 25th June 1833

My Dear Lord

I received your Lordship's Letter of the 22nd Inst. yesterday – I assure you my dear Lord, that I am tremblingly alive to the very critical situation of our position at this moment, and can only say that I will devote myself to the *Service*, and will leave nothing short, which is within my power to accomplish, to get matters placed in an improved, and more satisfactory footing. But be assured, that all things are so completely thrown out of joint, by the convulsed state of the Coal-trade, that it will be no easy matter to get them set right again.

God knows what may turn up at our meeting tomorrow[17] – it strikes me that the most prudent thing we could do, would be to establish as a preliminary step – a partial, or *sub*-regulation on the following principle. All freighting giving away Coals, and bribing of Capt[ain]s &c. to cease immediately. The 4/- taken off on the 13th Inst. to be put on again on Thursday, and the Coals to be worked bona fide at that price for the present – with a view to a further advance when matters arc more matured.

No limitation of Vends to take place in the first Instance. This is the outline of my plan which may be filled up and modified according to circumstances. But qu[er]y if it will meet the approbation of the other parties – my only hope is that they may be as sick of seeing their Coals *thrown* away as I am at this moment. We are going on here, at the average of 50 Keels a day, but it is truly distressing to see so many fine Coals carried away, without leaving a shilling of profit behind them.

If I possessed the faculty of divesting myself of reflection and forethought I should be the happiest mortal on earth. Such a gratifying, & delightful scene here – all bustle and business, and everything going on to one's heart's content, that regards the Harbour. The Hall too, and all about it looks like a little paradice [*sic*] – I wish my Lady could have seen it, as I saw it yesterday in passing, I am sure she w[oul]d have been charmed with it – without meaning anything offensive – in point of situation, & scenery, at this season, I don't think Rosebank is to be compared with it.

17 Minutes in NRO 263/A2.

No news since my last – only Attwood[18] Larkin Fife & Co. keep incessantly stirring up the pitmen, and seem as if they would shortly succeed in getting them all to join the N[ew]castle political Union.[19] A new radical paper is I am informed to be published this day by Mackenzie & Attwood has advised them to form themselves into Clubs of 7 each to subscribe 1d a Week each to purchase this paper – which is to *tell them the truth* – to shew them clearly how they are robbed of their wages by taxation and to shew them how to procure redress. They are to have 3/-for 1/6 worth of work and corn at half price. They are first to proceed by petition to obtain their object but if that won't do – they are to resort to open force. Fife said at the meeting at Scaffold Hill, last Sa[turday] Week, that all the military in the Kingdom would only be a *breakfast* for the Political Unions, and that as to the Yeomanry (meaning Bell's Corps) their Wives and Bairns would be a match for them. All this is tending to unsettle the minds of the pitmen very much – especially those who have short employment.

The Marq[ues]s of Londonderry   I have the honor [&c.]
London   J[no] Buddle

127.

D/Lo/C142/27 (61)   Newcastle 28[th] Aug[us]t 1833

My Dear Lord
    I received your Lordship's Letters of yesterday this morning, and with respect to a retrospective reference I think your Lordship takes up very strong ground. I have had a full discussion of the subject with Morton and Hunter – Morton rejects the retrospective principle also, and is determined not to submit to the Hettonian dictation any more than ourselves. And he is anxious to form an alliance offensive and defensive with us, as against the Hettonians and all other assailants. He has entered into, and signed an agreement, to join us in the advance of Walls-end on the 1st Sep[tember] and will also aid us in every way he can in getting our Coals shipped at Sunderland.

---

18   Charles Attwood, radical candidate for Newcastle in 1832.
19   For radical and working class agitation in 1833–9 see J.T. Ward, *Chartism* (London, 1973), pp. 46–66.

In short he is dispose[d] to act cordially with us in every way for mutual protection and benefit.

I have written the squire, and Tennyson, to urge them to join us in the advance, and I would treat the Hettons with utter contempt on the occasion. We shall have a struggle in the first instance, but will succeed with our advance in the end, and then the Hetton Co. will sneak after us, in the advance or be disgraced by admitting their inferiority, which selling below us would establish.

I agree with your Lordship that as a new era has arrived in the affairs of the C[oal] T[rade] that a change of measures has become necessary – particularly as the chance of a beneficial regulation seems hopeless. The leading feature of the change seems to be the abolition of the fitting system – for now it seems when weighed in the scale, it will be found wanting. The Shipping by Spout at Sunderland is the next point, and no time will be lost in bringing it to bear. As to the *factoring* department in London, that requires very much consideration, for reasons which I will explain personally. In talking the subject over with Morton, we cannot find out any advantage we could derive from Regulation on the plan proposed (*dictated*) by the Hetton Co. – we think we may just as well *indure* low prices without regulation as have them *forced* upon us by regulation. We do not, therefore, incline to concede the point of *retrospective* regulation.

Hunter will see your Lordship tomorrow at Seaham, and I will, if I can reach in reasonable time, be with you on Sa[turday] Evening – at all events I will be there on Sunday morn[in]g with an acc[ount] of all that passes on Saturday. And at all events we must hold a Council on Sunday – as to the line to be pursued with the Fitters &c

The Marq[ues]s of Londonderry   I have the honor [&c.].
Wynyard   J[no] Buddle

128.

D/Lo/C142/27 (87)   Pensher 6[th] Nov[ember] 1833

My Dear Lord

I dined at Lambton yesterday, but there was a party, and I had very little conversation with Lord D[urham] and that of a general nature – not a word on the Coal-Trade. The party consisted of Lord & Lady Grey – and their youngest Son and daughter

Mr and Mrs Ord[20] – late Member for Morpeth
Mr & Mrs W[illia]m Ord[21]
Dr & Mrs Headlam
A daughter of L[or]d Althorp
Capt. Bowlby   Addison Fenwick
B. Ogden, W[illia]m Bell, J[oh]n Carr – the fitting agent, Lord D's
secretary, Morton & myself.

Nothing could be more affable than the two Lords, but not a single word of politics was uttered – the conversation was general – or rather chit-chat. I had a conversation with Lord Grey on the Coal-trade – he attributes it's depression like that of other trades, to over-production, and does not think any remedy can be devised, but that it must go on, 'till the cheap working Collieries drive those who cannot compete with them, out of the trade. He seems disposed to give up the export Duty, on small Coals entirely and I think, if the point is pressed upon him next session, he will do so.

Lord Durham had heard, how well our Harbour Works stood the Storm of the 1st, and thinks after such a test, it may be considered proof against any thing. Lord D. seems in remarkably good health, and spirits, as does Lord Grey also, but the latter regrets that he cannot remain longer in the North.

The Weather still continues stormy and unfavourable, which keeps us without Ships, and a very slack Vend, which puts us all out of heart, but as soon as the Weather takes up we expect to get on briskly, as the Walls-ends in London, keep up at 21/-.

I have received Pearsall's[22] acc[oun]t of Importation into London for the mo[nth] of October, from which it seems that the total importat[io]n is 55,849 tons short of the quantity imported up to the same period last year. But the Tyne seems to have got far ahead in point of quantity, as he states the Tyne at   114,957 tons

Wear	51,750
Stockton	15,513
Blyth Scotch &c.	9,177

This shews a great excess from the Tyne to London, and I believe

---

20 William Ord of Fenham and Whitfield, 1781–1855, MP for Morpeth 1802–32, for Newcastle 1835–52. *Hist. Parl. 1820–32*, vi, 579–81.

21 William Ord, 1803–38, son of the above.

22 Unidentified.

there is still a greater excess to the Coast which shews the desperate struggle the inferior Collieries are making.

The Durham and Shields Rail-way. Your Lordship expressed your hostility so decidedly to this measure, the last time I mentioned it, that I decided to relinquish the Engineering of it, and acquainted Mr Clayton with my decision accordingly. They are however determined to go on, and Morton told me last Evening, that Lord Durham will permit them to come thro' his property, from the Dean & Chap[ter] property at Rainton, by Biddick, and Fatfield, to join the Stanhope Line,[23] in his Fatfield estate. T. Harrison[24] is engaged as Engineer, and Sopwith is surveying the Line. Morton did not tell me the terms, but I think I will learn them thro' another Channel in a day, or two. It is on the principle of a certain ann[ua]l Way-leave rent, similar to the Stanhope Co's plan. By this plan the Dean & Chap[ter] and Lord D. may bring them all the way, from Broomside to the Stanhope Line, in Fatfield, without passing thro' any other property whatever. When I learn more about this matter, I will inform your Lordship all I know about it. Morton, and I presume Lord Durham are very hostile to the Hartlepool, which together with the great benefit they will derive from the Shields Line, is the cause of their countenancing it.

The Marq[ues]s of Londonderry   I have the Honor [&c.]
Gordon Castle   J^no Buddle

129.

D/Lo/C142/27 (88)   Walls-end 7th Nov[ember] 1833

My Dear Lord

I met Mr Clayton this afternoon, on my way through N[ew]castle. He asked me if I was prepared to pay him Hildyard's Interest. I replied that our rents would not be received, I understood, until the 20th Inst. and that of course I could not be prepared for him, 'till then which put him off for the present.

This meeting gave me the opportunity of asking him what was doing in the Durham and Shields Rail-way affair. He said Lord

---

23 A project for a railway to link limestone quarries at Stanhope with coal at Medomsley, and thence to the Tyne, was launched in 1831. Work on the line began in July 1832. Tomlinson, *North Eastern Railway*, pp. 211–18.

24 Thomas H. Harrison, engineer to the Stanhope line and the Durham Junction Railway.

Durham had consented to grant them Way-leave, through all his property by Biddick at the rate of £200 per Mile per Ann[u]m for an unlimited quantity, and a Bonus for the annoyance to Biddick Hall (which they pass close on the E. Side) and for his old materials. He added it was necessary to obtain an Act for the Bridge over the Wear, and that the notice for the application to Parliament must be advertised in the provincial papers next week, as it must not be later than the 15th.

I inquired if they are bound to any specific Line – he said they were not as Lord D. has given them the option of selecting any line they may think best – only it must pass East of Biddick Hall. I then asked him, if in the event of your Lordship taking a different view of the case, Lord D. would object to the Line passing through Chilton-moor and Pensher, which I think a better Line. He thinks his L[or]d-[shi]p would not object to such a change, but is apprehensive there is not now time to negotiate with your Lordship, as the notice for the Bridge must be advertised next Week, and it's situation defined.

I informed your Lordship yesterday that I had washed my hands of this affair, seeing that my having any thing to do with it was not agreeable to y[ou]r Lordship – altho' I never thought of taking any interest in it beyond the ordinary professional remuneration. I there-fore now, consider myself *entirely* independent of it, and feel it my duty to your Lordship and Family, to offer my opinion as follows freely, & without reserve, for your Lordship's deliberate consid-eration without the least wish, to bias your judgment, or warp it from any decision that your Lordship may consider best, and most prudent under all circumstances.

1st. That the Line can be carried into execution, totally independent of your Lordship.

2nd That your Lordship, therefore, risks all the Injury to Seaham Harbour *if any* (which I do not apprehend) that this project can inflict, without the chance of participating in any of the benefits to be derived from it.

3rd. Then q[uer]y would it not be the best policy to make a 'virtue of necessity', and participate, in the advantages to result from it, by granting Way-leave with sale of materials on the same terms as Lord Durham?

It is to be regretted that there is not more time for the further consideration of this matter, but there is no help for it – still if your Lordship can decide & let me know by return, I will do the best I can, as the advertisement may be delayed 'till next Thursday.

I had almost forgot to mention, that Clayton said Lord Durham would guarantee 100,000 Ch. ann[ua]ly from his Coll[ierie]s to the Sunderland Branch, but would not guarantee any specific quantity to Shields. The Bridge is to cross the river from Biddick haugh into Lord Durham's Fatfield Estate, thro' his Staith there. If the Line were to pass thro' Pensher the Bridge would cross the river at Low Lambton.

The Marq[ues]s of Londonderry	I have the honor [&c.]
Gordon Castle	J[no] Buddle

130.

D/Lo/C142/27 (92)   Pensher 13[th] Nov[ember] 1833

My Dear Lord

I have this morning rec[eive]d your Lordship's *private* Letter of yesterday from Edinbro', by which I am glad to learn you are so far advanced on your return. I am so occupied with various matters here, that I cannot see Clayton before next Saturday but in consequence of what your Lordship writes on the subject of the Durham & Shields rail-way I have written Clayton a Letter of which I enclose a copy. What course he may take upon it. I cannot guess – whether he may reckon on making terms with your Lordship, and take the Pensher Line, or take the Biddick Line, I don't know, but he must decide without delay, as the advertisement for the notice to Parliament must go to the papers tomorrow. That your Lordship and family may derive great benefit from this project I cannot doubt, or I certainly should never have brought it under your L[or]d[ship]s consideration. The immediate advantage to your Lordship w[oul]d be the getting quit of a mass of old materials as a fair valuation, and the sale of a large quantity of Stone from the quarry for Bridge *Pedestals*, Culverts &c. The advantage permanently to the Family would be Way-leave rents, and the shipping of Pensher, and Barmston Coal at Shields, at a cheaper rate than they can be shipped at Sunderland.

If £12000 or £15000 could be got for the old Wagg[on]-Way – Staiths & Machinery, it would afford the easiest, and best mode of paying off Coutts' mortgage of £10,000 on the Stock and would *liberate* the remaining part of the Coll[ier]y Stock from their grasp. The residue might be applied in various ways, as in aid of Lady Eliz[abeth] Pratts'[25] £10,000 Banks Amory &c. all of which *we know*,

---

25   A cousin of Lord Londonderry, daughter of the Marquess of Camden.

as sure as death, will have to be met in some way, or other, as they best can. As to stopping those projects either in parliament, or out of it, I have little confidence, as past experience has proved how difficult it is either for individuals, or parties to oppose such projects with effect. Such oppositions only incur expence, trouble, and vexation. My deliberate opinion, therefore, is, that as we don't possess the absolute power of knocking this project on the head – it is most prudent to make as much out of it as we can.

The Marq[ues]s of Londonderry   I have the honor [[&c.]
Edinburgh   J^no Buddle

131.

D/Lo/C142/27 (96)   Pensher 25th Nov[ember] 1833

My Dear Lord

I have been at a Comm[ittee] meeting at Newcastle this morning,[26] where things look rather *blue*, in consequence of the fall of 1/- to 1/3 a ton in the price of Coals at London, last Friday altho' only 7 fresh Ships had arrived, but they *expected* a Fleet, which was a sufficient reason for this great reduction.

The Tyne Comm[itt]ee are much puzzled what to do, as the whole trade on the river, is nearly in a state of mutiny and rebellion, against the price regulation, and the Comm[itt]ee have found it necessary to grant Licenses to freight (on as moderate a scale as possible) to prevent an *explosion* – the cry being for a regulation of Quantities, or entire free trade again. It has been decided to invite the Wear Committee to a conference next Friday morning to state the impossibility of maintaining the Price Regulation on the Tyne, and to ascertain how far all parties may *now* be in the mood, and to endeavour to get the ground cleared for laying the foundations of a regulation of Quantities and prices for the ensuing year, as it is admitted on all hands that nothing else, can save the trade from absolute bankruptcy, and ruin. Yet there are a few reckless pig-headed ones, who will be very bad to manage, on any way. On the Wear, I don't think we shall have much difficulty, unless it be with the Hetton Co. I will call upon John Wood tomorrow, on my way to Seaham, and endeavour to feel how his pulse beats on, on this point. And between this and Friday,

26 Minutes in NRO 263/A2.

I shall see Morton, but I don't apprehend much difficulty – if any, with him.

I was glad to find the waggons rattling briskly on my arrival here – Sherraton Dunn, our Waggon regulator was advised of 90 keels being due at Seaham this morning, and has sent 50 down, and at the staith here, there are 20 keels – 12 for W[alls-]end, and 14 for Eden. This looks something like ourselves again, but the Eden-main, to Sunderland at present prices, are literally *thrown away* – we don't make a penny by them. We must if possible have W[alls-]end up to 28/6 and Eden to 24/6, which together with the shipping by *spout* at Sunderland will make us *flourish* again – even at 100,000 Vend.

Hunter will I presume bring me your Lordship's directions as to Amory Chisholme, Clayton, and Sherwood, tomorrow.

The Marq[ues]s of Londonderry   I have the honor [&c.]
Wynyard Park   J^no Buddle

132.

D/Lo/C142/27 (105)   Pensher 12th Dec[ember] 1833

My Dear Lord

I have delayed writing 'till the last moment this Evening, as I thought it not unlikely that my friend Donkin might give me a call, on his way home from the meeting of the Hetton Co. He has not however called, and I presume that I shall remain in ignorance of the decision of the Co. as to their future line of policy 'till we meet J. Wood at Chester tomorrow.

The great decline of prices last Monday in London, and the report of the factors, that Coals are almost unsaleable, at any price, w[oul]d one would imagine, produce a strong impression on the *Anarchyst* party, unless they are entirely reckless. As it must now be clear to the most obtuse, that nothing but a regulation of the supply, at this end of the trade, can ensure remunerating prices at the other end. The question therefore lies between regulation, or wide sweeping ruin. By carrying on the War of extermination, the Hetton Co. may undoubtedly succeed in shutting up a few of the most inferior Collieries on both Rivers, but still there are some, on the Tyne I *know*, which neither can or will be put down. Those fighting Coll[ierie]s have the power to make up any quantity that the subdued Coll[ierie]s may leave short, so that the Hetton Co. will not get the gap to fill up, and if they were as strong as Hercules, their allies will bring them to their *marrow bones*.

My occupation in this quarter, has not permitted me to attend the Comm[itt]ee meetings – but I rec[eive]d a Letter from Hugh Taylor this morn[in]g to inform me what they had done. I enclose this Letter in another cover, which will apprize your Lordship of the proceedings of the Comm[itt]ee.

Our vend is going on very slowly, I am sorry to say, from the want of Ships, it is impossible they can load at present prices, as Stewart's W[alls-]end is not leaving more than 21/- and where is the Shipowner that can afford to carry them at a loss of 5/- or 6/- per Ch. – it is quite out of the question to expect it, and our Vend of W[alls-]end must be bro[ugh]t nearly to a stand, 'till prices advance again in London, or we reduce to 21/- – there is no alternative. The regulation of price cannot relieve us in this respect, as the Tyne will force their Coals upon the market, on better terms to the Ship-owners, than they can obtain of us, and therefore they will go to the Tyne. I don't know what may turn up at Chester tomorrow – but if no opening is made towards a regulation of quantities, I consider the regulation of prices cannot be maintained during the next three months. Your Lordship may expect a Bulletin from Chester by tomorrow's post to say what our prospects are.

There have been *Warlike demonstrations* in this quarter in the beginning of the Week – but fortunately neither Powder burnt, nor Blood spilt.

A copy of the Newcastle press with the report of the speeches at Attwood's ruffian-like radical meeting,[27] was sent to Lord Durham, and another copy to Mr Hed[worth] Lambton, who was on his way to London. Some parts of Attwood's speech were so offensive to the earl and his Brother, that they both decided to demand an explanation, or 'the alternative'. Harland the M.P,[28] was deputed by Hed[wor]th Lambton, and W[illia]m Williamson (of mail coach memory) by the earl, to wait upon Attwood for the object above stated. Harland had got his answer some time before Williamson arrived. The radical chief, it seems, did not relish the smell of gunpowder but preferred 'eating his words' – as is (if my information be correct) to appear in the provincial papers tomorrow. If your Lordship has not already

27 A dinner was given at Gateshead on 2 December for Charles Attwood, unsuccessful candidate for Newcastle in the 1832 election, and Thomas Doubleday, secretary of the Northern Political Union. The price was kept low, and attendance was large. Radical speeches were made. Attwood's speech included an attack on Hedworth Lambton. *Newcastle Chronicle*, 7 Dec. 1833.

28 William Charles Harland, MP for Durham City 1832–41.

heard these particulars, you most likely will, but it may be as well not to notice them as coming from me.

I shall expect to hear from your Lordship on Sa[turday] morning at N[ew]castle, as to your Seaham movements. And I will regulate mine accordingly, as far as circumstances will permit, but if the meeting of the Hetton Co. of this m[ornin]g should have declared for Peace, the consequent measures may possibly require my attendance at some meeting on Monday, or Tuesday, but of this I shall most likely be able to apprize your Lordship tomorrow.

The Marq[ues]s of Londonderry   I have the honor [&c.]
Wynyard Park   J^{no} Buddle

133.

D/Lo/C142/28 (5)   72 Jermyn St. 5th Jan[uar]y 1834

My Dear Lord

Your Lordship's Letter of the 2nd did not reach me 'till 8 o'clock last Ev[enin]g and as I foresee, that my out of town business after post arrives in the morning will leave me but a brief interval for writing, in the afternoon, I think it best to write a few lines at the present moment.

It appears from Dunn's letter to Grey that there are two ways of telling the same story – he throws the blame altogether on the waywardness of the Hetton Co., concealing entirely the declaration of the *proprietory* that they would *not* consent to regulate, on their old basis of 40,000 on *any account* whatever. Which declaration must of consequence have been grounded on his own calculations and advice, and to which he was therefore a party. It can not therefore be fair, and candid in him to conceal this material fact from Mr Grey – a party so deeply interested, as it conveys an erroneous idea of the real state and bearings of the affair.

I am glad your Lordship has written to Lord Durham, as I think it will open the road to that state of good neighbourhood and friendly intercourse, which cannot fail to be beneficial to both families, and I have reason to know that Lord D. entertains an excellent opinion, and kindly feelings to my Lady, and also to your Lordship, in the character of a private Gentleman – politics being out of the question. I should advise your Lordship by all means to see old Arthur – 'necessity brings us into comp[an]y with strange bedfellows' – no possible harm can result from the interview, but good possibly may, and I wish the interview might take place before the Co. meet on the 7th. In such an interview I am sure your Lordship will be guarded in not quoting me on any of the pecuniary affairs of the Co. as it might interrupt the channel thro' which I receive the information.

As to poor Hunter's peccadillo,[1] I am glad your Lordship views it so charitably – it was a slip, unguarded, at an unlucky moment,

---

1   Hunter had been absent for some days on account of drunkenness. See C.M. Hiskey, 'George Hunter (1792–1851): an Industrial Biography', in *Durham County Local History Society Bulletin*, no. 23 (Aug. 1979), pp. 48–56.

and by no means the effect of a vicious habit. For many months he has been in a very nervous irritable state, and has more than once declared to me, that he could not endure the worry & distress of mind and body, which the incessant drudgery of the Bill renewing & money transactions, over and above his legitimate Coll[ier]y work, inflicted upon him, and that he must either give up his situation, or break down. I have soothed and encouraged him all I could with the hope of better times – but unless he is relieved shortly I am sure, that one or other of the above results will ensue, When I left he was fretting about Chaytor's £2000 under the conviction that if it was not paid in a few days, they w[oul]d inevitably proceed to extremities which w[oul]d certainly be the most fatal thing that could happen to us. They might proceed by *Poney* which is a brief summary process, and in 24 Hours might have executions in every part of the property. I do not know what to advise, I see the inexpediency of your Lordship running your acc[oun]t at Coutts' aground; but *tremble* for the consequences that must, and will result from Chaytor's proceeding – as future arrangements might in the event be put entirely out of our own power and control. Not being able to advise, at this distance, I can only trust in your Lordship's judgment, and discretion, to decide for the best.

Monday 6th January in Continuation. I have seen the Duke's and Sir R, Peel's answers to your Lordship's application relative to the Pictures,[2] which corroborates all the information obtained by Mr McDonnell[3] and myself on the same subject. And it is but too clear that there is not the least chance of raising money upon them in any shape, or way, to meet the exigency of the moment. And I am grieved to say, that I see no mode whatever, of preserving the property from almost certain destruction, but an immediate assignment, as stated in a former letter, and I hope your Lordship will decide & see Gregson & Hunter, as to the mode of carrying the measure into effect before the bank, or Chaytor take measures, as it may then be too late. I am glad your Lordship has had a meeting with Lord Durham, as I have no doubt it will bring a good understanding, beneficial to both.

I have no further information as to the probability of selling, or letting the Houses, but from all I hear, there is little chance of effecting either the one, or the other within any definite period. I will

---

2   Lord Londonderry was attempting to borrow money from the government against the pictures at Holderness House.

3   Edmund McDonnell, 1770–1852, second husband of Lady Londonderry's mother the Countess of Antrim.

endeavour to sound Bigge tomorrow as to a discounting of Bills, but
have no hope of success – he has a dishonoured Bill lying in his desk,
for about £380 at present. & I don't see how I am to set about asking
him, as a *mere tradesman* to discount long dated Bills – he will naturally say – 'go to your Bankers, discounting Bills is not my trade'.
Such an application is much more likely to bring him upon our backs
for p[ay]m[en]t of the overdue Bill which he holds – the payment of
which he may enforce any day, under his 'Warrant of Attorney'.

I send in another cover, a very kind letter from Sir H. Browne – I
only wish he had been nearer to us, in this hour of such need. I will
write to him tomorrow, or next day.

The Marq[ues]s of Londonderry   I have the Honor [&c.]
Wynyard Park   J^{no} Buddle

134.

D/Lo/C142/28 (7)   72 Jermyn St London 7th Jan[uar]y 1834

My Dear Lord
    Your Lordship's minute details of the meeting with Lord Durham
at Pensher, are mainly in accordance with what passed on the same
subjects with his L[or]d[shi]p, Stephenson, and Morton, and myself
at the castle. Before any thing is attempted with respect to reforming
abuses, here, and making so essential a change in the system of
management, we must have a thorough good understanding, and
mutual confidence established, and *confirmed*, amongst ourselves at
home. I am by no means of opinion that the contemplated *experiment* of the triple, or quadruple, association, to regulate for 6 months,
will answer any beneficial purpose. I am rather inclined to think the
contrary, and that it will just be so much valuable time thrown away
– especially if the prices are fixed at 24/6 and 20/6. At these prices
I think I know enough of the Tyne, to pronounce, that they will not
support any such regulation, by a corresponding measure. And I am
further of opinion that unless the proposed regulation on the Wear, is
supported by a similar measure on the Tyne, it will inevitably prove
abortive. At 26/6 and 22/6 I believe the Tyne would be satisfied &
would co-operate with the Wear.

I know the plan of great quantities and low prices, is a *pet* with
Morton, and might suit Hetton & Lord D—m but recollect, their
Coal, is mixed with Main Coal & other seams, and not so fine in
quality as our Hutton *pure* as 'Eden-main'. Our Eden has a decided

preference in the next best market to London, Lynn, and few of them go to London, while great quantities of Primrose & Lyon's Main go there. These Coals are intrinsically not so good as E[den] Main, and to force off a quantity, it may be necessary to reduce the price to 20/6. But I feel satisfied there is no necessity to reduce Eden-m[ain] to 20/6. Why then should we sacrifice 2/- per Ch. – unless the other parties allow us an equivalent in quantity, but which I think impracticable, as by increasing our quantity 1/10 per Ch. w[oul]d go into the pocket of the D[ean] & C[hapter]. I feel that under any circumstances, I should hardly consent to take less than 22/6 for Eden-main.

The necessary inquiries into the abuses here, must be set about in the most prudent & cautious manner, and will require much time. I really could not expect to feel my way in it so as to arrive at any satisfactory result in less than a fort[nigh]t or 3 Weeks – giving my *whole* individual attention to it. It was my intention to have started for the North tomorrow, but y[ou]r L[or]d[ship]'s Letter on this subject will detain me 'till Sat[urda]y to receive y[ou]r decision whether it is most important that I sh[oul]d remain here, or return home at this juncture. It w[oul]d seem most prudent I think to defer this inquiry 'till we get affairs at home into a better shape, then Morton, Wood & myself might come and devote ourselves to the business of inquiry.

I have not seen Stephenson since I came – he is to call upon me tomorrow and 'till today, I have never been able to go into the City, so that I am perfectly ignorant of the state of the Coal Exchange. I would observe, that your Lordship may quote my opinions to Lord Durham as freely as you please, only don't, pray, hand him any of my Letters, as it would put a great deal of constraint on my communications.

The Marq[ues]s pf Londonderry   I have the honor [&c.]
Wynyard   J[no] Buddle

135.

D/Lo/C142/28 (15)   Pensher 21[st] Jan[uar]y 1834

My Dear Lord

Since our discussion of yesterday, the melancholy and pressing state of our affairs has never for a moment been out of my mind; and I have thought, and pondered over them, 'till I have nearly lost the power of reasoning, and find my head addled. I would therefore rather depend upon the opinions I formed yesterday, or prior to yesterday, than on any opinions I might form today, as I really feel my head as heavy as lead.

I have drawn out a statement of which the enclosed is a copy, to lay before Batson and Grace[4] tomorrow – but I *seriously* dread, and doubt their thinking that they can, with so small a *probable surplus* venture on the plan of a Trusteeship. If they do not I must enjoin them to *secrecy* and not to expose our weakness – but of what avail will this be? It can only keep matters snug for a few days – certainly not beyond the end of this month. For if even they make the Pay on Friday, they will not take up any of the accept[ance]s for Feb[ruary] but will send them back, and probably take hold of Pittington, which will cause an explosion and will ruin us all. As on turning the subject over, and over in every shape, and way 'till my mind is entirely bewildered, I can neither make more nor less of it than, if Pittington is alienated, either by the bank taking possession, or by sale, that Rainton Colliery, and the rest, will be *utterly inadequate* to meet the remaining charges, and that the property will become the prey of the other creditors, & their Lawyers, and be torn to pieces and destroyed.

The profits of Rainton Colliery, and the Rents, cannot in prudence be taken at more than £25,000 a year, at the utmost, and this is all we have to stand against the Interest of Mortgages, and personal Debts of every kind, and for the payment of debts – save the Bank Debt, and Amory's, which must, of course adhere to Pittington exclusively, let it fall into what hands it may. Pittington with its incumbrances being alienated, the remaining part of the property would have the following payments to provide for viz

My Lady	£2000
The Countess of Antrim[5]	1500
Mrs Taylor[6]	500
Trust Fund including	
Russell's Int[erest]	3120

---

4   Thomas Batson and Nathaniel Grace, joint managing directors of the Joint Stock bank.

5   Anne Macdonald, 1775–1834, mother of Lady Londonderry, Countess of Antrim in her own right, married (1) Sir Henry Vane Tempest, Lady Londonderry's father, and (2) Edmund McDonnell.

6   Frances Anne Vane, b. 1769, sister of Sir Henry Vane Tempest, married Michael Angelo Taylor, MP.

Harbour Interest redemp[tion]	4250
Interest on Mortgages	7110
Ditto – on personal Debts	5100
Life Insurance	<u>370</u>
	23950

Thus it seems that under the most favourable point of view, in which I can possibly place the subject, and without making any charge whatever, for the enormous expence of keeping so large a personal debt afloat, by renewing of Bills, or taking into acco[un]t any of the Colliery tradesmen's debts, or Acceptances, that an ann[ua]l surplus of £1050 only is left to bear the whole burden!!! The thing is physically *impossible* – as well might we set a straw to prop up a hay Stack, as attempt to save the property under such circumstances, without at once fairly, and boldly, meeting the Storm, by Sale and *assignment – If possible*. My decided, and confirmed opinion is, after the deepest reflection and intense consideration, that it has been in my power to give to the subject, that *nothing short of sale & assignment combined can save the Family*. And that no more time is to be lost in scheming, and temporizing. This is my undisguised and solemn opinion, and decision – made after a sleepless night, in the sincerest spirit of friendship, and devotion to the interests of your Lordship and your family. It is this feeling which has compelled me to express my sentiments, and opinion with such entire freedom, and unreserved, as I am under the conviction, that I should not be acting honestly, were I to conceal my *true opinions* from your Lordship, at so critical a crisis, and connive at the adoption of any temporary and hollow scheme, which might at the moment palliate, but in the end produce inevitable ruin. Rather than act thus, I would, in spite of that attachment which so firmly binds me to the interest and welfare of your Lordship, and the family, solicit your Lordship's permission to retire, as I cannot bear, to stand by, tamely and see ruin over-running the family, with rapid strides, without having the power, more than a helpless infant, of averting it. The long, and the short of it is, that it would kill me out right.

I will go to Batson, and Grace in the morning, and sound them, on the affair of the trust, but I dread the meeting. If they reject the project, I shall feel quite discomfited, as I have not been able to devise a succedaneum. If they won't adopt it I must endeavour to get them to ponder upon, and not reject it at once, as the gaining of a few days is an object to us. We may get Clayton's offer, and be able to make something of it. Thorman[7] tells me, Harrison[8] the Engineer has been here, to look at the waggon-way, Staith, Machinery &c. to form his opinion of their Value.

Hunter is at Durham, on the pitmen's dispute about the measure of the Corve. They are evidently concocting mischief.

I cannot hear any thing of the Hetton meeting 'till I go to Morton's and shall not be able to inform y[ou]r Lordship what is passing 'till tomorrow evening post. Our Vend is going on but slowly I fear, but I have not been able to get out today, to look about me. Spence is better, but Thorman tells me, he had not yesterday been out of his Chamber. We had a terrible *incendiary* fire, in this neighbourhood last night. *Tommy* Elliot's (one of our Fitters) stack yard was set on fire last night, and the Wind being high, all the stacks were consumed. 100 tons of Hay and £900 worth of Wheat is destroyed – all the stacks had been fired at the same time, as the flames burst our simultaneously in every part of the premises. Some blackguard keelmen are suspected.

I have thought it best to send the boy with this, as if your Lordship should have any thing to communicate you can write by him in the morning.

The Marq[ues]s of Londonderry   I have the honor [&c.]
Wynyard Park   J[no] Buddle

136.

D/Lo/C142/28 (16)   Pensher 23[rd] Jan[uar]y 1834

My Dear Lord

I received your Lordship's affecting and affectionate Letter of last night by the boy this morning. I am deeply impressed with the solemnity of the sentiments which it conveys, as they shew that the best of hearts lies in the best of breasts. I feel quite inadequate to express the true state of my feelings, on the occasion, and can only repeat the declaration, which I have so often before made, of my entire devotion and attachment to the welfare of your Lordship and the family. And can only add, that under the important determina-

---

7   John Thorman, engineer to the Londonderry collieries.
8   T.E. Harrison, engineer of the Durham Junction Railway.

tion your Lordship has come to,[9] you will find me, as well as in prosperity – through good or evil report, and through all vicissitudes of our mortal condition, more I cannot say. I also feel most sensibly for my Lady – her fortitude and moral courage under the very trying circumstances of our case is beyond all praise, and must impress us all with sentiments of the most profound respect, and esteem. Her admirable constancy and firmness in the midst of our troubles is consoling and encouraging in the highest degree, and inspires feelings of hope, and confidence on the approach of better times.

I went to Newcastle this morning, have had a *day's work* with the bank, and have only this instant 8 o'clock returned. My plan is to be with your Lordship in the morn[in]g by 10 o'clock, and to bring Gregson with me. I shall not therefore, go into detail at present, but merely state that I *think* the bank Directors are disposed to listen to the project of the Trust, but Carr their solicitor having thrown out many technical Law difficulties, no progress can be made until Gregson goes with me to meet Carr, and the Directors to meet all points. The Directors are decidedly favourable to the plan of a Trust, but are timid about entering into it under the very heavy liabilities of the property, and the small ann[ua]l surplus. Nothing will reconcile them to it, but sales to a large amo[un]t to reduce the amo[un]t of personal debts. £400 of acceptances are due tomorrow, which they will not pay unless Fitters Bills can be got to cover them. Hunter must, therefore, be off to Sunderland in the morning, to raise the Wind if possible.

I called upon Clayton – he promised that I should receive his offer at Wynyard in the morning.

I return Mr McDonnell's Letter in another cover – I will not now make any comments, as I don't wish to detain the Boy. I also enclose J[no] Wood's Letter – Donkin and Percival Fenwick dined at Morton's

---

9   The idea of putting the properties into a trust to preserve them from Lord Londonderry's creditors had been developing since 1824. In December 1833 the Joint Stock Bank decided that unless the Londonderry overdraft was reduced immediately they would seize the collieries. Under a trust deed signed on 21 March 1834 (D/Lo/E51) all the English estates except Holderness House and Seaham Hall were transferred to trustees – Edmund McDonnell, Richard Batson of the Joint Stock Bank, and Robert Scurfield the fitter. The trust could be wound up when £200,000 had been raised and applied to the discharge of Lord Londonderry's debts excluding mortgages, and to the reduction of the overdraft. A new deed was executed in 1835. R.W. Sturgess, 'The Londonderry Trust, 1819–1854', *Archaeologia Aeliana*, 5th ser., x (1982), pp. 179–192; Hiskey, 'John Buddle', ch. 13.

yesterday – the meeting of the Co. continued in debate *seven* hours, and the question of regulation was carried in the *affirmative*. John Wood is invested with discretionary powers, to act with Morton, and myself, as he may see fit, without reference to the Co. and Donkin thinks all will go right – only this is not to be divulged 'till it is announced *officially*. Donkin says, some of the parties are jealous of his communicating the business of the meetings to Morton & myself. Old *Arthur* stated at the meeting, that the Marquess of Londonderry knew everything that passed at their meetings so that it was certain some one had *blabbed*.

Morton and I have fixed to meet J^no Wood at Chester next Monday. We think it best to meet by our three selves, in the first instances to arrange our plans, and not to have any thing to do with Matt[hias] Dunn, 'till we see our way a little, as he is a troublesome haggling sort of person.

We shall be with your Lordship in good time tomorrow, as I must return here in the Evening again.

The Marq[ues]s of Londonderry	I have the honor [&c.]
Wynyard	J^no Buddle

137.

D/Lo/C142/29 (13)   Walls-end 10th Mar[ch] 1834

My Dear Lord

The melancholy tone of your Lordship's Letter of yesterday, has so distressed me, that I feel utterly at a loss how to express my feelings on the occasion. I cannot however suffer myself to contemplate that separation of interest, and intercourse, which has now subsisted between us for fifteen years – within a few days – of the best days of our lives. It cannot – must not happen – for altho' the arrangement which imperious necessity has forced upon us, will introduce a third party into our councils, it does not follow, that it is to interrupt, much less to close, the channel of communication between your Lordship and myself, or that you are not to be apprized of, and consulted in all material, and essential matters in the administration of your own affairs. I entirely mistake the matter, and the men, we have to deal with, if in all matters your Lordship's views, and opinions, will not be attended to, with the utmost deference and delicacy. As to myself, notwithstanding I may have differed in opinion, with your Lordship on many occasions, as to the administration of your affairs, yet I never could impugn your Lordship's motives – but on the contrary, was always ready to give your Lordship full credit for the integrity of your intentions.

The determination of the Bank Directors has undoubtedly placed your Lordship in a most uncomfortable situation, 'till the Irish rents are relieved from that state of sequestration in which they are placed by Andrews' acceptances. But I cannot bring myself to believe, that they will adhere to the letter of their declaration – I really think, with the p[ay]m[en]t of the picture money, the execution of the Deed, and the brighter prospects of the Trade, they will relax, and virtually act on the advice & recommendation of the trustees, as to the requisite supplies for family purposes – altho' they will not allow a bargain to be driven upon the point.

I will be at the Bank this morning as soon as it opens to deliver y[ou]r Lordship's Letter, and talk to the Directors, and will write again by post this Evening. I hope Mr McDonnell will reach Wyn[yar]d to day, & make an appoint[men]t for seeing us all, as soon as possible as the Wear meet[in]g for the final arrang[emen]t of the Regulation is fixed for Thursday, and as the Tyne co-operation will have to be settled immediately afterwards I anticipate meeting at N[ew]castle on Friday. I hope to hear from your Lordship by tomorrow's post if Mr McDonnell has arrived, and what arrangements you have made for our meeting.

The Marq[ues]s of Londonderry   I have the honor [&c.]
Wynyard Park   J[no] Buddle

138.

D/Lo/C142/29 (36)   Seaham Harbour 15[th] Ap[ril] 1834

My Dear Lord

I attended the Commission meeting this morning at Sunderland, when a petition against the 'Junction' (So. Shields) rail-way to both Houses was agreed to, and signed by all the Sunderland Commissioners. I opposed, but Morton being prevented from attending I was left in a minority of *one*. The petition does little more than pray for the protection of the Commissioners rights, and will I think, be innoxious [*sic*] as regards the Bill.

All matters are going on very well here – with plenty of Ships for the regulated vend but the Pittington Pitmen, and part of the Rainton men, are very feverish, and we have reason to believe are swearing, and sworn into the National Trades' Union. The Pitmen of nine different Collieries So. of the Tyne, and on Wear, sent in their adhesion to *the Cock* last Sat[ur]d[a]y and shortly there is little doubt but the whole body will be obliged to join by intimidation. All the Ship-Carpenters, Ropers &c on the Tyne have joined. A large meeting of the Union was held on N[ew]castle Town-moor yesterday – none of the Radical leaders attended but *our friend* Hepburn took a conspicuous position. I have not heard any acco[un]t that I can depend upon of what passed – but it is said, the King is to be *commanded* to dismiss the Ministers, and in the event of non-compliance another meeting is to be holden, on Whit Monday – against which time, the plan of a *new constitution* is to be submitted to the meeting, and *we* are to take the affairs of the State into *our own hands*. Some state the number assembled on this occasion at 8000, others at 12,000. I passed a Body of about 800 on the Shields road, mostly pitmen, with music & colours, On one of the latter was painted, in large letters, 'Nail your colours to the Mast, Death, or Liberty'. It is quite clear that all this sort of work cannot go on long without mischief, and it is full time that parliament was looking to it.

I met Rawsthorn, Bradyll's attorney by chance in N[ew]castle last Saturday – he told me, that he had had a conversation with an eminent Lawyer at York Assizes, who informed him, that during the late proceedings in Robertson's affair, some new light had been elicited by the production of some letters of your Lordship's which had given a different complexion to the affair. I told him I had never heard of any thing of the kind – it may however, be as well to inquire of Cowburn, if there is any truth in this, or whether it is merely Lawyers' *gossip*. I am just going to the Collieries, but I will defer the investigation of Hikely and Newby's disagreeable affair, till Hunter's return.

Perceval Forster has made some sort of communication to the Wear Comm[itt]ee I understand, which may lead to a compromise, but I don't yet know what it is exactly. I believe he offers to take 40,000 basis for the present year.

The Marq[ues]s of Londonderry   I have the honor [&c.]
Holdernesse House   J^no Buddle
London

139.

D/Lo/C142/30 (1) Pensher 12th June 1834

My Dear Lord

I received your Lordship's letter of the 7th with Claytons, and Mitchell's enclosed, and of the 9th with Broooks' enclosed. I hope we are in a very fair way, to have Harbour room sufficient at Seaham, for all our purposes, in less than twelve months – and I don't exactly see that Brooks' Harbour of refuge will confer all the collateral benefits on us which he anticipates – but like most projectors he is partial to his own *Bantling*. He is I understand, a very decent sort of man, and I think your Lordship had best write him a civil acknowledgement of the receipt of his Letter and plan, and refer him to me; as to the eventual advantage which Seaham may derive from his project.

The Weather has been favourable, and T. Nicholson & Thorman, have made good progress with their work, during my absence. Eleven ft. In height, viz one half of the Coffer Dam (the large cast iron dam) is now fixed in its place, but the Wedging of the Joints is not yet completed, it looks exceedingly well, and I have the greatest confidence in it's complete success. The excavation of the So. Harbour, the Dock Wall, and the finishing of the Glacis, at the root of the N. Pier are all progressing, and by the time your Lordship returns to the North, I hope you will find the whole of the Works in a very satisfactory state.

At the Collieries, with the exception of some troublesome work in the Broom side Pits, all matters are going on very well. We only want more liberal monthly Issues – and an advance of 2/- per Ch. to set us upon our Legs again. The former I hope we may obtain next month, but from all I hear I doubt we shall find much difficulty in achieving the latter. There are still several dissatisfied parties, and altho' they are bound by the regulation, they do not *draw kindly in harness* – amongst others, i apprehend we shall have much trouble with Perc[eva]l Forster. We have a meeting of the Wear at Chester tomorrow, to endeavour to get all parties to sign the regul[ation] Contract and to give their Pro[missory] Notes, to cover penalties for *peccadillos* but Morton tells me, he thinks *Percy* will shirk then, and not attend the meeting. I viewed the Broom side pits this morning, and regret to say, that I do not find the situation of the Under ground affairs, so satisfactory as I could wish. The Seam & Strata are shattered by several dislocations running in various directions, and altho' none of them are of material magnitude, they are large enough to injure the Coal materially, and to cause spoils the lustre

of the Coals, so that, as yet no Walls-end have been obtained altho'
on the first getting of the Coal, it had a most flattering aspect. I have
pointed out such measures as I think best calculated to obviate these
defects.

I expect Harrison, in the morning, and will make all the way with
him I can towards an arrangement for the sale of the stock to the
Junction R.W.Co., but I am sadly afraid we shall not be able to get on
quick enough, to satisfy Sir E. Banks' impatience, and it will require
all Mr McDonnell's skill, and exertion to keep him quiet.

The Joint Stock Directors have had a special meeting on the state
of the *old* Ba[lanc]e and have passed some strong resolutions. They
insist upon an immediate reduction, or they will proceed to sale. I
hope, and trust Mr McDonnell will shortly be able to make further
sales – to keep feeding them a little. I will speak to Batson on your
Lordship's affair on Sa[turday] but he has been under the necessity
of remitting Amory another £1000, which with the Pay tomorrow,
will run the Trust Fund *far* in arrear. This is like struggling between
sinking & swimming, but the necessarily small Issues of vend will
not for the present do better for us.

The Marq[ues]s of Londonderry   I have the honor [&c.]
                                                  J^no Buddle

140.

D/Lo/C142/30 (17)   Walls-end 10th Aug[us]t 1834

My Dear Lord
I received your Lordship's letter of the 8th Inst. this morning,
together with Mr McDonnell's, and one from Groom of the same
date, at Seaham all of which I will answer tomorrow. I was at the
Harbour, in consequence of an accident to our Coffer dam on Friday.

On the 18th & 19th Ulto. a Gale of Wind, from the N.E. and very
high Sea carried away the screen of Timber work which had been
placed, just within the entrance of the So. Harbour, for the protection
of the dam, while building. The dam not being properly secured, at
the time, received a violent shaking, from the action of the Sea which
injured the Hemp Bolts so much in the two top lengths of Segments,
that we were obliged to take them off, to have them re-fitted. At
the same time, the N.W. quarter of the circle of the Dam was flat-
tened a little, but not so much so, as to require it's being taken down,
and adjusted, as we were all of opinion, that it might be effectively

secured by staying, and laying a Buttress of Clay, and Spoil, round the outside of it. But this could not be done 'till the Flooring, and Piers of the Intake gate, were laid & the Pier got a course or two above low Water-mark. This was accomplished last Thursday, when I fixed all matters with Tommy Nicholson for the securing of the dam, which were to be completed, before the pressure was laid upon it. Thorman being engaged with Harrison in the rail-way was not present, and was not apprised of my design and unfortunately gave directions to shut the bottom Sluices on Friday morn[in]g to try the pressure of the Tide against the dam. The water rose to within a foot of the top, of the Dam, when one of the Joints, in the flat part of the Circle opened inwards – like the opening of a Dock gate, and the Water instantly rushed in, with such force, as to drag in other segments – forming a breach, of about 40 ft. in width. The damage is not however, of much extent, only 8 segments broken, and none of the Frame Work injured, and altho' it may take a Week to repair the Dam – it will not retard the laying of the Foundation of the Gate Piers & Flooring, more than 2 or 3 days. Fortunately the Excavators had left work about 15 minutes before, so that no one was hurt. I feel annoyed at this interruption, small as it is, as both the Season, and our Money is spending very fast

I thought it best to give your Lordship this detail, as ten to one, but a very alarming account may be given in the Papers.

The Marq[ues]s of Londonderry   I have the honor [&c.]
London   J^no Buddle

141.

D/Lo/C142/30 (24)   Walls-end 28th Aug[us]t 1834

My Dear Lord

I am happy to learn by your Lordship's Letter of yesterday that you have arrived safe at Wynyard, and found our young friends, on their return from Seaham quite well. My Lady's kind attention to Lady Durham, will no doubt be taken, as it is meant – most kindly, and will be appreciated accordingly.

I have been to Percy-main Colliery this morning (the very *Hotbed* of the Union) and was glad to find the Unionists completely crest-fallen, in consequence of the failure of Hepburn, Pile, and Perkins' mission to London. Those workers returned last Saturday, the trades Unions in London, having refused to admit the Pitmen, or accept their alliance. The grounds of objection taken by the *Gen[era]l* meeting, as far as *my friends*, at Percy-main will yet speak out – to the Pitmen as allies is, that their employment is so hazardous, they might be too burdensome to the Fund, and because *only* 3000 of this whole Body are yet sworn in. I should hope from this, that this infernal combination will decline, and that this expedition of Hepburn & Co. to London, has been a last effort, to keep up the Esprit de Corps.

I am summoned to attend a meeting of the joint Comm[itt]ee on Sa[turday] 'to take into consideration, an important communication from the Coal Exchange'. I anticipate what it is – the Factors find it impracticable to continue *their* regulation, under the pressure of Ships which *we* heap upon them, and from the Coal-buyers, delivering their own Ships *on arrival*, without waiting their fair turn. An accumulation of 180 Ships remained unsold at last Friday's market – that is to say as many as should be sold during the next succeeding 5 market days. This has thrown the freighted Ships under demurrage, and the Ship-owners, having Ships laden, on their own acc[oun]t are suffering from the detention of their Vessels. Some plan must be devised for remedying these evils, or it is impossible for the Factors to maintain their regulation. The difficulty is, how to send a sufficient supply to the Coast, without sending too great a quantity to London. And how to get out of it I really cannot tell, as we cannot prevent the captains from going to any port they please when they have got the Coals on board.

I have had conversation with Rob[er]t Clark the factor,[10] on advancing the price of Coals – he thinks we would just vend as many Coals at an advance of 2/- as at present prices, but I fear there will be no moving the Hetton Co.

I am anxiously expecting to hear from Mr McDonnell on the Pittington affair, as I am apprehensive from his silence, some hitch may have occurred. I shall be happy to pay my respects to your Lordship, and my Lady the first opportunity, but cannot name the time before Saturday.

The Marq[ues]s of Londonderry   I have the honor [&c.]
Wynyard Park   J[no] Buddle

---

10 Robert Clarke, coal factor, London. Raymond Smith, *Sea-Coal for London: History of the Coal Factors in the London Market* (London, 1961), p. 369.

142.

D/Lo/C142/31 (10) Newcastle 8th Oct[ober] 1834

My Dear Lord

I got home last Evening and came here this morning to hear Coal-trade & other news. As far as regards the general aspect of the trade I think it more favourable than when I left home. The no. of Ships remaining unsold at market, by the day's letter, is reduced to 39, and the prices of the Wear *best* Walls-ends are up to 21/9, which will cover the advance of 2/- here, and if we do but conduct the affairs of the trade, in the Comm[it]tees with ordinary tact and prudence, I am *quite sure*, we may henceforward maintain the advance with *all ease*. But unfortunately the *needy*, *greedy*, and *knavish* in the trade, so far outnumber, the *easy moderate*, and *honest*, that it is difficult to conjecture, whether we may be able to continue on the fair line of march, which we are just entering upon. On this point I cannot but entertain *very great doubt*.

The stoppage of Tom Brown[11] *here*, and the stoppage of Clark & Burgess[12] on the Coal Exchange, consequent thereon – altho' long expected, has caused a very great sensation in the neighbourhood. *Our* Bankers are the principal sufferers, and I regret to say that there is a very feverish feeling in the town, with respect to the Bank. Lockwood is off to London on the occasion, to keep peace with old Jews if he can. I found Batson cool & competent, as usual but Grace very sick, and rowing us to the non-reduction of the Bal[anc]e – the Directors at their meeting yesterday having made a complete *blow-up* about it, and unless relief is speedily attained by Groom's exertions, Grace declares that come what may they the Directors, in justification of themselves, will be *obliged* to resort to the remedies they possess. This is all very gloomy, but I still hope Groom will place the matter in the best point of view he can, with Sir J. Beckett[13] – as he cannot but be impressed with the vast importance of the subject to the family. I have written to him, a gentle *whether* by this post, and to inform him that the Land Valuers have nearly finished – that he will have their report in a few days, and that I will be glad to hear from him, as to the progress he is making &c.

---

11 Alderman Thomas Brown, Sunderland businessman and banker.
12 Robert Burgess, coal factor, London. Smith, *Sea-Coal for London*, p. 159. For Clarke, see n. 10.
13 Sir John Beckett, trustee of the Londonderry marriage settlement.

I will be able most likely to say tomorrow, or Friday, what sort of a job the Land valuers Ben Johnson & *Ned* Grace are likely to make of it – they wish to see me, on some points.

Bobby's[14] withdrawing from the Trust is a good thing – particularly if Col. Wood[15] will fill the vacancy. *Bobby* was evidently out of his element, and not at home in the affair.

I do not write Mr McDonnell to day as I am pressed with various matters, and your Lordship can communicate the contents of this to him.

I have heard this morning through a most *confidential channel*, that Lord D—h—m's Bills are *seeking* to be *renewed* – this is a *rara avis*, and shews that the advance of 2/- could not be a matter of such perfect indifference as Morton at first affected to think it – however this must not go further at present, by-and-by it will be heard of in other quarters.

The Marq[ues]s of Londonderry	I have the honor [&c.]
Wynyard Park	J^{no} Buddle

143.

D/Lo/C142/31 (20)   Newcastle 2nd Dec[ember] 1834

My Dear Lord

I have received your note with the extract of your Lordship's letter to Col. Bradyll on the affair of the harbour. It is all very well as a private communication from one gentleman to another, but I must own I wish the last sentence 'I propose to you to ship any quantity of your Coals, after June next cheaper than you can get an offer for from any other port' [*sic*][16]

Under our existing agree[men]t with Bradyll, and all other circumstances connected with the question, I cannot but think this direct *cheap offer* premature and uncalled for. And it will I doubt tend to increase the difficulties of our future negotiations with the S. Hetton Co.

They have never complained of the 1/10 per Ch. being too much for the Harbour – their complaints have always been confined to

---

14 Robert Scurfield, one of the original trustees of the Londonderry trust.
15 Unidentified.
16 This sentence seems to be incomplete.

the *apprehension* of the Harbour not being capable of shipping their quantity during the *Winter months*. Your Lordship's proposal ought not, therefore, to have gone beyond *quantity*.

Your Lordship will please to consider that your position with respect to Seaham Harbour differs essentially from all the other ports or Harbours we shall have to compete with. They are in the hands of Companies, who are also the proprietors of the rail-ways leading to them, while your Lordship possesses the Harbour *only*. Your Lordship must, therefore, have a larger amo[un]t of tonnage on the Harbour than they will, or need *numerically* to charge, because they can amalgamate the tonnage of the Harbour with that of the rail-way, and thereby give the appearance of the harbour dues being very low. The Stanhope Co. for instance only charge 6d per Ch. at Shields for shipping, but then they find their account in the rail-way tonnage. The Hartlepool Co. also put a low rate of tonnage for the Harbour, and make it up in the rail-way dues.

The matter must be considered as a joint common Rail-way and Harbour – the question with Bradyll ought to be, how much will Rail-way, Harbour & Spouts cost at Seaham & what will they cost at other places? But as your Lordship's proposal merely specifies the *shipping of the Coals* I'm apprehensive, that Bradyll or at least his adviser may sink the consideration of the rail-way, and stick to the *shipment* at the Harbour *only*. At any rate I'm afraid it will afford them grounds for quibbling.

I was under a mistake as to the Comm[itt]ee meeting to day – it is tomorrow, when I may probably see P. Forster, but of course I shall be *mum* on your Lordship's proposal to Bradyll. Clayton will pay the £1400 on a Bond of indemnity, so that I have little doubt, in a few days the money will be forth coming.

The Marq[ues]s of Londonderry   I have the honor [&c.]
Wynyard Park   J[no] Buddle

144.

D/Lo/C142/32 (3)   Pensher 7[th] Jan[uar]y 1835

My Dear Lord

I asked Morton to breakfast with me this morn[in]g to talk the canvassing affair over, and to endeavour if possible, to find out how matters really stand in the Electioneering campaign, between your Lordship, and Lord Durham as from the good and neighbourly *business* terms which have for some time past existed between you, I expected that a sort of tacit understanding, as to *local* politics might also have been maintained. Morton totally denies the charge of having canvassed any of our men further than what occurred at Houghton, as stated in my former Letter – nor has he ever been on any of our premises to interfere with our people or to promise them work, as he had Lord Durham's positive orders to the contrary. As from the amiable terms which existed between your Lordship and Lord Durham, his L[or]d[shi]p was resolved to abstain from all interference. But Lord D. considered your Lordship's bringing Bradyll forward an infraction of the tacit non-interference understanding and therefore feels himself at liberty to pursue his own course, – especially after endeavouring to push Sir E. Grey[1] forward when all hope of success was at an end, which he attributes merely to a desire of causing unnecessary expence. Morton speaks of this affair of Sir E. Grey, as *matter of fact*, and says, it is reported, that your Lordship endeavoured to bring both old Greenwell of the Ford, and Cartwright[2] forward to cause Lord Durham's friends expence and trouble. Of the truth or falsehood of these reports your Lordship must know but I have no doubt of their having excited Lord Durham's utmost opposition...[3] or other, there is a complete misapprehension between Mr Trevor and Tommy Nicholson as to the information conveyed by this note. Mr Trevor says 'I hear Morton is making the most bril-

---

1   In the general election in January 1835 Trevor and Harland were elected for Durham City. Sir Charles Edward Grey stood as a candidate, but withdrew before the poll. He was MP for Tynemouth 1837–41. Heesom, *Durham City and its MPs*, pp. 43, 54.

2   William Greenwell of Greenwell Ford, Durham; John Crawford, Norton.

3   The text does not follow on here. 'Opposition' falls at the end of p. 1; 'or other' starts p. 2; some words appear to be missing.

liant promises. Nicholson is just come in with this alarming news'.
Now on asking Tommy about this news, this morn[in]g he says he
only heard of it from Geo[rge] Wooler[4] on his arrival at Durham!!!
Of his own knowledge, he knows nothing of any promises made by
Morton.

I have been round our Works all day, and have not heard any
electioneering news – only a *report* that *Tatie* gave up this morning
at Sunderland, which I think probable.

I have no letter from John Gregson to day, at which I am disappointed, as it keeps me in a state [of] suspense. Hunter continues
better to day, but is languid and nervous.

I must be at Newcastle early in the morning to confer with Batson
as to the means of raising our Pay money – which I see no way
of doing unless some one will become personally responsible for
the requisite Amo[un]t which under present circumstances is not a
pleasant affair.

The Marq[ues]s of Londonderry   I have the Honor [&c.]
Wynyard Park   J[no] Buddle

145.

D/Lo/C142/32 (11)   Pensher 5[th] Mar[ch] 1835

My Dear Lord
    I have the honor to acknowledge the receipt of your Lordship's
Letter of the 2[nd] Inst. I saw Mr Selby[5] in London, and got all the
information from him he could give on the foreign Coal trade, of
which he has had no experience himself, and the upshot of all he
c[oul]d say upon it was that if we w[oul]d consign a few cargoes to
his friends Messrs Belquarie & Co. of Bordeaux, or to the Ho[use] of
Van Omersen at Amsterdam he w[oul]d write a letter of recommendation or introduction to them – remarking at the same time that the
success of the adventure would hinge entirely on the Coals meeting
the purpose for which their customers the Glass makers &c. might
want them.

The season for exporting Coals is just now opening, and I will see
Spence abo[u]t freighting a Ship to Bordeaux – but I assure y[ou]r
Lordship that Spences coming to London on such a business w[oul]d

4   George Wooler, Fawnlees, Wolsingham.
5   London coal merchant.

not be of the least use – merely the expence of the journey thrown away – and at a time here when his whole time & attention is required at the Harbour. Indeed I see very clearly that when Bradyll's work increases and the Haswell Coals come to be shipped that we must have an active Harbour Master appointed to be constantly on the spot to keep the Pilots & Capt[ain]s in order as there is *rum work* when Spence is absent. We have had plenty of applications from the Merch[ant]s for our Small Coals for export[atio]n but at too low a price, and I have no doubt of selling all we make at a better price to 'comers & goers' than the regular merchants will give. However we will try the fate of 2 or 3 Cargoes to Mr Selby's friends, and when they are shipped I will write him.

The Haswell Co. got the Hutton Seam last Monday, in great perfection *they say* 5 ft thick. They will be ready if all goes well with them, to commence shipping their Coal about the latter end of May. I was at the Harbour yesterday & altho' the late bad Weather has retarded the Work very much yet I think we shall be ready to receive them, against they are ready to come. By hook, or by crook we must get ready for them, as if they come I am pretty sure they won't leave us again, and they will agree to come for 3 years *certain*. I calculate on getting the whole of their Coals, as well as Bradyll's, which will be a capital job for us – as if the Collieries prosper so as to enable them to work & vend what their *Caliber* entitles them to it will shew us a Harb[ou]r revenue of £10,000 or £12,000 a year. Besides all the Material business and benefits which such an increased scale of business must necessarily bring to the Town & Estate.

I hear from pretty good authority (though *private*) that the D—l is to pay on the Hartlepool concern – the Excheq[ue]r Bill Loan Office has refused to grant them a loan. After their application to the Board, the business seemed to go on tardily & Tom Wood wrote a *private* and *confidential* Letter to one of the Comm[issioner]s accusing Birkwood of being biassed against him by the Marq[ues]s of Londonderry and the Clarence R[ail] W[ay] Co!!! The letter was laid before the Board and fell into Birkwood's hands, and has made a regular *flare-up* between T. Wood and Birkwood. J[no] Burrell is now in Town trying his diplomacy with the Board – to get matters made up but with scarcely any hopes of success. I sincerely whish [*sic*] he may fail, and then I think we shall have our *Brace* of *Black Grouse*, at Snippers Gate and Haswell quite safe.

The Marq[ues]s of Londonderry   I have the Honor [&c.]
                                                              J[no] Buddle

146.

D/LO/C142/32 (19)   Newcastle 18th May 1835

My Dear Lord

I have your Lordship's Letter of the 16th this morning, and have the pleasure to inform your Lordship that the Haswell Co. having completed their arrangements with P. Forster for the conveyance of their Coals, I was enabled to conclude an agree[men]t with them for their shipment last Sat[urday]. A minute to that effect is entered in their Book, and I will have a Mem[orandum] of Agree[men]t signed at their meet[in]g next Sat[urday]. They have fixed the 21st June for the ship[men]t of their first cargo. Perc[eva]ll is to exert himself to get his way ready by then, and I think there is no fear of us being ready to receive them. I fully expect to let the Water into the So. Dock next Springs but one – say 9th June. I do not intend to fill it *for good* then, & to float the Ships into it, but for the purpose of trying the effect of screening the Channel from the Dock Gates out at the mouth of the Harbour. We will let the Water in, at the high Spring Tides, and at dead low-water, open the 6 sluices in the gates, and allow the Water to rush out under a pressure of 16 or 17 perpendicular, which will afford a fine practical experiment of the effect of screening. It will be an interesting sight, well worth seeing.

As to the means of completing the *essential* parts of the Harb[ou]r for the accommod[atio]n of the Haswell Co. Bradyll's increase, N. Hetton (sh[oul]d we catch them) as well as *our own Work* – the sum ment[ione]d in my Letter of the 13th to y[ou]r L[or]d[shi]p will reach the mark, and I expect that the Int[eres]t due from the Bank for the use of the Excheq[ue]r Bills – together with the sale of the Lime from the Stone dug out of the Dock, will nearly about pay the Cost. If these means should fall a little short the difference must be squeezed out some how or other, as we must not break down, *half a neck length* short of the Winning Post. As to Light Houses, Parapet &c. they must remain in abeyance, until better times. The only point which gives me anxiety, is the state of N.E. pier-end, which still remains *headless*, and I am by no means quite satisfied of it's *entire safety*. The channel is gradually deepening, which together with the effect of the frequent heavy rolling Sea from the N.E. threatens the safety of the Foundation. If possible I should wish to expend £600 to £800 on securing this part by putting in the foundation of the pier-head this summer – my mind would then be quite at ease on all the *essentials* of our Harbour.

As to the shipment of the proprietary Coals, we shall soon be in a situation to accommodate them also – but then they have no access to the Harbour – nor can they have any *beneficial* access, until Gregson's way is completed, which cannot be in less than 12 mo[nths] but may be more, as matters are not running quite smooth in this affair. In the first place I learn that money is rather scarce, and in the next place the Hetton Co. have stopped their proceedings in the Eppleton farm. They actually pulled up the way, and stopped the progress of the work there last Friday

Again it is said that the Proprietary. are actually in Treaty with the Hetton Co. for the sale of N. Hetton & that J^{no} Burrell is now in London to endeavour to strike the bargain. Mr McDonnell may probably find out from J. Gregson if this is really the case, as if it is so, the proprietary are not in a state to treat with us for the shipment of their Coals.

Cartwight's information respecting Thornley is correct, and his inference probable. Up to last Friday no change for the better, or any appearance of improvement, in the exploratory Hutton Seam drifts had taken place. As far as I can judge from the late Borings at Ferry-hill, Coxhoe & from what is reported of Mason's Borings near Rush-yford – the Thornley Pit seems to be beyond the line of Demarcation, where the Hutton Seam becomes deteriorated. This line lies some where between Haswell & Thornley, and from information I have rec[eive]d as to the surface level between the two places, the respective depths of the Pits &c. I am of opinion, it is formed by a large Slip Dyke, or dislocation of the Strata. There is no doubt but this failure at Thornley will greatly enhance the value of the Collieries possessing the best Coals – but will they have the prudence to avail themselves of the golden prospect which is opening before them? This is the question. I am apprehensive, that spirit of cupidity which has always pervaded the Trade, and mangled it's prosperity from time to time, ever since I knew it – though slumbering at present, is still alive, and will at no distant period rear it's head again, and run it's usual career of mischief.

The mischief will most likely commence on the Tyne, amongst the inferior Collieries. For some time past there has been a deep growl of dissatisfaction in this class, which has occasioned many meetings and angry discussions, and nothing but being *bound* by the rules of the regulation keeps the Trade together at present. But it is 'pig in hatter' like work, and unless some sort of conciliatory measures can be devised before the 31 Dec[ember] the Inferior Class will secede at all risks. The cause of their dissatisfaction is briefly this. The best Coll[ierie]s who can always sell their quantity press for larger issues

& obtain them too, than the inferior Coll[ierie]s can vend. But as they will not – indeed many of them cannot afford to be short of their quantities, owing to the smallness of their Bases – they are obliged to freight their Coals to the London Market as the Coal merchants will not buy them so long as they can have a supply of the better Coals. This throws a glut of inferior Coals into London, and reduces them to so low a price, as not to leave those Coll[ierie]s any profit, and several sustain loss. They therefore, allege that the reg[ulatio]n is merely for the benefit of the best Coll[ierie]s, and that if it continues on the present system it will ruin them. This they will not stand – for if ruin is to be their lot, they will be ruined as Free-men & not perish in the *Fetters* of regulation.

The remedy in my opinion is not very difficult, and I have been talking for some time quietly to Morton & Wood, about it. It is simply to put other 2/- per Ch on our W[alls-]end Coals – which according to the comparative prices in London, they will very well bear & still pay the Ships better freight than the 2nd class. This w[oul]d curtail the Vend of the W[alls-]end Coastwise and leave the inferior sorts an opening in their legitimate markets & relieve the pressure which they occasion on the London market.

Morton & Wood are now satisfied of the entire humbug of the interference of the Yorkshire, Scotch, and Welch Coals, with the W[alls-]ends, and begin to lend a favourable ear to my admonitions with respect to putting 2/- more on our W[alls-]ends – indeed I think I may say that I have made a complete convert of Morton, and [he] w[oul]d I have no doubt join in the advance. Wood is also *more than half inclined* and but for the awkward position in which he is placed with the Co. would I firmly believe join in. It is understood that he has to quit the managem[en]t at the end of his year's notice. Scully & his party L[or]d Dundonel[6] & Major Cochrane are as hostile as ever to Regulation & high prices, and he is at daggers drawn with Arthur. So I doubt it will be rather up-hill work to get them to join in an advance. I am however so convinced of the propriety of the thing, that I will lose no opportunity of pushing it, and don't quite despair of getting it effected on the 1st July.

Your Lordship is undoubtedly right as to a moderate tonnage at the Harbour – still there is no occasion for us to value our position too cheap, & give ground, until it is *turned* by fair competition, which cannot happen for 12 mo[nths] at any rate. let us therefore shew a

6   Thomas Cochrane, 1775–1860, tenth Earl of Dundonald, admiral. *ODNB*.

bold front as long as circumstances will permit. The time for quitting Thompson has not yet arrived – we cannot well quit him with the *Meadows* Pits N. of Benridge, but we may *moderate him*.

The Marq[ues]s of Londonderry   I have the honor [&c.]
London   J^{no} Buddle

147.

D/Lo/C142/32 (24)   Walls-end 3rd June 1835

My Dear Lord

I have your Lordship's *private* Letter of the 1st Inst. this morn[in]g with Mother C—'s long treatise on the *Black art*.[7] Her reasoning is grounded on false principles, consequently her deductions, although plausible, are erroneous.

Like many others, she does not seem clearly to understand the true principle of regulating the Coal-trade – she evidently views it only as a *partial* measure, contrived merely to prop up the inferior Collieries, by cramping the vends of the best Collieries. This is by no means the principle of regulating the Trade – the true spirit, and principle of a regulation is, that it should benefit *all* classes, and make the *whole* trade move harmoniously, and beneficially as if it belonged to one large joint stock Co. How then can any individual possessed of common sense, and a justly balanced mind think to pursue his own particular interest, to the prejudice of the Body? Has not this been tried again &, again, by the powerful, the obstinate, or the presumptious [*sic*], in every Class of the Trade, and has not the result been invariably the same – a *complete failure*. What has occurred in the trade, it may be asked, in 1835 to render the principle of regulation, which has been proved to be correct for the preceding century inapplicable? On the contrary have not the difficulties, and complexities of the trade greatly increased of late, and if it is to be carried on under regulation at all, is it not the more necessary that the true principle should be regularly adhered to? I am so satisfied of this, that I feel no difficulty in prophesying that if the 3 great Collieries persist in pressing such large Issues, as they have hitherto done, to the great prejudice of the Inferior Collieries, that there will very soon be an end of the Regulation, and further, I have reason to

---

7   Neither 'Mother C' nor her Treatise have been identified.

believe, I would say to *know* that the first hostile movement will be made by some of the inferior Collieries, as they feel, that the existing Regulation, as at present conducted, is operating almost exclusively for the benefit of the best Collieries.

I am quite aware of the pettifogging feelings of jealousy which my endeavour to maintain the principles of the regulation, have excited in certain parties, altho' those endeavours have operated mani-fessedly to the benefit of those who opposed them. And without meaning to give myself airs, or taking more merit than is due to me, I believe it is mainly owing to that spirit of moderation, and justice, which I have endeavoured to maintain, that the regulation has been extended to the end of the year.

Mrs C. seems to set her mind on *quantity* and does not object to advance the price provided the vend is not curtailed – how sensible this is!!! But I can assure her, that whether she advances the price, or not, the quantities *will have to be reduced*, or there must be another scramble. The Market is already over-done with best Coals, and how in the name of common sense, are the best Coll[ierie]s to keep up their present quantities when Bradyll's increase, and Haswell, *entirely additional*, is pressing in upon them – it is folly to expect it, and the proper line to take, is to advance the price, and to take the quantity which the legitimate demand of the market may require let it be little or much. As to the *Cuckoo* cry, of existing competition from other quarters, by advancing our Walls-ends other 2/- it is nonsense – from whence is the competition to arise? It is our second, & inferior, Coals, that we have to meet competition with, and I think I have fairly got Morton & J^{no} Wood out of the grasp of this *Bugbear*.

If I find the opportunity fitting at the Chester meeting tomorrow (it is to be a meeting of the Comm[itt]ees of the 3 Rivers)[8] I mean to *start the hare* for an advance of 2/- and an extension of the regulation for another year, from the 31st Dec[ember] next. I w[oul]d have the present regulation to go on for the remainder of the year, and in the mean time have the general scale of Bases revised, and adjusted to the altered state of affairs. I cannot but think another year of peace highly desirable, for a thousand reasons, whether I look at the Trade as *one* great mercantile Concern, or take into consideration the situ-ation of several individuals who are deeply interested in it's pros-perity. I cannot now go into the freighting system and consignment

8   Some, although not all, of the collieries which shipped their coal from the Tees joined the regulation in 1834.

of the Coals to *one Factor*. It would answer Major Cochrane's purpose admirably, no doubt – but I have *great doubt* of it's answering either your Lordship's or Lord Durham's.

The Marq[ues]s of Londonderry	I have the honor [&c.]
Holderness House	J^{no} Buddle

I return the Mother's letter in another Cover, and your Lordship may rely on my secrecy & prudence in the affair. It is well to keep this channel of communication open – no harm, but good may eventually arise out of it. I by no means think a split in the trade at the end of the year improbable – indeed it seems certain unless we can get an extension of the reg[ulatio]n established so as to succour the inferior Collieries, as the present mode of procedure will drive them to a state of desperation. We don't meet at Chester 'till 2 o'clock tomorrow – we dine, and as there will be a long debate on my motion – most likely adjourned 'till *after dinner*, I scarcely expect to be able to report to your Lordship 'till Saturday's post.

I think J. Gregson must not have sufficiently explained the nature of the proposed change in the Securities to the Bank Directors, which has caused the demur, on their part.

It is *reported* that N. Hetton is not yet sold – the 'proprietory' are s[ai]d to ask £73500 – the Hetton Co. have to consider this offer & give their ans[we]r on the 11th Inst. so it is said, but I know nothing of it myself. A share, or shares of Hetton might be bought, but who unless to be a *sleeping* partner, w[oul]d go into such a concern? None but one whose taste it is to fish in muddy water would join the pack.

148.

D/Lo/C142/32 (30)   Walls-end 20th June 1835

My Dear Lord

When I wrote your Lordship from Seaham last Thursday I little dreamt of the afflicting catastrophe, which had occurred here, just about that time. On my way up to Pensher I met a messenger, to inform me that a great accident had happened at W[alls]End but could state no particulars – only that the pits had blasted, that no one had escaped, and that no person could get down the Pits owing to the great eruption of *after-damp*. Eight bold, and experienced men had attempted to go down by the pit, in front of my house, but had nearly lost their lives. On reaching the place I found the working

Pit checked up for 40 f[atho]ms with the wreck of the *air Brattice*, and the air stoppings &c. so smashed in the other pits that it was impossible to gain access, and it was quite evident that any creature who was below at the time of the explosion must have perished. No time was lost in devising means of gaining access to the places where the people were – at 2 o'clock yesterday morn[in]g we gained access to one division of the Work[ing]s and by six in the Even[in]g succeeded in getting out 21 of the dead Bodies, which is all within 2 or 3 that were in this Division. To day we are making slow progress towards another division, in which between 30 and 40 Bodies are lying and I hope during the night, if all goes well, to get them out.

When those in the 3rd Division may be got at *if ever* I don't know – the case is most complicated difficult and dangerous – but my subordinates that have escaped, are all prime gallant fellows, and will do all that human power can accomplish, and my professional acquaintance are flocking in from all quarters to render all the assistance they can.

This miserable affair will prevent me from leaving here for some days, altho' it will be a great relief, to leave such a scene of horror – as soon as circumstances will permit.

All we have been able to discover is *where* the explosion occurred, but we are in the dark as to *how* it happened, and will most likely, for ever to remain so. We are sure however that it could only happen either from some act of negligence, or an accident to a davy lamp, as no other light was used in the Division where the explosion occurred. It is impossible to say what the ultimate result of this affair may be, as to re-opening or putting an end to the Colliery, until we see further, but it is distressing to think that the business cannot be carried on without the imminent risk of such an expenditure of human life.[9]

This will be a great case for Jos[ph] Pease's Commit[tee][10] and

9   Buddle read a paper giving a full account of the disaster to the Natural History Society of Northumberland, Durham and Newcastle upon Tyne on 16 November 1835. It was published in the *Transactions* of the Society, vol. 11 (1838), pp. 346–83, 'A Narrative of the Explosion which Occurred at Wallsend Colliery on the 18th of June 1835'.

10 A select committee of the House of Commons on Accidents in Mines, whose members included Joseph Pease, MP for South Durham. Buddle gave evidence to it on 1, 2, 3 and 8 July. He described his work on ventilation, and his high opinion of Davy's safety lamp. The committee's report was published as *Report from the Select Committee on Accidents in Mines*, Parliamentary Papers (1835), vol. 5 (605).

will afford an opportunity of giving complete details of the nature
of such accidents.

N. Wood & G. Johnson Lord Ravensworth & M. Bell's Viewers
have gone off this Evening to attend the Comm[itt[ee They have
given me all the assistance they can in this affair, and will be able
to explain it so far as we have yet made progress, but I presume my
attendance will not be dispensed with. I will write again shortly.

The Marq[ues]s of Londonderry   I have the honor [&c.]
                                                        J[no] Buddle

149.

D/Lo/C142/32(32)   *Confidential*   Walls-end 24[th] June 1835

My Dear Lord

I have your Lordship's Note of the 22[nd] this morn[in]g. Nothing
could have happened at a worse time than this horrible affair here.
We have now got all the dead Bodies but 5 out – 101 in all, but
no peace or respite from exertion can take place until they are also
found.[11] The measures requisite for that purpose require constant
change and contrivance, and occupy my almost undivided attention
in directing them. I am therefore labouring under a load of great
responsibility and feel that I cannot quit my post with propriety till
the way is made as clear as circumstances will permit for getting out
the remainder of the Dead. This I think there is a reasonable prospect
of getting done tomorrow and next day, so that I may be able to start
on Sa[turday] Evening for London.

We are however, unfortunately in the hands of the most stupid of
the human race, as a Coroner – scarcely capable of understanding
the most plain & simple statement – much less of combining two
ideas, in his head at the same time. I am therefore obliged to attend &
watch him, to prevent his misinterpreting the evidence and putting
down arrant nonsense, and representing the Witnesses to have said
what they never meant. He sat yesterday & the day before, and is to

---

11 The 'official' death toll was 102 men and boys, aged between 8 and 76. In spite
    of disasters such as this at Wallsend, or that at Rainton in 1823 (see above,
    pp. 88–9), the death rate in mining accidents in the North East was declining
    fairly sharply in this period. See P.E.H. Hair, 'Mortality from Violence in
    British Coal Mines, 1800–1850', *Economic History Review*, new ser., xxi, no. 3
    (Dec. 1968), pp. 545–61.

sit again tomorrow. I will do all I can to push him on, and if possible get him to finish on Friday and Sat[ur]day.

As to the amo[un]t of damage done to the Colliery by this accident, or what may be the ultimate result it is impossible at present to estimate. Everything below Ground is blown to atoms, and what the cost of restoring the Ventilation and putting matters to rights again might be I have not yet attempted to estimate. But when I consider the great expence which would attend a restoration of the Colliery – the small profit which it might eventually produce, and the great risk which must inevitably attend it's future working, I cannot feel justified, on my own responsibility in recommending it's continuance. I therefore think of proposing a meeting with Mr Russell in London, now when all the most experienced Colliers in England are in Town, and bring the case before them, and let them, in Council assembled decide the question as to continuing, or abandoning the Concern.[12]

I have not yet proposed this to Mr Russell and do not know if he will adopt the suggestion, but I feel that I cannot undertake the responsibility of carrying on the Concern unless under the sanction of some such authority.

The Marq[ues]s of Londonderry   I have the honor [&c.]
London   J[no] Buddle

I court Pease' inquiry, as I feel the utmost confidence in being able to satisfy every person who is competent to understand the subject, that no defect in system, nor laxity of discipline has occasioned the accident.

150.

D/Lo/C142/32 (41)   Walls-end 16[th] Aug[us]t 1835

My Dear Lord

I made an experiment of the scouring power of the Water from the Dock on the Channel at Seaham Harbour last Wed[nesday]

---

12 The High Main seam at Wallsend, which had been the source of its top-quality coal, was exhausted in 1831. The colliery was now working the less valuable Bensham seam: Northumberland County History Committee, *History of Northumberland*, vol. 13 (Newcastle upon Tyne, 1930), p. 51. After the disaster the colliery was advertised for letting, but in the absence of offers Russell decided to continue working it.

by opening the Sluices, with a pressure of 6 feet of Water, in the basin. The result was most satisfactory, and shewed clearly that the scouring power is ample for keeping the Channel completely clear of depositions of sand at all times.

We are now loading small Vessels regularly in the Dock, and during the next Springs I hope the rock will be removed and the Channel widened, so as to admit the larger vessels when the Dock will come into full operation – to the extent of two loading berths.

On Thursday, we had a party to Hartlepool – consisting of Morton, Donkin, T. Nicholson, Thorman, and myself.

So far, they are making great efforts to form a Channel from the Harbour, past the end of the old pier to low Water mark in the Bay, by their powerful dredging Mach[in]e and by taking up the Stones and gravel by manual labour. These operations aided by an enormous scouring power of back Water, which is let off through the sluices at the last quarter of the ebb Tide, have succeeded to a considerable extent in deepen[in]g the Channel. But whether by dint of scouring and dredging, a practicable Channel for the larger class of Colliers, can be maintained against the efforts of those natural causes which have a constant tendency to fill it up, the experience of time – say next Winter, can alone shew.

In the formation of the Channel, they are much favoured by a crust of strong gravel from 2 to 4 ft. thick, in the bed of the old Harbour. This crust of gravel prevents the sides from being washed away by the *scour*, and confines it's force to the clearing of the Channel, which is of great service. All this is favourable as far as it goes, but a Bar is forming in the Bay, in front of the Channel, by the Sand which is washed out, by the force of the scouring current. To what extent this may go, or what it's effects may be in the harbour remains to be seen. In the present state of the thing, it may be considered as a trial of what can be effected by *main force* unaided by science, against the constant efforts of natural causes. I therefore remain of the same opinion viz. that without the formation of a proper *Embouchure* this cannot be an efficient harbour.

They have got one Drop erected in the Harbour, and are shipping about 7 keels a day, of the Thornley Five-quarter Coals, in small Coasting Vessels. These Coals are round but *very coarse*, and nothing but the length of the turn, at the other harbours induces the Capt[ain]s to take them. We rode up the rail-way from the harbour to Castle Eden – it is in a wretched state. It is with the utmost difficulty that 7 Keels a day can be got down, and when Wet Weather sets in, it will be impassable. Nothing can be so absurd as the opening of this way – it cannot be completed for the regular transport of Coals in less than 9 or 12 mon[nths] and it should not have been sooner opened. Altogether, this concern is the most discouraging thing I ever saw.

We met with Gully[13] at Hartlepool – Morton introduced me to him, and we had a *talk* on Coal-trade affairs – he is still for low prices, but is willing to join the best Collieries, in a separate regulation. To this I believe we shall have to come, after the end of the present year, as including Bradyll & the Haswell Co. I reckon an additional supply of nearly 200,000 Chs. coming into the market ann[ua]lly and how this is to be provided for, under regulation I cannot imagine.

The Marq[ues]s of Londonderry   I have the Honor [&c.]
Holderness Ho[use]   J[no] Buddle

151.

D/Lo/C142/32 (43)   Pensher 27[th] Aug[us]t 1835

My Dear Lord

Nothing of material importance has occurred in this quarter since I last wrote. I am in correspondence with J. Gregson respecting the shipment of the N. Hetton Coals at the harbour, but he wishes to drive a hard bargain. We agree as to the rate per Ch. but he objects to be bound to time, and wants to be quit at 6 mo[nths] notice, as they may probably sell the Colliery. I don't however think this likely, and my last offer is, that the Co. should be bound for 32 years certain unless they should sell in the mean time, and then to be at liberty in that case to quit at 6 mo[nths] notice after the sale has actually been made.

I met Dunn their Viewer, and Husdell[14] their Fitter at the harbour yesterday – to shew and explain to them the Shipping accommodation we could afford them. They were very well satisfied on this point, but Husdell does not like the notion of quitting Sunderland alleging that they will sacrifice their Small Coal-trade by doing so. There is, however, a more potent reason than this for his not wishing the Co. to quit Sunderland – he has £400 a year for fitting the Beamish Coals, and £300 for N. Hetton, and if the latter comes to Seaham, he may not be able to manage both.

13 John Gully, partner in the Hetton Co. and Thornley Co.
14 Jacob Husdell, Sunderland fitter.

There is yet no approximation between the Committee and the Stanhope Co. toward regulation and matters continue to wear a war-like appearance. Morton & I have frequent discussions as to our plan of partial regulation in the event of War, and we are shortly to have a conference with J[no] Wood, and Philipson on the subject.

I have with other 4 or 5 neighbouring Viewers been served with a subpoena, to give Evidence in a very important Coll[ier]y cause which has been referred from the Liverpool Assizes, and we have to appear at a place called Newton half-way between Manchester and Liverpool at 10 o'clock, on Sa[turday] morn[in]g. We are therefore obliged to start from Newcastle this even[in]g. I have no idea how long I may be detained, but will make my stay as short as possible, The pitmen are again shewing symptoms of discontent – the spirit has not yet reached this quarter, but 2 or 3 Coll[ierie]s on the Tyne are struck or at limited work. This may arise from the appearance of so many new Collieries opening. *Kit* Morton[15]it is said has got a branch of rail-way laid from the Clarence to his Colliery – he is sending Hand Bills about the Country inviting Pitmen to his Colliery and threatens to drive all before him – he tells Morton that nothing less than 100,000 Ch. a year will satisfy him. This is nonsense and rodomontade. His Coals are the merest rubbish, yet every Chaldron which he can force into the market, will displace a Chaldron of some other Coal.

W[illia]m Lambton[16] has come to Biddick, and is going to reside there, it is said. The Weather has set in very wet here, and will cause my Lady an unpleasant journey I fear.

The Marq[ues]s of Londonderry　　　　　　　I have the honor [&c.]
London　　　　　　　　　　　　　　　　　　　　　　　J[no] Buddle

15　Unidentified.
16　William Lambton, 1793–1866, brother of Lord Durham.

152.

D/Lo/C500 (1)   Pensher 18th Jan[uar]y 1837

My Dear Lord

I had the honor to receive your Lordship's letter of the 14th Ulto. on the 2nd Inst. but have delayed writing in expectation of several important matters which are hanging in the wind, being bro[ugh]t to a close, and Mr McDonnell being on the spot, and in frequent communication with your Lordship rendered my writing the less necessary.

In the first place, I beg to assure your Lordship that nothing has occurred in your Lordship's observations relative to the affair of Lord Durham[2] which has in any degree disturbed my mind beyond the feeling of regret, at the time, that your Lordship should for a moment have been impressed with the idea, that any little collateral business of that nature should alienate my attention or zeal from the duty which I owe to your Lordship's concerns. I am, however, entirely satisfied with what your Lordship says in allusion to the subject, and feel, that I can communicate with your Lordship, without embarrassment, or reserve, as usual., and that altho' an occasional breeze may occur, in the voyage of Life, to ruffle the surface, yet the deep stream of attachment, steadily continues it's course, and is not to be turned aside by minor causes.

Mr McDonnell is now here, labouring with all his might, for the good of our affairs. He is indefatigable, but I regret to say, his health is very indifferent. He has been suffering from the prevailing epidemic, which has visited this country with a heavy hand, scarcely an individual, much less any family having escaped it. Hunter and Newby, are both laid in their Beds at this time by it.

---

1   No letters for the year 1836 have been found in the Londonderry Papers. Their absence for the first half of the year is not explained. In August Lord and Lady Londonderry and their eldest son left England for a tour of northern Europe and Russia, and had now reached St Petersburg. Lord Londonderry had been offered the embassy to Russia in 1835 but had had to withdraw in face of hostile criticism in Parliament. This was a private visit.

2   In late 1836 Buddle was asked to advise Lord Durham on a particular problem. Lord Londonderry evidently took exception to the connection. He seems to have accused Buddle of disloyalty but later to have apologised.

I am by no means comfortable about Lord Seaham, he has undoubtedly outgrown himself, and I wish we had him safe in England again. The climate of Petersburgh is, I fear, too severe for him, in spite of all the artificial means of Stoves, and Fires, which art and science, can devise to modify and improve it.

The Winter, here, has so far, been more severe than for many years past, and altho' it has moderated a little, there is every appearance of it's continuing. It is, however, *Harvest Weather* for us. The only drawback, is the great scarcity of ships, during the tempestuous weather, which from the want of depots at Sunderland, and at Seaham has thrown us 5200 Ch, short of our year's Vend. This arises from the ships having been thrown into *clusters* – they won't wait for Coals a single day, almost, and as it is impossible to lead them from the pits with sufficient rapidity, to load them as quickly as they wish, they won't wait at Seaham, but run to Sunderland, or Shields. Thus it is always, either a Feast, or a Famine at Seaham – either working night & day for life and death, for a short spell, or standing still. Nothing can remedy this, but getting a depot made at the Harbour, which we must, at all events accomplish next Summer. This is the more necessary, as Spence has now ships to provide for North Hetton as well as ourselves.

We are now far advanced with the Seaton Coal arrangements[3] – when completed the details will be forwarded to your Lordship.

The Kelloe Way-leave affair must remain in abeyance for the present, until the schemes of the various companies of speculators are further developed. Mr McD[onnell] and I keep our eye upon it. The new S. Durham R[ail]W[ay] Co.[4] are making a great swagger, in the newspapers, yet I am certainly informed that money is exceedingly scarce with them, and that the share-holders of the old Co. are in great pecuniary difficulties, as to the settlement of the expence of last year's parliamentary campaign. It seems the *ready money* for that job, was chiefly raised by certain of the promoters drawing Bills on

3   Negotiations were in progress with Lord Durham and the Hetton Coal Co. for a partnership to work the coal at Seaton and Seaham.

4   A bill for a railway from Frosterley and Willington in Weardale to join the Byers Green branch of the Clarence Railway and the Wingate branch of the Hartlepool Railway, opposed by Lord Londonderry and other coal owners, was defeated in the House of Lords in June 1836. It was now revived in a new form and under a new name. The first proposed line went through Kelloe, needing a wayleave from Lord Londonderry. Tomlinson, *North Eastern Railway*, pp. 286, 289, 290, 298.

each other, which answered very well, while money was plentiful, and those Bills could be renewed, and discounted. But since money has become scarce, and the Bills cannot be discounted, the *Paper Mill* is stopped, and the *manufacturers* are thrown upon their backs. I learn too, that several Bills accepted by the Directors of the Hartlepool Co. are lying over-due at our *ex-Friends*[5] and other banks, and the question is – who is to pay them? The immediate remedy, I believe, is against the Chairman – this won't suit *old Rowley*.

Perc[eval] Forster, J[no] Burrell, Rawsthorn & Co. have begun to sink at Garmondsway, from which it may be inferred, that they have completed their *Way-leave* agreements for their Line to Hartlepool. I shall shortly procure a plan of their Line and be able to inform your Lordship of it's precise route.

All the other Companies mentioned in my former letters, are pushing on, with their new Collieries, and the ground being now about all taken up in the Co[unty] of Durham, the spirit of Colliery adventure, has been extended into Northumberland. The Bedlington, and Sleekburn Coal-fields, on the N. Banks of the Blyth River are let to companies, and sinking has commenced. The Hawksley Coal, on the E. Coast, near Alemouth is also let, and a Harbour is to be made at Alemouth for shipping the Coals. And even Lord Grey's Coal-field at Howick, is talked of – should this also be let Northumberland will be as completely over-run with new Colliery adventurers as Durham

Mischief and disturbance to the established, and regular trade of the Country cannot fail to follow all this – it is distant but still the cloud is gathering – black and heavy, and the tempest must inevitably burst upon us, in due time. It therefore behoves us, in the mean time, to set our shoulders, sturdily to the wheel, and endeavour, by every possible means to get our waggons lifted out of the rut, before the road we have yet to travel is broken up by the Storm. My present notion is, that unless we can bring our *Bark*, into smooth water, and safe moorings in the course of the present, and the two following years, she will break *a-drift* of us, in spite of all our exertions to save her. She must, therefore, be aided and supported, by the utmost stretch of saving, and economy, and every sort of extraneous aid that can be given to her.

Our Books for 1836 will be balanced shortly, when it will appear, what the exact result of the year's work has been. Much pressing personal, and other debt has been paid, but still we have been obliged

5   Backhouse's.

to run a large bal[anc]e with the bank, who has certainly had a hard bargain of us. I know it to be the fact, that they discounted our Ship-Bills, at Backhouse's during the greater part of the year, at 5 per cent, to enable them to meet our payments, while they were only charging us 4 per cent discount on the *same* Bills. This arose from their want of sufficient capital, the share-holders having refused to advance any more money at the ann[ua]l meeting last Feb[ruary]. And if they do not consent to make a large advance, at the ann[ua]l meeting on the 10th of next mo[nth] the Directors must *shut up Shop*, as they cannot go on, but to *great loss* with their present amo[un]t of capital. They refused to discount a £2000 Bill for Mr Bell M.P. the other day, in consequence of which he removed his Colliery acc[oun]t to Lambton's.

Our pitmen still continue in a very ticklish state, and the new Collieries are all wanting recruits, and are holding out flattering inducements. I therefore anticipate a very troublesome Binding in April.

I have been to Sunderland to day, to an election of 3 new Commissioners to fill up the vacancies, occasioned by the decease of the late Sir M.W. Ridley, Dr Eden, and *Tommy* Thompson. We have elected Sir M.W. Ridley,[6] Mr McDonnell, and a Mr Hen[ry] Johnson – a man of small, but independent fortune who we expect will not attach himself to the *Dock* party. We got Sir W. Chaytor to propose Mr McDonnell, which he did very cheerfully, as *'t Marquess had been very polite to him, and he was glad to have 't opportunity of returning 't compliment'*. And old *Arthur* seconded the baronet's nomination. This is all very well & I think we should now *sink the Tatie* – the Election was carried *nem. dis.* Sir Hedworth[7] came too late, or perhaps we should not have got so easily through the business. I met *Cuddy*[8] whom I have not seen for an age, in the Commission room. He is suffering from a complaint in his eyes, and believes he must go to London to consult Travers on his case which alarms him. He is busy writing the Life of Queen Elizabeth, of whose original letters and other curious documents he has got a large collection from the archives of the Bowes family at Gibside. A considerable sensation has been caused in Sunderland & N[ew]castle to day, by the intelligence of the stoppage of Esdaile's

---

6   Sir Matthew White Ridley, fourth Bt, 1807–77.

7   Sir Hedworth Williamson.

8   Sir Cuthbert Sharp. The book, published in 1840, was *Memorials of the Rebellion of 1569*, a collection of documents from the Bowes Papers, not a life of Queen Elizabeth.

Bank.[9] Altho' the Bank of Eng[lan]d has agreed to let them easily down, until they can *wind up* – the Bankers, & mercantile people cannot tell where the straggling shot may fall, or who *spent Balls* may hit – our sly Quaker acquaintance, have not drawn upon them these 3 or 4 years – those Quakers have wonderful keen noses, for scenting danger at a distance. I beg my most dutiful regards and best wishes to my Lady, and should be glad that we had her Ladyship & Lord Seaham safe in England again.

The Marquess of Londonderry   I have the honor [&c.]
St Petersburgh   J[no] Buddle

Our bankers have cashed your Lordship's cheque for £30, and my Lady's for £20 for the Seaham Church Subscription.[10] I will either forward the receipts or keep them 'till you return, as your Lordship will please to direct.

153.

D/Lo/C500 (4)   Pensher 7th April 1837

My Dear Lord

I am happy to have the gratification of acknowledging the receipt of your Lordship's very interesting, though rather gloomy Letter of the 15th Ulto. from Berlin – received on the 25th as it looks as if your Lordship were bending your way home-wards again.

Well may your Lordship ask, in reference to my Lady – 'What English fine Lady has ever done, or gone through so much.' Tracing your long route on the map, even at the *fire-side*, at this season, is enough to make one's teeth chatter, and that you have all achieved such a journey during so inclement a season *unscathed* is marvellous, and I most sincerely congratulate you all – especially my Lady, on such an achievement. I am happy to learn so good an account of

---

9   A London bank, amalgamated with Smith, Wright & Co., and connected with Backhouse's Bank. See John Clapham, *The Bank of England*, vol. 2 (Cambridge, 1944), p. 156; Phillips, *History of Banks*, p. 349.

10 A new parish church for Seaham Harbour was built between 1835 and 1840. See A.J. Heesom, 'Problems of Church Extension in a Victorian New Town: the Londonderrys and Seaham Harbour', *Northern History*, xv (1979), pp. 138–55.

Lord Seaham's health – his young blood is warm, it flows freely, and won't easily freeze.

I am glad your Lordship has turned your active and intelligent mind to the internal resources and statisticks of Russia, and that you contemplate the publication of your researches,[11] as since Dr Clarke's time I don't think we have had any account of the interior resources of that vast Empire, but he saw every thing with a jaundiced Eye and wrote with a prejudiced pen.[12]

I had correspondence some years ago with Prince Leven,[13] on the Coal mines of Russia and sent a person out to explore the Country. He found Coal in the province of Toula, but it was of too sulphurous a nature for smelting iron, which was the object of the Government at that time. I have no doubt but Coal of better quality might be found, but it certainly would not be for the benefit of England that Coal fit for the smelting of iron should be found in Russia.

The highly distinguished reception which you met with from the Emperor, cannot but have been most gratifying to my Lady, as well as to your Lordship. It is also highly gratifying to your Lordship's friends in this Country – but *Gall* to your political Foes, and they trump up all sorts of stories, no matter how absurd, in consequence. At a dinner given to Cuddy Rippon[14] by his radical constituents at Gateshead on the 27th Ulto. it was *talked* that the Emperor of Russia had given your Lordship a *million* of money to return two Conservative Members for Durham. I hardly think, however, that the said Cuddy will be able to keep his Seat as the Manchester Insurance Co. have taken possession of his estates, and appointed a receiver for a mortgage of £80,000, and a London Jew is in possession of all the personals at Stanhope castle, and the general opinion is, that he is an irretrievably ruined man.

This electioneering dinner brings me to your Lordship's inquiry, as to my opinion of the probability of your being able to bring in Mr

11 Lord Londonderry published in 1838 a two-volume work, *Recollections of a Tour in the North of Europe in 1836–1837*. He included some material on Russia's population, resources, and trade.

12 Edward David Clarke, *Travels in Various Countries of Europe, Asia and Africa, Pt 1: Russia, Tartary and Turkey* (6 vols, London, 1810–23). Clarke (1767–1822), was an antiquary and mineralogist. He was in Russia and Turkey in 1799–1802 collecting antiquities and minerals. He took an unfavourable view of most of what he saw in Russia, from the arbitrary government to the Orthodox Church. *ODNB*.

13 Prince Christopher Lieven, Russian ambassador in London 1812–34.

14 Cuthbert Rippon, MP for Gateshead 1832–41.

McDonnell, with Mr Trevor for the City. This is a subject on which I don't feel myself at all competent to give an opinion of any value as in the first place I am almost wholly ignorant of politics – either general, or local, and least of all with those of Durham – further than what I have seen of the freemen, I believe them to be the most corrupt and morally depraved of their species, that whether a candidate be Conservative, Wig [sic] or Radical, matters not a straw – the Man who will most freely afford them the means of indulging their beastly appetites during Election time, and allow them to leech him afterwards, is the man for them. It is not, therefore, from them, that an observant By-stander can judge of the state of public feeling. This can only be known from those of a different grade, who are not influenced by such feelings. And as my opportunities of learning the sentiments of such people about Durham, are few I cannot form any estimate of the state or strength of the different parties there.

In Newcastle I think I can form a somewhat better notion, as I there see and hear more of men of all parties. The result of my observations is that radicalism is decidedly on the decline, that Toryism is not gaining ground and that the moderate, or rational reform party, greatly predominate. The conservatives incline to the Wigs[sic] for fear of the radicals, and the radicals will, I think, support the Whigs also out of spite to the Conservatives. Whether matters may stand in the same sort of way in Durham I cannot say. In Newcastle I think the probability is that the present members will be returned (according to *present appearances*) next Election, as I cannot think the radicals will be able to bring in a Member, unsupported by the Whigs. The whole no. of Electors for Newcastle is about 4000 and when the radicals sent a requisition to Sir W. Molesworth[15] they could only muster something above 300 signatures – not a tithe of the whole number of electors, and their late meet[ing]s have been very thinly attended, I am informed.

With respect to the practicability of your Lordship returning both members for the City, I don't feel myself competent to form any thing of an opinion, beyond mere *conjecture* – grounded on what I imagine to be the state of public feeling in the neighbourhood. The notion, so founded, which I entertain is, that your Lordship could

---

15 Sir William Molesworth, eighth Bt, 1810–55, radical politician, MP for East Cornwall 1832–7, Leeds 1837–41. First Commissioner for Works 1853–5, Secretary of State for the Colonies 1855. *ODNB*.

not return two members, and that the attempt would be attended with great expence.

On the other hand, I think if no such attempt were made Mr Trevor would find little difficulty, and that the battle would lie between Harland, and Granger. I would not, however, have your Lordship to attach any value to these observations but would advise you to seek the opinion of some confidential friends (not blinded by the zeal of party feelings) who have better means of observing the feelings and strength of parties than I have. And your Lordship will please to recollect, that in this sort of business I always take a cautious – a timid view, as considering the dreadful sacrifices which have been made by the family in their Electioneering contests, and which have contributed so largely to form the embarrassments under which we are now all suffering so severely. The bare idea of incurring further expence, and waste of money in that way, makes me tremble, and makes a *very coward* of me. If, therefore, the prospect of obtaining your Lordship's object *without expence*, is not as clear as the sun at noon-day I would implore your Lordship by all that is just and prudent not to risk a contest.[16]

Your Lordship asks, Why is not Biddick and Herrington sold, and why not proceed in every possible way to redeem me from the galling situation of a dependant?

Mr McDonnell will, I presume, have informed your Lordship that as Herrington is in progress of paying for it's self he thinks it most prudent to keep it for the family, and Biddick will be sold to Lord Durham if we can agree with Morton and Stephenson about the price. But they are rather shy about it without Herrington, the latter being their chief object on account of it's giving them a way-leave to Sunderland entirely independent of your Lordship. I expect shortly to bring the negotiations on Biddick to a point, but have great doubts of their giving us our own money for it.

As to exertions being made to relieve your Lordship from the

16 In the event Lord Londonderry did not attempt to bring in another Conservative candidate for Durham City in the 1837 election, but left the two Liberal candidates, William Harland and Thomas Granger, to compete for the second seat. Trevor came top of the poll, Harland second. Lord Londonderry did, however, encourage a Conservative candidate for North Durham, the Hon. Henry Liddell, to break the Liberal control of the two County seats. He issued a letter to all his agents, employees and tenants asking them to work for Liddell. The letter leaked after the election and was published by the *Durham Chronicle*, causing a furore. See Alan Heesom, 'The "Wynyard Edict" of 1837', *Durham County Local History Society Bulletin*, no. 21 (1978), pp. 2–7.

existing state of things, I can most conscientiously affirm, that I believe every official individual in your Lordship's concerns from Mr McDonnell downwards to the last link in the chain, is exerting himself for the attainment of that object, as zealously, as if it were his own personal affair. And with respect to myself, supposing I were brute enough to be influenced by feeling alone that would be a sufficient stimulous [*sic*] to the utmost exertion as it is not to be supposed that I am not suffering inconvenience, and loss from the want of the money which is due for arrears and for what I advanced to the support of the concerns, in time of need. I can assure your Lordship that I have been deprived of the opportunity of making £1500 at least during the last 18 months, by only having £1000 of the £2600 which I advanced in Jan[uar]y 1835 before the great advance in the price of shipping took place, and also prevented the earning of the ship in one of the best years, 1836 that was ever known for the shipping. Several other persons have suffered serious loss and deprivation from wanting their money, but I merely mention these matters to shew your Lordship, that more persons are deeply interested in having you replaced, unencumbered, and unfettered in the administration of your affairs than your Lordship might probably be aware of.

I have delayed closing my letter for several days, to wait the decision of the magistrates at the Durham Session, as to the Byers-green Branch of the Clarence rail-way being finished according to the terms of the Act of parliament or not, on the 3rd Inst. as if it should not be finished on that day, the powers of the Co. cease, and they cannot afterwards, if opposed, finish either it, or the Durham, or Sherburn branches.[17]

I went over the line with some other Engineers on the 3rd Inst. and found it in an unfinished, and inefficient state, and when the Co, found, that we were ready to give evidence to that effect to oppose their obtaining the requisite certificate from the Bank of it's being finished, they slunk off without moving the Court to be allowed to give evidence of it's being finished according to the terms of the Act. It seems they may do this at any time within 6 mo[nth]s so they will most likely allow the matter to stand over, and take all chances, at the July sessions – we shall however be prepared to meet them. Their anxiety to finish this Branch within the period specified by the Act is to give them fresh grounds to go to parliament again for a *fresh* Act,

---

17 See Tomlinson, *North Eastern Railway*, pp. 311–12.

to empower them to borrow £60,000 more. It is a *fresh Hare* started to enable them still further to *humbug* the public – if they succeed, it must be by the aid of *Witch-craft* I think.

I have also delayed this letter for a few days more, 'till I could have communication with Morton, Hugh Taylor & Donkin who as well as your Lordship are deeply interested for the parties they represent, in the question of Church Leases, especially those of Collieries & Mines, now under the consideration of Government.[18]

This is a question of very great importance to the Lessees of the Bishop & the Dean & Chapter's Collieries in the Co. of Durham – especially as the Lessees of the Land, are looking very keenly after their own interests with respect to the *Way-leaves*, which places their interest, and that of the Colliery Lessees to a certain degree in opposition. We therefore find it requisite to act independently of the Landowners in this affair.

After several previous meetings and discussion we met at Donkin's yesterday, and drew up a statement with which Donkin and Morton are to proceed to London tomorrow evening, to lay before Lord Lord [*sic*] Howick & Spring Rice &c. to put them in possession of the actual state and nature of the Church Coal property in the County, from the want of an accurate knowledge of which they might easily fall into errors, that might operate greatly to the prejudice of the Coll[iery] Lessees. Our statement is unavoidably, rather long and explanatory, but it's essence is, that we recommend the way-leaves, and Mine leases, to remain in the possession of the Church, or to be vested in the hands of Commissioners – renewable as at present. The Lessees of the Collieries to have the option of purchasing, but the property not to be sold to any other than the parties at present in possession. The way-leaves i.e. the power of granting way-leaves, not to be sold to the Land-owners, but it is left for consideration whether they should not have a *qualified* interest in them, but by *no means* to have the *veto*. This is the chief point on which friend Gregson, and

---

18 As part of the process, after 1832, of examining and reforming the finances of the Church of England, a select committee on Church leases was set up in 1837. Its first report, that year, contained details of all properties leased by the Bishop of Durham and the Dean and Chapter (*Report from the Select Committee on Church Leases*, Parliamentary Papers, 1837, vol. 9 (538)). Buddle and Nicholas Wood gave evidence to the committee on 2 July 1838, describing the system of leasing collieries and suggesting a method by which they could be enfranchised equitably (*Report from the Select Committee on Church Leases*, Parliamentary Papers (1837–8), vol. 9 (692).

the other Land-lessees are at issue with us – they have an *itching* to be placed in a position to enable them to *grab* the way-leaves – we must therefore, watch their movements carefully. Gregson is gone or going to London forthwith to look after the business on the part of the Land-lessees. Your Lordship will comprehend our reasons for the line we have taken but I will send you a copy of our statement as soon as I can, as the subject is one in which your Lordship is deeply interested, and I hope you will be in London to attend to it, when the Bill goes before the Lords – *if it should get on for this session.*

The Comm[itt[eee of the Coal trade have instructed J[no] Gregson to watch the several *refuge* Harbour Bills now before Parliament[19] and also Alderman Wood's City improvement Bill. Bridlington, Lowstoff, Scarbrough, and Hartlepool all have Bills at Comm[itt]ee to enable them to impose a passing toll of ¼ d per Ch. of 50 cwt. each, on all vessels, passing from the Northward with Coals. The vend from the Tyne may be stated at 700,000 Ch. and that from Sunderland and Seaham at 500,000 – together 1200,000 Ch., which at ¼ d amounts to £1250 for each, or £4800 but which, considering the short weight, assumed for the Ch. viz. 50 cwt. instead of 53 may be stated at £5000 per annum at least.

Then Alderman Wood proposed to lay a tax of 6d per ton upon all Coals imported into London – the ann[ual] import may be taken at 2,300,000 tons which at 6d as proposed by the worthy alderman would amo[unt] to £57500 per annum. Then again the projectors of the Warkworth Harbour wish to impose a duty of 6d per register ton, on all vessels passing within two miles of the Harbour, so that there is no end of these innovations, and we must oppose them by every means in our power.

The Weather still continues as bad as possible – continued gales of Wind, with Frost & Snow – the Wind generally from the N.W., North, and N.E. which interrupts the navigation so much, that we cannot get the vend up at Seaham – up to the 31st March we are 14434 tons short. As this miserable Weather must have an end shortly, it is to be hope that we shall have time enough to make up our shorts before Midsummer, and as we are progressing with the staith at the Harbour, I don't expect we shall again be so circumstanced.

The Country is also suffering from the long protracted winds – the lambs are dying nearly as fast as they are produced, and the cattle are starving for want of fodder. Hay is £8 per ton in Newcastle

---

19   Minutes of a meeting, 15 Apr. 1837, NRO 263/A2.

market, and £13 at Morpeth. If we had been thrown upon the market for our supply of Hay we should have been ruined – oats are up to 27/- and 28/- per quarter. This with the advance on the pitmen's wages will make a hole in our profits this year I fear.

I must apologise for this long letter, but from the broken nature of our correspondence, I find so many things press upon me, when I take pen in hand to write your Lordship, that I scarcely know where to stop, and after all I find that I have omitted many things I should have mentioned. I hope, however, your Lordship will shortly be within a more tangible distance. I beg my most respectful compliments to my Lady & hope she has recovered from the fatigue of the tremendous journey. I don't recollect whether I named in my last letter that we had positively closed with Grey for his Silksworth Coal – this completes our *arrondissement* for the Seaton Coal.

A tremendous gale drove 11 ships on shore between Sunderland and Seaham, on the 3rd last Monday afternoon – no lives lost, nor no damage at Seaham. At Sunderland the damage to the vessels in the harbour and it's entrance is terrible.

The Marq[uess] of Londonderry　　　　　　　I have the honor [&c.]
　　　　　　　　　　　　　　　　　　　　　　　　　　Jno Buddle

154.

D/Lo/C142/33 (2)   Newcastle 11th Aug[us]t 1838

My Dear Lord

I am glad to inform your Lordship, that there is now a prospect of an amelioration in the state of our trade taking place – the London market being at length cleared of ships, & prices getting up to a proper standard.

We had a full meeting of the United Comm[itt]ee of the 3 Rivers, at Chester, last Monday[1] – all the Collieries except Thornley represented – a Letter was rec[eive]d from Tom Wood to say that there w[oul]d be a gen[era]l Meeting of the Company on the 13th Inst. to decide the question of their coming into the regulation, which decision w[oul]d be communicated to the trade, in due course. The general opinion is that they will decide to join the regulation. I apprehend, however, that they will demand conditions which will not be complied with & unless they will consent to leave the fixing of their basis to reference, in the usual way, I think we shall be all at Sea again. In the mean time all the other new Collieries have agreed to leave the settlement of their Bases, to the Committees of their respective Districts – so that the only Screw which is now loose, as to the Regulation, is Thornley. And whether that Co. will have the hardihood to set the whole trade at defiance, remains to be seen.

The abolition of freighting, & other irregular modes of vending Coals, were decided to be abolished, which will greatly benefit the Trade – but it was not thought prudent to issue more than 25 per cent for the 1st Fort[nigh]t of the month. Hopes are, however, entertained that we shall have a much brisker trade during the remainder of the year – still I see no likelihood whatever of our being able to make up our £20,000 arrears during the remainder of the year, – only now about 4 working months – so that I sincerely apprehend that our profits will fall far short of last year. Considering the immense number of new Collieries which have come, and are coming into the trade – even supposing them all to come into regulation, the Bases must necessarily be so increased as to reduce all our vends, *rateably* to a comparatively low scale, & of course reduce our profits accord-

---

1   Minutes in NRO 263/A2.

ingly. This is undoubtedly a sombre view of the case, but it seems to me inevitable.

The Marq[ues]s of Londonderry   I have the honor [&c.]
                                                J^{no} Buddle

P.S. Just as I was sending this to the Post Messrs Marreco & Barnard,[2] Directors of the Durham Junction Railway called upon me – to say, that it is their intention to open the *great* Bridge & Railway, some time during the Week of the meeting of the British Association here,[3] and to request me to ask your Lordship's permission, to allow them to lead & load their first cargo of Coals from Pensher. Those Coals are the Stewart's Steam-Boat Walls-end shipped at present by Lord Durham's spouts at Sunderland. They will not be included in this regulated vend, and if your Lordship approves of it, I think it will give us a little *éclat* to have the first Coals sent to Shields by this new route. And it will be well to shew all the parties with whom we have to deal in leading & shipping our Coals at Sunderland, that we have *two strings to our bow*.

155.

D/Lo/C142/33 (5)   Pensher 18th Sep[tember] 1838

My Dear Lord

I received your Lordship's Letter of the 16th enclosing an extract of a Letter from Mr McDonnell, by which his sentiments appear to coincide with your Lordship's – that any Fine to be paid for the renewal of Rainton[4] shall be provided by Sir J^{no} Beckett's Trust. The estates are certainly deeply encumbered already – but the great bulk of the encumbrances was brought on by the necessity of paying £100,000 for Pittington to prevent the whole Coll[ier]y concern from being broken up and ruined, and a very small proportion of the mortgage Debt only has been occasioned by the Rainton Renewals. In truth

---

2   Antonio Marreco, Thomas Barnard.
3   The British Association for the Advancement of Science, founded in 1832, held its meeting for 1838 in Newcastle. Buddle was a member of the local organising committee, and gave a talk on the structure of the North East coalfield. The Durham Junction Railway line was opened on 24 August.
4   Negotiations in 1838 for the renewal of the Rainton lease were unsuccessful. They were taken up again in September 1840.

there would have been no debt at all on the Rainton acc[oun]t if the Pittington purchase had not been made, and if the Rainton lease had been renewed in due course, in 1826,instead of being left un-renewed 'till 1831, and if the £11000 then paid for the N. Hetton privileges (the benefit of which y[ou]r Lordship rec[eive]d in the sale) had not been placed on the Settled Estates.

Mr J. Gregson and I have given a very full and deliberate consideration yesterday & to day, to those topics regarding the trade, & it's probable fluctuations which appear to weigh on your Lordship's mind; and the enclosed paper records our joint sentiments as to the proposal which ought to be made to the Dean & Chap[te]r. We have forwarded a copy to Mr McDonnell recommending that if it meets your Lordship's approval, and his, the paper should be forwarded by Mr McDonnell, direct to Mr Chaytor, to lay before the Chapter at their meeting on the 28th Inst. Your Lordship will perhaps think it desirable to communicate your sentiments thereon, to Mr McDonnell and Mr J. Gregson, & I will meet your Lordship at Seaham, or elsewhere (if you wish it) to afford any explanation, or receive any suggestions that may occur. The £3321.3.4 seems, however, in our humble opinion, too much of a *bagatelle*, compared with past transactions, to be put in the way of keeping the Family hold upon this valuable & important property for 21 years to come.

The Rainton Coll[ier]y & Farm Fine in 1820 was £51000 and in 1832 £42000 odd – and though we should be most reluctant to recommend an addition of any amo[un]t like those sums to the present Debt, we can have no hesitation in pronouncing it to be for the interest of the family that the smaller sum should be paid.

The renewal, however, can only proceed on your Lordship's & Lady Londonderry's request to the Trustees – it is therefore for your Lordship's decision what may be the most prudent course to pursue on this important occasion. You can scarcely receive Mr McDonnell's answer before next Tuesday, or Wednesday, on either of which days Mr J. Gregson, and I, will wait upon your Lordship, at any place you will please to appoint. J. Gregson goes to Durham, to old Gregson's, to day – 19th Sep[tember].

I am going to Durham and Auckland tomorrow, but will return to Newcastle on Sat[urda]y morning. I should have sent this by last night's post, but could not get the enclosed copied in time.

I have the honor [&c.]
J[no] Buddle

J^{no} Gregson informs me by a note, that he has enclosed your Lordship the copy of the d[ra]ft of the proposal which I intended to have enclosed in this.

The Marq[ues]s of Londonderry

1839

156.

D/Lo/C142/33/(16)   Pensher 31st Jan[uar]y 1839

My Dear Lord

I this morning received your Lordship's Letter of yesterday – and yesterday rec[eive]d Ritson's[1] statement from Mr McDonnell. I gave this to Hunter, who will be with your Lordship to day, that you might interrogate him upon the various allegations which it contains. At present I will say nothing further, on the subject, than that I am persuaded when the *truth* comes to be investigated, as to the giving away of Coals – loading Walls-end for Eden-main &c. much of the information contained in this statement will assume a *very different* appearance – but documents & dates must be referred to. The Fitting Books will shew the quantity of Coals taken in by *every ship* which has been loaded at the Harbour since its commence[men]t & from which it will be seen who were favoured, and who were not fairly treated. In the terrible years of 1832–3 *great* measure was generally given at all the ports – by the Coal-owners to induce the capt[ain]s to load – instead of money bribes. On the Tyne & at Sunderland also, I believe, this abuse was carried to a great extent – ships of 9 Keels were loaden for 8, but the most usual mode was by loading the Waggons excessively, by putting 26 or 27 Bolls of Coals into them instead of 24 – and this we were obliged to do as well as our neighbours. The practice was notorious & I think I can obtain from Morton & the Hetton Co. an acc[oun]t of what they did in this way, and Hindhaugh[2] must know very well the great extent to which the practice was carried on the Tyne. A comparison of the quantities charged to Robinson's ships – with the quantities charged to others, at the same period – which can be had from the Fitting Books, will shew to what extent he has been favoured. This Hindhaugh with the assistance of the clerks can soon accomplish. As Mr McDonnell as well as Hunter will be with your Lordship tomorrow – it will be best to have the affair of the *missing receipts* distinctly understood.

It is impossible for me to express the extent of the chagrin I feel at

1   Unidentified.
2   Nathaniel Hindhaugh, a fitter on the Tyne, appointed auditor for the Londonderry trust.

all this malversation, which has been carrying on – and I can only say, that I have been deceived & duped by sneaking duplicity – as many other people have been. I am not of a suspicious disposition, and never dream't of such nefarious conduct in a person who had your Lordship's entire confidence & seemed almost to be attached to the Household – it is positively disgusting. As to Nicholson & Thorman – they must be dealt with as your Lordship & Mr McD[onnel]l may see fit – only it will not do to dismiss Thorman at any rate 'till we can see how to replace him. He has an immense quantity of machinery under his charge – especially in the conveyance of our own as well as Lord Durham's Coals & it would be highly injurious to entrust it's management to a novice. Thorman is unquestionably an able man in his department, and I apprehend great difficulty in finding a proper person to succeed him.

The road to Seaham is so blown up with snow, & this day has been so stormy that I have not in my present state of health been able to go to the harbour as I intended. I hope to meet with Mr McDonnell there next week – say Tuesday to go into all matters – preparatory to your Lordship's return – when a Council must be held for the purpose of endeavouring to get matters put upon a satisfactory footing, as they cannot remain in their present state.

A line from Hindhaugh this morn[in]g informs me of your Lordship's order that any salary due to Spence may not be paid – his last quarter has not been paid at the Colliery office but it is possible Hunter may have paid it by cheque – this he can inform your Lordship.

If this wretched man has made any thing like the money by holding back petty accounts & by Keels, which is important to him it is a mystery what has become of it, as he is in debt to every body – he never appeared to be a man of any expence, and I never saw him, to all appearance, with a shilling in his pocket. This storm has put a stop to all Coll[ier]y operations – but good will result from it. Consumption will increase & supplies will be held back.

In point of health I am pretty much the same – I must undergo strict discipline for 3 or 4 days, which will I expect set me all right again – the warm bath is recommended. I am afraid your Lordship is going to have but indifferent Weather for your journey.

The Marq[ues]s of Londonderry   I have the Honor [&c.]
                                                                    J[no] Buddle

157.

D/Lo/C142/34 (4)   Pensher 12th Aug[us]t 1839

My Lord

I am glad to inform your Lordship that the *whole of the* Collieries on the Wear – with the exception of Thornley went to work this morn[in]g as usual. But on the Tyne 18 were off – but no rioting, or breach of the peace has been committed.

At Seghill, that hot-bed of all sorts of mischief, the men commenced firing guns at 3 o'clock this morn[in]g – which was responded to from Cramlington. On inquiry I learnt that a meeting of the Cramlingon, Seghill, W. Cramlington, Holywell Hotspur & Cowpen men was to take place at 10 o'clock in the Forenoon – to decide whether they should stop the other Collieries which were at work, or return to work themselves. I sent an express to the magistrates at the Moot-hall to apprize them of what was going on, and to suggest the expediency of their proceeding to disperse the meeting with a military force, and to give protection to the men who were at work at the neighbouring Collieries – particularly at Backworth Colliery, which is in the very centre of the insurrection. The meeting was held at a place called Whiteridge, near to Seaton Delaval. Sir M. White Ridley & Mr C. Bigge proceeded with a Troop of Cavalry – followed by a Detachment of Infantry – to the place of meet[in]g but the meeting was dissolved just as the cavalry came in view. The magistrates however fell in with several groups of the men who had attended the meet[in]g who all declared that they – the Chartists[3] had resolved not to interfere with, or interrupt the men who were

---

3   The People's Charter was published on 8 May 1838. It called for manhood suffrage, the ballot, payment of MPs, abolition of the property qualification for members, equal constituencies, and annual elections. Large meetings were held in various parts of the country, including Newcastle in the summer. A national petition was presented to Parliament in July 1839, but the House of Commons declined to consider it. After this the movement faded. See Malcolm Chase, *Chartism: a New History* (Manchester, 2006). For Chartism on Tyneside, see W.H. Maehl, 'Chartist Disturbances in North-Eastern England, 1839', *International Review of Social History*, viii, no. 3 (1963), pp. 389–414; *idem*, 'The Dynamics of Violence in Chartism: a Case Study in North-East England', *Albion*, vii, no. 2 (Summer 1975), pp. 101–19; D.J. Rowe, 'Some Aspects of Chartism on Tyneside', *International Review of Social History*, xvi (1971), pp. 17–39; *idem*, 'Tyneside Chartists', *North East Group for the Study of Labour Bulletin*, no. 8 (1974), pp. 30–45; *idem*, 'Tyneside Chartism', in N. McCord (ed.), *Essays in Tyneside Labour History* (Newcastle, 1977), pp. 62–87; and John Rowland, 'Physical Force Chartism on Tyneside in 1839', in M. Calcott and R.

willing to work – and left every one to do as he pleased. All were willing to converse with the Magistrates, except the Seghill men – they were sulky & would not talk any. The Viewer summoned them to meet him at 6 o'clock this even[in]g to ascertain if they mean to go to work tomorrow. If he does not get a satisfactory answer, he is to come forthwith to the Magistrates who will grant warrants for 10 or a Doz[en] of the ringleaders for absenting themselves from their work – they will be apprehend tonight & committed for 3 months tomorrow. These proceedings will, if followed up, put an end to the affair – as it is clear that the great Body of Pitmen is averse to a strike – and no other class of workmen, have struck. A sharp look-out must however, be kept on the Seghill malcontents.

The Marq[ues]s of Londonderry   I have the honor [&c.]
                                                 J[no] Buddle

158.

D/Lo/C142/34 (5)   East Rainton 4 o'clock p.m. 14[th] Aug[us]t 1839

My Lord

    I have this instant received your Lordship's Dispatch of this morn[in]g & am glad to learn that y[ou]r Lordship has put the Durham magistrates on the qui vive. For altho' the Flame of Chartism is beginning to burn more dimly – the Embers are far from being extinguished.

    All our Pits are working to day and Little-town & Sherburn resumed work this morn[in]g. This has arisen out of the meeting of the Council at Sunderland last night. At this Council it was after a long debate (as Liddell our Pittington Delegate reports) resolved, that as other Classes of Workmen had not come forw[ar]d to join the Pitmen, in commencing 'the saved month' – it w[oul]d not be politic in the Pitmen to persevere in the strike at this time, and therefore, that they should continue to work. This is all very well so far as it goes, but as the leaven & spirit of the system still continues – nocturnal mischief such as cutting Incline Ropes on the railways – setting fire to Engine Houses, hay Stacks &c. is to be dreaded, and we ought to have some plan of protection devised. Morton got 4 of the Littletown Ringleaders committed last night for a Fortn[igh]t for neglecting

Challinor (eds), *Working-Class Politics in North-East England* (Newcastle, 1983), pp. 8–16.

their work. I have not rec[eive]d any authoritative acc[ount]s from the Tyne, to day – but am informed, that Seghill & sev[era]l other Coll[ierie]s are still off work, and that the Police & military went to Seghill last night to apprehend some of the ringleaders.

I shall be at Seaham tomorrow where I should be glad to meet your Lordship to receive your advice, and opinion as to some system of protection against the nocturnal mischief of these villainous Chartists, which we have reason to apprehend. I have to be at Newcastle by 12 o'clock on Friday, which would prevent my being at Seaham that day.

The Marq[ues]s of Londonderry   I have the Honor [&c.]
                                                                        J[no] Buddle

159.

D/Lo/C142/34 (7)   Seaham Harbour Thursday ½ past 2 o'clock
                                                  15[th] Aug[us]t 1839

My Lord

I have rec[eive]d your Lordship's packet of this morn[in]g with your excellent Letter to the Magistrates, which I have copied and forwarded according to your Lordship's orders. I entirely approve of every word & sentence your Lordship has written in this Letter – as it is quite to the point.

I enclose a Letter which I received from Dr Fenwick this morn[in]g with my answer which I sent by a messenger. This copy will convey to your Lordship my wishes as to the establishment of a Police Force at the Collieries. If a couple of regular police men were established at each Coll[ier]y they might easily be concentrated at any point in case of need – and would form a strong Body, and would also give great confidence to any Body of Special Constables which it might be necessary to raise as an auxiliary Force.

I am apprehensive that I shall be detained too late at a meet[in]g of the special Comm[itt]ee appointed to examine into the *splitting* of Collieries and other abuses, to be able to reach Seaham 'till too late on Sat[urda]y Even[in]g, as the meeting does not take place 'till 2 o'clock. But if your Lordship will be so good as to inform me at what time you will be in Newcastle on Sunday, for the Train,[4] I will be glad

---

4   It is not clear where Lord Londonderry was going. If it was to Ireland, he
      could have taken a train to Carlisle, that line having been opened in 1838. The

to meet you, as I should wish much to have your Lordship's opinion, on the establishment of a Coll[ier]y Police – and at the same time to give you all the information I may collect in the mean time relative to the state of affairs.

The Marq[ues]s of Londonderry   I have the Honor [&c.]

                                                           J^no Buddle

160.

D/Lo/C142/34 (14)   Pensher 5th Oct[obe]r 1839

My Lord

   The intelligence conveyed by your Lordship's Note, of the 22nd Ult, (received on the 3rd Inst.) has excited feelings of very opposite natures in my mind. In the first place I am rejoiced beyond measure that you have arrived safe – so far, on your voyage[5] – and in the next place I feel the deepest regret that you should have been exposed to such imminent danger. What a horrid affair it would have been if the steamer had been holed by striking the wreck – you might have all gone to the bottom, without it's even being known what had become of you – the idea of such a catastrophe makes one tremble – it has indeed been a providential escape. Crossing the Bay of Biscay during the autumnal Equinox must always be attended with great discomfort, at any rate – independently of any unusual accidents. I can readily imagine the state of suffering my poor Lady & the young ladies must have endured, during such a tempestuous voyage, & the alarm such a terrific accident must have given them. And I most heartily congratulate them, on having reached terra-firma in safety. I sincerely wish you were safely through the Straits of Gibraltar as at this season the navigation of the Atlantic along the coast of Spain, must at best be but a precarious, and uncomfortable affair & I heartily wish you well through it.

---

line to York was not opened until 1844. Tomlinson, *North Eastern Railway*, pp. 314–18.

5   The Londonderrys visited Spain and Portugal, with an excursion to Tangier. Lord Londonderry's *Journal of a Tour in the Southern Part of Spain, including Tangier, Ceuta, and Tetuan*, was privately printed in 1840. Lady Londonderry's longer *Journal of a Three Months Tour in Portugal, Spain and Africa* was published in 1843.

Since your Lordship left England, nothing of material importance – either of a public, or private nature has I think occurred in this quarter. On the whole the aspect of the Coal trade has improved – the energetic exertions of the Comm[itt]ee in enforcing the strict observance of the rules of the regulation has inspired more confidence – about £1000 of fines have been levied *and paid* for violations of it's rules, which has bro[ugh]t the trade into a more healthy state, in 'the home department' – and the *novices* are feeling the propriety of submitting to the wholesome discipline of the regulation, so that at present there is evidently a more kindly feeling towards it's continuance than existed some time ago, and I think there is a prospect of it's going on for another year. The Thornley Co. seem likely to be the only *Thorn in it's side*. The Issues have been better the last & present month, and we have had a brisk demand for the Stewart's Steam Boat Walls-end – so that I fully expect all our resting heaps of them will be run off during this month. Marreco informs me that those Coals have got a good character at Lisbon & up the Mediterranean, and I should not wonder if your Lordship hears something of them in the course of your travels.

Mr Mc Donnell will have informed your Lordship of J^{no} Gregson's discussions with me at Pensher on the purchase of the Seaham Railway & the Seaton & Seaham Coal affairs. The purchase of the Railway seems a matter of vital importance & Gregson thinks he can manage to raise the money for the purchase.

Nothing further has been done in the Seaton Coal affair, it is our policy to delay it, but the other parties are pressing for a decision. I am *hanging fire* & staving them off as well as I can, but Lord Durham came to Lambton last Wed[nesday] the 2nd Inst. & I presume he will be pushing for a decision. Morton broke his right arm by a fall from his gig, this day week & is hors de combat for the present. But this won't delay the business if L[or]d D. pushes it.

The pay[men]t of Tanner & Scurfield's Bal[anc]e is not yet effected. J. Gregson writes me, on the 1st Inst. that he has not yet rec[eive]d the D[raf]ts of the Deeds to enable him to complete the business & complains of the tardy movements of the lawyers!!! This delay is very embarrassing, as we cannot both fulfil our engagement with Tanner & Scurfield & send the Coals to Seaham.

Stewart's W[alls-]end is now the favorite Coal in London generally leading the rest 3d or 6d per Ton – and the consequence is that we always have plenty of ships waiting for them at the Harbour, but none come for Bradyll's except Davison's and their own ships – their Coals are standing very bad at market. They have got their

Dalden Pits sunk thro' the limestone, into the sand below – & have met with an enormous feeder of Water – they have been pumping 2000 gall[on]s of Water per night for some time, without making the slightest impression on the feeder & are stopped until they get their large pumping Engine started.

The Brandling Junction Railway from Gateshead to Sunderland is now in operation[6] & in 3 weeks trains are to run from Gateshead, Sunder[lan]d & Shields by it & the Durham Junction, by Pensher, to Rainton Meadows where a station is to be established & overbusses are to be established between this station, and Durham & Houghton, so that Passengers will be taken from the Mead[ow]s to N[ew]castle in an hour & from Pensher in ¾ of an hour. This will be a convenience to us in getting our Horse Corn from Newcastle, by the D—m Junction & Brandling Lines – some parties have been vending a few cargoes of our Stewart's Steam Boat at the Wearmouth Dock – and there is a prospect of our vending a considerable quantity in this way.

This opening of the Brandling Junction and connecting it with the Durham Junction, has revived the notion of bringing the Great N. of England that way, instead of taking it by Durham & Chester-le-Street.[7] It is proposed that the Line should diverge at Thinford Mill, and proceed E. of Shincliff by our Broomside Pits, Belmont – through the Grange & so join the Durham Junction at Morton a quarter of a mile N. of Chilton-moor. This Line *must* I conceive come through the Grange, and hold out the prospect of driving a good bargain for the Land. This Line may be executed in less than half the time, and at half the expence of the Line by Durham & Chester, and will probably supersede it. This would preserve the Old Durham Estate in statu quo – in which case we should both have 'eaten our cake & have it' as the land is to revert to the proprietor if the Railway is not made thro' it, in Five years. This job seems to be worth the favourable consideration of your Lordship. The projectors of this scheme, are to have a meeting with the Directors of the Great N. of England R[ail]W[ay] Directors [*sic*] at Durham on the 15th Inst. on this affair.

---

6   The line was opened on 5 Sep. 1839, with a connection to the Durham Junction Railway as described. Tomlinson, *North Eastern Railway*, pp. 327, 330, 332–3.

7   See Tomlinson, *North Eastern Railway*, pp. 300, 432. At this time work on the Great North of England railway was concentrated on the stretch between York and Darlington.

I hope your Lordship's next communication will inform me of your safe arrival at Naples, or some other resting place in that part of the world, where Lady L. and the young Ladies, may recruit their health, after so long a sea voyage. I beg to present my dutiful respects to my Lady, and with every good wish, have the honor [&c.]

The Marq[ues]s of Londonderry   J^no Buddle

161.

D/Lo/C142/34 (15)   Pensher 20th Nov[ember] 1839

My Lord

I had the honor to receive your Letter of the 24th of Oct[obe]r from Gibraltar, on the 9th Inst. and heartily congratulate you, on your escape from the turbulent Atlantic, and safe arrival within the limits of the more tranquil Mediterranean. My Lady is really a Heroine – to cross into Africa, without scarcely allowing her feet to touch terra-firma, after so long & tempestuous a sea voyage. I am, however, glad to learn that your visit to Tangiers, was so gratifying, & repaid you for the time & trouble it cost. We know very little of the country round Tangiers, I believe, & nearly about as little of the people – the Moorish people present an instructive example of the rise, & fall, of human Institutions, Civilization, & National Character, & Power – they were no doubt a powerful people, but borrowed the sciences they possessed from their more eastern neighbours. They have long been immersed in barbarism and I hope they will still keep it, on their *own side* of the water, *much longer*. I could go on, moralising on this subject, & others connected with it, but feel that it is not the proper time, & place, for the purpose, and will proceed to matters which more nearly concern us.

Tanner & Scurfield were, I am glad to say, paid off on the 21st Oct[ober] – it is true, that it has increased Mr McD[onnel]l's responsi-bility, but it has rendered us independent of Sunderland – & repaying Coutts loan of £6000 to Mr H. costs us no more, than paying off these Fitters. The Bal[anc]e was struck on the 31st July, as we expected to have been prepared to have paid it, on the 1st Aug[us]t – and from that day to the day of pa[ymen]t the Fitters paid *in full* for all the Coals they needed in the mean time, which made the Bal[anc]e larger on the day of p[aymen]t than it w[oul]d otherwise have been. The Bal[anc]e of payments were as follows

Scurfield's Bal[an]ce		£3540. 14. 4
Paid by Mr McDonnell's order	3000.0.0	
Hunter's cheque on J[oint] S[tock] Bank	540.14.4	
		3540. 14. 4
Tanner & Beckworth's Bal[anc]e		3348. 7. 4
So that the whole amo[un]t of this Bal[anc]e was		6889. 1. 8
which was paid by Mr McDonnell's order on		
Coutts for		6000 0. 0
Hunter's cheques on Bank		889. 1. 8
		£6889. 1. 8

So this transaction was closed.

Your Lordship will have seen from the newspapers how scarce money has been & still continues to be for commercial purposes. The resolution of the Bank of Eng[lan]d not to discount the Bills of, or negotiated by, the *Issuing* Banks – Joint Stock or private – that is to say, Banks issuing *their own* notes – has injured many concerns & *ourselves* amongst others.[8] *Our* Bank was amongst the *proscribed* for issuing it's own notes; it was, therefore, obliged to re-discount it's paper at other Banks who dealt with the Bank of England – they have to pay equal to 6¼ per cent, including Comm[ission] to those Banks. It was therefore impossible for them to keep Mr McDonnell's Bal[anc]e lying as a *dead* security – hence the necessity of his giving them Bills on which they could raise money by paying the high rate of discount. They were driven to this by *necessity* & without it, they could not have gone on. But the extra expence is serious – they are now charging us 6¾ per cent discount, including comm.[issio]n – they pay 6¼ themselves for re-discounting – so that they have only ½ per cent to cover all the expences of their business, which is *very poor* indeed. Our old Friend Longshot & *Friends*, have fine times of it – they have a bargain with the Bank of England – not terminable under 12 mo[nths] notice – to have the bank paper, to any extent they may require – at 3 per cent. This makes it a fine trade to them, as they screw up such poor D—ls as are obliged to go to them, to any extent they please – nothing under 6¼ per cent – but in some instances much more. The Bank of Engl[an]d refused to discount the Lambton Bank Bills, as they would not depart from their general rule on any account whatever.

The regulation still goes on, and no regular notices have been

---

8   See Clapham, *Bank of England*, ii, 138–42.

given, by any party to the Comm[itt]ee of their intention to quit it at the end of the year. The Thornley basis was settled by reference at 70,000 which is most unsatisfactory to Gully & Tom Wood. Gully bullys, & blusters, & swears he will sell his share of the Coll[ier]y rather than submit to be so *tied up*. This is the same sort of game he played at Hetton – but after a while, he took to drawing in harness very quietly – and it is probable he may do the same at Thornley. They cannot not now quit the Regulation before the 30th of June next, as 6 mo[nth]s notice, from the 31st Dec[ember] next must be given. We have had contrary winds, bad weather & high seas for a month past, which has occasioned a scarcity of ships at the Harbour & has caused us to fall 20,000 Ch. short of our Vend up to the 15th altho' 240 Ch. had been vended at Sunderland. We must avoid sending *best* Coals to Sunderland as much as possible, yet when ships cannot be got at the harbour & may be had there, we must either send the Coals there, or lose the vend.

At the harbour 3 course of Blocks have been laid on the Pier-head which has raised it up to the level of the neap tide low-water mark & its beneficial effects upon the Channel are already felt. We are now nearly at a stand for want of Blocks & Lee[9] & Usher[10] are on the qui vive, to get some bro[ugh]t round from Pensher, but have not yet been able to get anything done. The new Steamer answers very well & the old one, is now undergoing repair – when finished we shall be able to do *all* the work of the harbour & Bradyll's steamer will be sent to Hartlepool or sold we shall then do his business *for hire*, which will help to pay the expence of the steamer.

Railways

We are & shall soon be 'all running on wheels' in this quarter. The opening of the Brandling Junction Line from Gateshead to Sunderland has formed a communication with the Durham Junction Line, at W. Boldon. The Durham Junction Co. are forming a station at our Meadows Pit, from whence omnibusses[11] are to run past the Adventure Pit, to W. Rainton & so on by the turnpike to Durham & to join the Clarence at Black Gate. Omnibusses are also to go to Houghton from a station near Chester Moor. A station is also to be established

---

9   M. Lee, fitter at Seaham.
10   William Usher, harbourmaster at Seaham.
11   The vehicle, and this name for it, first appeared in England in 1839, having originated in France the previous year. *Oxford English Dictionary.*

here, so that we may go to, or come from Gateshead in 25 minutes. This plan will be in operation by Christmas and I expect it will make a considerable Saving in our cartage. Ultimately I think it probable that the Great N. of Eng[lan]d Line will come this way. Money has got *very* scarce in this concern & I hear that they have great difficulty in getting funds to carry on the work – all they seem to reckon on at present, is to complete the Line to Croft, against next September – this will bring them to Darlington by the Croft branch of the Darlington Line. They purpose going to Parliament next spring for an extension of time – to complete the Line from Darlington to Newcastle.

If however the Bill for the projected Line, from the Durham Junction at Chilton-Moor, to meet the Great Northern, at Thinford Mill could be got passed next session – that part of the Great N. Line from Darlington to N[ew]castle will certainly never be executed. The damp, however, which the scarcity of money is throwing on all adventures of this kind, will I apprehend, check this project also. It is estimated to cost as follows viz

Cost of the proposed branch from Thrislington Gap, to the Junction Line at W. Rainton 10 miles	£220,000
Ditto from the Durham Junction to the Brandling Junction 5 miles	50,000
Branch to Durham	40,000
	310,000
Engines & coaches	40,000
	£350,000

The cost of the Great N.. Line from Darlington to Newcastle will cost £700,000, and will require from 7 to 9 years to execute it.

When on the subject of Railways I will advert to the purchase of the Seaham railway. Notwithstanding the scarcity of money J[no] Gregson seems to have no doubt of being able to borrow the money for his purpose. I do not look upon the borrowing of the money, in the light of an ordinary Loan, or Mortgage. It is, properly speaking, borrowing to purchase a 'mercantile' property, which possesses within it's own resources, the power of *self* redemption. Under the proposed plan, the Coll[ierie]s will not be called upon to make a larger ann[ua]l payment – to effect the purchase, than they w[oul]d do, if the agree[men]t for the lead[in]g was renewed – & then in the end we should *still have the purchase to make*[12]

---

12 The letter ends here, without a concluding form.

162.

D/Lo/C142/34 (24)   Pensher 3rd Nov[ember] 1840[1]

My Lord

I had hoped long before this to have been able to inform your Lordship that the valuation of the Seaham Railway had been completed – but after *waffling* on for 3 Weeks the umpire decided that all the earth-work machinery, fencing &c. should be included!!! It was therefore necessary to have the time extended to the 20th Inst. as this is a work of labour & will require time. Ten days have been lost by Blacknowes (Perkins & Co's measurers) absence in London, but they are now hard at work, and I do hope they will finish by the 20th – especially as J. Gregson has the money all ready to pay as soon as the valuat[io]n is completed. This decision of the umpire will greatly increase the amo[un]t of the valuation. Still I expect it will not much exceed the sum we originally supposed.

I must own I was staggered at the decision of the umpire – it is everything that Perkins & Co. could have wished and we might as well have had no umpire at all. I am however glad to say that J. Gregson has induced Mr Pennant's[2] solicitor to dispense with with [sic] the extension of the N. Hetton leading agreement, as recommended by N. Wood, which has saved us some trouble, and expence – besides binding us to an engagement which might not eventually have proved best for the interest of our Rail-way & Harbour. This brings me to the *Durham & Sunderland Railway Co.* This concern, it seems, has got into a *mess.* The Directors have addressed a circular to all the land proprietors on the Line pressing for an abatement of the Way-leave Rents – the gross amount of which is £7000 per ann[um]. They state that the share-holders have advanced £140,000 – that the Directors have contracted a debt of £135,000 more – that a great proportion of this is upon *running* acceptances, and that part of it is immediately, and peremptorily demanded by the bank. And further that the Income has fallen £3000 per ann[um] short of paying the interest on the debt and the expence of working the Line. Unless,

---

1 Only seven letters from Buddle between January and September 1840 are preserved in the Londonderry Papers.

2 George Pennant, one of the wayleave proprietors for the Seaham railway.

therefore, they can obtain the abatement of rents prayed for, they must *give up the concern*.[3]

Some of the Way-leave proprietors will no doubt accede to their wishes, but we *certainly ought not*, and Mr McDonnell has very properly, directed accordingly. Our policy is, to *knock this concern on the head, if possible* – as I consider it to have been much more injurious to our harbour than even Hartlepool. With this prospect in the *wind*, the getting possession of our Railway, becomes the more desirable, and the altering of it, and assimilating it to a public Line, by securing the way-leaves, on a more permanent and *general* footing, becomes a matter of grave consideration. I am *wide awake* to the importance of this plan, and will endeavour to devise some scheme for its accomplishment. The knocking up of this Concern would render it much more difficult for any speculators to step in between the Dean & Chap[ter] and us, in the renewal, or retaking of the Rainton Coll[ier]y lease – an event which I look to with very gloomy forebodings.

The Coal-trade – continues in quite as unsatisfactory a state as when I last wrote your Lordship on the 22nd Sep[tember]. The provisional Executive Comm[itt]ee met twice every week – exerting themselves to the utmost, to keep the regulation on its legs – but whether they may be able to carry it on to the end of the year, seems questionable. The breaking up of the Fitters' regulation, by the end of the year seems inevitable, or even sooner, and the general regulation being able to survive it's fall is scarcely to be expected. Indeed I don't see how we are to live under the regulation in it's present form, as the small Issues which w can obtain under it, are dwindling down our Vend in an alarming degree. I see little prospect of our vend exceeding 79,000 to 80,000 Ch. this year, and if it goes on, on the same declining scale as they would probably be in an open trade. If some plan, therefore, cannot be devised to make the Regulation work more beneficially for the best Collieries – it will not be worth their while, in my opinion, to continue to be parties to the general Regulation, and they must endeavour to fall back upon a sub, or partial Regulation amongst themselves. That is to say, they must not go to Logger-heads amongst themselves.

The Issue of Vend in 1837 was 778 per mo[nth] on our Basis of 138,000. In 1838 the Issue was 695 per mo[nth], in 1839 it was 639 per mo[nth], and this year 1840 it does not appear that it will exceed

---

3   See Tomlinson, *North Eastern Railway*, p. 471. The company obtained sufficient relief to allow the work to continue.

575 – being 195 per mo[nth] less than in 1837 – 120 less than in 1838, and 64 less than last year. That is to say, our Vend this year will be less by 26910 Ch. than in 1837, 16,560 Ch. than in 1838, and 8833 less than last year. This is an alarming *wearing* down and if it goes on for two years longer, will completely cripple us.

We are not, however, not [*sic*] alone in this retrograde race as every one is falling back in the same proportion, according to their Bases – and very few, indeed, except the best Collieries, are making any profit. Yet the Demon of reckless adventure is as active as ever, or even more so.

Since I last wrote your Lordship *three* very large new Collieries have been commenced – at Castle Eden, E. Wingate, and So[uth] Wingate, including a large tract of Coal, about Sheraton. These specu-lations have all been *jumped into* in consequence of L[or]d Hawdon's[4] Wingate Colliery having turned out so much better than was antic-ipated. The Castle Eden Coll[ier]y is taken by a Co. consisting of *Dick* Greenwell (one of y[ou]r Lordship's late Fitters, & a man of the name of Farrar in Sunderland, Richardson of Castle Eden, & a person named Marshall whom I don't know. But the great monied partners are Cook & Gladson – and Greenwell (Dick's brother) all silk mercers in London, and reported to be enormously rich. They have taken 3500 acres for which they have agreed to pay a Certain Rent of 30/- per acre & 30/- per ten. The Certain rent will be £5350 per ann[um].

The So[uth] Wingate Coal is taken by Metcalf Jun[io]r a ship-builder at So[uth] Shields – the ex[ecutor]s of the late Tennant of Stockton[5] (not Kit) and Wilson & Thompson, of Darlington –Old Votum of Stockton and Seymour the Viewer.

The E. Wingate Coal is taken by the two Metcalfs,[6] father & son, ship-builders of So[uth] Shields – wealthy people – Marshall the Coal-factor, and some others whose names I don't know.

The two latter Royalties are taken at the same rate of certain, and tentale rents, as Castle Eden but I don't know their extent – further than that they are very extensive.

Each of these Winnings is calculated to cost £150,000 – at Castle Eden, they have commenced to create the largest pumping Engine in

---

4   Cornwallis Maude, third Viscount Hawarden, 1780–1856.
5   Thomas Tennant, a director of the Clarence Railway. Christopher Tennant was a prime mover in launching that railway.
6   Thomas Metcalf & Son, shipbuilders, South Shields.

the Country I believe. These parties must entertain a most magnificent notion of the Coal-trade, and will discover their mistake in due time.

The rumour of war, and hubbub in France[7] has completely paralyzed our Coal-trade, with that Country, so that for the present our Steam Coal trade is nearly *done-up*. The French merchants don't send their Vessels, and the English ship-owners dare not send their ships to France for fear of detention. Our Bank has been in some difficulty from the sev[era]l Coll[ier]y & other acco[unt]s it has on hand, but it now seems to be getting more at ease again. It has taken possession of the Fawdon Colliery and has advertised it for sale. Report states it's bad Debts, at £188,000 since it's commencement in 1833 and it is surmised, that it may wind up it's concerns at no very distant period – but without loss except to the share-holders. It will however have to call upon all it's Customers who owe it money to pay up their Balances. Mr McDonnell is aware of all this, & will be turning his attention to the removal of the acco[un]t to some more stable concern.

The release of the Building Ground at Seaham has not yet been effected but J. Gregson informs me it is going on, & nothing but the Law's delay is retarding it's completion.

Bradyll's people are increasing their shipments at the Harbour, and I am glad to say that the Pier-head is *completely finished* & the framing removed. Olsher has shewn great zeal and energy in pushing this job to completion.

Nothing has been said about the Seaton Coal-affair for a long time – 'till the other day. Morton has been in London on Lady Durham's affairs[8] and on his return, he resumed the old cry 'we must have something done about the Seaton Coal'. He says Lord Grey, whom Lady Durham consults is uneasy about it, as he does not understand it. We, i.e. Morton & N. Wood, & myself are to have a *talk* about it shortly – but I don't anticipate that at most we shall yet begin the boring thro' the limestone *talked* about before.

I hope this will find your Lordship and my Lady, all safe, and in good health where ever you may be. I have not received any commu-

---

7   The British and French governments were seriously at odds over policy on Syria, where a Turkish-Egyptian war had begun in 1838. Eventually an agreement was reached by which a settlement was imposed, Turkey recovering northern Syria while Mehemet Ali kept the south for his lifetime. M.S. Anderson, *The Eastern Question 1774–1923* (London, 1966), pp. 88–109.

8   Lord Durham died on 28 July 1840.

nication from your Lordship since you left England,[9] but learn from Hunter that you had arrived safe at Vienna. I begin to feel anxious, to hear from your Lordship, and hoping soon to receive a good account, I have the honor [&c.]

The Marq[ues]s of Londonderry   J[no] Buddle

163.

D/Lo/C142/34 (25)   Pensher 31st Dec[ember] 1840

My Lord

I had the honor to receive your Lordship's letter of the 6[th] Ulto. on the 2[nd] Inst. and was very glad to learn that you had reached Constantinople in safety, after so many privations and perils which my Lady endured with her wonted fortitude and constancy. I see by the news papers that you have had a most flattering reception by the Sultan – at a very interesting epoch too – just when the news of the brilliant achievements of the English in Syria had arrived. This is all very well, but I shall be very glad to hear of your safe arrival at some place nearer home in a Christian country.

I have deferred writing until the tedious affair of the Seaham railway Valuation could be brought into shape. The award was not signed 'till the 12[th] Inst. – the amo[un]t £22721.16.1 – after this the mortgage deeds to Mr Pennant had to be signed by Mr McDonnell & myself as your Lordship's attorney. At the moment of signing the award Mr Pennant was taken seriously ill. J. Gregson therefore immediately dispatched one of his clerks to Mr McDonnell & myself to get the deeds signed. And fortunate it was that he did so. Mr Pennant died within about 24 hours after the deeds being executed, I understand. Had he died before we would have been nonplussed as his ex[ecutor]s could not have lent the money, and we should have had no quarter from Perkins & Co. The only delay is waiting 'till the ex[ecutor]s prove the Will which Gregson expects will not be many days. In the mean time Perkins & Co. refuse to give us possession of the way & we are likely to have difficulty, and bother with them

---

9   The Londonderrys went on another tour in 1840, up the Rhine, down the Danube to the Black Sea, to Constantinople and back by Greece. Lord Londonderry published an account in *A Steam Voyage to Constantinople by the Rhine and the Danube* (London, 1842); Lady Londonderry published *Visit to the Courts of Vienna, Constantinople, Athens, Naples etc.* (London, 1844).

in getting the acco[un]t for leading settled, from the 30th of June up to the time we shall get possession. J. Gregson purposes in the event of difficulty arising on this point, to pay the money into the Court of Chancery which will most likely induce Perkins & Co. to settle the leading acco[un]t without delay, or further haggling, as I believe the purchase money is much wanted – their Colliery concerns being anything but flourishing, and I hope that these matters may be so arranged, as that we may get possession of the Way in a few days, as I sh[oul]d not like the Co. to trail on into the new year, with their old leading acco[un]t.

I have not yet got anything settled with Morton, as to future plans for the mutual leading & shipping of our Coals, and altering our Railways to the Parliamentary gauge – as those matters depend on sundry collateral considerations which cannot yet be bro[ugh]t to bear. But I have all matters in my own mind nearly arranged, when the proper time arrives. The chief impediment to the altering of the way to the parliamentary gauge, is the *expence*, to make the requisite alteration in the way & wagons, will cost *us* about £4000, and Lady Durham *more* – and I *guess* that her Trustees are pretty much in the same state as our own, and that such an expenditure would be equally inconvenient to her Ladyship as to us. This project will therefore I presume remain in abeyance at least 'till we see what turn the present most unsatisfactory state of the Coal trade may take.

I deeply regret that I have great cause to groan at the very unsatisfactory and declining state of our trade – at a time when I should have been but too happy, to have cheered your Lordship with tidings of prosperity, and better prospects. But I am bound to give your Lordship a true & faithful acco[un]t of matters, as they really are, without putting any false gloss upon them.

We have now closed the Vend for the year 1840 – the Issue on the Basis has only been 550 on the Thous[an]d, being 89 per ann[um] less than in 1839. The consequence is, that the gross Vend of 1840 is 241,175 Ch. less than in 1839 and the receipt of money is £16,289.17.10 less. This your Lordship will perceive, is a most serious defalcation, and I dread the effect it will produce on the year's profit, when Hindhaugh gets the acco[un]ts balanced.

I should not have thought so much of this had it risen from any accidental cause, & that I could have seen brighter prospects behind it. But this is not the case – it arises from the enormous Cloud of new Collieries which like a flight of Locusts has been seen, gradually approaching for some time, and is now lighting upon and devouring the old ones. No human effort, or stretch of economy in management, can avert the consequences of such a state of things – nothing but a proportionate extension of market can possibly relieve us, and that seems a very remote contingency – if not altogether hopeless.

The system of general Regulation seems fast breaking under it's own weight – the number of new Collieries continually being heaped upon the Basis has reduced the Issues so, as not to leave a living Vend for each – the Vend of W[alls]end & Eden-main this year is only 77,457 Ch. being 10,796 less than it was last year. And under general regulation I see no reason to expect that it may not continue to retrograde in the like ratio for an indefinite period to come. This progressive diminution of Vend is particularly oppressive to us – as it brings us under the standard quantity of 60,000 Ch. for Rainton, and 30,000 for Pittington on which we have *already paid the tentale or mine Rent in advance whether we vend the quantity or not*.[10]

The harmful effect of this diminished Vend upon us, is therefore *twofold*, as we not only lose the profit on the short quantity, but we also lose the *purchase money* upon it, in aggravation of the increased expence of working, occasioned by the reduction of the quantity, as it is impossible to effect a proportional reduction on the working charges.

The only palliative (for a remedy seems hopeless) seems to be the establishment of a separate regulation of the best Collieries, as has already been stated to your Lordship. But the arranging of such a scheme is not without it's difficulties, as the first question which arises, is *where to draw the line* of demarcation between the best, and inferior Coals? There are now so many Coals ....[11] best Collieries have agreed to maintain their full prices coute que coute, 'till the effects of the *shock* subsides. The deputation will return, in time to report progress to the general meeting on the 23rd when it will be decided whether we are to *trail on* with the present regulation for another year, or to break it up. In the latter event the first class Collieries will endeavour to form a separate regulation as stated in former letters.

---

10 The lease of Rainton and Pittington Colliery was renewed on 28 Sep. 1841 (DCM, B/BA/103). Negotiations in 1838, the normal seven-year interval, having failed to reach agreement, the Dean and Chapter made a fresh approach in September 1840. Under the terms of the new lease, Lord Londonderry was entitled to work 60,000 Ch. per annum of best coal from Rainton and 30,000 Ch. from Pittington for the remaining eleven years of the lease, plus 30/- per ten for quantities in excess. The fine was £10,000. D/Lo/B242.

11 The text seems to be incomplete here. The first sheet ends the with the word 'Coals'; the second begins with 'best Collieries'.

All our Works, except for necessary repairs, have been at a stand since the 24th Dec[ember] till this morn[in]g when we recommence for the new year.

I hope this will find your family party all comfortably assembled, at Naples, and I hope also that your Lordship's next letter, will enable me to congratulate you, on this happy event. I only wish that the *Gathering* had been in 'old England'.

By the bie Mr Russell seems disposed to 'keep it up' at Brancepeth, during his Sherriffalty[12] – he is now there hunting, and the castle is full of Company. His mother, the Honble Mr & Mrs Hamilton[13] &c. are staying with him – with members of the neighbouring gentry – so that all is gaiety at the Castle. I have to spend a day or two with him, (not to hunt) after the meeting of the 23rd.

I beg to present my most respectful comp[limen]ts to my Lady, the young Ladies, and Lord Seaham who I presume will be at Naples, as soon as this. I shall be anxious to hear of your Lordship's and my Lady's safe arrival at Naples, and hoping to receive a good account after so much fatigue, and privation of comfort.

I have the honor [&c.]
Jno Buddle

Bradyll's Vend, at Seaham Harbour

1839	12197 Ch.	at 4/6	£914.14.0
1840	17959	do	1346.18.6

I expect they will increase their quantity considerably this year.

Nothing further done about the Borings at Seaham.

The Marq[ues]s of Londonderry

---

12 Russell was Sheriff of Co. Durham for the year 1840–41.

13 The Hon. Gustavus Hamilton, 1797–1872, married to Emma Russell, sister of William Russell. She inherited Brancepeth on Russell's death in 1850. He succeeded as seventh Viscount Boyne in 1855.

164.

D/Lo/C142/35 (8)   Newcastle 14th Aug[us]t 1841

My Lord

I have received your Lordship's vituperative Letter of this morn[in]g.[1]

I can conscientiously assert that the *true Interests* of your Lordship, and the Family, have always been most faithfully & zealously attended to by me, as abundant facts will testify. I therefore feel, that I do not merit the censure which it now is your Lordship's pleasure to inflict upon me.

Your Lordship's recent conduct towards me, renders it necessary, that I should conduct myself in my management under the Trust with the greatest circumspection.

I do not therefore, feel, that I can exercise any discretionary power in the matter, as I am aware that I may again be called upon, to answer charges of a similar nature to those of which I have already had a specimen. I can therefore, in the position in which I am placed, only forward your Lordship's Letter to Mr McDonnell, and request his instructions thereon.

The Marq[ues]s of Londonderry   I have the Honor [&c.]
                                                    J^{no} Buddle

165.

D/Lo/C142/35 (10)   Newcastle 8th Nov[ember] 1841

My Lord

I have the honor to acknowledge the receipt of your Lordship's note of the 4th Inst. and beg respectfully to explain, that the reason of my not having reported to your Lordship, for some time past, on the state of your Collieries & other matters is – that after the uncomfortable interview which I had with your Lordship, last May, at Holderness-house, and your Lordship's subsequent unkind & harsh

---

1   For the breach between Buddle and Lord Londonderry see Introduction, p. xxiii.

communications, I did not feel, that I could with propriety write to your Lordship – lest I should subject myself to further painful communications. But as your Lordship desires it I will now, cheerfully, resume my communications, on all your Lordship's concerns under my superintendence, as usual.

This is the more necessary, as the affairs of the Coal-trade seem to be rapidly approaching a crisis. And the Seaham Winning,[2] as well as the partial working of the Seaton Coal, by the Hetton Co. are also pressing towards a decision and require great consideration. I wrote Mr McDonnell from London on the 24th Oct[ober] very fully on these matters, and he will most likely forward the letter to your Lordship, as it contains matter for grave consideration.

I am here, to day, attending a meeting of the Executive Comm[itt]ee who have very difficult cards to play, to keep the Regulation on it's Legs, & I scarcely think it can possibly go on beyond the end of the year.

We have spent the most of this day with the representatives of L[or]d Howardson's Coll[ier]y on certain points of difference with the Comm[itt]ee without being able to reconcile them – and at present, this affair wears the appearance of breaking up the Regulation, if nothing else does.

The Marq[ues]s of Londonderry   I have the honor [&c.]
                                                                         J[no] Buddle

166.

D/Lo/C142/35 (14)   Newcastle 22nd Nov[ember] 1841

My Lord
    The result of the special meeting to day, of the United Committees, is that the executive Committee are directed to make their *final* report on the 20th of December. In which if in the mean time they are not able to effect satisfactory settlements of Fines for over Vends, and other matters in dispute with certain Individuals – they are to *shew up* the names of the delinquents. And the United Committees are then to decide on the measures to be taken, as to calling a general meeting &c.

---

2   The High Pit at Seaham was won by the Hetton Co. in 1840, Lord Londonderry's Low Pit in 1849.

Great difference of opinion exists, on the question of breaking up the general, and establishing a separate regulation of the best Collieries. But here a great difficulty presents itself in the out-set – in consequence of Thornley and Wingate Grange being amongst the delinquents, & the most refractory parties to deal with at present. If, therefore, they cannot be reduced to reason, a separate regulation, of the best Collieries will be impracticable.

The Hetton & Haswell Cos. seem inclined to temporize, and hang by the regulation however imperfect it may be, as they think if the best Coals can hold their ground, so as to enable them to obtain their present prices & Vends it will be better than running the risk of a break up. Perhaps they may be right, and I am inclined to think, that so long as we can see our way to make about £20,000 profit we had better stick to the old regulation *if we can*. Morton is in a very wavering & unsettled state of mind on the subject. The price of best Coals in the London market still keeps very firm at about 22/- with a good demand.

I have seen Ryle relative to the manage[men]t of the Colliery Farms, and I expect to be able to make a satisfactory arrangement with him, as stated in my Letter of the 18th.

The Marq[ues]s of Londonderry   I have the honor [&c.]
                                                                            Jno Buddle

167.

D/Lo/C142/35 (15)   Pensher 30th Nov[ember] 1841

My Lord

I had the honor to receive your Lordship's packet of the 23rd in the afternoon of the 27th Inst. and on the 28th forwarded your Lordship's Letter and observations on J. Gregson's Letter to Mr McDonnell, and on my Letter to your Lordship – to J. Gregson with a request that he would forward his observations to Mr McDonnell without delay.

I now enclose a copy of your Lordship's observations which I have perused but find them too elaborate, and containing matter of too much moment for me to venture a hasty opinion on – especially as the important subject they embrace are for the most deliberate discussion, and which must be carefully weighed and examined according to the various *phases* they may present when exhibited in different points of view.

Paragraph I. The whole affair as respects your Lordship's present and prospective Interests is involved in great difficulty – *and is beyond my powers of reasoning to devise any feasible and satisfactory mode of extrication*. As so much depends on numerous contingencies of which I neither possess a competent knowledge, or have any control. I shall, therefore, confine my observations for the present to a few points in the meeting of the 17th Inst. on which your Lordship has animadverted. And first as to J. Gregson and myself *seemingly* having lost sight of the *partition* project, and dissolution of the partnership.

II. We took this course advisedly, and deliberately, and to the best of our judgment, as we considered by pressing the measure at the meet[in]g it would betray an anxiety on our part, and enhance the importance of the object *to us* in the estimation of the other parties. And at the same time we considered that better opportunities might and undoubtedly would occur during our negotiating the terms of the partnership Deed for accomplishing this object should it finally be decided on under all circumstances, as the best course to adopt. And that we should most likely be able to bring the proposition *from them*, which would undoubtedly enable us to make better terms than if we were the *suppliants*. But above all, it would have been premature, before your Lordship had had time to consider duly, and decide so very important a point.

III. With respect to the name – 'the Seaham Coal Co.' I take the blame of this entirely upon myself, and if I have erred, I have done so, under the mistaken idea that I was acting for the best, on your Lordship's behalf. The other parties pressed for the adoption of the name 'the Seaton Coal Co.' – this struck me as being highly improper, and inconsistent. To sink the name of Seaham, as if no such place were in existence, when the Winning was to be made in the estate, appeared to be derogatory, and detracting from the importance of Seaham, and that it would be distasteful to your Lordship. I therefore pressed or rather insisted on the title of the Co. being *Seaham*. Being well aware, that if the name *Seaton* once got currency – the name 'Seaham' with all it's associations, would be wholly lost sight of. If however your Lordship thinks otherwise, and would wish to have the name changed, there will be no difficulty in doing so.

IV. As for the Buildings, and Erections for the Winning it is usual for the Co. to farm as much Land, of the proprietor of the estate, at a fair rent, & for a term co-extensive with the Coal lease, as will be sufficient for Pit-room, Engines, Shops & Pitmen's houses &c. (if the Co. build them) and for pasturage for the Colliery Horses. But if the Landlord chooses to build the Houses, the Co. take them of him at an ann[ua]l Rent.

If it should not be agreeable to your Lordship to have the pitmen's houses built on the Seaham Estate there are Brough's, Thompson's, Carrs, Bond's &c. freeholds close at hand, and I have no doubt, any, or all of them would be glad either to build the houses themselves on their property or to let or sell building sites to speculators – which is the way in which most of the Collieries in the neighbourhood have stocked with pitmen's houses.

As the Colliery buildings will be chiefly cottages for the workmen they will not give Votes – if any should happen to be of sufficient value to qualify Voters – the probability is, that they would vote in the Interest of the landlord of the property.

V. The appointment of Agents, Under-Agents &c. would as is the case in other partnerships to be directed by the majority, unless an agree[men]t was made to the contrary.

VI. The question of continuing or dissolving the partnership is one of great moment, and requires your Lordship's most serious consideration. The reasons for first entertaining it, are so fully detailed in my paper of the 8th Jan[uar]y 1840 that it is unnecessary to add any thing more on that subject at present. In the opposite scale may be placed, assuming that it should be dissolved, and that the agree[men]t for the Seaham Coal, as well as the Agreements for all those parcels of the Seaham Coal which might be wro[ugh]t by the Seaham Winning were surrendered to your Lordship. The effect would be the loss of ⅔rds of the Seaham Coal rent, and saddling your Lordship with the whole amo[un]t of the Seaton Coal rents of the portion to be attached to Seaham.

VII. If then the Winning of Seaham were deferred, the dead rents of the Seaton Coal would rapidly *roll up*, while every year that the Winning was delayed, would be cutting short the term in those leases, and thereby rapidly diminish the Value of the property. And would lessen also the chance of *working up the shorts* – if not to render it impossible to do so.

Your Lordship would then have no choice left, but either to make the Winning, or give up the Seaton Coal, with the loss of all the money and interest which had been paid for it. These considerations were a sufficient bar to a hasty declaration of your Lordship's wish to dissolve the partnership – without first having time to give the subject all that consideration which it's vast importance demands.

If it were physically certain that the Seaham Colliery would prove as successful as to realize our best expectations, then indeed it might warrant such an effort as the property may be capable off making to accomplish it. But as no human foresight can presume to guarantee such a result, it must, like all mining speculations, be attended with a certain degree of risk, and uncertainty. Making the necessary effort would therefore seem to be *hazarding too much on the cast of the Dice* – should the *throw* prove a failure it might inflict a fatal blow on the property.

On the other hand should it prove a failure in the partnership, the loss would be comparatively small, while if it should be successful, the advantages to your Lordship would be *certain* to the extent originally contemplated – see paper of 8th Jan[uar]y 1840.

This affair is too vast for me to venture an opinion on, but I have endeavoured to place it in as clear a point of view before your Lordship as I can – to enable you to form your own opinion, and to draw your conclusions accordingly. And on your Lordship's return, I shall be glad to give you any further information, ot assistance in my power, to aid your Lordship's endeavours to adopt that course which may appear to be the most judicious.

Since the 17th neither Morton nor Wood have said a word to me about the Plans & estimates for the Winning &c. and I do not feel that I am called upon to move in the matter 'till they urge me to it. And I would rather have it remain in abeyance until your Lordship's return.

I have nothing satisfactory to say about the Coal trade. Now towards the close of the year the complaints of the want of profits, are loud and general. Bankers are *holding hard* and pressing for the balance of over-drawn acc[oun]ts to be paid up, and are charging 6 per cent disc[oun]t. In short I never heard so much groaning and complaining before amongst Coal-owners, Ship-owners, Bankers, & Tradesmen of all kinds. Yet the importation of Coals into London this year has exceeded the last by 10 per cent, and our Issues of vend up to the end of this year are 13 per cent more than they were last year. The increase of the London Importation is attributable to the cheapness of the 2nd class and inferior Coals – which has driven the canal & inland Coals, *back*. The price of Small Coals on the Tyne has been reduced to 4/- per Ch. This is affecting the trade on the Wear, and if the Tyne people cannot be bro[ugh]t to spring their prices again, the Wear must come down. The decline in the price of Small Coals is owing to the decline of the iron & Glass &c. trade, most of the manufacturers of these articles being nearly at a stand. The Iron Masters in England, Wales and Scotland have agreed to reduce their *make* ¼ for the present, as the present prices won't pay the expence of making the iron. The Belgians are cutting us out of the Iron trade on the Continent – they have got 55 Blast Furnaces and within the last 2 mo[nth]s have contracted for a railway in Germany at 3/- per ton under the lowest tender from England!!!

Morton has received intelligence of Lady Durham's having been nearly dying as possible from an attack of inflammation in the throat on her way to Geneva. If she had died, what would have become of our partnership during the young Earl's minority? I have a letter from Mr McDonnell of the 22nd from Marseilles, by which I regret to learn that he is not much, *if any* better.

The Marq[ues]s of Londonderry   I have the Honor [&c.]
                                                          J^no Buddle

168.

D/Lo/C142/36 (1)   Coal-trade Office Newcastle 3rd Jan[uar]y 1842

My Lord

The United Committees have finished the outlines of their report to day – to be laid before a Meeting of Representatives, on the 12th Inst. – the Comm[itt]ees to meet again on the 10th to prepare all matters ready for the Meeting on the 12th.[1] The report of the Comm[itt]ee is in favour of a continuation of the regulation – an Executive Comm[itt]ee of 7 to be appointed for the management of the monthly Issues, and other matters of detail, on which they are to report to the United Comm[itt]ee fortnightly, or oftener if necessary. The executive Comm[itt]ee to be elected from the United Committees of the 3 Rivers. In order to keep the market regularly supplied – so as to prevent a glut at one time, and a scarcity at another, it has been resolved to form a scale of the monthly Issues for the whole year, at once – subject, of course, to such modifications from month, to month, as circumstances may require. By adopting this plan, it is expected, that much difference of opinion, and confusion will be avoided, when the Comm[itt]ees meet to fix upon the Issues. This scale has been formed by taking the average monthly Vends for the last 4 years, making due allowance for the increase during the last two years.

The total Basis of the regulated Coll[ierie]s is 7,848,000 tons

New Collieries	795,000
Total working Basis for 1842	8,643,000

This when divided by the estimated Vend for the year, gives an Issue of 540 ½ per m[onth] which is the *expectancy* for the current year. This when apportioned to the monthly Vends, according to the averages of the last 4 years – gives the quantities as stated on the margin, in whole numbers & decimals.

Jan[uar]y   27.75   By this scale being placed in the hands of the
Feb[ruary]   33.6   Coal-owners, they will have an idea what vend
Mar[ch]   43.03   they have to expect, and will be able to regulate

---

1   Minutes in NRO 263/A2.

Ap[ril]	44.59	their workings accordingly.
May	45.58	The co-operation of the factors and ship-owners
June	44.39	will be requested with a view to maintain the
July	46.26	selling prices of the *best Coals*, as the standard
Aug[us]t	51.92	for all the rest, at the following rates

Sep[tember] 53.40   From the 1st of Oct. to 1st April 22/9 per ton
Oct[ober]   52.05   1st April to 1st June   22/-
Nov[ember] 54.39   1st June to 1st Sep.   21/6
Dec[ember] 43.50   1st Sep. to 1st Oct.   22/-
            540.47

These prices in the London market would allow the ship-owners a proper amo[un]t of freight, and enable them to pay the Coal-owners their present prices. If this plan can be fairly worked out, it will undoubtedly be better than *breaking-up* – reduced as the monthly issues will be.

There will, however, be great difficulty in bringing all parties to concur, as some of the second rate & inferior Collieries think the regulation does not benefit them, but rather the contrary & therefore protest against continuing any longer, under it.

The Committees of the 3 Rivers, are now out of office, and new ones are to be elected by Ballot against the Comm[itt]ee meeting of the 10th that is when the old Comm[itt]ees meet to finish their report & to resign their office.

Our pits are off work, & railway &c. will all remain idle 'till the 13th or 14th – we must therefore defer sending your Lordship's cargo, until we can get *fresh wrought* Coals. And it would be well if in the mean time your Lordship could ascertain as nearly as you can, the no of tons which you can store, at H[oldernesse] H[ouse] that the quantity may be sent accordingly. As these Coal-trade meetings will occupy me on the 10th & 12th and as our Pits &c. won't resume work before the 13th your Lordship would not be able to see our *great machine* in operation as I should wish you to do, before the 13th. I could meet your Lordship at Seaham on the 13th or any time during the following week that might suit your Lordship's convenience, as we would then be in full operation – that is to say as full as a small issue will permit.

By Lady Durham's Will,[2] the whole of the Property, real & personal is left to the young Earl – subject to a charge of £70,000

---

2   Lady Durham died on 26 November 1841.

for the Daughters' fortunes, and also the property lately bo[ugh]t of
your Lordship – which is left to the Ladies. In the event of the young
Earl's death, the whole of the property, subject to the above charges,
goes to William Lambton.[3] The amo[un]t of the probate duty paid
at L[or]d Durham's death was £3500, and it will not be less on the
present occasion.

The Marq[ues]s of Londonderry   I have the honor [&c.]
                                                          J[no] Buddle

169.

D/Lo/C142/36 (40)   Pensher 25[th] Jan[uar]y 1842

My Lord

I have the honor to acknowledge the receipt of your Lordship's
letter of yesterday enclosing Jacky Legge's[4] *long spun yarn* of the
22[nd]. It is true that Morton, & I, have found it necessary to unite
our efforts to put a stop to the abuses which had crept in, in the
expenditure of the money collected under the *guise* of Church rates.[5]
Your Lordship's, & the Lambton Collieries, from the high scale at
which they are rated pay the greatest proportion of all the parochial
rates, and the great no. of shop keepers, & the petty rate payers in
Houghton forming a powerful body of Voters at the parish meetings,
used to lay on rates, at their pleasure, under the name of Church
rates – to play at Ducks, & Drakes with – as so *very small* a share
of the Expence, came out of their pockets. The Church Steeple was
raised & a Bridge built out of the Church rates – to please the Rector,
J. Legge & Co. But these we could not at all understand to appertain
to the 'necessary repairs of the Church'. We have put a stop to these
proceedings, but at the same time, do not object to the levying of
Church rates to be applied to their legitimate objects.

It is a long time since I gave up this troublesome scribbling, creature Legge. He has no occupation, & will write you a *quire* in the day,
if you would attend to him.

I send the enclosed, received this post, and I submit, that it would

3   William Henry Lambton, 1793–1866, brother of the first Earl.
4   John Legge, Houghton le Spring.
5   Rates levied, by the vestry, on all occupiers of property in a parish for the
     upkeep of the church and its furnishings.

be better to wait 'till March, as Walker[6] suggests, as no work can be done at the Harbour 'till after that time. And he will also be able to do more work in a day then, than in two at this season. And we must have as much out of him as we can get, during his stay; as his professional charge will be no joke. It may probably be advisable, in the mean time, to have a fresh survey of the Harbour made by a regular surveyor. But this we can discuss at meeting.

We are completely blocked up with snow, to day – our post lad could not get up from the harbour this morn[in]g, but as your Lordship's Letter of yesterday, has come to hand this even[in]g I expect mine of yesterday will have reached your Lordship. I also had a Letter from Mr McDonnell yesterday, to the same effect as he has written your Lordship.

I hope the weather will improve, and the roads be open, so as to enable your Lordship to reach Seaham to dinner on Thursday. I won't answer Watkin's[7] letter till I hear from, or see, your Lordship.

The Marq[ues]s of Londonderry   I have the honor [&c.]
                                                                   J[no] Buddle

170.

D/Lo/C142/36 (22)   Newcastle 7[th] May 1842

My Lord

I had the honor to receive your Lordship's letter of the 5[th] at Pensher yesterday with 'the statement' of the 27th Ulto., your Lordship's remarks thereon, Mr Gregson's answers and your Lordship's rejoinder.

I have perused the documents, but feel that they embrace too many difficult and complicated circumstances & considerations, for me to hazard a written opinion upon. So many collateral objects spring out of almost every branch of the various points embraced, and which may be placed in such various, and even anomalous points of view, as would involve a labyrinth of writing without eliciting a satisfactory result. Nothing but personal discussion, when ideas may be freely interchanged, can I think lead to any satisfactory result – on these complicated and important affairs.

6   Unidentified.
7   Unidentified.

If I comprehend your Lordship's object rightly it would be to raise the £45000 to liberate the personal trust, by mortgage on the Harbour and railway – instead of by selling the Grange Coal. This if it could be accomplished would in my mind be the more eligible plan, as it would enable us to keep, and work the Grange, by some means or other, as a separate and independent Colliery – altho' if the Regulat[io]n continues (which is, however, most problematical) there might be some difficulty in accomplishing.

We must always bear in mind that we are essentially a Coal family, and that therefore nothing but the most urgent necessity should by rights impel us to alienate any of that description of property. Which be it remembered, when brought into activity, gives infinitely more political influence than the mere landed property under which it lies.

If the Grange could be retained as a separate Colliery it would undoubtedly, in the end prove more beneficial to your Lordship than by sale.

I observe that the money proposed to be raised by the sale of the Grange Coal, is to be appropriated in the first instance, to the satisfying of the Trust liabilities. And the residue is to go to the winning of Seaham. It must however be remembered, that after satisfying the former object, the residue will be utterly inadequate to the latter.

I submit that your Lordship will be best able to arrive at some definite and practicable plan of arrangement at the present crisis of affairs, by personal communication with Messrs McDonnell & Gregson.

I enclose a statement of our Vend for the first 4 months of the year, by which your Lordship will perceive, that export trade of Steam Boat & Small Coals cuts no mean figure, and has greatly aided in keeping our wheels moving during the slack demand of the spring months, for best Coals. If the imposition of the 4/- duty takes place, it will inevitably greatly abridge this branch of our trade, and throw a greater weight of cost upon the working charges of the best Coals. In short it will be a *bad job* for us.[8]

By the by, there is a very good article in the Morning Post of

---

8   In his Budget statement on 11 Mar.1842 Peel proposed a duty of 4/- per ton on the export of all coals, to replace the existing (since 1834) duty only on exports in foreign ships. After objections and lobbying by the trade, the duty was altered, on 14 June, to 4/- for foreign ships, 2/- for British ships, and 1/- for small coals. *Parl. Deb.*, 3rd ser., lxi, cols 448–9, 474; lxiii, cols 1545–81. The duty was abolished for British ships in 1845 and for foreign ships in 1850.

yesterday, on the affair of the Coal Duty. The question is very fairly stated, and the observations upon it are sensible.

The Factors' Letters, to day, state that the plans agreed upon, this day week, have prevented a fall of 2/- per ton in the price of the best Coals. And if we only supplied them properly from this end, they entertain no doubt of being able to maintain the prices at such a standard as will remunerate the ship-owners, and maintain the present prices to the Coal-owners also.

Our Comm[itt]ees meet on this, & other business on Monday, when we must endeavour to get matters put right amongst ourselves on this matter. Nich[olas] Wood & Geo[rge] Johnson have come over to my way of thinking upon it. And Morton who is expected home tomorrow, will hardly, I think, with 3 or 4 more hold out against us.

The Marq[ues]s of Londonderry   I have the honor [&c.]
                                                             J[no] Buddle

171.

D/LO/C142/36 (49)   Pensher 9[th] May 1842

My Lord

I had the honor to receive your Lordship's Letter of the 7[th] yesterday, and I have this morn[in]g seen in the *Times* the report of what passed last Friday in the Ho[use] of Lords relative to the employment of Boys & Girls in the Collieries.[9]

Nothing could be more judicious & correct than your Lordship's statement – it was as proper, as it was prompt, and the Coal-owners of this Country ought to feel greatly obliged to your Lordship for having placed the matter in its true point of view.

Neither Women, nor Girls are *ever employed* in the pits under-

---

9   *Parl. Deb.*, 3rd ser., lxiii, col. 197. A Royal Commission had been appointed in 1840 to enquire into conditions of child labour. Its first report, published early in 1842 (Parliamentary Papers (1842), vol. 15 (380): *Children's Employment Commission. First Report of the Commissioners: Mines*) dealt with the mining industry. Petitions asking for government action were presented to Parliament. In the House of Lords on 6 May Lord Londonderry protested, on behalf of the North East coal industry, against the implication that women were everywhere employed in degrading conditions. On 7 June Lord Ashley (later seventh Earl of Shaftesbury, *ODNB*) introduced in the House of Commons a bill to forbid the employment of women and girls, and of boys under the age of thirteen.

ground in this district – and in your Lordship's Collieries, no Women
or Girls are even employed about the Pits *above ground* much
We don't employ Boys underground, as *Trappers*, under 8 years of
age – Drivers 11, and Putters from 14 to 22.

None of our Seams are under 3 ft 3 in. thick, and we have them
of various thicknesses up to 6 feet. The Children's Employment
Comm[[ission] have all those things stated in their Returns made
according to their own forms, & directions. In the course of the Week
I will send your Lordship copies of those returns – if they should
be of no other use, they will give your Lordship some interesting
statistical information.

At our Committee meeting to day we received a copy of the Resolutions of a meeting of the Ship-owners' Society of South Shields
– approving of the re-establishment of the factors' regulation &
requesting *our* aid in carrying it into effect. We have called the attention of the Ship-owners Societies, at N[orth] Shields, Sunderland,
and Stockton to the subject, and expect to receive their favourable
answers against next Sat[ur]d[a]y.

On looking over the returns of the Vends for last mo[nth] I observe
that we are 496 tons 1 cwt *over* – while Hetton is 5519 tons 19 cwt and
Lambton 5965 tons 10 cwt *short* of their Issues for the month – this
made me *chuckle a bit*.

The Marques]s of Londonderry   I have the honor [&c.]
                                                      J^no Buddle

P.S. The Drifts, or galleries, in which our putter-lads work, are 2,3,
and 4 yards wide – none less than *two*.

172.

D/Lo/C142/36 (50)   Walls-end Sa[urday] Evening 14th May 1842

My Lord
    I had the honor to receive your Lordship's Letter of the 12th by
yesterday's post, and in the first place beg to thank your Lordship
for the very high compliment you have paid me *personally*.

I however, hope that the line which your Lordship has adopted,
with respect to the Duty on Coals, has been the result of due reflection – and convention as to the impolicy of this measure. After all
the evidence which has now been elicited – it seems impossible that
any unprejudiced mind should not discover, that in proposing this

tax, as a source of revenue, Sir R. Peel must have laboured under an erroneous opinion as to the real nature, and bearing, of our foreign export trade in Coals. And I can hardly doubt, from the information which he has received on the subject – backed by the opinion of your Lordship, and other influential persons, but he will give it up. I learn from H. Taylor *privately* that the Duke of Northumberland has taken the same line, with Sir *Robert* as your Lordship has done. I have received a Letter from a friend in London by this Post in which he says, that he has learned, through a confidential channel, that Sir Robert *has given up the notion of the Coal-duty altogether*. I hope this may prove to be correct, as it will render any prejudicial change in our arrangements at the Collieries unnecessary. But 'we must not holler before we are out of the wood'.

On the question of the Coal tax I beg to recommend to your Lordship's perusal a pamphlet published in London – entitled 'Observations on the proposed duties, on the Exportation of Coals, &c.' I have desired our Coal-trade Clerk in London to send your Lordship a copy – it contains much valuable information

The employment of Females in Collieries &c. I brought your Lordship's suggestions on this affair under the cons[ideratio]n of the Executive Comm[itt]ee to day, who expressed their admiration of the bold manner in which your Lordship has taken up the Cudgels for the trade. And on Monday the matter will be brought before the general Comm[itt]ee. And in as short a time as possible your Lordship will receive an official communication on the subject.

With respect to the employment of Girls in Pits, the article in the Chronicle I think only refers to Staffordshire, Lancashire, and Yorkshire. *No such practice exists in* Durham, & Northumberland – if the contrary should be stated, it may be refuted by referring to Leifchild's[10] report to the Children's Employment Comm[ission]. It is to be found in the Appendix Part the 1st, page 513.

Leifchild was the sub-commissioner appointed to investigate, the nature of the Children's employment &c. in the Collieries of our District, but he did not find a single girl employed in the Pits. This abomination, belongs to other Coal Districts in England Wales &

---

10 J.R. Leifchild, one of the Commissioners enquiring into the employment of children, and part author of the first report. Leifchild confessed to Buddle that the Report was 'most imperfectly developed' even though it was the result of 'slavish labour'. He acknowledged that Durham did not disclose the 'painful instances' so common in other areas. Leifchild to Buddle, 18 May 1842 (National Coal Board Manuscripts, DCRO, NCB 1/JB/1783).

Scotland – the Charge is too true – I have myself witnessed it, in all those places.

Girls worked in the Pits, formerly in this Country – when a Boy I knew some old Women, who had been brought up, 'Pit Lasses' – in the Pits. But the practice began to decline a century ago – and totally ceased 50 years since.

The Marq[ues]s of Londonderry   I have the honor [&c.]
                                                                                          J^{no} Buddle

I shall write from Pensher, on Monday or Tuesday, on other matters.

173.

D/Lo/C142/36 (51)   Pensher 16th May 1842

My Lord

The time of the united Committee has been so entirely taken up with the affair of the factors' regulation, and correspondence with Ship-owners, Societies on this subject – that nothing more could be done about the report of the Childrens Employment Commissioners, than to appoint a special sub-committee to examine it and the Evidence on which it is founded. This Committee is to meet next Friday morn[in]g and in the mean-time the members are to collect such information as they can – to enable your Lordship to disprove any erroneous statements that may be made in the Lords, on the subject – and Mr Bell & other members will attend to it in the Commons. What we have to guard against is any obnoxious legislative interference in the established customs of our peculiar race of Pitmen. The stock can only be kept up by *breeding* – it never could be recruited from an *adult population*. It is like bringing lads up to the sea – only the Pit Lad's life is incomparably better and more comfortable than the sailor's. But if our meddling – morbid *humanity mongers*, get it infused into their heads, that it is cruel, unnatural, slavery to work *in the dark* – and to be *imprisoned* 12 hours a day, in the Pit – a *screw* in the system, will be let loose, and there will be no knowing the end of it.[11]

---

11 On 13 June the united committee resolved that the proper lower age limit
      for the employment of boys should be ten, and that Buddle should lobby
      Lord Ashley. The latter saw both Buddle and North East MPs, and expressed

We are all going on well here, and have abundance of ships for our small Issues (only 42 per thou[sand] this month) but Lambton, & Hetton, are very short. Morton is in the *dumps* about it, and unless the factors' regulation, bring those parties up, into *position* again, I am apprehensive of their being compelled to freight, give extra measure, lower prices or some other mischief – which may bring evil upon us.

The Marq[ues]s of Londonderry   I have the honor [&c.]

                                                  J^no Buddle

174.

D/Lo/C142/36 (25)   Pensher 18th May 1842

My Lord

I am glad to learn by your Lordship's letter of yesterday that you have got all matters so satisfactorily settled with Sir John Beckett & J. Gregson – and that your Lordship can honor us, with your presence – to break the ground at the Grange Winning.

I however find it advisable to delay this operation a while. On going carefully through the investigation of the mining surveys & sections, I find that I cannot fix upon the precise spot, as the most eligible situation for the Winning without ascertaining the depth of the Hutton seam, at the River-side, near the Wood-well House. This can only be done by Boring; but as I don't expect the depth will exceed 20 fath[om]s it will be accomplished in 3 weeks or so, as there are no difficulties of quick sands &c.

Great benefit may result from this Boring, as it may prevent us from making a false step, in the outset, and we shall lose little, by the delay, as the machinery, & apparatus, for commencing to sink may be collected on the premises in the mean time.

Probably too, this delay may better suit your Lordship's convenience – it will bring us nearer the 30th of June – an *auspicious day*. And why should we not break ground on the day your Lordship takes the field again, as *Commander in Chief*?

As I understand it to be your Lordship's plan, to celebrate L[or]d Seaham's Birth-day in August – this Grange affair might, therefore, be considered as the prelude to it. And I submit that your Lordship

willingness to accept an age limit of ten provided that boys only worked alternate days.

had better dine here privately – as if you dine at the Waterloo your Lordship will be beset by the Freemen, and more expence will be incurred than need be. However there is time enough to arrange all this.

I have just returned from Seaham where there is an *abundance of ships* to carry off our *Issue* & Foreigners for Steam Boat & Small – as many as we can work. A bad accident occurred there, on Monday – One of the Waggon Riders – one of the best of the men, & a very decent fellow – slipped his foot & fell before the waggons – 3 of the wheels crushed one of his legs to attoms, and injured the other – this was about 11 o'clock, in the fore-noon, and by some blundering, a surgeon was not procured 'till 7 o'clock p.m. when the limb was amputated. But the poor fellow was so exhausted by the loss of blood that he died immediately after the operation. He has left a widow and 3 small children.

I met Morton yesterday – almost in a state of despair – the ship-owners are still holding off, and in addition to his shorts of last mo[nth] he is more than 3000 tons short – so far this mo[nth] – he sees no remedy but reducing the price 4/. per Ch. This must however be avoided if possible.

I know nothing about T.M. Videan but will inquire about him, when I go to Newcastle tomorrow.

The Marq[ues]s of Londonderry   I have the honor [&c.]
                                                                    J^no Buddle

175.

D/Lo/C142/36 (62)   Walls-end 17th July 1842

My Lord

I have the honor to acknowledge the receipt of your Lordship's Letter of the 15th with it's Enclosures.

I congratulate your Lordship on the successful result of the noble *stand-up fight*, which your Lordship has made for us against such fearful odds, and cordially thank your Lordship for having, thrown your protecting Shield over me, against Lord Clanricarde's attack.[12]

---

12 On 24 June Lord Londonderry presented in the House of Lords a petition from the North East coal trade against Lord Ashley's bill (*Parl. Deb.*, 3rd ser., lxiv, cols 338–42). He quoted a letter from Buddle stating that he himself had started pit work at not quite six years old. The bill received its third reading

Your Lordship has certainly taken the *sting* out of the Bill, as regards the Northern Collieries – but I see that the clause for underground Inspection remains. I scarcely think it will ever be acted upon – yet retaining the power is not so well.

I will see the Times newspaper at the Central Exchange to-morrow – and will endeavour to get your Lordship's speeches inserted in the Newcastle papers – as the only means of letting the trade know generally – the noble Efforts which your Lordship has made on this occasion.

The business of the Assizes is hampering me exceedingly. I expected to have been done with it yesterday – but am engaged on a Special Jury cause – to-morrow – a tedious case of succession, which is expected to last the whole day. This is bothering & throwing me very much back in my legitimate occupation, as I have not yet been able to get through N. Wood's paper – nor to examine James Walker's plans & report of the Har[bo]ur which arrived on the 13th.

The C[oal] T[rade] Comm[itt]ee meet to-morrow – but my engagement at the Court, will not I apprehend allow me to attend. I will however manage to put your Lordship's dispatches of the 15th into the Chairman's hands, as the sooner the Committee, are apprised of the efforts your Lordship has made against this obnoxious Bill the better.

The Issue for the remainder of the month, will be given out to-morrow. It will I apprehend, from the large arrears of *shorts* – at Lambton, and the two Hettons &c. be very small.

The Marq[ues]s of Londonderry   I have the honor {&c.]
                                                                        Jno Buddle

in the Commons on 4 July. On 12 July Lord Londonderry presented in the Lords an amendment to make the lower age limit for boys ten instead of thirteen. In the Lords debate on the second reading he argued for delay and further investigation, but failed to divide the House (*Parl. Deb.*, 3rd ser., lxv, cols 101–29). Some amendments regarding the date of entry into force of the ban on the employment of women were accepted by the Commons, and the bill received its third reading in the Lords on 1 August. A.J. Taylor, 'The Third Marquess of Londonderry and the North Eastern Coal Trade', *DUJ*, new ser., xvii (1955–6), pp. 21–7, is somewhat unfair on Buddle's conduct, as is O. Macdonagh, 'Coal Mines Regulation: the First Decade, 1842–52', in R. Robson (ed.), *Ideas and Institutions of Victorian Britain* (London, 1967), p. 62. Cf. A.J. Heesom, 'The Northern Coal Owners and the Opposition to the Coal Mines Act of 1842', *International Review of Social History*, xxv (1980), pp. 236–71; *idem*, 'Lord Ashley's Coal Mines Act, Social Reform, and "Social Control"', *Historical Journal*, xxiv (1982), pp. 69–88.

176.

D/Lo/C142/37 (3)   Walls-end Sa[turday] even[in]g 27th Aug[us]t 1842

My Lord

I beg to congratulate your Lordship, on the successful manner in which our *Grand Shew*,[13] at both the Collieries & Harbour went off.

The immense multitude of Strangers at Pensher, as well as our own people, separated (and dissolved like snow in a gentle thaw) in the even[in]g in the best possible good humour – highly delighted with the entertainment they had received, & all they had seen. And notwithstanding the immense croud of Strangers from the neighbouring Coll[ierie]s which surrounded our tables, not a single act of intrusion, or irregularity was committed.

The harbour affair passed off equally well. Agreeably to your Lordship's request I addressed the men at the tables, in a style suited to the occasion, & the Company. After apologizing for your Lordship's not being able to address them in person, I complemented them, on their respectable appearance, and good behaviour – complemented them also, on their abilities as capital *trencher-men* &c. and concluded by expressing a hope that they would receive ships into the Harbour and exert themselves so, as to enable us to *clear* our Pit-heaps of Coals, as *clean* as they had *cleared* their Plates of the Beef. Great applause.

The moral to be drawn from the scenes which we have witnessed on this occasion, at the Coll[ierie]s & Harbour is, that if the high aristocracy of the country were more frequently to find occasions to bring themselves into personal intercourse with the working classes, and shew them a little countenance, & kindness, Chartism, and all other absurd causes, of political excitement, would evaporate like the white mist in September before the sun-beams. In this respect your Lordship has shewn a brilliant and laudable example. And it would be well if other Noblemen would follow it, on fitting occasions – it would be the means of verifying the old English proverb, that 'Giff-gaff, makes good fellowship'.

I now turn to a less agreeable subject – the gloomy state of the Coal-trade. The price of Stewart's W[alls]end, has fallen to 20/- per

---

13   To celebrate Lord Seaham's coming of age: he was born on 21 April 1821. The Duke of Buckingham, even more impecunious than Londonderry, had a week of festivities at Stowe in 1844 for the coming of age of his eldest son, the Marquis of Chandos. See David and Eileen Spring, 'The Fall of the Grenvilles, 1844–48', *Huntington Library Quarterly*, xix, no. 2 (Feb. 1956), p. 165.

ton in London & Lambton's, Hetton &c. to 19/9 & 19/6 – with nearly 600 ships in London loaden & discharging their cargoes. At 20/- per ton in London, the ship-owners, are only making 6/- per ton freight – which considering that they have to lie from 3 to 5 weeks before they can get delivered is absolutely ruinous. As at the prices of 19/6 & 19/9 Lambton, Hetton &c. would only pay 5/6 & 5/9 freight – they cannot get a single ship to load on their own acc[oun]t and are therefore obliged to freight, and are paying 7/- per ton. The consequence is that our best customers are leaving us, and I *foresee* – that in a short time we shall be totally without ships, unless we either freight – *uphold* i.e. guarantee the same freight, as others, are paying or reduce the price of the Coals – to the equivalent standard of the *freighters*.

The cost of our Coals to the ship-owner including prime cost of 11/6 per ton – coast lights & other charges, is 14/- and whatever the Coals sell for beyond that sum is left to him for freight. Consequently, at the present sell[in]g price of 20/- only 6/- is left for freight. But Lambton, Hetton, Haswell, So[uth] Hetton &c. are giving 7/- freight – and as their Coals are only selling for 19/9 and 19/6 – say 19/6 – they are losing 1/6 a ton, or 3/11¾ per Ch. as to pay 7/- freight the Coals ought to sell at 21/. As Stewart's W[alls]-E[nd] always sell at 3d per ton more, it would require an abatement of 3/3 ¾ per Ch. on them, to pay the ship-owner as well as the 7/- freight.

As it is but too clear what must be the result of this state of things, unless an immediate stop is put to the freighting system, I have called a meeting of the representatives of all the best Wear &c. Collieries – next Friday – to see if they can adopt some plan to prevent the necessity of your Lordship reducing the price of your Coals, which must be the immediate consequence, if this freighting system is continued, as my apprehension is, that the parties *will not be able* to discontinue the freighting. I must request the favour of your Lordship's Instructions for my government at the meeting. There are 3 modes of procedure open to us – *all bad*, viz. freighting, upholding freight – or reducing the price of the Coals, & the question is, which should we prefer. If there were a chance of this only being a temporary depression, I would prefer upholding – but if it were likely to be permanent, then I would at once reduce the price 2/- 3/- or 4/- per Ch. as the necessity of the case may require. I shall be glad to receive your Lordship's advice, on this matter before next Friday & have the honor [&c.]

The Marq[ues]s of Londonderry   J[no] Buddle

177.

D/Lo/C142/37 (7)   Walls-end Sunday morn[in]g
                                        11th Sep[tember] 1842

My Lord

After a long and tedious negotiation yesterday, we came to the enclosed arrangement with Morton, Wood, Donkin & Philipson – for the purpose of putting an end to the Seaham & Seaton partnership affair – without *Law*.

I hope your Lordship will approve of the terms, as we have obtained all our chief objects – without parting with any *money*. All that we concede is the working of 3000 tons of Coals – and the letting of 100 acres of our Seaham Coal to the Seaton Co. for which they are to pay a tentale of 30/-

J. Gregson assisted me in the negotiation, but Mr McDonnell was not present, and is not yet informed of the result of our meeting, as he had gone off to Ravensworth, before we broke up. And I understand he intends to start for Glenarm by the Carlisle train this morn[in]g, and J. Gregson went to Durham last night on his way to London.

At our Committee meeting yesterday we received the report of the Durham *Detailment*, which on the whole was favourable, as all the reporting parties except 2 or 3 who from unavoidable circumstances could not attend – agreed to put themselves under control, and to act upon provisional Bases – until their permanent Bases can be fixed by reference. It is therefore possible that on Wed[nesday] a *cobbling*-up of the Regulation may be made – so as to prevent the ruinous consequences of an immediate rupture. I however consider a reduction of 4/- inevitable & all I anticipate from the most favourable result of Wed[nesday]'s meeting, is that it may let us *more easily down*, and avert this *frightful* consequences that will result from a further decline of prices in London – on our *up-held* ships.

We have all this mo[nth] upheld 7/- freight – which requires the price in London to be 20/9 – to give us our full price of 30/6 for W[alls]end.

The price in London last Wed[nesday] was only 19/9 – or 1/- per ton below the standard which reduces our price 2/8 per Ch. But if a break-up of the trade takes place it is expected – with upwards of 300 ships at market, the best Coals will fall to 16/- which would incur a loss of 4/9 per ton or 12/7 per Ch. on the cargoes of all our up-held ships. The idea of such a result is really terrific, and we must if possible avert such a catastrophe. We had better lie upon our oars (I mean the *whole* trade) for a fortn[igh]t and not Vend any Coals at all – in order to get the market cleared rather than risk such an over-whelming loss. I really believe the Owners of the best Collieries, will submit to any limitation of Issue, whatever, for the remainder of the month, in order to get the market cleared – every body is *dead beaten*, and nonplussed. And the Banks are *holding hard* so that no assistance can be had from them.

I am going to York by the train[14] this morn[in]g, but expect to return tomorrow eve[nin]g or Tuesday morn[in]g, and I shall be anxious to communicate the result of Wed[nesday]s meeting to your Lordship with the least possible delay.

The Marq[ues]s of Londonderry   I have the honor [&c.]
                                                            J[no] Buddle

178.

D/Lo/C142/37 (34)   Walls-end 6[th] Nov[ember] 1842

My Lord

I have the honor to acknowledge the receipt of your Lordship's Enclosure of yesterday with Mr Burdon's letter, and your Lordship's answer.

The reasons urged by Mr Burdon, embraces the very principle on which I declined the appointment of Magistrate, so long, & at length with considerable reluctance accepted it. I was named at the same time Morton was – and I knew at the time from a friend on the Bench – the strong objections which were taken by the Magistracy to the appointment of Agents. But in addition to this, there was an insuper-able difficulty opposed to Morton's appointment – as an *uncertified Bankrupt*. In my case however it rather looks like straining at 'gnats & swallowing camels' as on referring to the list your Lordship will find several individuals quite as thorough-going Agents & Managers of Collieries as I am. I might mention Stobart of Etherley, Lamb of Ryton, W[iilia]m Bell & Ramsay of Derwenthaugh. They look to the *swarm* that are Coal-owners and Coal-proprietors – even Mr Burdon himself a Coal-proprietor – living close upon his Lessees Collieries where he is liable to be called upon daily to adjudicate between them

---

14 It was possible to go by train from Gateshead to York from 30 March 1841, with several changes and two omnibuses. A continuous link was not open until 1844. Tomlinson, *North Eastern Railway*, pp. 430, 432.

and their workmen. In short, is their [*sic*] any man on the Bench, that may not in some way or other be open to the imputation of *partiality*? Fortunately however, the jarring Elements, and Interests, which assemble on the bench, will always operate as an effectual safe-guard & guarantee, against any undue partiality. I was told by a friend on the bench that my appointment by your Lordship[15] had been the subject of animadversion – not so much from being in violation of the *principle* alluded to by Mr Burdon – as being considered a *satellite* of your Lordship's. I told my friend that I felt I had been placed upon the Bench by your Lordship's good opinion – that I felt confident, I should do nothing to discredit that opinion – and that I certainly should not *sneak off* again merely because my appointment, as an Agent was thought to be in violation of a principle laid down – by whom?

I assisted at the Petty Sessions at Gateshead on the 23rd Ulto. and at Houghton last Thursday – there was not a single case in either instance in which I could be supposed to have the least personal Interest, feeling, or bias – If any such case should occur I can have no difficulty in keeping myself clear of it.

I think your Lordship's answer to Mr Burdon is excellent it is written 'suaviter et fortiter', and as regards the allusions to myself I feel deeply indebted to your Lordship.

The Marq[ues]s of Londonderry   I have the honor [&c.]
                                                   J^no Buddle

179.

D/Lo/C142/37 (53)   Pensher 27th Dec[ember] 1842

My Lord
    I had the honor to receive your Lordship's paper of Observations on the proposed Rules for the future regulation of the Coal trade – dated the 22nd Inst. I have read your Lordship's remarks and opinions, which you have given at considerable length, with great attention, and think the *pith* of them may be condensed into two brief statements viz.

---

15 Lord Londonderry was appointed Lord Lieutenant of Durham in 1842. See A.J. Heesom, 'Problems of Patronage: Lord Londonderry's Appointment as Lord Lieutenant of County Durham', *DUJ*, new ser., xxxix (1977–8), pp. 169–77.

1st. If all parties sign these Rules against the next meet[in]g your Lordship may be disposed to continue in the gen[era]l regulation.

2nd. If not, your Lordship would for *one year*, try the experiment of a regulation or arrangement of the best Collieries – if it should not succeed – then fall back upon our former position.

My present conviction is, that we *shall not* get all parties to sign against the next general meeting, and therefore that we shall either have to fall back upon the 2nd position or have a general scramble. I am afraid there will be as much difficulty in bringing some of the best Coll[ierie]s into *Line*, as there will be in arranging a gen[era]l Regulation.

I have very little doubt of Lambton, Hetton, N[orth] Hetton & probably S[outh] Hetton going hand in hand with us. But I very much doubt Thornley, Cassop, Crow-trees, Wingate-grange, Castle-eden &c. Several of the latter I apprehend won't come into any reasonable Bounds, until they are *thrashed* into them. Then have we the power of *thrashing* them? Again what are we to do with the Quakers on the Tees – who plainly tell us, that they cannot (say won't) abstain from freighting. The whole affair is so beset with difficulties, that I really do not at all see my way clear.

A project for establishing a Factors' regulation for the best Coals *only* is now under the cons[ideratio]n of the Com[itt]ee as without some such measure, it is believed that prices will fall to a ruinous extent. Whether this scheme may be rendered practicable I cannot yet tell. The London market still continues in the same *gorged* state. Last Friday 430 ¼ cargoes remained unsold. There were 41 cargoes of Stewart's, and only *one* sold at 21/3, 11 of Lambton's & 3 sold at 21/- and 29 of Hetton & only 2 sold at 21/- It therefore appears that there is a sufficient supply of Coals, in London, for the whole month of Jan[uar]y without a single cargo more being sent. Nothing can be more discouraging than this – the fineness of the season is no doubt the chief cause of this state of things, in London. And the foreign demand for Steam Coal, being almost wholly at a stand, the Coll[ierie]s supplying it, are pouring it into the London market which aggravates the evil.

I am afraid that poor fellow, Smith[16] has got into the *wrong box*, with his Gas Scheme at Seaham. I send his letter to me with his proposal for a Light Ho]use] together with Lee's remarks thereon. And I really don't see what we can do for him. If he could have

16 Unidentified.

lighted the Harbour, as cheap as we light it ourselves we might have given him a preference altho' the whole of our *staff* on the place are unfavourable to the Gas even on equal terms, in point of expence.

I send the Boy with this, as in case your Lordship or Mr McDonnell should have any thing to communicate, I can receive it a day sooner by him than I should by the Post.

The Marq[ues]s of Londonderry   I have the honor [&c.]
                                                              J^{no} Buddle

180.

D/Lo/C142/38 (21)   Newcastle 4th Feb[ruar]y 1843

My Lord

I had the honor to receive your Lordship's Letter of the 2nd this morn[in]g with the enclosed. I hope we may shortly be relieved by a great order for Steam Coal – else I don't know what is to become of us as our best Coal-trade seems to be going headlong *to the Dogs*.

Your Lordship's observations, as to the apparent want of decision in the trade, as to putting an end to the regulation at once, is very true. But at the same time it must be taken into consideration that so decisive & important a step should not be taken rashly, and that it is more prudent to temporize, so long as any reasonable hope of averting so great a calamity – both individually & collectively – remains. The matter is now however in my opinion hopeless, and I expect nothing but a breaking up of the whole system this day week. We may therefore calculate on a fall of prices to or even below *zero*, as the best Coals making anything like a *rush* to vend an extra quantity or even to support prices at more than 24/- is in the present state of the market *utterly out of the question*. If we can get our Receipts to cover Wages – it will be as much as we can expect, until the Storm abates – but remittances, or surpluses, *cannot be looked for*.

At yesterday's market there were 111 cargoes of best Wear Coals for sale, and only twelve sold for the annexed list – the highest price 20/- !!! The second class sold more freely and supported better prices. This shews clearly that the best are at, or rather above their fair competitive price. If therefore they maintain present prices they risk being supplanted by the second class. It therefore appears but too plain that no other course is left open to the first class, but to reduce their prices so low, as that the 2nd class cannot *afford* to meet them in the market. And I think that reduction must in the first instance be 6/- per Ch. This, no doubt, will be a desperate *plunge*, but I don't see that anything short of a miracle can avert it. I met some of the recusants to day going to the Office to sign the Agree[men]t – but still there are other matters to be arranged as well as merely signing the rules which will I am persuaded set us all *adrift*.

This state of things has for the present put a stop to all the talk about the Seaham Winning – and it certainly is not for us to press it. By the Agree[men]t we have got the load of the Seaton Certain Rents

(£1760 I think from memory) off our shoulders. We can therefore lie *upon our oars*, without expence as long as the Seaton Co. please. And in the mean time the Int[eres]t on the amo[un]t of the Certain Rent, which we have paid, is *accumulating* for our benefit.

I am very much of your Lordship's opinion, that it will not be convenient to some of our Neighbours to commence the Seaham Winning, with the best Trade last year, and the great expenditure on new Railway &c. Raising money otherwise than by *borrowing* for this object is impossible, and who without collateral security will lend money for such a purpose?

The Darlington & N[ew]castle R[ail]W[ay] Co. have broken ground in the Grange & are pushing on with great vigour.[1] I expect to let the Grange Quarry to the contractor on advantageous terms.

The Marq[ues]s of Londonderry   I have the honor [&c.]
                                               J[no] Buddle

Best Coals at market 23[rd] Feb[ruar]y 1843

Stewart's	19	none
Lambton's	20	4
Hetton	36	2
Haswell	7	1
Bradyll	7	none
Caradoc	12	3
Tees	10	2
	111	12

41½ cargoes in all were sold. Consequently 29½ cargoes of *inferiors* were sold. 271 ships remained unsold.

181.

D/Lo/C142/38 (27)   Walls-end Sunday morn[in]g
                                     26[th] Feb[ruar]y 1843

My Lord
    I just have time to save post to inform your Lordship that a

---

1   See Tomlinson, *North Eastern Railway*, pp. 432–5, 438–41, 449–50. The section of the line between Rainton and Belmont was opened on 15 April 1844.

gen[era]l meeting of Coll[ier]y Viewers & Agents was held, at Newcastle yesterday – to establish a reduced scale of Wages. The Binding of the Pitmen is fixed for Sa[turday] the 18th of March.

The guaranteed wages of the Pitmen are reduced from 15/- to 13/- per week.

How the Pitmen may take all this remains to be seen. On their part they are not idle – they are meeting constantly – precisely as they did prior to the great strike in 1832 – their precise object is not yet know [sic] but there are some active delegates from Wakefield amongst them – which augurs no good.

At present matters have a gloomy aspect and unless trade opens out, so as to give the Pitmen better employment – nothing but starvation stares them in the face. In many instances they are only working 2 or 3 days in the week & earning 9 or 10/-. This we know they won't long endure with patience, and an outbreak may be expected.

I have little to add on the general affairs of the trade, prices in London advanced 3 on best Coals, last Friday – pulling Stewart's up to 20/- but only about 6 cargoes of best Coals, in all sold.

The sole cause of this depression is the idea that our Regulation will be broken up, on the 1st March & that there is no sort of understanding amongst the factors as to the scale of prices they are to adopt, each market-day. They all declare there is no necessity for keeping prices so low.

More signatures have been obtained to the Agree[men]t for continuing the Reg[ulatio]n. I am not certain whether *all* who are within reach of post have not signed or undertaken to sign.

At the meet[in]g of the Comm[itt]ee to morrow – if this should be found to be the case, an effort – as *a last effort* is to be made to get a Factors regulation without rotation as planned at Sunderland, carried into effect. If this fails the Reg[ulatio]n *must* cease. My own feeling I own is for *breaking up* & reducing prices, as the only chance of extinguishing the *Ephemera* which are working our prices like a slow paralysis. I however feel that I cannot take such responsibility upon myself, as this decisive step would incur. I expect Morton home in the course of the week & if he joins me in this & your Lordship & Mr McDonnell approve it – I would strike the Blow – but query whether our Bankers should not be sounded – they are deeply interested in the consequences. I had a letter from Hunter yesterday, he says he is very busy & does not expect to get home before the end of this week. I hope he will not be longer detained, as he is much wanted at home.

The Marq[ues]s of Londonderry   I have the honor [&c.]
                                                              J[no] Buddle

Our friend Anderson[2] is now beginning to get contract ships for Steam Coal.[3]

182.

D/Lo/C142/38 (38)   Walls-end 2[nd] Mar[ch] 1843

My Lord

   I have your Lordship's several letters of the 27th & 28th Ulto. On the affairs of the Coal-trade I do not feel that I can add any thing to what I have already said. If the regulation goes on (of which however I still entertain great doubt) it must unquestionably be conducted strictly in accordance with the Rules. I am sure it cannot be carried on beneficially unless supported, the plan prepared for the management of the market, of which I enclose a copy of the heads. But when we look at the list of Collieries who are to be brought into this measure it is impossible not to doubt the practicability of carrying it into effect. We shall however be better able to judge, after we receive the answers of Individuals to the enclosed circular, on Monday. I have had a letter from Morton in London, who will be at home to day. He sees nothing for us, but to reduce our prices to 24/- to enable us to regain possession of the market by driving the 2nd class out. This will be a terrible sacrifice but if it becomes necessary, it must be submitted to. I shall see Morton, Wood, H. Taylor, Donkin & Philipson on Monday – for a consultation s to the course we should pursue with the best Coals in the very embarrassing position in which they are placed. My feeling I own, is for breaking up the gen[era]l Regulation, but unless they should concur with me in this I do not think I could be justified, in taking so great a responsibility upon myself – independently of certain prudential consid-

---

2   Robert Anderson, Newcastle fitter.
3   The draft of a reply is written on this letter. Lord Londonderry regarded the decision to reduce wages as perfectly wise. The magistrates and constables must keep the peace. The cost of provisions had fallen so that hardship would be less. In the circumstances of the trust, he had no power to act on regulation, but Mr McDonnell would act for the best on the question: if Morton and Wood agreed with Buddle, and the best collieries stood by each other, it seemed madness not to attempt to crush the ephemera.

erations alluded to in a former letter. If the regulation can be firmly established we might try it another year – as we should certainly make *some profit* under it. But if broken up – our making any profit at all, for 12 mo[nths] is *more than doubtful*.

I should much question the prudence of publishing your Lordship's letters to the Committee, under any circumstances. It w[oul]d only shew that there was disunion amongst the Coal-owners – which is just what the Public wish for. And I cannot see any possible good that would result from it.

I was not aware that the valuation of the Collieries at the time of your Lordship's marriage pressed. It will be a laborious task, as to shew the increase of the property, all the changes which have taken place, in the mean time must be accurately traced which will give occupation to an expert accountant for some time, as all the Books & acc[ount]s for 23 years will have to be referred to. Probably, your Lordship may be able to get Cowan to undertake the job under my direction, as it is not possible for me to undertake the labour of it without neglecting every thing else.

I don't know what has become of Hunter. I have only had a single note from him saying that he was very busy & did not expect to get home before the end of this week. I hope he will not be longer detained as he is wanted at home.

The Marq[ues]s of Londonderry   I have the honor [&c.]
                                                 J^no Buddle

183.

D/Lo/C142/38 (34)   Walls-end Sunday morn[in]g 5th Mar[ch] 1843

My Lord

Just as I was leaving N[ew]castle yesterday afternoon I received a large packet from Mr Walters[4] with a message for me to forward it – which I now do accordingly.

I also rec[eive]d your Lordship's letter of the 3rd and have nothing to say on the miserable state of the Coal trade, further, than that I think the regulation will not survive over tomorrow's Comm[itt]ee meet[in]g. And in anticipation of this event, I have called a *private* meet[in]g of the rep[resentative]s of the principal best Collieries to

4   Unidentified.

endeavour to devise some plan to prevent our going by the ears together, and running down our prices ruinously low. Nothing can stay the breaking up of the Regulation, except the improving state of the London market – but this would merely be clinging to a straw.

Hindhaugh has balanced last year's acc[oun]ts & I enclose the result, which shews that under Regulat[io]n *with all it's faults* we can still make profit. Without it we shall I fear make little or none for a length of time. There only appears to be one line for us to take – viz. to put down prices *so low* that none but the comparatively cheap-working Coll[ierie]s can live –and the rest must be *killed off*. This will be an effectual remedy, but it will be a tedious & costly one. I cannot however devise any other & we can never again contemplate our present scale of prices.

I have nothing further to observe relative to your Lordship's Letters to the Comm[itt]ee – the prudence, & expediency, of publishing them is entirely for your Lordship's consideration. But I cannot comprehend what possible good can result from such a step.

I do not comprehend your Lordship's mean[in]g as to it's 'being desirable that Messrs Robson[5] & others should be discharged'. If your Lordship thinks the Coll[ierie]s can be carried on *without Viewers*, I must at once honestly & frankly tell your Lordship that they can not – and I could not incur the responsibility of such a state of things, where life & property is so extensively risked. Your Lordship will please to take into consideration the *long period*, which your Collieries have fortunately gone on, without any serious catastrophe whatever – and then I think your Lordship will feel disposed to think something more favourably of the services of the Viewers.

I will set about the statem[en]t of the Coll[ierie]s when I go to Pensher tomorrow & it will be completed with all the expedition circumstances will permit.

I send the enclosed Letter of Cloves, the Coal merchant, to Lee as a specimen of what we have to expect under a fighting trade. The *assumed* complaint against Stewart's is most exaggerated. I am sure the complaint of Stewart's being *coarse & full of dross* is false. Since they first sunk in price every possible attention has been paid to send them of better size. clean & good –the screens have been widened so as to take 8 to 12 Ch. of small *more* out of Stewart's per day at the Alexandrina pit alone which [is a][6] prodigious sacrifice.

---

5   John Robson, viewer at Rainton.

6   A couple of words seem to be missing at the turn of the page.

But the truth is, that from the large proportion of Pillar working we have, our Coals cannot be produced so lumpy & large as Hetton, & Lambton. It is the fineness of the quality alone, which has hitherto supported the character of Stewart's.

I enclose a letter from Morton, which shews his feelings on the affairs of the trade. If the Reg[ulatio]n is broken up, to-morrow I don't see any course for us to take but to adopt a general system of freighting in the first instance, as expecting the ship-owners to load on their own acc[oun]t at any price we may reduce the Coals to, is out of the question. We must either, therefore, freight, or stand still and heap up the Coals at the Pits – which will be attended with great additional loss.

The Marq[ues]s of Londonderry   I have the honor [&c.]
                                                            J[no] Buddle

184.

D/Lo/C142/38 (45)   Pensher 27[th] Mar[ch] 1843

My Lord

I send your Lordship the enclosed from Storrow the surgeon. On arriving here, this morn[in]g I found that Hunter had gone to his Friends at Winlaton near Ryton last Sa[turday] Evening, with his amanuensis Nicholson the young man, your Lordship saw at Wyn[yar]d. I have ex[amine]d Mrs Hunter this morn[in]g very closely, as to Hunter's conduct, and state of health, and have made out from her that from the worry he is in about the p[ay]m[en]t of these Bills – but more especially from one of these periodical tippling fits, to which he is unfortunately addicted – he is not in a fit state, at present to proceed with the payment of the acc[oun]ts. As soon as the drink is kept from him, he recovers in 2 or 3 days, but this can only be done at Winlaton. In his own House, his Wife can keep the Drink from him, but she says he goes out some where – certainly not to the public Houses, and will return in an hour –not to say drunk – but in a state of stupidity & unfit for any sort of business – and without the aid of his amanuensis would not be able to get on at all. Hunter's fort is that of a *Pitman* – and I do not know of a better one. But these fits of inebriety might overtake him at a time when his services might be most needed. And I really don't know what course to take with him – such conduct, is to me most inconvenient, offensive, & disgusting. Since his return from London, I have not had the least assistance from him, which has entailed upon me all the details & minutiae of his office and which with the general movements of our great machine at this critical time, is really too much for me. His Wife tells me, that he feels these money transactions of your Lordship so onerous and so much out of his line, that he intends to give up his situation. Towards the end of the week I make no doubt he will have come to his *sober* senses, and I must know what he really means on this point, as it will be necessary to look out for a successor to him – as we have no person in our own body to succeed him. There are plenty of *half-bred Pitmen* – young Viewers, which have been reared in the new *mushroom* Collieries. But we require a thorough-bred one of experience and resource, with some Brains in his head, a description of man which is not to be picked up every day, as all those of character and name are engaged. I assure your Lordship that all this is a source of great anxiety, and discomfort to me.

I have the honor [&c.]

J^no Buddle[7]

P.S. I hear that the new harbour of our Friend Sir J. Rennie & the *great* Radcliffe Colliery dependent upon it – have proved an *entire failure* at Warkworth.[8]

---

7   In a note on this letter Lord Londonderry wrote that he had a high regard for Hunter, as an excellent viewer and wholly honest in accounts and money matters; but he would be disquieted about any man whom tippling fits rendered incapable of doing his duty. Hunter should therefore be replaced unless he entered into a solemn undertaking that he would never again resort to this habit. There should be no difficulty in getting a good viewer, and a clerk would always be available for paying the bills. See Christine M. Hiskey, 'George Hunter (1792–1851): an Industrial Biography', *Durham County Local History Society Bulletin*, no. 23 (Aug. 1979), pp. 48–56.

8   An Act for building a harbour at the mouth of the River Coquet was obtained in 1837. There were a number of different designs, the one eventually adopted being by Rennie. Construction took place between 1838 and 1849. The harbour was eventually given the name of Amble. The project for the harbour and one to develop the small Radcliffe Colliery, two miles distant, were mutually interdependent. NEIMME, NRO 3410/Bud/48/13, 18 Aug. 1841.

185.

D/Lo/C142/38 (51)   Pensher 24th May 1843

My Lord

I had the honor to find your Lordship's Letter of the 11th waiting for me on my return from Glenarm[9] yesterday, afternoon.

I am glad the extinguishing Engine sent to Wynyard met your Lordship's approval. And I concur with your Lordship that the *Apron* of the dam ought to be completed, and made secure, lest the Expence which has already been incurred should be lost money. We must not lose the Hog 'for a halfpenny's worth of tar'. The job must therefore be completed as soon as circumstances will permit.

With respect to the stone for Lord Durham's memorial,[10] I will make the Inquiries your Lordship requires – I only wish our affairs had been such as to have enabled your Lordship to have carried out your liberal and magnanimous intentions – in shewing respect to the memory of a political adversary.

I am glad to say that I find all our works in good order – the widening of the Railway was completed & the waggons at work upon it, *last Thursday*!!! The job has been completed in a remarkable short space of time and does great credit to Thorman and all the *staff*, for their judicious arrangements and great energy, and exertions.

Those interminable east winds, however, have put us, as well as all our neighbours entirely out of ships. The Pits are in consequence off work today & as the wind continues to blow from the E[ast] with rain, I don't expect we shall have any ships to-morrow.

A large meeting of Pitmen took place on Sheddon's hill last Sa[turday], when it seems our men joined the Union, as they have since restricted their work. It is by no means unlikely that further mischief will arise out of all this.

I was detained in Dublin till Friday afternoon at 5 o'clock – hanging on, in Court and after all, was not called. Owing to some technical objection taken by the Plaintiff's Council – the Judge directed the Jury to give the verdict for the Plaintiff – so, as far as regards the Trial, I might as well have staid at home.

I took the mail from Dublin on Friday night, & got to Glenarm on

---

9   Edmund McDonnell's house.

10 Penshaw Monument, a Doric temple on top of a hill above the village of Penshaw near Lambton Castle, erected in 1844 by public subscription. Buddle subscribed £25: NEIMME, NRO 3410/Bud/48/12. 20 Aug. 1840. Lord Londonderry evidently contemplated donating the stone from his quarry.

Sa[turday] at 3 o'clock in the afternoon. I staid & discussed matters with Mr McDonnell, 'till 12 o'clock next day – then took the mail to Belfast – slept there and made the best of my way next morn[in]g by mail & packet to Carlisle, from thence by train to N[ew]castle where I arrived at 1 o'clock yesterday. I met with Sir J^{no} Rennie at Belfast, we spent the ev[enin]g together – next day he accompanied me, to Portpatrick, where he took me round the Harbour & shewed me all his plans and works – nothing could be more kind, and courteous than he was. He wants £30,000 more to complete the Works.

I arranged with Mr McDonnell to join him in London, soon after his arrival – to hold council with your Lordship, on all matters under the present extraordinary state of affairs generally – when no man knows what to do, or what to advise for the best.

I found a letter, on my arrival from Perceval Forster, with an offer for the North Nook of the Kelloe Coal. It is put in the shape of the D[ra]ft of an Agree[men]t and the terms are such as, I think, as will lead to a Bargain. Some of the Articles will require attention and modification, and I have written *Percy* that I shall have an opportunity of submitting the offer to your Lordship & Mr McDonnell in the course of a Fortnight or so, when he will receive a communication on the subject. No harm will take place from the delay, as the term is to commence on the 13th Inst. I enclose your Lordship a copy of this offer. I have not yet seen Morton, Wood, Donkin, Philipson, nor any other of my Colleagues of the Committee, to learn what 'news' at the Coal trade Office.

The Marq[ues]s of Londonderry   I have the Honor [&c.]
                                                            J^{no} Buddle

186.

D/Lo/C142/38 (52)   Walls-end 28th May 1843

My Lord

   Nothing of any material interest has occurred in our Concerns this week, nor in the affairs of the Coal-trade generally. Owing to the contrary winds which have so long prevailed little business has been doing, but Rob[er]t Sanderson has managed to dispatch the small cargo of Steam Coals to Brest, and I hope they will give satisfaction, as they are of the best quality – my only doubt is as to their size as they are not quite so *lumpy* as some of the first-rate Steam Coals from the Tyne.

The organization of another formidable union is progressing rapidly amongst our Pitmen, and I expect your Lordship will have seen the reports of their proceedings in the provincial papers – with a copy of their Petition to parliament. They have restricted their Work, in every Coll[ier]y in the District, I believe, except Backworth – where the men have refused to join the league, or to attend the district, or general meetings. They have therefore become obnoxious to the Body, and are threatened to be driven off by brute force to the next general meeting. I don't see how this is to be prevented, as there is no police establishment in the Neighbourhood and the parish Constables are inadequate to the duty.

I have got one of my old spies engaged to give me information of their proceedings. He knows little of their secret proceedings yet – but the talk amongst them is, that a general strike is to take place, in the Autumn, when the Potatoe & Turnip crops are advancing to maturity. This strike is to extend to every class of the working population thro' England, Wales & Scotland (Ireland does not seem as yet to be included) and the ultimate object is 'the Charter'.[11]

Wakefield, as regards the Colliers, seems to be head quarters, and Emissaries from there are sent to all the Colliery Districts. One of these fellows, of the name of 'Swallow'[12] has been in this Neighbourhood, since about Christmas. He travels about from Colliery to Colliery – lecturing, & exciting the men and organizing them privately, and has at length succeeded in inducing them to unite, and subscribe to the general Fund.

There is every appearance of this agitation arising to a serious crisis, as there are no means of checking it – they take care to keep within the pale of the law, and will not commit themselves to partial out breaks before their grand plan is ripe for execution. I will keep your Lordship advised of all the information I can gain.

The Marq[ues]s of Londonderry   I have the honor [&c.]
                                                              J^{no} Buddle

---

11 After Parliament's second refusal to consider the Chartist petition in May 1842 the movement split, the northern wing becoming largely industrial but weakened by an economic upturn, the southern more politically radical. Ward, *Chartism*, pp. 164–7.

12 David Swallow, Chartist agitator.

187.

D/Lo/C142/38 (58)   Pensher 27th June 1843

My Lord

I found all matters here, on my return, pretty much in the same state as when I left home. I have not yet seen my *spy* on the Tyne, to learn what is going on, on that River – but in this quarter altho' Mr Swallow & his coadjutors, are very active in getting up meetings and *lecturing* in this neighbourhood, I do not find that any further progress has been made, or any political features manifested itself in the Union. The Viewers report that the family men are getting very much dissatisfied with the limitation of wages imposed by the rules of the Union, and I think it not unlikely that this discontent will either hasten a strike, or break up the combination shortly.

The women are forming a Union to bring down the prices of Butcher's meat, Milk, Butter, Potatoes, &c. This I think a capital burlesque on the Pitmen's Union and will aid in breaking it up, as they won't long be content to abstain from the *Flesh* – and the women certainly will not be able to carry their point, and obtain it at the maximum price 4½[d] per lb at which they have fixed it.

We had a long day's work at the executive Comm[itt]ee meeting yesterday, and I see that we shall soon bring matters to a crisis. That is to say, we shall either enforce a strict observance of the rules of the Regulation – or break it up. I apprehend the latter – as I scarcely see how we can maintain the present prices of the best Coals in London. It is true, that the Factors Board Reg[ulatio]n has kept up the price to the proper stand, but the view of it is, that by keeping up the prices so – it has brought a deluge of inferior sorts into the market, which otherwise could not have *shewn their faces* there. And I fear there is no mode of checking their intrusion but by lowering our prices. But before this should be done, we ought to have the market cleared of the present enormous accumulation, or the loss will be frightful. This subject is occupying the attention of the Rep[resentative]s of all the best Collieries.

I have just been to the Harbour which owing to the contrary winds, is entirely out of ships – but the whole month's Vend is up, within 190 Ch. which is insignificant. The vend of oversea for the month up to last night is Steam W[alls]end 560

Double Screened Small   631

Single ditto   <u>199</u>

1390

Poor Lee seems to be going quite out of his mind, & his family entertain apprehensions that he may commit violence upon himself. He
goes away for a day, or two, but comes back again & looks into
the Office, and expresses an apprehension of receiving his dismissal.
Morton has just called in passing, he says they have not had a ship
since last Thursday & their Over Sea trade is entirely at an end. This
is not to be wondered at, as he has set the whole host of brokers and
exporters against him by sending out his own traveller to take their
customers from them. It is an 'ill wind that blows no body profit'
and several of his old customers are coming to us. They say he has
also lost a large sum for last year's Coals, in bad debts – £2000 is
mentioned, but I do not think this can be true.

The Marq[ues]s of Londonderry   I have the honor [&c.]
                                                              J^no Buddle

188.

D/Lo/C142/38 (54)   Walls-end 9th July 1843

My Lord

The general meeting of the Pitmen took place yesterday, at
Shaddon's hill, but I am not yet informed what resolutions were
passed. But another gen[era]l meeting on N[ew]castle Town-moor,
next Sat[urda]y is *talked of*. The report is that a general strike of all
classes of the working population of the kingdom is organizing. And
partial strikes of the pitmen, at different Coll[ierie]s are constantly
taking place. The Wingate Grange men have been off work for some
time, to oppose the introduction of a flat wire rope for drawing the
Coals.[13] They keep one hemp rope in the pit for the men to ride
on, but this does not satisfy them, and they insist on the wire rope
being taken off. They are supported by subscription, and I enclose a
copy of one of their begging letters, which was intercepted by a spy
of my nephew's[14] – it was addressed to the men at Seaton Delaval
Coll[ier]y where he is the manager. It shews the spirit and tone in
which the communications are made.

As to the state of the trade it gets the longer the worse, and my
present feeling is that the regulation cannot be continued after the

---

13 See Welbourne, *Miners Unions of Northumberland and Durham*, pp. 65–6.
14 Robert Atkinson, viewer at Seaton Delaval.

gen[era]l meeting on the 25[th] but a more correct opinion may probably be formed on this point after the meeting of the Executive Comm[itt]ee to-morrow. A last call has been made to all delinquents to appear at this meet[in]g to settle their acc[oun]ts for Fines &c. on pain of being *shewn up* at the gen[era]l meet[in]g as the Comm[itt]ee don't possess any other power of coercion. My opinion is, that many are not able, even if they were willing to pay. I don't therefore see how we are to get over it, as all must fare alike, or all be excused.

But this is not the only difficulty. Such a number of Coll[ierie]s, mostly new ones, have put in claims for references for an increase of their bases, on the ground of having sunk new Pits, or having found new seams &c. that the gen[era]l Basis is rolling up so, as to cut down the Issues to such a degree, as to cramp the old Coll]ierie]s beyond endurance.

The trade has committed great error in appointing lawyers for umpires. The trade appoints a Viewer, it's referee – the Coll[ier]y appealing appoints another Viewer it's referee. The former names a low quantity, the latter a very high one. The matter is then referred to the Umpire, who knowing nothing *practically* of the subject, he can only judge according to *such evidence*, as is put before him & in most cases – splits the difference so that the appealing party almost always give an undue increase. I opposed the appointment of Lawyers from the first but was over-ruled – but the Comm[itt]ee have now seen the mischief of it, when too late.

All this together with clandestine deviations from the factors' regulation – has br[ough]t the regulation into such a state, that the honourable part of the trade, will not, I believe, be able to make any profit under it. In reference to our own position, I find that up to the 30[th] of June, our Vend of best Small & Steam Coal is short of what it was up to the same period last year, and our receipts, are £13000 less. If therefore matters go on in this way, during the remainder of the year (and I see no better prospect) we shall certainly make little, or *no profit*. It is really not to be endured, to see new Collieries, sinking new pits, for the sake of establishing claims for increased Bases, while by the diminution of the Issues, the old Coll[ierie]s are obliged to shut up Pits, or to reduce their workings so, as greatly to enhance the price of working. Morton & the Hetton Co. see this as well as I do, but the Lambton Ex[ecutor]s are timid, & afraid to lead in any decided measure, and the Hetton Co. are always disposed to temporize. But matters have now reached a crisis, and it behoves us, really, to give our whole mind & con[sideratio]n to what is best to be done, in your Lordship's Coll[ier]y affairs. I am, therefore, anxious to have a full discussion with your Lordship, & Mr McD[onne]ll before the gen[era]l meeting of the 25th and which I submit would be best at Wyn[yar]d or Pensher. But at the same time, I will attend any where that will best suit your Lordship's convenience.

There are so many collateral points to be taken into cons[ideration] in discussing the great question as to 'what is best to be done' – that I consider *personal communication* quite indispensable.

The Marq[ues]s of Londonderry   I have the honor [&c.]
                                                 J^{no} Buddle

189.

D/Lo/C142/38 (68)   Pensher 28th July 1843

My Lord

After I came home last Eve[nin]g I wrote the enclosed, which is as nearly as I can make out the facts relative to the proceedings of our peoples, in the affair of the Election last Tuesday.[15] No doubt Purvis' party used every exertion fair, & foul, to seduce our freemen from their allegiance.

Two rascals, in our employ – Adamson a mason, & Adamson a painter (no relations) became most active partizans for them – treated our Agents with the utmost insolence, and carried off some of our freemen to vote for Purvis, in spite of their teeth. These two fellows have had constant employment with us – the painter is a

15   In April 1843 one of the two MPs for Durham City, Robert Fitzroy, resigned his seat on being appointed Governor-General of New Zealand. In the resulting by-election Lord Londonderry put up the former MP Arthur Trevor, now Lord Dungannon. He was elected, but made the mistake of distributing 'hand money' to those who had voted for him, a practice formerly normal but now made illegal. Dungannon was unseated on petition. Thomas Purvis, a local lawyer and landowner, having initially sought Lord Londonderry's blessing, now declared himself independent. Londonderry, incensed at this disregard for his position and the large sums of money he gave the local Conservative Association, instructed his voters to remain neutral. Purvis was elected, along with the Liberal John Bright. The Tories in the City were split, Londonderry was dropped as chairman of the Conservative Association and in 1847 the Conservatives did not secure even one of the City seats. David Large, 'The Election of John Bright as Member for Durham City in 1843', *DUJ*, new ser., xvi (1954–5), pp. 17–23; Heesom, *Durham City and its MPs*, pp. 25, 44; *idem*, ' "Legitimate" vs "Illegitimate" Influence: Aristocratic Electioneering in mid-Victorian Britain', *Parliamentary History*, vii (1988), pp. 298–300.

lazy scoundrel, and I have often been out of all patience with, & on the very point of turning him off. If I were to follow the bent of my own feelings, and inclination at the present moment – they should not again return to their work but in this I shall be governed by your Lordship's decision – but they really deserve to be made examples of.

I saw Rob[er]t Anderson before I left Durham yesterday – he told me that the Conservatives were talking of calling a County meeting to take into con[ideratio]n your Lordship's conduct in respect of the City Election. He wishes to be furnished with the facts of the case so as to be prepared in case of need to say something in vindication, and justification of your Lordship at the *talked of* meeting.

The *Clique* at Durham are quite *rabid* – but the *paroxysm* will subside like a nine days' wonder, and I should not advise your Lordship to take any steps while the *Ebullition* lasts (unless attacked) but to wait the attack & then your Lordship will be better able to decide on the most judicious line to take. When the poll is published we shall see who were friends & who were Foes.

I will write on other matters in a day, or two – mean time, I have arranged a plan to increase the Vend of Eden-main & to curtail the Vend of Stewart's – 'till the great load of ships in London are sold off. As in the event of the regulation going to pieces after the 15th Aug[us]t & a consequent reduction of prices we should sustain a frightful loss, on the unsold Coals in London. We receive 26/- per Ch. *net* for Eden-main to the coast – which is nearly as much as we now get for Stewart's in London. But it is much more than we shall realize by Stewart's in London if the Regulation is broken up. I am therefore anxious to reduce the risk of loss, on Stewart's & to *slide out of the stock* in London as easily as possible.

The Marq[ues]s of Londonderry   I have the honor [&c.]
                                                                    J[no] Buddle

190.

D/Lo/C142/38 (71)   Walls-end Sat[ur]d[a]y evening 29th July 1843

My Lord

On returning from Durham to Pensher, on Thursday even[in]g I went to Hunter to endeavour to obtain some information from him relative to the Electioneering transactions of Tuesday – before I wrote my letter of that Even[in]g to your Lordship, and also to communicate to him your Lordship's message to me by Mr McDonnell for his dismissal. I however found it impossible to obtain any information from him – as although not drunk and having been in the house all day without drink[in]g I found him in a very nervous & excited state, and completely in *Babbleshire*, evidently from the effects of previous inebriation – much in the state, I presume, in which he appeared before your Lordship and Mr McDonnell, the previous Evening.

I have very little doubt he had been in a stupidly drunken state, at Durham, on Monday night, and Tuesday, as I am not aware of any sufficient reason for his remaining at Durham on Monday night. Now really a man, on such an occasion, not being able to restrain himself from the indulgence of such a brutal & beastly propensity, shews decidedly that he is lost to every sense of decency & propriety of conduct, and that he is utterly incorrigible, and not to be trusted. I cannot, therefore but approve of your Lordship's determination to dismiss him.

I would, however, submit to your Lordship, that as is usual in the Trade, that he should have six mo[nth]s notice – say from the 30th June – to allow time for him to wind up any matters he may have in hand for your Lordship, and also to allow me time to look out for a proper person to succeed him, as at present I have no one in view that I should think fit for the purpose. And if the Seaham Winning goes on we shall require more assistance in his line.

I some time ago mentioned to Mr McDonnell the propriety of having an infusion of *young blood* into our Concerns. For altho' thank God I possess as sound a constitution, and as good health, as any man can possibly be blest with, yet time is rolling on, and at last, I must yield to it's natural consequences. I therefore wish your Lordship, at leisure, to give this matter your serious consideration. Should your Lordship approve of my suggestion as to giving Hunter six mo[nth]s notice, I will feel obliged by a Letter to that effect, that I may *shew to him.*

I have agreeably to your Lordship's direction written Lee's dismissal – & enclose a copy of my Letter to him.

I have to day concluded an agree[men]t with Potter for 301 acres of his Kelloe Coal, at the certain ann[ua]l Rent of £1250, and I expect a proposition from him in a few days, giving us the option of substituting £3000 per ann[um] certain rent for the *whole estate.* I am inclined to prefer the latter, as I think it the *very outside* value of the Coal, and it would put an end to further *pottering* about it.

Mr McDonnell was at Newcastle to day, & had a meeting with Morton & Nich[olas] Wood, on the subject of the best Collieries *sticking* together in the event of the Regulation breaking-up on the 15th of next mo[nth]. They concur in this idea and we are to discuss it further on Monday m[ornin]g when Mr McDonnell will see them again, on his way through Newcastle. Almost all the arrears of Fines & Contributions, have been *paid* up at the C[oal] T[rade] Office since the meeting last Tuesday. Indeed the Clerk informs me that *all* have been paid up except a very few which are under reference!!! This shews that there must be a great dread of the consequences of breaking-up the Regulation.

I enclose a note from Morton in answer to one from me requesting him to meet Mr McDonnell & Wood this morn[in]g. It states his opinion briefly on two points viz. the meeting of the 25th and the Durham Election – on both I think he takes the right view. The Postscript alludes to Perc[eva] Forster. When he was old Arthur Mowbray's clerk, Arthur used to call him 'our prick-eared Lad' – by no means an inappropriate application. As *mouth-piece* to the Durham Conservatives *John Hodgson Hinde* seems to have *opened his mouth wider* than there was any occasion for.

The Marq[ues]s of Londonderry

I have the honor [&c.]
J^no Buddle

191.

D/Lo/C142/38 (88))   Newcastle 9th Sep[tember] 1843

My Lord

The Pitmen's Delegates held meetings, at their head-quarters, at this place, on Friday, Sa[turday] & Monday & Tuesd[a]y last. The result is not known – further than that an address to the Coal-owners (of which I enclose a copy) was agreed to and printed. And it was resolved not to have a general strike – but to adopt a system of annoyance by petitioning the Coal-owners individually for advances in the hewing-price &c. and to stop particular Collieries if their demands are not complied with.

It was also resolved that a gen[era]l meeting of the Tyne-men should be held on Scaffold-hill, and of the Wear & southern Collieries on Pittington-hill, this day week. The object of those meetings I have not learnt, but if they are for nothing else, they serve to keep up the agitation.

Mr Roberts[16] received £200 last Sa[turday] as the 1st instalment of his £1000 for his first year's Salary – and is to receive £200 more to day. I learn however from all quarters that there is much difficulty & grumbling about getting the *Brass-relieve* collected, and the office of *local* delegate, has become so unthankful & irksome that in some Coll[ierie]s they are obliged to choose the delegate by lot. The lot last week fell upon a putter lad, only 17 years old at Benwell Colliery. The restriction of work too, is objected to at some Collieries. All this looks well and I should not be surprised e'er long to see the Miners' Union[17] fall to the ground – and the whole affair either resolve itself into a Chartist agitation or be given up altogether.

I have just rec[eive]d the list of yesterday's Coal-market – prices of best Coals a shade lower but better sales. Stewart's and Lambton 19/-, Hetton 18/9, Haswell 19/6 Tyne best Coals 16/- – 192¾ cargoes left unsold.

The Blaydon-main Colliery-men have stopped & it is reported that the Hetton men have also stopped, but this requires confirmation. Hoping soon to have the pleasure of seeing your Lordship at Seaham,

The Marq[ues]s of Londonderry   I have the honor [&c.]

                                                          Jno Buddle

192.

D/Lo/C142/38 (90)   Pensher 18th Sep[tember] 1843

My Lord

The transactions of this day's meeting have brought the affairs of the regulation to a crisis. For some time past the Comm[itt]ee have been carrying on a correspondence with Tom Wood on behalf of the Thornley Co. who has feared off from signing the Agree[men]t on the ground of disapproving of certain parts of it, but at the same time virtually obeying it's provisions by strictly abiding by the Issues – indeed up to the 31st Aug[us]t the Vend of the Coll[ier]y is 22337

---

16 W.P. Roberts, solicitor, represented pitmen in a number of criminal cases; editor of the *Miners' Advocate*. See R. Challinor, *A Radical Lawyer in Victorian England: W.P. Roberts and the Struggle for Workers' Rights* (London, 1990).
17 The Miners' Association of Great Britain and Ireland, formed in 1842: see R. Challinor and B. Ripley, *The Miners' Association: a Trade Union in the Age of the Chartists* (London, 1968).

tons short for this year, so that in fact the Comm[itt]ee have nothing to complain of. Still his signing of the Agree[men]t was considered indispensable to the correct establishment, and firm consolidation of the Regulation, and he was called upon, either to sign the Agree[men]t on, or before this day, or to declare that he would not sign. A Letter was received from him, this afternoon, declining to sign, and proposing a new set of rules for the government of the trade.

The Committee were so disgusted with this communication, in addition to all the former trouble, & vexation, they have had with this Cox-comb, that they resolved to put an end to further temporizing, and decided to break-up the regulation. For which purpose, a general meeting of Rep[resentative]s is to be convened to-morrow week. The Com[mitt]ee to meet this day week to devise the best mode of proceeding to render the *blow* the least destructive. I do not think the breaking-up of the regulation could, all matters considered happen at a better time, as I think prices are nearly about as low for the best Coals, as they can be, and we may possibly get an increase of Vend.

We shall suffer most in the reduction, on Eden-main, as I think prices to the Coast will fall to a very low figure.

Neither Wood nor Philipson were at the meeting, and I had no opportunity of talking to Morton, as to the line *we three* should adopt under those circumstances, and must take an opportunity for discussing this very important matter with them, before the explosion actually takes place. I however foresee difficulties in the way of an arrangement of this kind, which in *conversation* I shall explain to your Lordship.

The sales of best Coals, last Friday, were brisker than they had been for a long time before – 7 cargoes of Stewart's were sold out of 23 – but at declining prices 18/6 and 18/3, and I am sorry to say, Stewart's are complained of for being *small*. I am apprehensive their [*sic*] may be cause for this, arising from improving Eden-main, for the Coast, by taking the *round* out of Stewart's. This, however, *won't do*, and I must look after it immediately, & *remedy it*.

It seems the gen[era]l meeting of the Wear Pitmen, at Pittington is put off, till next Sa[turday] – to afford Messrs Roberts & Beasely[18] the

---

18 William Beesley, Chartist agitator and clerk to the 'Pitman's Attormey', W.P. Roberts.

opportunity of attending – they were occupied at the Scaffold-hill meeting last Sa[urday] – it was a very numerous meeting.

I have not yet been able to obtain any correct information respecting the proceedings, but hear that it was resolved not to have a general strike. Partial strikes are however to be continued – the men at certain Collieries are to petition for an increase of wages, and reductions in the working regulations, which it would be absurd to comply with – and of course will be refused. But the refusal on the part of the masters will form a pretext for the strike. From all I hear, & observe, I have no doubt these meetings are merely a sort of *drilling* preparatory to a Chartist movement.

I enclose a statement of the Wear Vend from the 1st Jan[uar]y up to the 31st of Aug[us]t last – by which your Lordship will see, that the *shorts* far exceed the *overs* and that on the whole the Vends have been as correctly observed as can be expected, in so large a scale of business. I also enclose a comparative statement of our Vend for the same period between the last and present year, which shews a woeful falling off in the latter. A reduction of £13575.2.4 in the receipt of money is a very serious affair.

I am very glad to learn by your Lordship's Letter of the 15th that some day next week will be convenient to your Lordship, to give me a *Business Audience* – as I have many matters to submit to your Lordship's cons[ideratio]n, and I have full occupation here this week.

With respect to what is doing, at the Harbour, I will not enter upon it now, as it is one of the points which I have to bring under your Lordship's notice, more at leisure & more fully than I can now do.

As to the Seaham Winning, it is decided on, but the time of commencing is not fixed. I have been occupied for the last month, all the time I could spare to it, in planning the Pit, Machinery &c. and estimating the Cost – and have them almost ready to submit to N. Wood for his approval, on behalf of the other parties. When it is considered that this Winning is to be a source of revenue to the Family for a Century to come, and also to be the *main-stay* of the Harbour for a similar period, it is obvious that it ought to be planned, and executed on the most improved principles, that the advanced state of science, and mining experience, and practice will afford. This I have endeavoured to do, and if N. Wood approves of what I have done (he has not yet seen the plans &c.) I presume ground will be broken forthwith. Errington the engineer alluded to was engaged by N. Wood – to assist Thorman in drawing the plans from my designs – making models &c.

Before ground is broke, N. Wood & I will have to meet on the ground to set out the site of the Pits &c. according to the Plan finally agreed upon between us.

The United Comm[itt]ee have to meet at Newcastle this day week – and the gen[era]l meeting is to take place next day,[19] which will occupy me both those days. But I will be glad to wait upon your Lordship on the Wed[nesday] Thursday or Friday, at any place, or time you will please to appoint. Or if agreeable, I will be proud to see your Lordship here.

I had an opportunity to day, just barely to hint at the *confidential affair* to Morton – a mere 'breaking of the ice' without being able to pursue the subject – his manner of receiving the hint, was not repulsive. He says he *hears* that Burdon declared he will stand for the Co[unty] in opposition to your Lordship's int[eres]t, and that he will oppose your Lordship in all public, as well as local affairs. What can have made this man so determined & bitter a Foe?

I am informed that at the D[uke] of Northumberland's audit, there were upwards of £6000 arrears on the ½ year's Rents. The Farmers expected an abatement of 20 per cent – none was made, & they were bitterly disappointed.

The Marq[ues]s of Londonderry   I have the honor [&c.]
                                                                                              J[no] Buddle

---

19 Minutes in NRO 263/A2.

BIBLIOGRAPHY

Unpublished Sources

Durham, County Record Office:
    Londonderry Papers
    National Coal Board Deposit 1: Buddle Papers
Newcastle upon Tyne, North of England Institute of Mining and
Mechanical Engineers:
    Buddle Collection
Woodhorn, Northumberland Archives:
    Northumberland and Durham Joint Coal Owners Association Papers

Parliamentary Papers

Report of the Select Committee of the House of Lords on the State of the Coal Trade (1830), vol. 8 (9)

Report of the Select Committee of the House of Commons on the State of the Coal Trade (1830), vol. 8 (663)

Report of the Select Committee on Accidents in Mines (1835), vol. 5 (603)

Report of the Select Committee on the State of the Coal Trade (1836), vol. 11 (522)

Report from the Select Committee on Church Leases (1837–8), vol. 9 (692)

Children's Employment Commission. First Report of the Commissioners: Mines, 1842, vol. 15 (380)

Printed Works

Anderson, M.S., *The Eastern Question* (London, 1966)

Arbuthnot, Mrs., *The Journal of Mrs Arbuthnot 1820–1832*, ed. James Banford and the Duke of Wellington (London, 1950)

Banham, John, 'Arthur Mowbray – Adventurer or Entrepreneur: a North East Business in the Industrial Revolution', *Durham County Local History Society Bulletin*, nos. 48–9 (1992)

———, *Backhouse's Bank of Darlington 1774–1830*, Papers in North Eastern History (Durham, 1997)

Bean, W.W., *Parliamentary Representation of the Six Northern Counties of England 1603–1886* (Hull, 1890)

Borroughs, Peter, 'The Northumberland County Election of 1826', *Parliamentary History*, x, part 1 (1991), pp. 78–104

Brock, Michael, *The Great Reform Bill* (London, 1973)

Buddle, John, 'A narrative of the explosion which occurred at Wallsend Colliery on the 18th of June 1835', *Transactions of the Natural History Society of Northumberland, Durham and Newcastle upon Tyne*, xi (1838), pp. 346–83

Calcott, M. and Challinor, R. (eds), *Working-Class Politics in North-East England* (Newcastle, 1983)

Challinor, R., *A Radical Lawyer in Victorian England: W.P. Roberts and the Struggle for Workers' Rights* (London, 1990)

Challinor, R. and Ripley, B., *The Miners' Association: a Trade Union in the Age of the Chartists* (London, 1968)

Chase, Malcolm, *Chartism: a New History* (Manchester, 2006)

Christiansen, Rex, *A Regional History of the Railways of Great Britain, Vol. 7: the West Midlands* (Newton Abbot, 1973)

Church, Roy, *History of the British Coal Industry, Vol. 3: 1830–1913* (Oxford, 1986)

Clapham, Sir John, *The Bank of England*, vol. 2 (Cambridge, 1944)

Clarke, Edward David, *Travels in Various Countries of Europe, Asia and Africa, Pt 1: Russia, Tartary and Turkey* (6 vols, London, 1810–23)

Dunn, Matthias, *An Historical, Geological and Descriptive View of the Coal Trade of the North of England* (Newcastle upon Tyne, 1844)

Fewster, J.M., *The Keelmen of Tyneside: Labour Organisation in the North-East Coal Industry, 1600–1830* (Woodbridge, 2011)

Fisher, D.R. (ed.), *The History of Parliament: the House of Commons, 1820–1832*, 7 vols (Cambridge, 2009)

Flinn, M.W., *The History of the British Coal Industry, Vol. 2: 1700–1830* (Oxford, 1984)

Fordyce, T., *Local Records, or Historical Register of Remarkable Events*, vol. 3 (Newcastle upon Tyne, 1867)

Fynes, Richard, *The Miners of Northumberland and Durham* (London, 1873)

Hair, P.E.H., 'Mortality from Violence in British Coal Mines, 1800–1850', *Economic History Review*, new ser., xxi, no. 3 (Dec. 1968), pp. 545–61

Heesom, A.J., 'The Duke of Wellington's Visit to the North East of England, September–October 1827', *Durham County Local History Society Bulletin*, no. 60 (1999), pp. 3–35

——, *Durham City and its MPs 1678–1992* (Durham, 1992)

——, '"Legitimate" vs "Illegitimate" Influence: Aristocatic Electioneering in mid-Victorian Britain', *Parliamentary History*, vii (1988), pp. 282–305

——, 'Lord Ashley's Coal Mines Act, Social Reform, and "Social Control"', *Historical Journal*, xxiv (1982), pp. 69–88, reprinted in T.

Boyns (ed.), *The Mining Industry* (4 vols, London and New York, 1997), i, pp. 266–85

———, 'The Northern Coal Owners and the Opposition to the Coal Mines Act of 1842', *International Review of Social History*, xxv (1980), pp. 236–71

———, 'Problems of Church Extension in a Victorian New Town: the Londonderrys and Seaham Harbour', *Northern History*, xv (1979), pp. 138–55

———, 'Problems of Patronage: Lord Londonderry's Appointment as Lord Lieutenant of Co. Durham', *Durham University Journal*, new ser., xxxix (1977–8), pp. 169–77

———, 'The "Wynyard Edict" of 1837', *Durham County Local History Society Bulletin*, no. 21 (Apr. 1978), pp. 2–7

Hiskey, Christine M., 'George Hunter (1792–1851): an Industrial Biography', *Durham County Local History Society Bulletin*, no. 23 (Aug. 1979), pp. 48–56

———, 'John Buddle (1773–1843): Agent and Entrepreneur in the North East Coal Trade' (M.Litt. thesis, University of Durham, 1978)

———, 'The Third Marquess of Londonderry and the Regulation of the Coal Trade: the Case Re-opened', *Durham University Journal*, new ser., xlv (1983–4), pp. 1–9

Jones, Carol, 'Experiences of a Strike: the North-East Coalowners and the Pitmen, 1831–1832', in R.W. Sturgess (ed.), *Pitmen, Viewers and Coalmasters: Essays in North-East Coal Mining in the Nineteenth Century* (Newcastle upon Tyne, 1986), pp. 27–54

Kirby, M.W., *The Origins of Railway Enterprise: Stockton and Darlington Railway 1821* (Cambridge, 1983)

Large, David, 'The Election of John Bright as MP for Durham City in 1843', *Durham University Journal*, new ser., xvi (1954–5), pp. 17–23

———, 'The Third Marquess of Londonderry and the End of the Regulation 1844–7', *Durham University Journal*, new ser., xx (1958–9), pp. 1–9

Lillie, William, *The History of Middlesbrough: an Illustration of the Evolution of English Industry* (Middlesbrough, 1968)

Londonderry, Charles, Marquess of, *Journal of a Tour in the Southern Part of Spain, including Tangier, Ceuta and Tetuan* (London, 1840)

———, *Recollections of a Tour in the North of Europe in 1836–1837* (London, 1838)

———, *A Steam Voyage to Constantinople by the Rhine and the Danube* (London, 1842)

Londonderry, Edith, Marchioness of, *Frances Anne: the Life and Times of Frances Anne, Marchioness of Londonderry, and her husband Charles, Third Marquess of Londonderry* (London, 1958)

Londonderry, Frances Anne, Marchioness of, *Journal of a Three Months Tour in Portugal, Spain and Africa* (London, 1843)

———, *Visit to the Courts of Vienna, Constantinople, Athens, Naples etc.* (London, 1844)

MacDonagh, O., 'Coal Mines Regulation: the First Decade, 1842–1852', in R. Robson (ed.), *Ideas and Institutions of Victorian Britain* (London, 1967), pp. 58–86

Mackenzie, E., and Ross, M., *Historical, Topographical and Descriptive View of the County Palatine of Durham* (Newcastle upon Tyne, 1834)

Maehl, W.H., 'Chartist Disturbances in North-Eastern England, 1839', *International Review of Social History*, viii, no. 3 (1963), pp. 389–414

———, 'The Dynamics of Violence in Chartism: a Case Study in North-East England', *Albion*, vii, no. 2 (Summer 1975), pp. 101–19

McCord, N. (ed.), *Essays in Tyneside Labour History* (Newcastle, 1977)

Mewburn, Francis, *The Larchfield Diary: Extracts from the Diary of the late Mr Mewburn, first Railway Solicitor* (London, 1876)

Mountford, Colin, *The Private Railways of County Durham* (Melton Mowbray, 2004)

Mussett, P., with Woodward, P.G., *Estates and Money at Durham Cathedral 1660–1985* (Durham, 1988)

New, Chester, *Lord Durham* (Oxford, 1929)

Northumberland County History Committtee, *A History of Northumberland*, vol. 13 (Newcastle upon Tyne, 1930)

Oxford Dictionary of National Biography (Oxford, 2004)

The Parliamentary Debates (Hansard), London

Parson, Wm. and White, Wm., *History, Directory and Gazetteer of the Counties of Durham and Northumberland*, 2 vols (Newcastle upon Tyne, 1827, 1828)

Phillips, Maberly, *A History of Banks, Bankers and Banking in Northumberland, Durham and North Yorkshire* (London, 1894)

Richard, Thomas, *Local Records of Stockton and the Neighbourhood* (Stockton and London, 1868)

Richardson, M.A., *The Local Historian's Table Book of Remarkable Occurrences*, Historical Division, vol. 3 (Newcastle upon Tyne, 1843)

Ridley, David, 'Political and Industrial Crisis: the Experience of the Tyne and Wear Pitmen, 1831–32' (University of Durham Ph.D. thesis, 1994)

Robinson, John Martin, *The Wyatts, an Architectural Dynasty* (Oxford, 1979)

Rowe, D.J., 'Some Aspects of Chartism on Tyneside', *International Review of Social History*, xvi (1971), pp. 17–39

———, 'Tyneside Chartism', in N. McCord (ed.), *Essays in Tyneside Labour History* (Newcastle, 1977), pp. 62–87

———, 'Tyneside Chartists', *North East Group for the Study of Labour Bulletin*, no. 8 (1974), pp. 30–45

Rowland, John, 'Physical Force Chartism on Tyneside in 1839', in M. Calcott and R. Challinor (eds), *Working-Class Politics in North-East England* (Newcastle, 1983), pp. 8–16

Sharp, Sir Cuthbert, *Memorials of the Rebellion of 1569* (London, 1840)

——, *Seaham and Seaham Harbour* (1928)

Smith, Raymond, *Sea-Coal for London: History of the Coal Factors in the London Market* (London, 1961)

Spring, David and Eileen, 'The Fall of the Grenvilles, 1844–48', *Huntington Library Quarterly*, xix, no. 2 (Feb. 1956), pp. 165–90

Sturgess, R.W., *Aristocrat in Business: the Third Marquess of Londonderry as Coal Owner and Port Builder* (Durham, 1975)

——, 'The Londonderry Trust 1819–54', *Archaeologia Aeliana*, 5th ser., x (1982), pp. 179–92

Sweezy, Paul M., *Monopoly and Competition in the English Coal Trade 1550–1850* (Cambridge, MA, 1938)

Sykes, John, *Local Records, or Historical Register of Remarkable Events* (2nd edn, Newcastle upon Tyne, 1866)

Tan, Elaine S., 'Market Structure and the Coal Cartel in Early Nineteenth-Century England', *Economic History Review*, new ser., lxii (2009), pp, 350–65

Taylor, A.J., 'The Third Marquess of Londonderry and the North East Coal Trade', *Durham University Journal*, new ser., xvii (1955–6), pp. 21–7

Thompson, F.M.L., 'The End of a Great Estate', *Economic History Review*, new ser., viii (1955), pp. 31–52

Thorne, R.G. (ed.), *The History of Parliament: the House of Commons, 1790–1820* (5 vols, London, 1986)

Tomlinson, William Weaver, *The North Eastern Railway, its Rise and Development* (Newcastle upon Tyne, 1914)

Venn, J.A., *Alumni Cantabrigienses*, pt 2, vol. 3 (Cambridge, 1947)

Ward, J.T., *Chartism* (London, 1973)

Welbourne, E., *The Miners' Unions of Northumberland and Durham* (Cambridge, 1923)

Welford, Richard, *Men of Mark 'twixt Tyne and Tweed* (London, 1895)

White, Francis & Co., *General Directory of the Town and City of Newcastle and Gateshead …* (Sheffield, 1843)

Newspapers

Durham Chronicle
Newcastle Chronicle

INDEX